the Candidate for goddess™

The Candidate For Goddess Vol. 5

Created by Yukiru Sugisaki

Translation - Alethea and Athena Nibley
English Adaptation - Mary Wolfman
Copy Editors - Suzanne Waldman,
Alexis Kirsch and Peter Ahlstrom
Retouch and Lettering - Abelardo Bigting
Production Artist - Vicente Rivera, Jr.
Cover Design - Patrick Hook

Editor - Rob Tokar
Digital Imaging Manager - Chris Buford
Pre-Press Manager - Antonio DePietro
Production Managers - Jennifer Miller and Mutsumi Miyazaki
Art Director - Matt Alford
Managing Editor - Jill Freshney
VP of Production - Ron Klamert
Editor-in-Chief - Mike Kiley
President and C.O.O. - John Parker
Publisher and C.E.O. - Stuart Levy

A 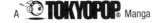 Manga

TOKYOPOP Inc.
5900 Wilshire Blvd. Suite 2000
Los Angeles, CA 90036

E-mail: info@TOKYOPOP.com
Come visit us online at www.TOKYOPOP.com

ISBN: 1-59182-751-5

First TOKYOPOP printing: December 2004
10 9 8 7 6 5 4 3 2 1
Printed in the USA

the Candidate for Goddess™

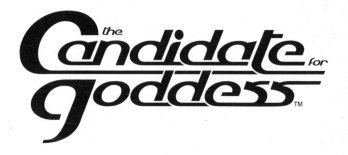

VOL. 5

BY
YUKIRU SUGISAKI

TOKYOPOP®

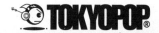

HAMBURG // LONDON // LOS ANGELES // TOKYO

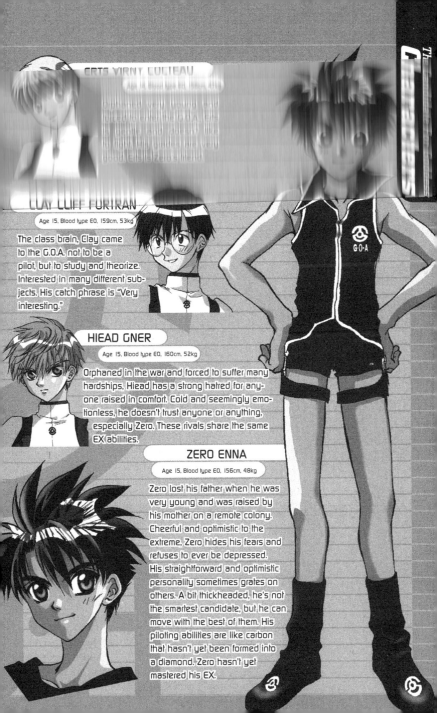

ERTS VIRNT LUCIEAU

Age 14, Blood type E0, 168cm, 48kg

CLAY CLIFF FORTRAN

Age 15, Blood type E0, 159cm, 53kg

The class brain, Clay came to the G.O.A. not to be a pilot, but to study and theorize. Interested in many different subjects. His catch phrase is "Very interesting."

HIEAD GNER

Age 15, Blood type E0, 160cm, 52kg

Orphaned in the war and forced to suffer many hardships, Hiead has a strong hatred for anyone raised in comfort. Cold and seemingly emotionless, he doesn't trust anyone or anything, especially Zero. These rivals share the same EX abilities.

ZERO ENNA

Age 15, Blood type E0, 156cm, 48kg

Zero lost his father when he was very young and was raised by his mother on a remote colony. Cheerful and optimistic to the extreme, Zero hides his fears and refuses to ever be depressed. His straightforward and optimistic personality sometimes grates on others. A bit thickheaded, he's not the smartest candidate, but he can move with the best of them. His piloting abilities are like carbon that hasn't yet been formed into a diamond. Zero hasn't yet mastered his EX.

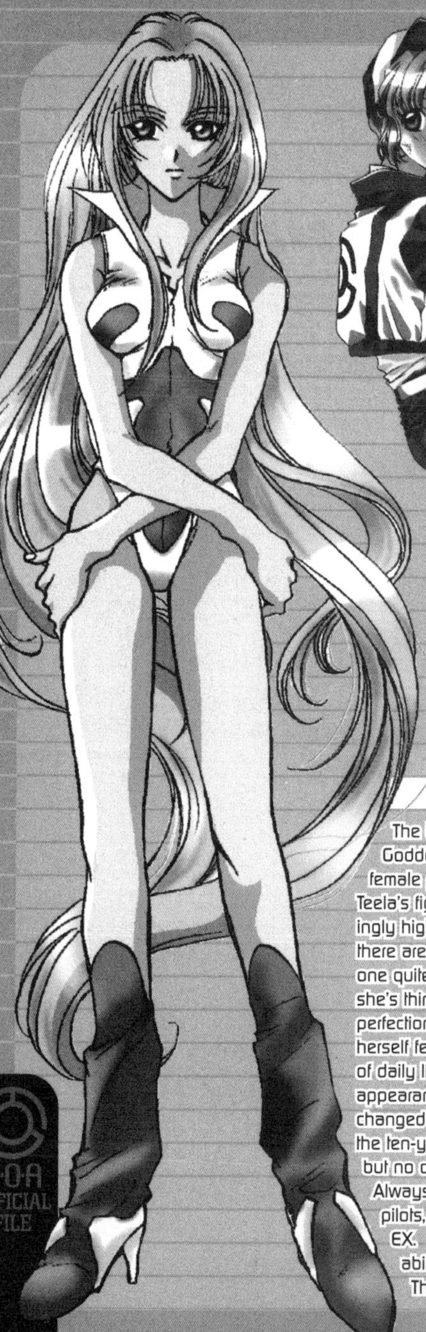

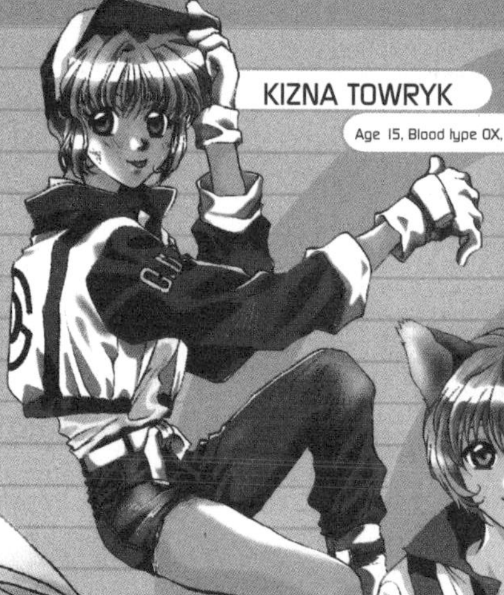

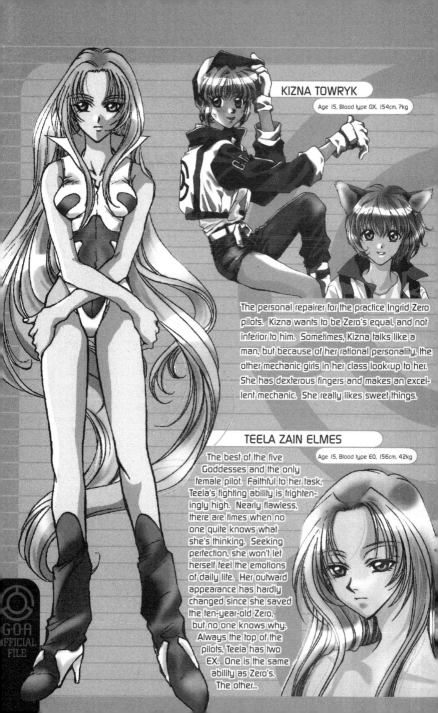

KIZNA TOWRYK

Age 15, Blood type OX, 154cm, 7kg

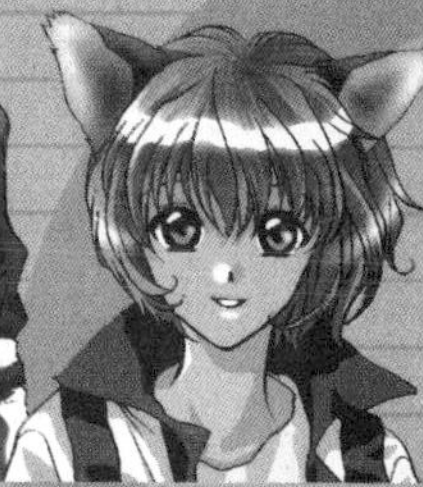

The personal repairer for the practice Ingrid Zero pilots. Kizna wants to be Zero's equal, and not inferior to him. Sometimes, Kizna talks like a man, but because of her rational personality, the other mechanic girls in her class look up to her. She has dexterous fingers and makes an excellent mechanic. She really likes sweet things.

TEELA ZAIN ELMES

Age 15, Blood type EO, 156cm, 42kg

The best of the five Goddesses and the only female pilot. Faithful to her task, Teela's fighting ability is frighteningly high. Nearly flawless, there are times when no one quite knows what she's thinking. Seeking perfection, she won't let herself feel the emotions of daily life. Her outward appearance has hardly changed since she saved the ten-year-old Zero, but no one knows why. Always the top of the pilots, Teela has two EX. One is the same ability as Zero's. The other...

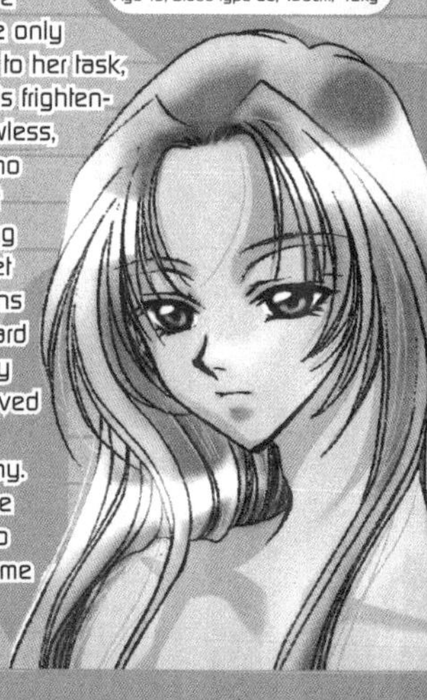

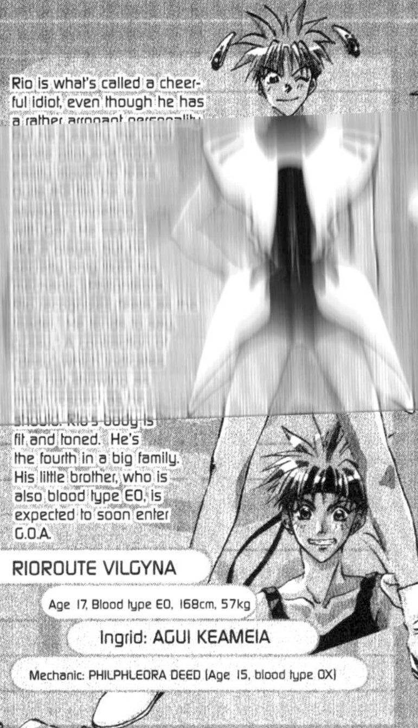

Rio is what's called a cheerful idiot, even though he has a rather arrogant personality

should. Rio's body is fit and toned. He's the fourth in a big family. His little brother, who is also blood type EO, is expected to soon enter G.O.A.

RIOROUTE VILGYNA

Age 17, Blood type EO, 168cm, 57kg

Ingrid: AGUI KEAMEIA

Mechanic: PHILPHLEORA DEED (Age 15, blood type OX)

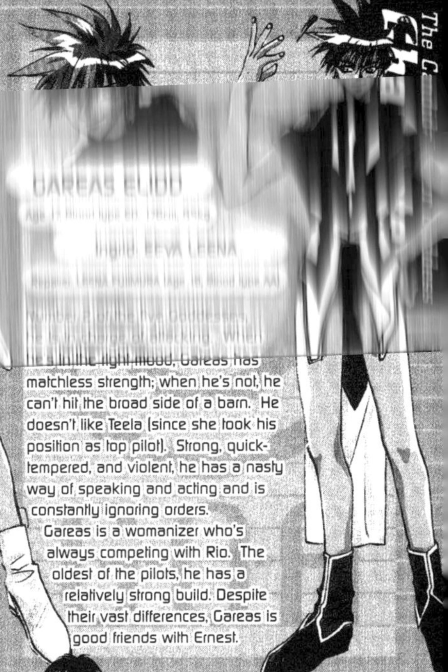

the right mood, Gareas has matchless strength; when he's not, he can't hit the broad side of a barn. He doesn't like Teela (since she took his position as top pilot). Strong, quick-tempered, and violent, he has a nasty way of speaking and acting and is constantly ignoring orders.

Gareas is a womanizer who's always competing with Rio. The oldest of the pilots, he has a relatively strong build. Despite their vast differences, Gareas is good friends with Ernest.

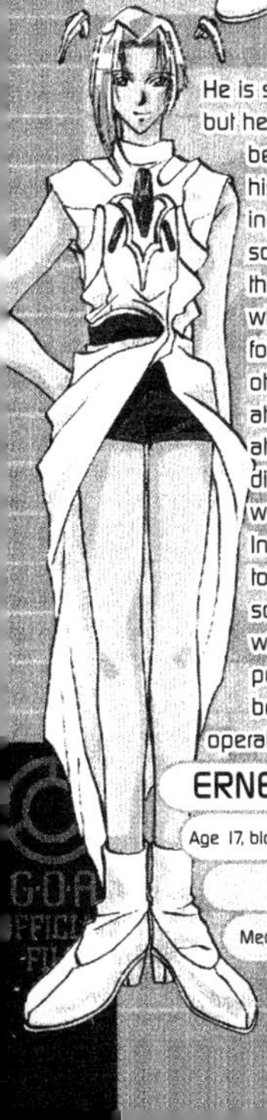

He is submissive and kind to everyone, but he has a complicated side that, while being lonely, likes his solitude. With his polite, careful way of speaking, Ernest is always the mediator if something bad happens between the Candidates. His EX is telepathy, which has caused a hard time for him when associating with others. But after meeting Gar at G.O.A., he started to look at things positively. Ernest dislikes his EX and often wonders why he has it. In battle, he uses his EX to support the Ingrids so they can fight with 120% of their power, as well as being in charge of operations.

ERNEST CUORE

Age 17, blood type EO, 170cm, 59kg

Ingrid: LUHMA KLEIN

Mechanic: TUNE YOUG (age 17, blood type AB)

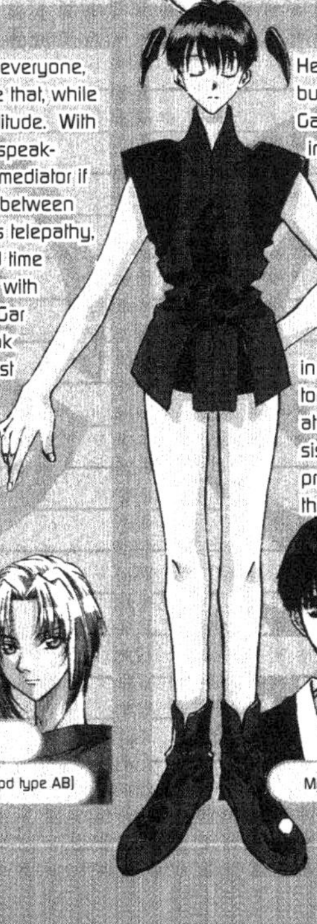

He's quiet and usually emotioness, but Yu is quite strong-willed. Like Gar, he is also in charge of attacking. Because of his calm judgment, the other pilots have great trust in him (his skills are also top notch). He has a rather young face and light complexion, and has a small build. There are rumors to the effect that, while enrolled in G.O.A., he nearly killed his instructor. When his home colony was attacked by Giseisha, he and his sister Kazuhi were rescued by the previous five Goddesses. To him, the most precious thing is his only family, his little sister.

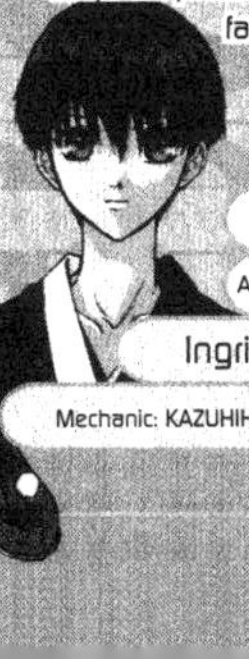

YU HIKURA

Age 16, Blood type EO, 160cm, 48kg

Ingrid: TELLIA KALLISTO

Mechanic: KAZUHIHIKURA (Age 15, Blood type OX)

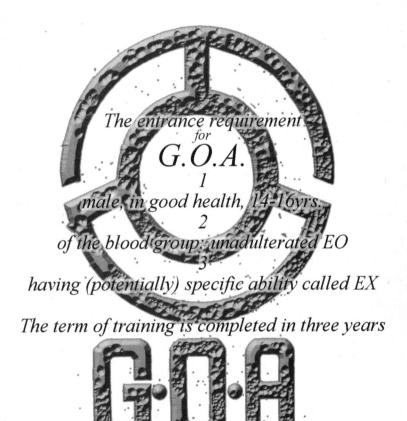

The entrance requirement
for
G.O.A.
1
male, in good health, 14-16yrs.
2
of the blood group: unadulterated EO
3
having (potentially) specific ability called EX

The term of training is completed in three years

WELCOME, EVERYONE.

THIS IS G.A. (GUARDIAN OPERATOR ACADEMY). THE FACILITY FOR TRAINING KNOWN AS HUMANKIND'S B.O.A. WITH YOUR FINE QUALITIES YOU WILL NO DOUBT LIKE THE THE ORGANIZATION THAT WILL BE ACTIVE IN A POSITION THAT WILL AFFECT THE FUTURE OF ALL MANKIND. LET THE KNOWLEDGE THAT IT IS THE YOU WHO HAVE PLEASURE THE FORTHCOMING FUTURE INDIVIDUALS BE SO BE GOOD CANDIDATES! YOU WILL SOON BECOME TRUE G.O.A. AIR PILOT **CANDIDATES!**

1
TO BE A HEALTHY MALE OF 14-16 YEARS OF AGE.
2
TO BE OF THE BLOOD-TYPE UNADULTERATED EO.
3
TO HAVE A SPECIAL ABILITY (EX) OR
TO HAVE THE POTENTIAL TO HAVE IT.

Eyes Only

YOU WILL BE ENROLLED FOR THREE YEARS.

THE TRAINING IS EXTREMELY HARSH, AND MANY OF YOU WILL PROBABLY DROP OUT.

FURTHERMORE, EVEN IF YOU PASS THE TRAINING, THERE MAY BE NO VACANCY AMONG THE CURRENT PILOTS (DUE TO DEATH OR RETIREMENT BECAUSE OF DEGENERATION OF EX). WHILE YOU ARE ENROLLED, THE CHANCES OF BEING CHOSEN AS A PILOT ARE EXTREMELY LOW.

HOWEVER,

ON THE OTHER HAND, IF YOU DISPLAY ABILITIES SUPERIOR TO THOSE OF THE CURRENT PILOTS WHILE YOU ARE ENROLLED, THE ROAD TO BECOMING A PILOT WILL OPEN FOR YOU.

WE WANT YOU TO BELIEVE IN YOURSELVES, BE DILIGENT IN YOUR TRAINING, AND WIN THE POSITION OF PILOT.

IF YOU HAVE DIRECTION AND AMBITION, WE HAVE NO PROBLEMS HELPING YOU.

WE WILL GIVE YOU THE KNOWLEDGE AND TECHNIQUES NECESSARY TO BE A PILOT.

WE HAVE BUT ONE ENEMY: A GROUP OF UNIDENTIFIED LIFE FORMS WE CALL GISEISHA.

IN THIS BATTLE TO PROTECT THE PLANET ZION, WE, THE LAST OF MANKIND, WILL TAKE NO OTHER PATH THAN VICTORY.

FAILURE IS UNACCEPTABLE.

IN THE BATTLEFIELD, THERE EXISTS ONLY ONE SIMPLE RESULT.

NAMELY, YOU WIN, OR YOU LOSE.

I SHOULDN'T HAVE TO TELL YOU WHICH ONE TO CHOOSE.

THE FUTURE OF THIS BATTLE RESTS ON THOSE WHO HAVE JUST BECOME PILOT CANDIDATES--YES, YOU.

YOUR NUMBER IS...

(EXCERPT FROM THE HANDBOOK FOR NEW STUDENTS)

G·O·A

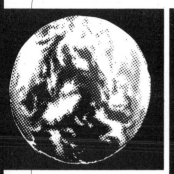

Z I O N

ZION IS THE LAST PLANET, OUR LAST REMAINING HOPE. ALL MANKIND WISHES TO SOMEDAY SET FOOT ON THAT PLANET. FURTHERMORE, AS ALL INFORMATION IS THOROUGHLY CONTROLLED BY THE GOVERNMENT, VERY LITTLE IS KNOWN ABOUT ZION. BUT THERE IS NO DOUBT THAT ZION IS TO US THE ONE AND ONLY "PROMISED LAND".

THE DETAILS OF THE FOUNDING OF G.O.A.

STARLOG 4088, DUE TO THE "CRISIS OF SYSTEMS (LOST PROPERTY)", WHICH INVOLVED FOUR STAR SYSTEMS, WE, MANKIND, HAVING LOST THE PLANETS ON WHICH WE LIVED, ESCAPED TO SPACE. HENCEFORTH, TO THIS DAY, WE HAVE BEEN FORCED TO LIVE IN SPACE COLONIES.

OUR LAST HOPE, THE PLANET ZION, REMAINS, BUT THE UNIDENTIFIED BEINGS, "GISEISHA," CAST A DARK SHADOW OVER THAT HOPE.

MANKIND CONCENTRATED ALL ITS EFFORTS INTO BUILDING THE GIANT HUMANOID WEAPONS, "INGRIDS (GODDESSES)," WHICH WE USE TO FIGHT THE GISEISHA. BUT ONLY THOSE WHO HAVE MET THE UNUSUALLY STRICT REQUIREMENTS CAN BECOME PILOTS OF THE GODDESSES. SO, TO FIND AND TRAIN THOSE FEW PEOPLE OUT OF THE MANY APPLICANTS TO BECOME A PILOTS, G.O.A. (GODDESS OPERATOR ACADEMY) WAS ESTABLISHED.

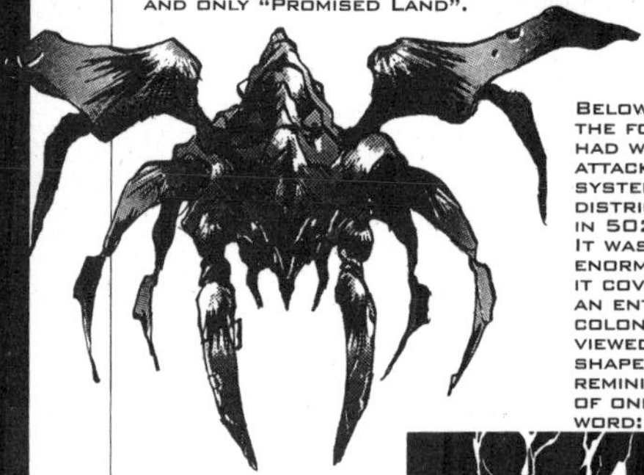

BELOW IS THE FORM IT HAD WHEN IT ATTACKED STAR SYSTEM 21NN, DISTRICT 128 IN 5025. IT WAS SO ENORMOUS IT COVERED AN ENTIRE COLONY. WHEN VIEWED, ITS SHAPE IS REMINISCENT OF ONLY ONE WORD: "DEVIL".

THE ENEMY: GISEISHA

GISEISHA IS THE GENERAL TERM USED FOR THE MYSTERIOUS LIFE FORMS THAT HAVE ATTACKED US. AS THEIR CONSTITUTION, SHAPE, AND ABILITIES VARY, THEIR TRUE NATURE IS COMPLETELY UNKNOWN. AS THEY MAKE REPEATED INVASIONS ON ZION AND ATTACK OUR COLONIES THAT ARE ON THEIR WAY TO THE LAST PLANET, THERE IS NO DOUBT THEY ARE MANKIND'S GREATEST ENEMY. WHY THEIR GOAL IS ZION, WHY THEY ARE ATTACKING OUR PEOPLE, EVEN THE REASONS FOR THEIR ACTIONS ARE UNKNOWN. BUT, SINCE THE FIRST CONFIRMED SIGHTING HAPPENED AFTER THE CRISIS OF SYSTEMS, IT IS SAID THAT THEY MAY BE A CONSEQUENCE OF THAT EVENT.

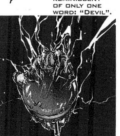

ABOVE, IS THE FORM THAT ATTACKED G.O.A. AS IT WAS CRUISING THE SURROUNDING SPACE NEAR ZION IN 5030. IT IS SMALLER IN COMPARISON, BUT AS A RESULT OF ITS TERRIBLE FIGHTING POWER, THE GODDESS AGUI KEAMEIA'S MANIPULATOR WAS DESTROYED.

G·O·A

G.O.A'S SYSTEM

...THEY WILL BECOME PILOTS. ONE OF THE CURRENT PILOTS MUST STOP BEING ABLE TO PILOT (DUE TO DEATH OR DEGENERATION OF EX), OR THE CANDIDATE MUST SHOW ABILITIES SUPERIOR TO THOSE OF A CURRENT PILOT. FOR A CANDIDATE TO BECOME A PILOT, THOSE ARE THE ONLY TWO PATHS.

FOR THE THREE-YEAR ENROLLMENT, G.O.A. HAS PUT TOGETHER VARIOUS CURRICULA.

IN LECTURE, EVERYTHING ABOUT G.O.A., THE INGRIDS, ETC. IS THOROUGHLY DRILLED INTO THE STUDENTS, STARTING WITH THE BASICS. WHEN NEW CANDIDATES ARE ENROLLED, THE LIMITS OF THEIR PHYSICAL ABILITIES ARE CHECKED, AND THEIR TRAINING PROGRAMS FOR THEIR PRO-INGS ARE ADJUSTED ACCORDINGLY.

FURTHERMORE, WHILE INSIDE G.O.A., ALL THE CANDIDATES' EX ARE NEUTRALIZED TO A DEGREE SO THEY CAN LIVE NORMAL LIVES.

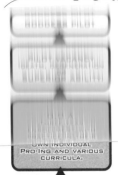

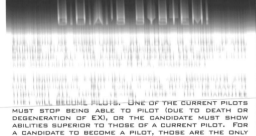

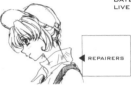

...OWN INDIVIDUAL PRO-ING AND VARIOUS CURRICULA.

APTITUDE
(MALE, AGE 14-16, HAS EX)

ALL COLONIES

THIS DIAGRAM IS A SIMPLIFIED VERSION OF THE ACTUAL SYSTEM.

◀ REPAIRERS

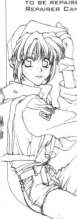

ALL THE NECESSARY PERSONNEL IN CHARGE OF REPAIRING THE PRO-INGS ARE WOMEN. UNLIKE THE GODDESS CANDIDATES, THEY ARE SENT TO G.O.A. TO TRAIN TO BE REPAIRERS; THEY ARE REPAIRER CANDIDATES. THEY STUDY EVERYTHING RELATED TO REPAIRING THE PRO-INGS AND ARE THOROUGHLY TRAINED TO THINK OF PROTECTING THE LIVES OF THE PILOTS AND THE MACHINES. LIKE THE CANDIDATES, THE REPAIRERS ARE REQUIRED TO WEAR UNIFORMS SUCH AS THE ONE SHOWN. THE HAT AND GLOVES ARE ALSO PART OF THE UNIFORM. WHAT THE MODEL'S DONE TO THE UNIFORM IN THIS PICTURE ORIGINALLY SHOULD NOT HAVE BEEN ALLOWED.

CANDIDATE ▶

THE GODDESS CANDIDATES ARE REQUIRED TO WEAR UNIFORMS LIKE THE ONE SHOWN ON THE RIGHT. AS IT IS THE CASUAL WEAR FOR ALL THE CANDIDATES, THEY WEAR IT UNDER ALL CIRCUMSTANCES EXCEPT TRAINING. ASIDE FROM THIS UNIFORM, THEY HAVE A PILOT SUIT WORN ONLY WHILE IN THEIR PRACTICE VEHICLES. AND FOR SPECIAL OCCASIONS, THEY EACH HAVE A SPECIAL JACKET USED FOR OFFICIAL EVENTS AND SUCH.

ABOUT THE UNIFORMS:

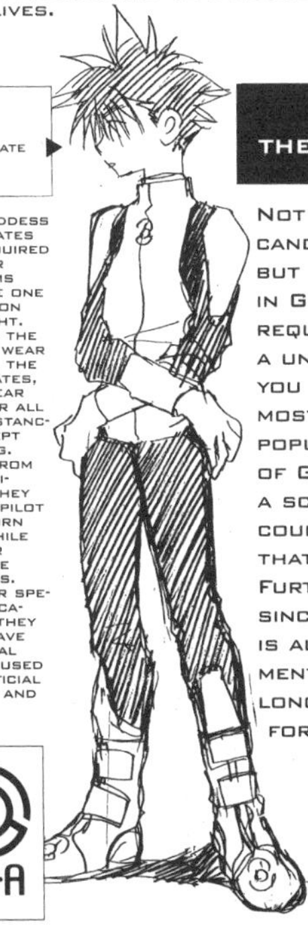

NOT ONLY THE CANDIDATES, BUT EVERYONE IN G.O.A. IS REQUIRED TO WEAR A UNIFORM. IF YOU THINK OF THE MOST DENSELY POPULATED PART OF G.O.A. AS A SCHOOL, YOU COULD SAY THAT THAT'S OBVIOUS. FURTHERMORE, SINCE CLEANLINESS IS ALSO A REQUIREMENT FOR PILOTS, LONG HAIR IS FORBIDDEN.

3
1
5
4
2

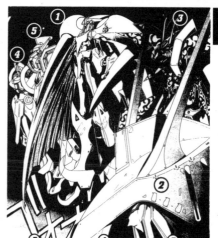

WHAT ARE THE GODDESSES?

THE INGRIDS ARE GIANT HUMANOID WEAPONS CREATED TO PROTECT ZION FROM THE GISEISHA. ULTIMATE WAR MACHINES, ONLY FIVE OF THEM EXIST. AS THEY ARE ALL BUILT IN THE FORM OF WOMEN, THEY ALL HAVE FEMININE NAMES. NICKNAMED "THE FIVE GODDESSES," THEY ARE ELEGANT AND MAGNIFICENT IN BATTLE. THEY CONTINUE TO FIGHT THE GISEISHA THROUGH GENERATIONS OF PILOTS.

5 LUHMA KLEIN: THE INGRID IN CHARGE OF DETECTION AND ANALYSIS PILOTED BY ERNEST CUORE. SHE CAN EASILY FIND THE ENEMY AND TRANSMIT TACTICAL DATA TO HER TEAM.	4 AGUI KEAMEIA: THE INGRID IN CHARGE OF DEFENSE PILOTED BY RIOROUTE VILGYNA. SHE CAN SPREAD A STRONG DEFENSIVE SHIELD.	3 TELLIA KALLISTO: AN INGRID IN CHARGE OF ATTACK PILOTED BY YU HIKURA. POWER IS VERY IMPORTANT TO HER, AS SHE SPECIALIZES IN ATTACKING DIRECTLY.	2 EEVA LEENA: AN INGRID IN CHARGE OF ATTACK PILOTED BY GAREAS ELIDO. SHE HAS SEVERAL GUNS FOR ITS INDIVIDUAL USE.	1 ERNN LATIES: THE INGRID PILOTED BY TEELA ZAIN ELMES. PUTTING THEM IN ORDER, SHE IS THE TOP OF ALL THE GODDESSES.	BASIC INFORMATION ABOUT THE FIVE GODDESSES:

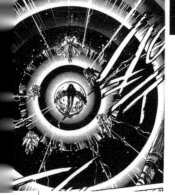

THIS IS A PICTURE OF THE FIVE GODDESSES IN 5025 AS THEY REMOVED THE GISEISHA ATTACHED TO COLONY K-01 IN THE 21NN SYSTEM, DISTRICT 128. AT THIS TIME, BECAUSE THE GISEISHA DID NOT ENGAGE THE GODDESSES DIRECTLY, THE BATTLE WENT MORE SMOOTHLY THAN A SIMULTANEOUS ATTACK IN WHICH ALL THE GODDESSES MUST COOPERATE.

BASIC INFORMATION ABOUT THE FIVE GODDESSES:

THE FIVE GODDESSES ALWAYS FIGHT TOGETHER AS A TEAM. THIS WAY, EACH GODDESS HAS A SPECIFIC ROLE, AND BY COMBINING THESE ROLES, THEY CAN WORK TO THEIR FULL POTENTIAL. CURRENTLY, THE ESTABLISHED PATTERN IS: LUHMA KLEIN FINDS AND ANALYZES THE ENEMY AND SIGNALS THE OTHERS; AGUI KEAMEIA SETS UP THE SHIELD; AND THEN ERNN LATIES, EEVA LEENA AND TELLIA KALLISTO ATTACK AND DESTROY THE ENEMY.

THE SYSTEM IS BASICALLY ONE PILOT (MUST BE MALE), ONE REPAIRER (MUST BE FEMALE), AND ONE INGRID THAT HAS BEEN ADJUSTED SPECIFICALLY FOR THE PILOT, ALL PUT TOGETHER AND USED AS ONE SET.

THE POSSIBILITY OF BECOMING A PILOT IS LIMITED TO THOSE WHO, OF THE FOUR BLOOD TYPES (AA, AB, OX, AND EO), HAVE TYPE EO (AN EXTREMELY RARE TYPE), AND WHOSE EX IS AWAKENED BETWEEN THE AGES OF FOURTEEN AND SIXTEEN.

G·O·A

THE EQUIPMENT OF THE PILOT

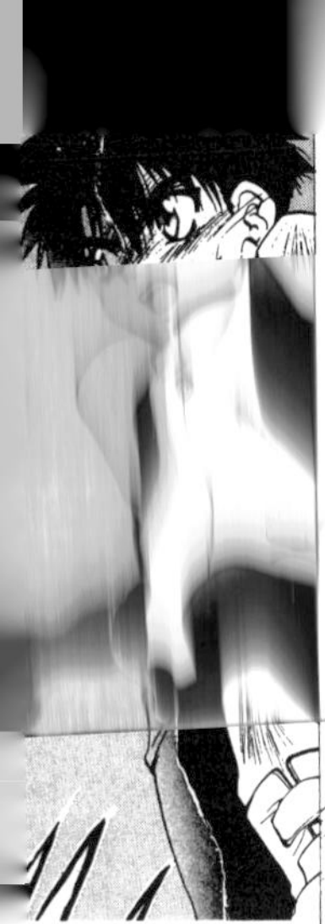

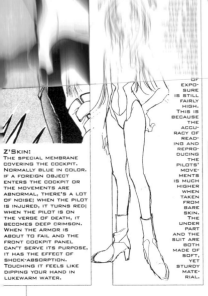

Z'SKIN:
The special membrane covering the cockpit. Normally blue in color. If a foreign object enters the cockpit or the movements are abnormal, there's a lot of noise; when the pilot is injured, it turns red; when the pilot is on the verge of death, it becomes deep crimson. When the armor is about to fail and the front cockpit panel can't serve its purpose, it has the effect of shock-absorption. Touching it feels like dipping your hand in lukewarm water.

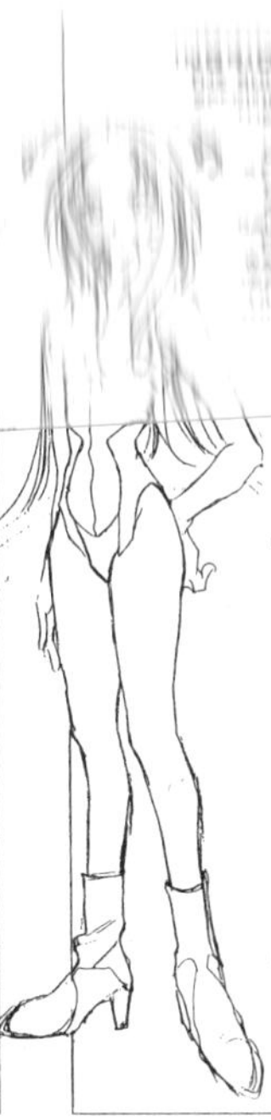

...of exposure is still fairly high. This is because the accuracy of reading and reproducing the pilots' movements is much higher when taken from bare skin. The under part and the suit are both made of soft, yet sturdy material.

...attributes of the Ingrids are so much better that the systems can't be compared. But in order to bring out that high power, special equipment is needed for each Ingrid. Here, we will introduce each piece of Ingrid equipment.

SCANNER:

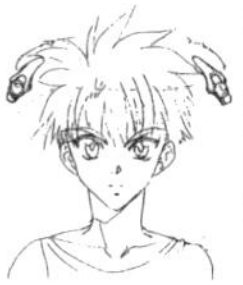

The mechanism that reads the pilot's brainwaves and connects them directly to the Ingrid. It could be compared to a second brain, and, to an extent, it can save the pilot's physical condition and emotions. Floating two centimeters above the ears and just above the temples, it can function even if there is something between it and the head. It also rotates around the head.

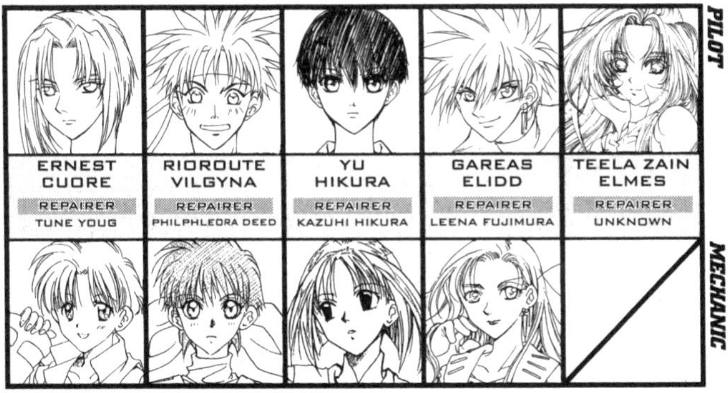
PILOT
ERNEST CUORE
REPAIRER
TUNE YOUG
RIOROUTE VILGYNA
REPAIRER
PHILPHLEORA DEED
YU HIKURA
REPAIRER
KAZUHI HIKURA
GAREAS ELIDD
REPAIRER
LEENA FUJIMURA
TEELA ZAIN ELMES
REPAIRER
UNKNOWN
MECHANIC

G·O·A

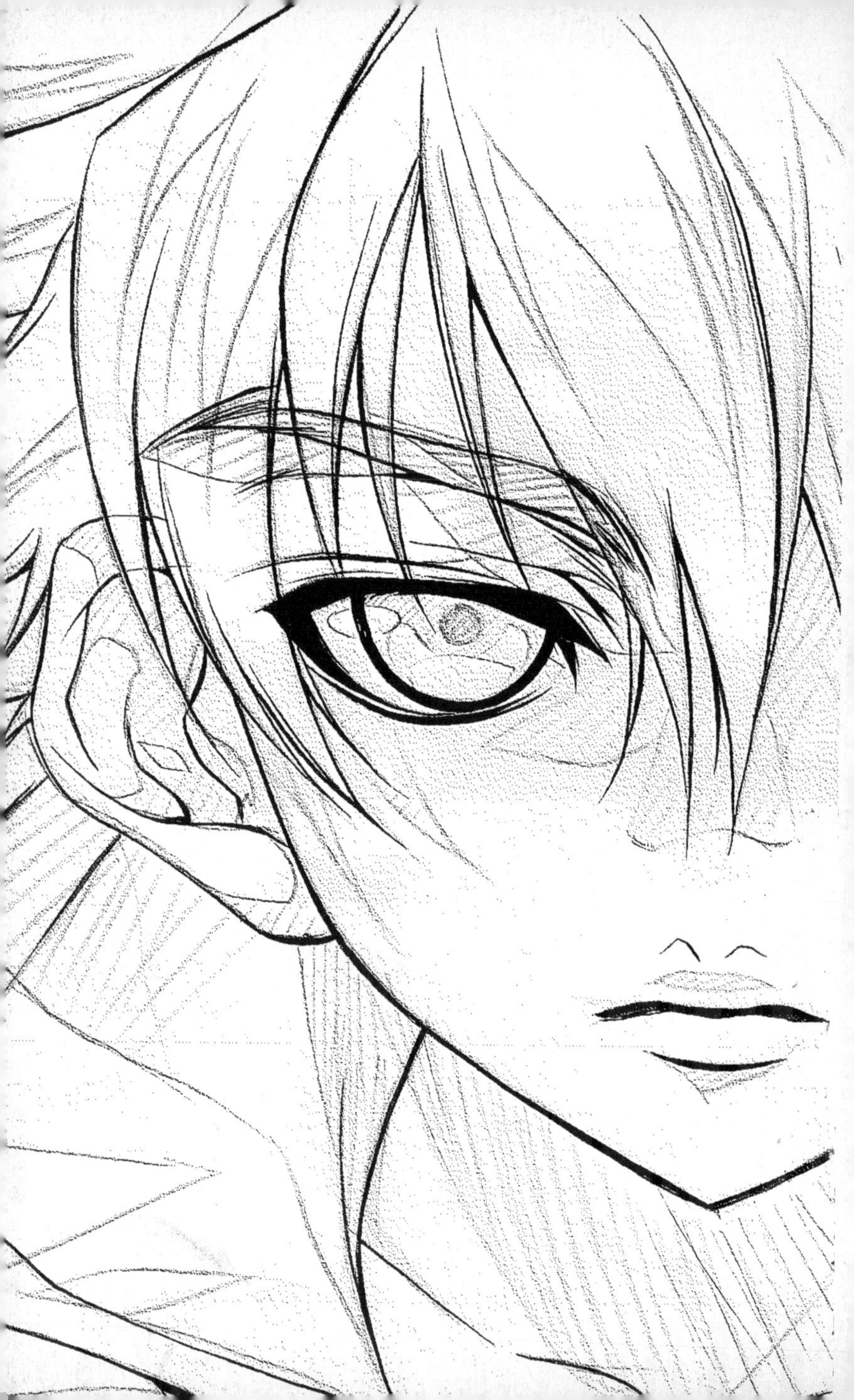

OUTLINE OF STORY

IT IS THE YEAR S.C. 5030. ALMOST A THOUSAND YEARS AGO, THE CRISIS OF SYSTEMS (ALSO KNOWN AS LOST PROPERTY), DESTROYED FOUR ENTIRE PLANETARY SYSTEMS AND FORCED MANKIND TO LIVE IN ARTIFICIAL COLONIES IN THE VASTNESS OF EMPTY SPACE. MANKIND'S LAST HOPE IS THE ONE REMAINING PLANET, ZION, BUT THIS PLANET IS ALSO BEING TARGETED BY UNKNOWN ENEMIES CALLED THE GISEISHA (A.K.A. THE VICTIM.) TO BATTLE THE GISEISHA, MANKIND CREATED FIVE GIANT HUMANOID WEAPONS, INGRIDS (ALSO KNOWN AS GODDESSES), BUT THE PILOTS MUST MEET SPECIAL REQUIREMENTS (MALE, IN GOOD HEALTH FOURTEEN TO SIXTEEN YEARS OLD; BLOOD TYPE EO; POTENTIALLY HAVING THE SPECIAL ABILITY OTHERWISE KNOWN AS EX). G.O.A. (GODDESS OPERATOR ACADEMY) WAS ESTABLISHED AS A FACILITY TO TRAIN THESE PILOTS, AND THE STUDENTS HAVE COME TO BE KNOWN AS CANDIDATES FOR GODDESS.

TWO OF THE NEWEST CANDIDATES ARE ZERO ENNA AND HIEAD GNER. WHILE ZERO TRAINED WITH UPPERCLASSMAN ERTS VIRNY COCTEAU, HIEAD SUDDENLY FORCED HIS WAY IN AND STARTED A FIGHT WITH ZERO. INSTRUCTOR AZUMA LEARNED OF THIS AND PUT BOTH BOYS IN THE "SELF-EXAMINATION" ROOM. DESPITE THEIR SHARED PUNISHMENT, THE RIVALRY BETWEEN THEM SEEMS ONLY TO HAVE GROWN STRONGER.

MEANWHILE, REPAIRER TUNE YOUG TRIED TO CONFESS HER SECRET LOVE TO GODDESS PILOT ERNEST CUORE, BUT THEY WERE INTERRUPTED BY AN EXTREMELY LARGE GISEISHA INVASION. AS ERNEST AND THE OTHER PILOTS RACED TO CONFRONT THE ENEMY, SEVERAL PILOT CANDIDATES WERE ASSIGNED TO ACT AS A LAST LINE OF DEFENSE OUTSIDE G.O.A. MUCH TO HIS DISMAY, ZERO WAS NOT ONE OF THEM.

THE FIVE GODDESSES FOUGHT A DIFFICULT BATTLE AGAINST THE VAST NUMBER OF GISEISHA. WHEN PILOT GAREAS BROKE FORMATION AND GOT INTO TROUBLE, ERNEST TOOK A DIRECT HIT WHILE TRYING TO HELP HIS COMRADE. MORTALLY WOUNDED, ERNEST BECAME LOCKED IN A DEATH GRIP WITH THE GISEISHA LEADER. IN ORDER TO DESTROY THE LEADER, GAREAS WAS FORCED TO KILL HIS FRIEND AS WELL. DISTRAUGHT BY THE DEATH OF HIS TEAMMATE, GAREAS IGNORED THE ORDER TO RETREAT AND GODDESS LEADER TEELA WAS FORCED TO TAKE CONTROL OF GAR'S GODDESS.

THOUGH ERNEST WAS KILLED IN THE BATTLE, HIS GODDESS, LUHMA KLEIN WAS SALVAGEABLE. LUHMA WAS RETURNED TO G.O.A. FOR REPAIRS AND A NEW PILOT. THE REPAIRS WERE HANDLED BY AN EMOTIONALLY WRECKED TUNE YOUG. THE CANDIDATE PROMOTED TO PILOT WAS ERTS.

THOUGH EVERY CANDIDATE WORKS TO ONE DAY BECOME A PILOT, PROMOTION DUE TO THE DEATH OF A PILOT IS A SOMBER OCCASION. IT'S EVEN MORE SO WHEN IT TURNS OUT THAT THE CANDIDATE AND THE PILOT IN QUESTION ARE ACTUALLY BROTHERS...

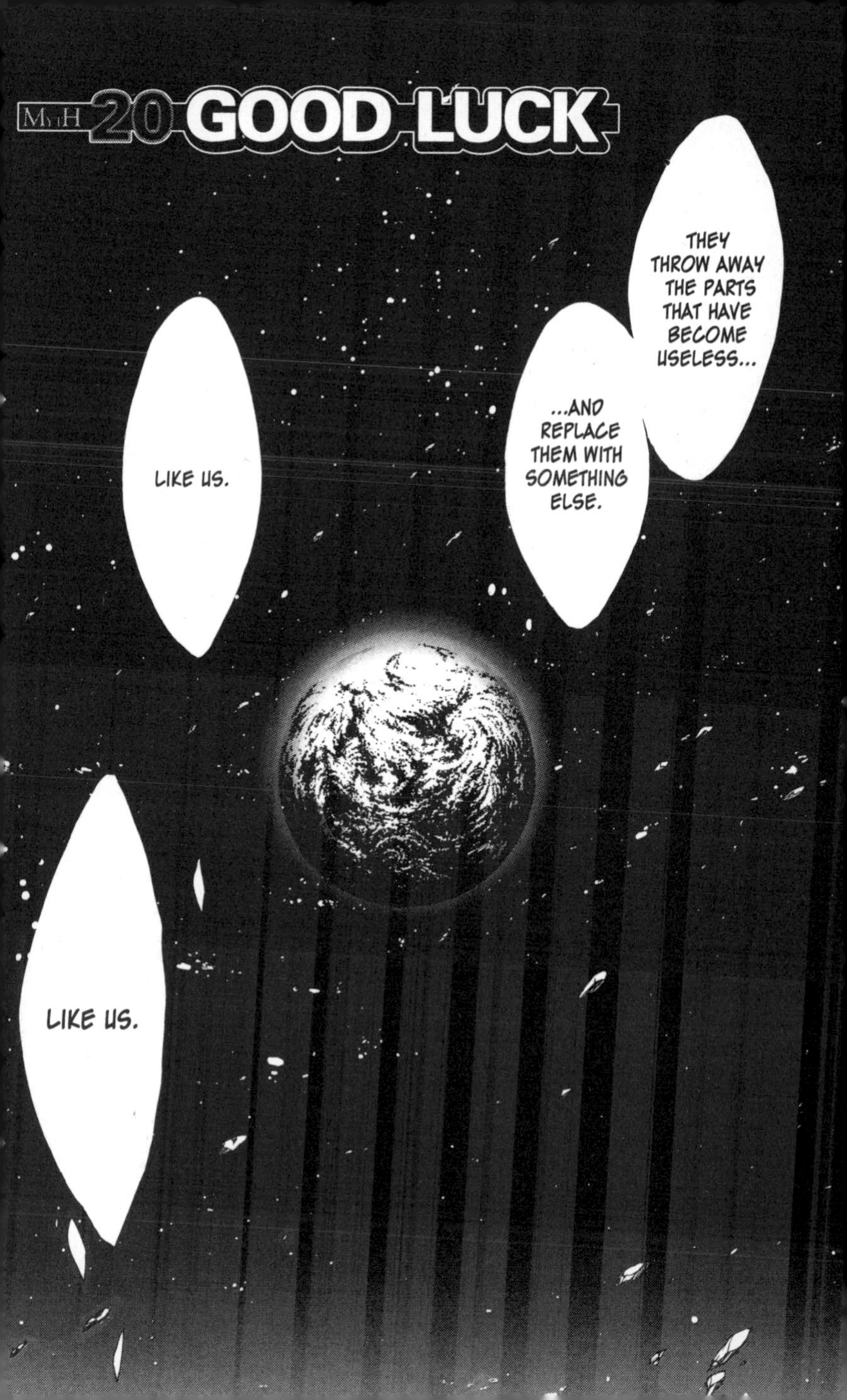
MYTH 20 GOOD LUCK
THEY THROW AWAY THE PARTS THAT HAVE BECOME USELESS...
...AND REPLACE THEM WITH SOMETHING ELSE.
LIKE US.
LIKE US.

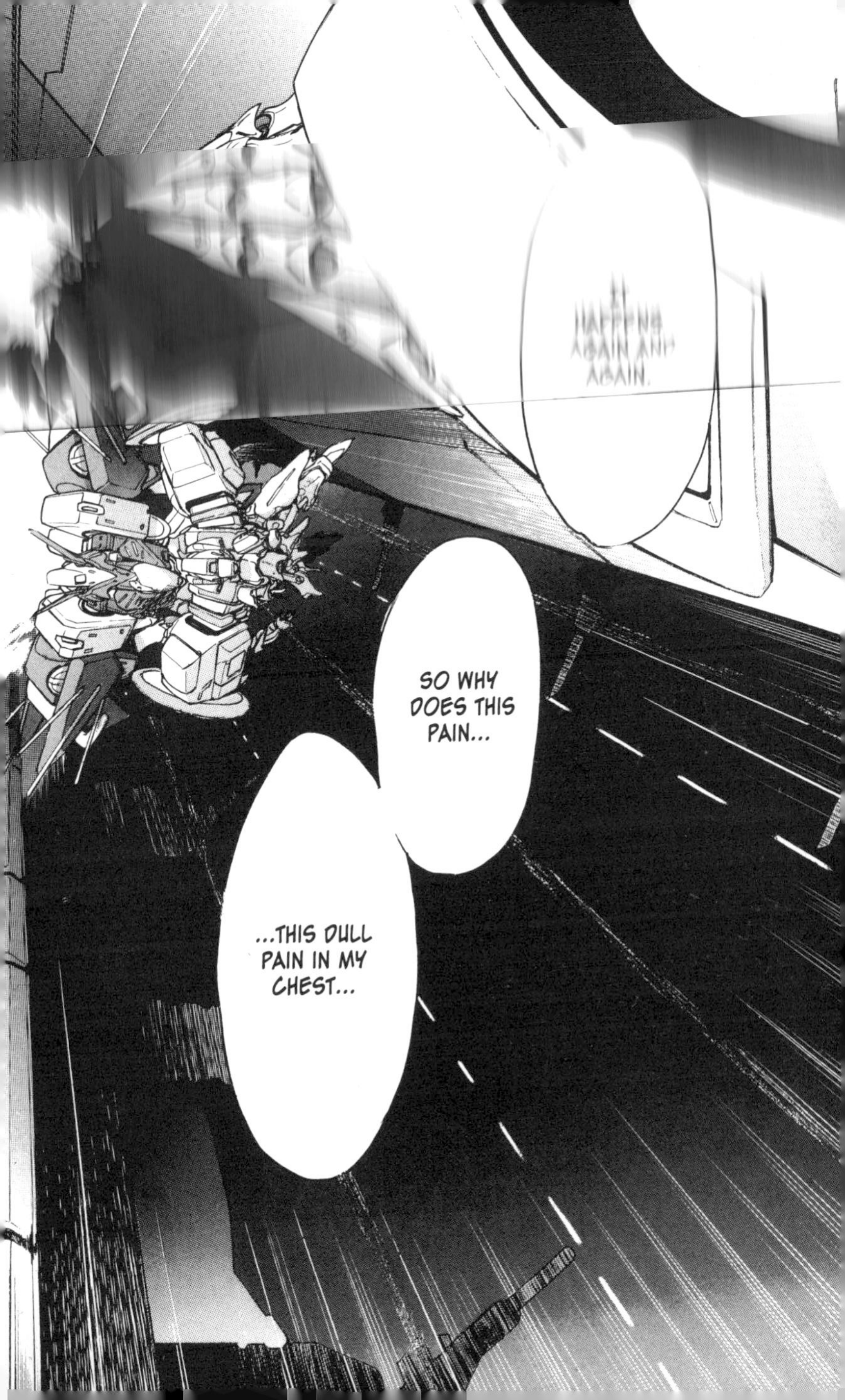
IT HAPPENS AGAIN AND AGAIN.
SO WHY DOES THIS PAIN...
...THIS DULL PAIN IN MY CHEST...

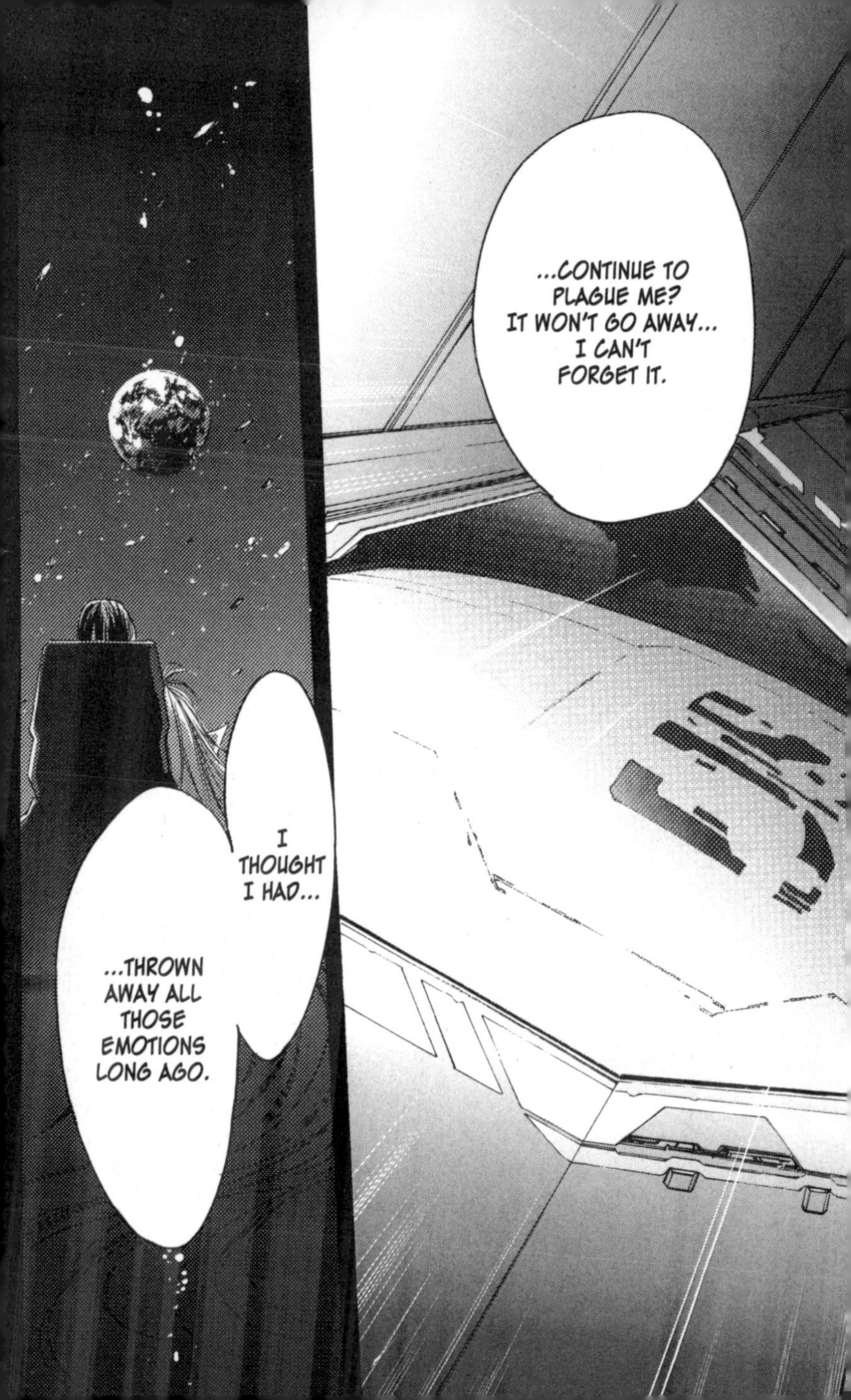
...CONTINUE TO PLAGUE ME? IT WON'T GO AWAY... I CAN'T FORGET IT.
I THOUGHT I HAD...
...THROWN AWAY ALL THOSE EMOTIONS LONG AGO.

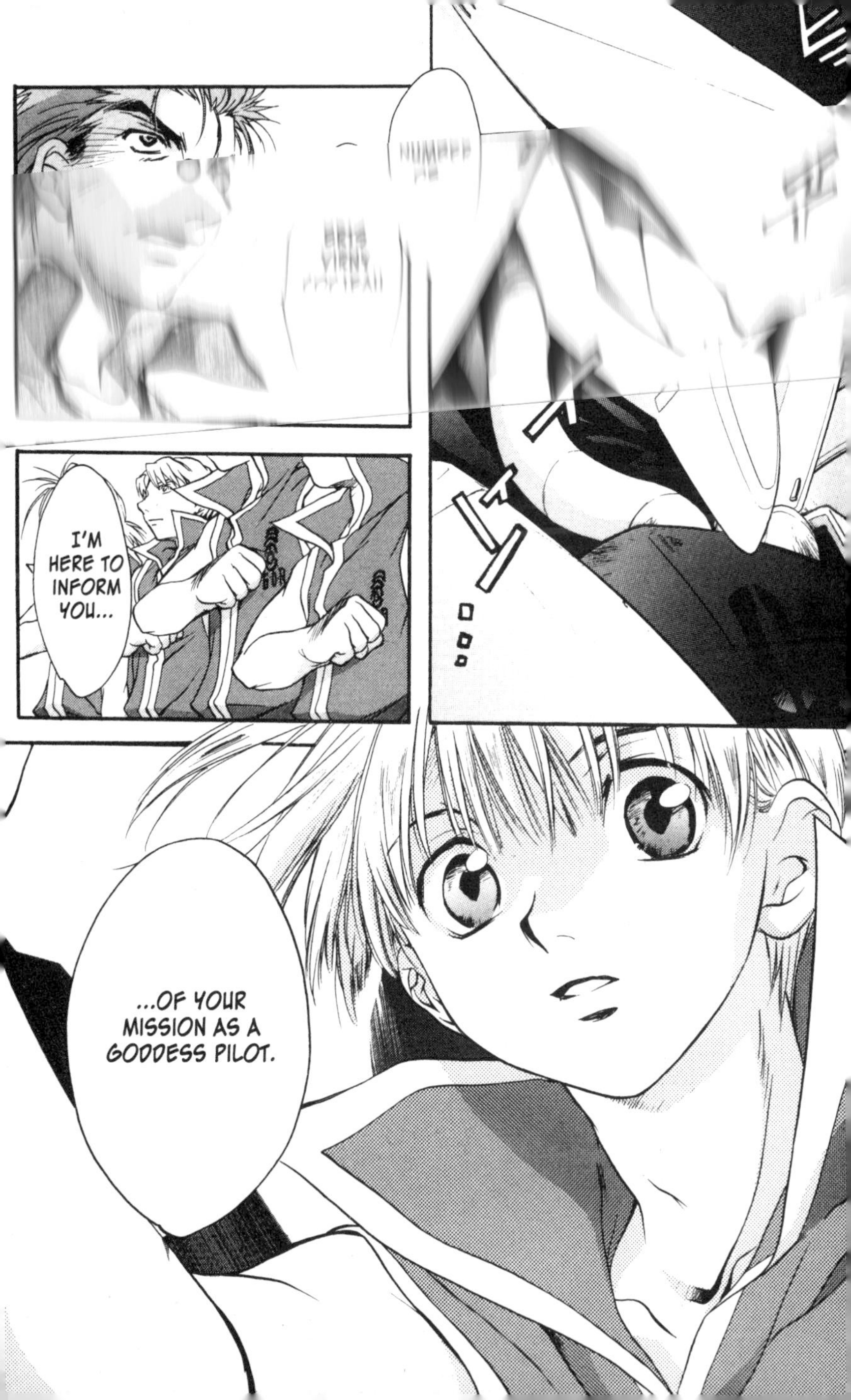
I'M HERE TO INFORM YOU...
...OF YOUR MISSION AS A GODDESS PILOT.

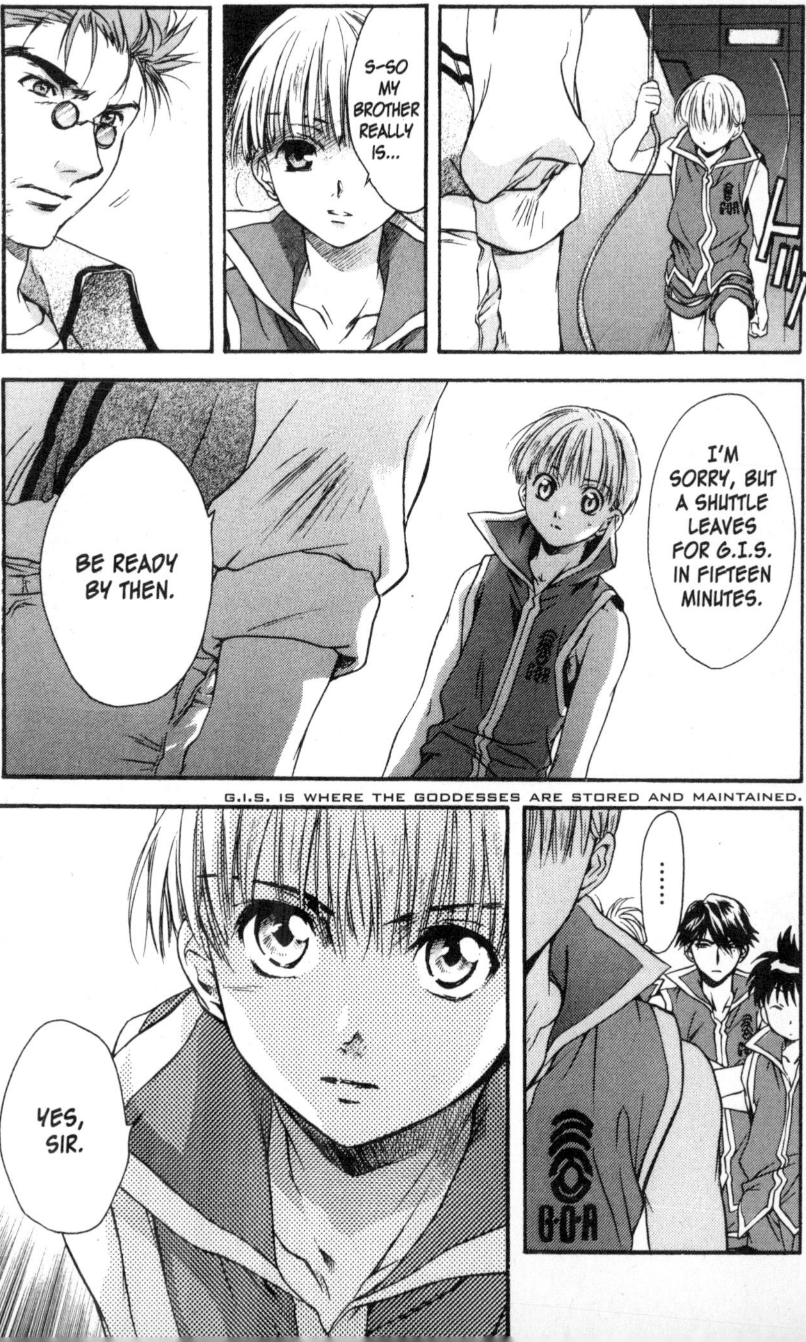
S-SO MY BROTHER REALLY IS...
I'M SORRY, BUT A SHUTTLE LEAVES FOR G.I.S. IN FIFTEEN MINUTES.
BE READY BY THEN.
G.I.S. IS WHERE THE GODDESSES ARE STORED AND MAINTAINED.
......
YES, SIR.

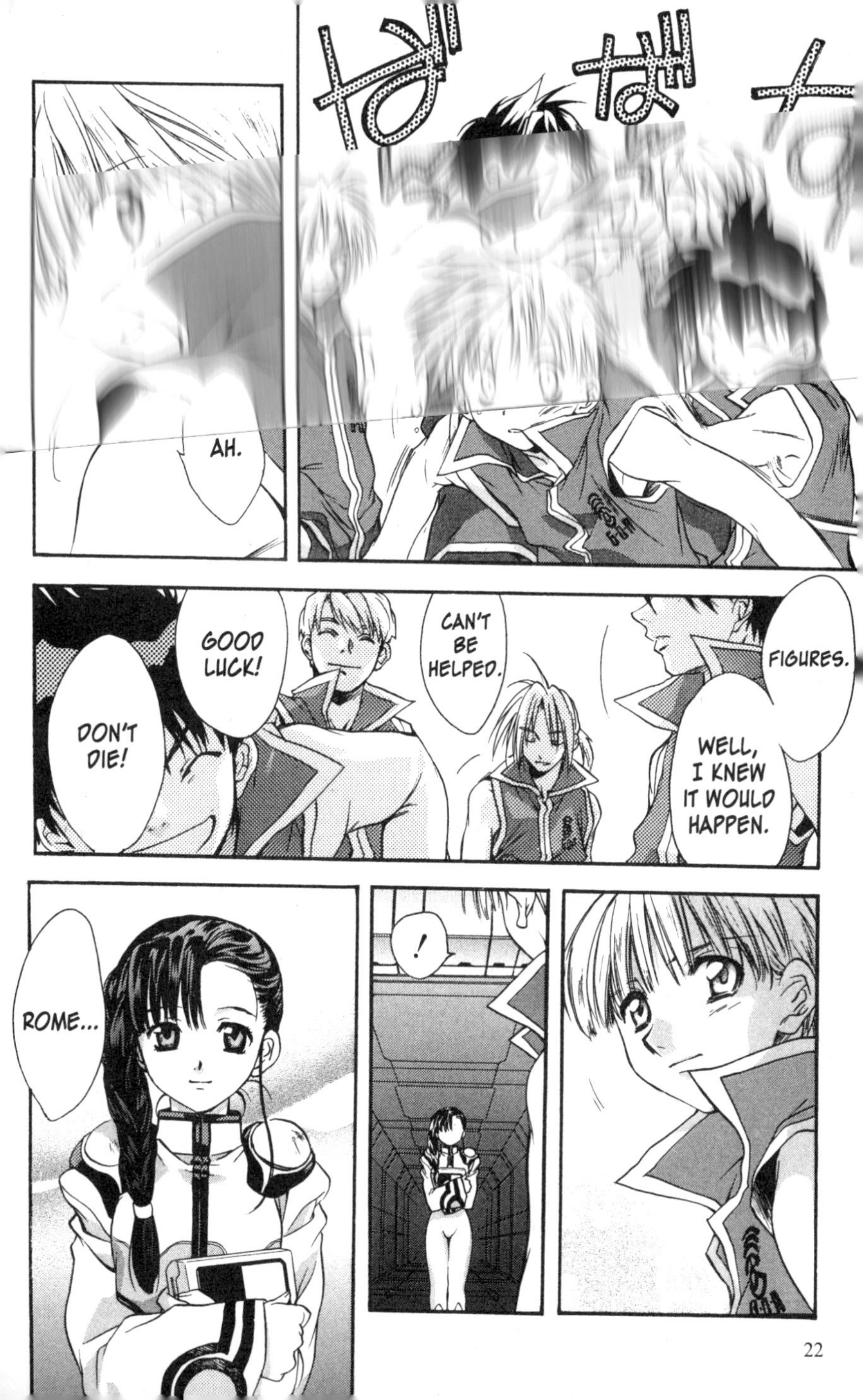
AH.
FIGURES.
WELL, I KNEW IT WOULD HAPPEN.
CAN'T BE HELPED.
GOOD LUCK!
DON'T DIE!
!
ROME...

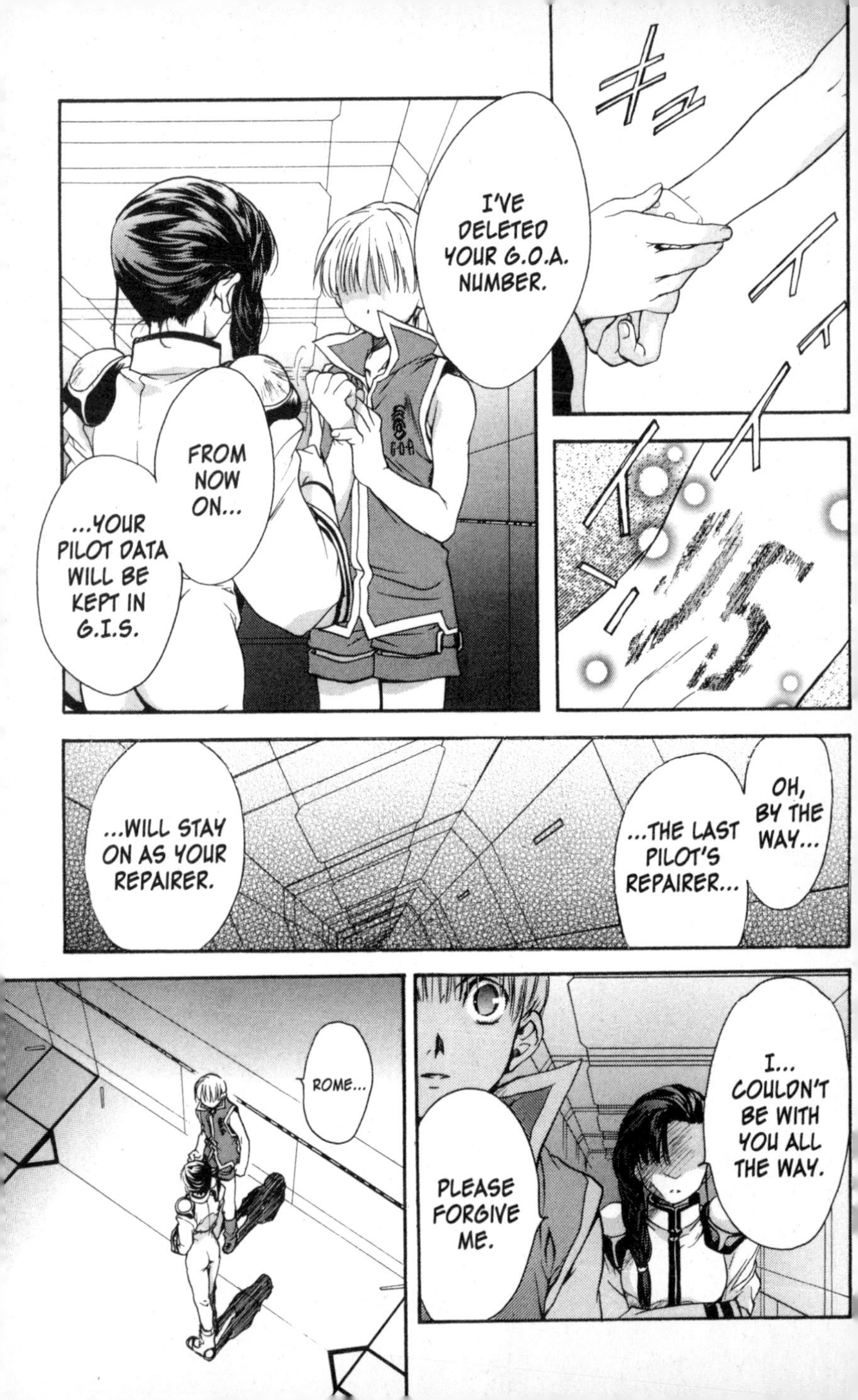
I'VE DELETED YOUR G.O.A. NUMBER.
FROM NOW ON...
...YOUR PILOT DATA WILL BE KEPT IN G.I.S.
OH, BY THE WAY...
...THE LAST PILOT'S REPAIRER...
...WILL STAY ON AS YOUR REPAIRER.
I... COULDN'T BE WITH YOU ALL THE WAY.
PLEASE FORGIVE ME.
ROME...

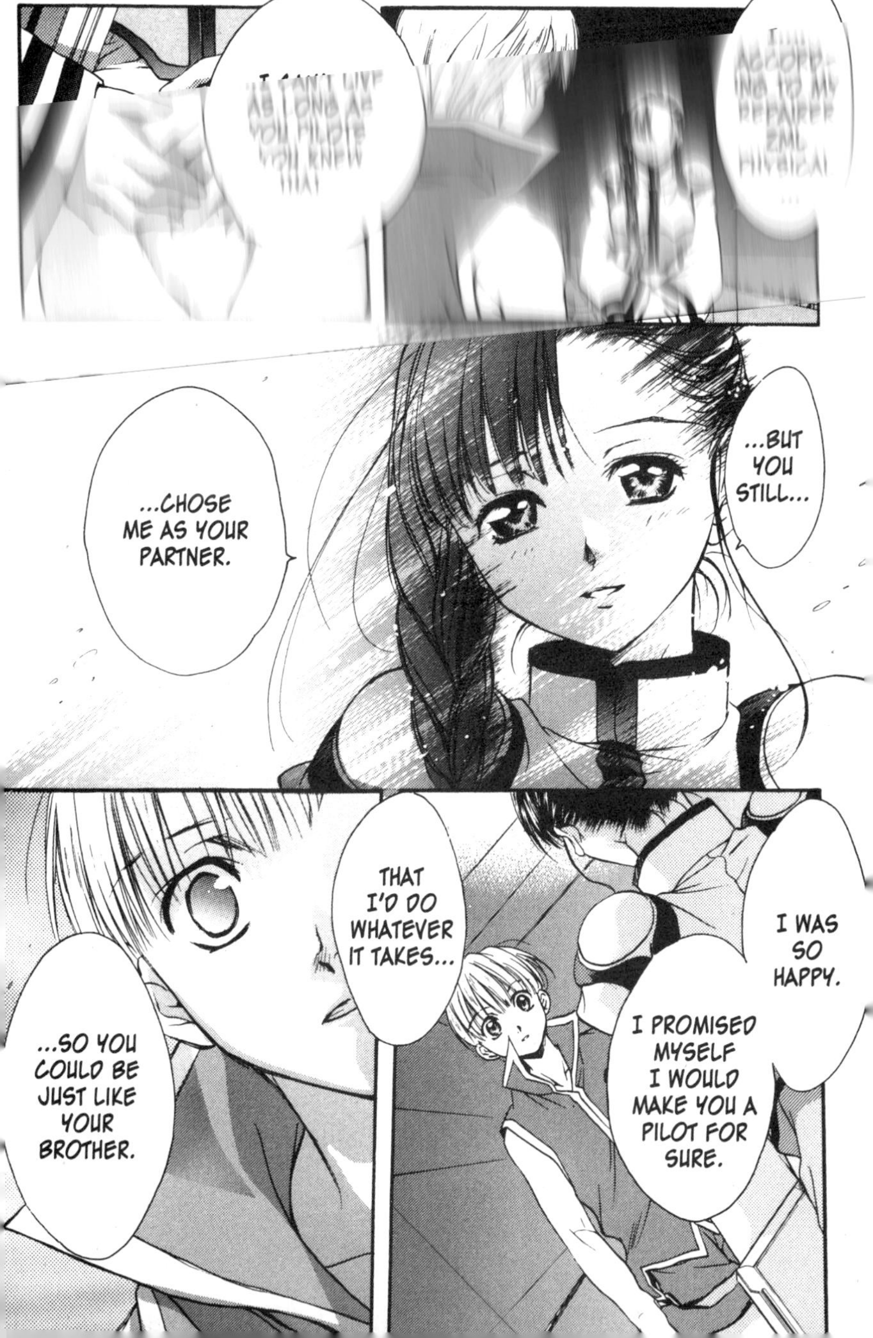
...BUT YOU STILL...
...CHOSE ME AS YOUR PARTNER.
I WAS SO HAPPY.
I PROMISED MYSELF I WOULD MAKE YOU A PILOT FOR SURE.
THAT I'D DO WHATEVER IT TAKES...
...SO YOU COULD BE JUST LIKE YOUR BROTHER.

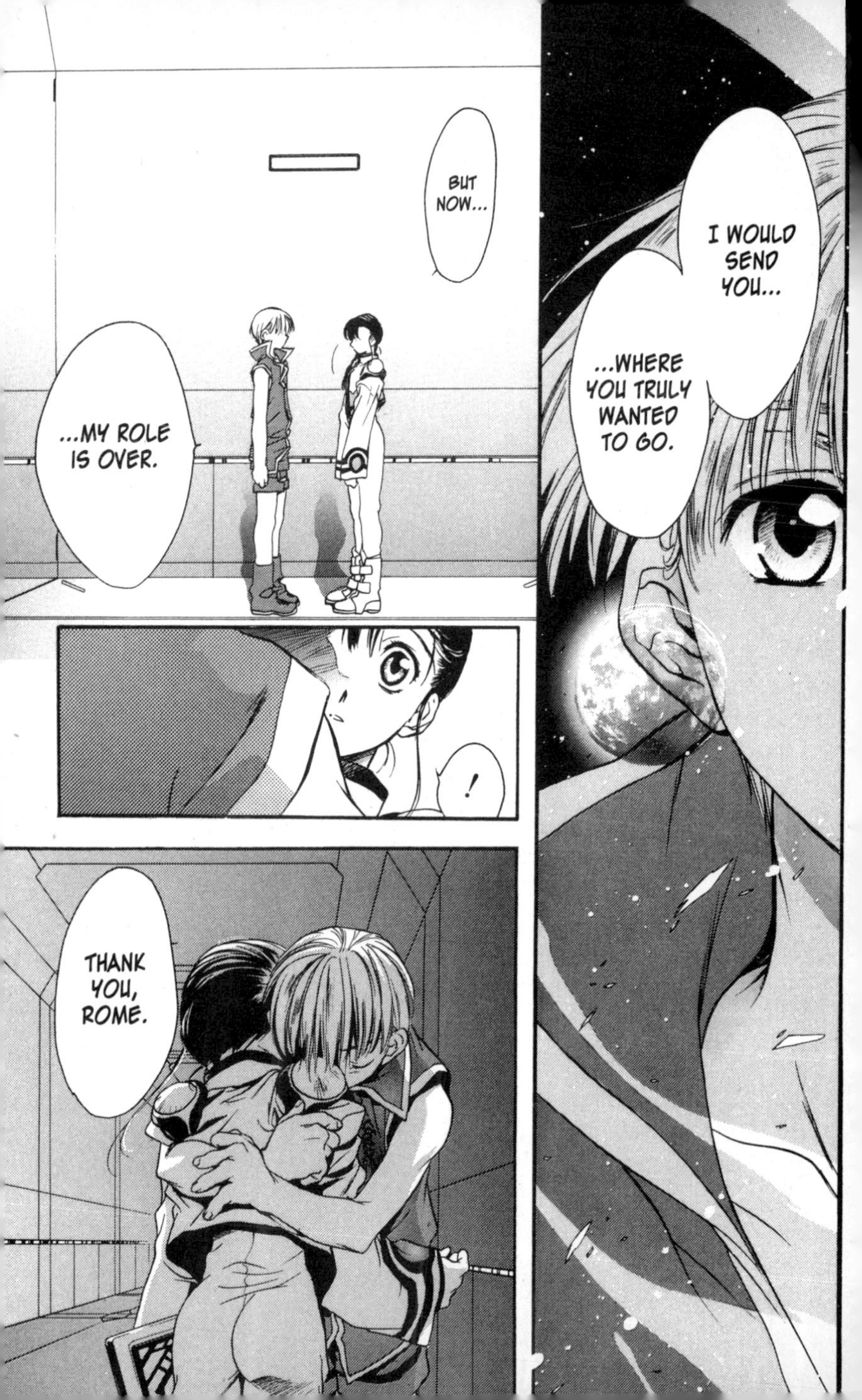

I WOULD SEND YOU...
...WHERE YOU TRULY WANTED TO GO.
BUT NOW...
...MY ROLE IS OVER.
!
THANK YOU, ROME.

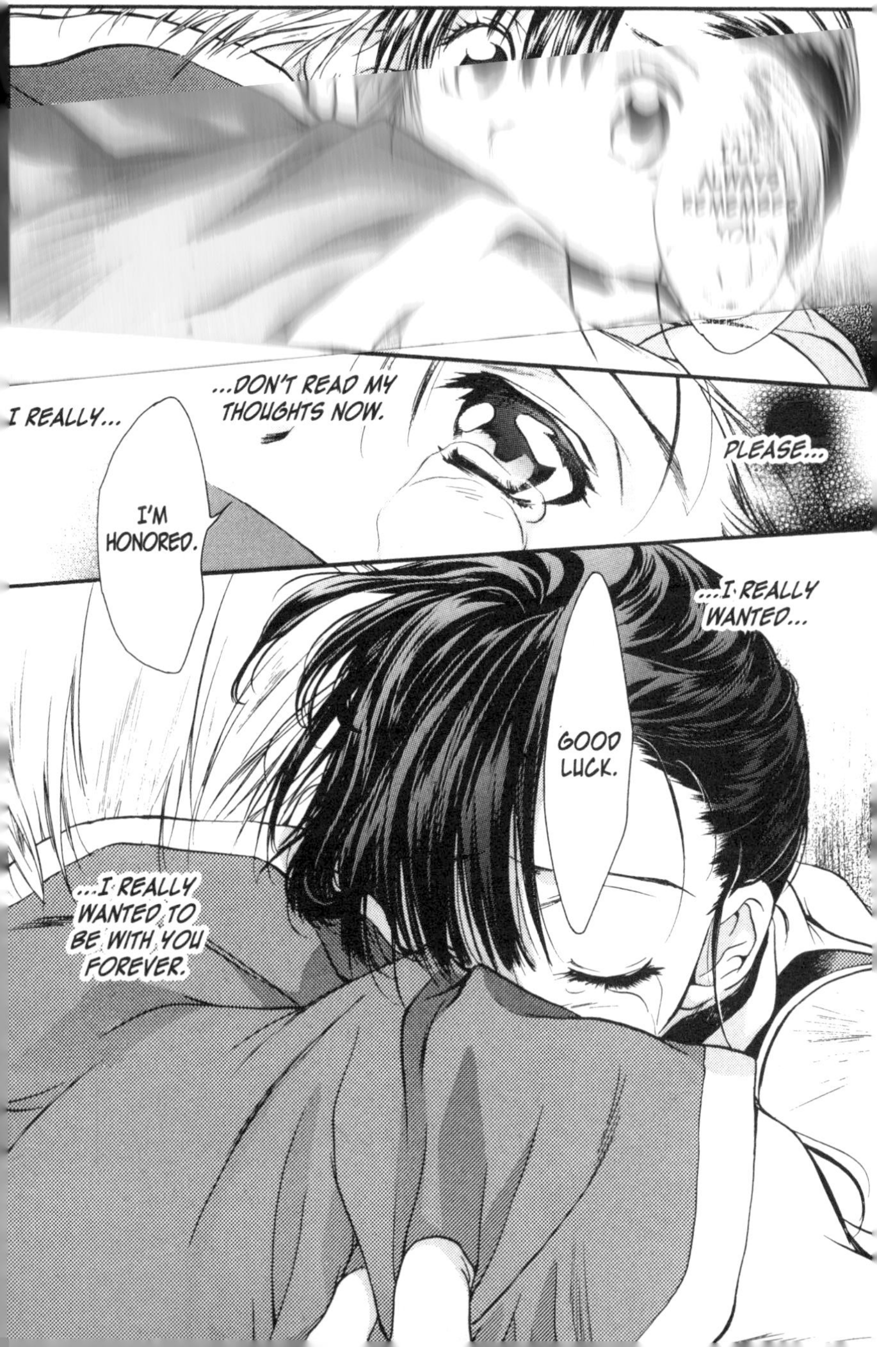
PLEASE...
...DON'T READ MY THOUGHTS NOW.
I REALLY...
I'M HONORED.
...I REALLY WANTED...
GOOD LUCK.
...I REALLY WANTED TO BE WITH YOU FOREVER.

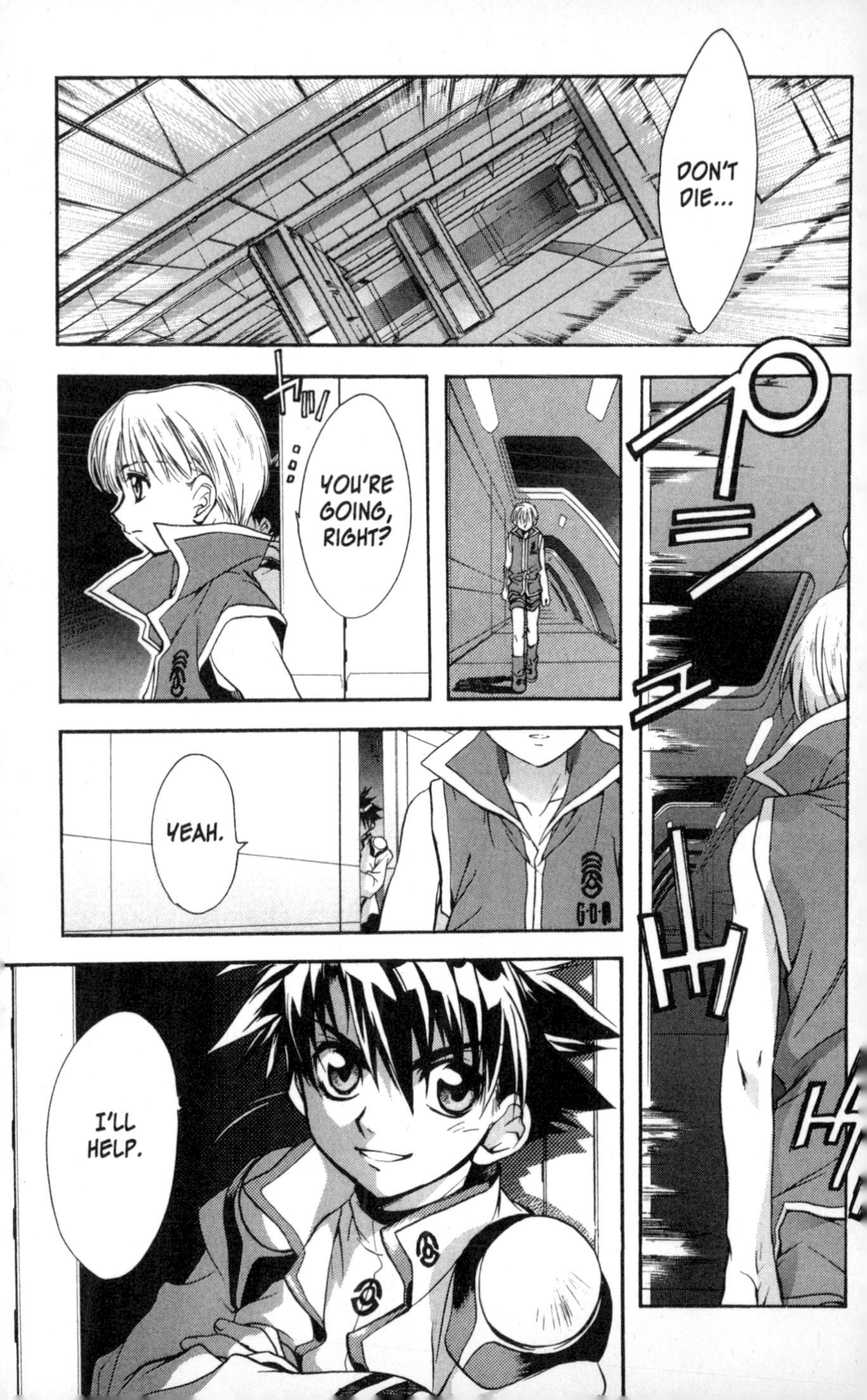
DON'T DIE...
YOU'RE GOING, RIGHT?
YEAH.
I'LL HELP.

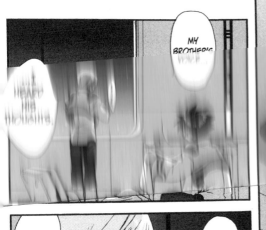

MY
BROTHER'S
VOICE

YOU'RE
NOT
SCARED OF
FIGHTING
ANYMORE
ARE YOU?

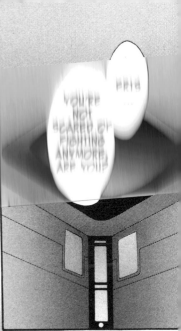

..."SPIN
HOPE."

ハイン
ハイン

HE
SAID...

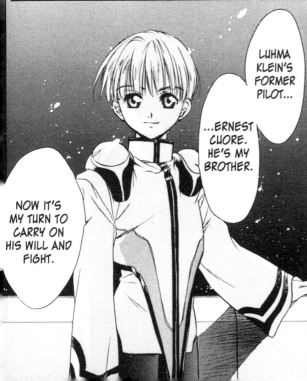

LUHMA
KLEIN'S
FORMER
PILOT...

...ERNEST
CUORE.
HE'S MY
BROTHER.

NOW IT'S
MY TURN TO
CARRY ON
HIS WILL AND
FIGHT.

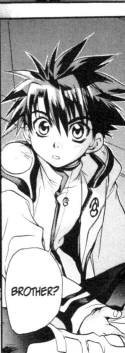

BROTHER?

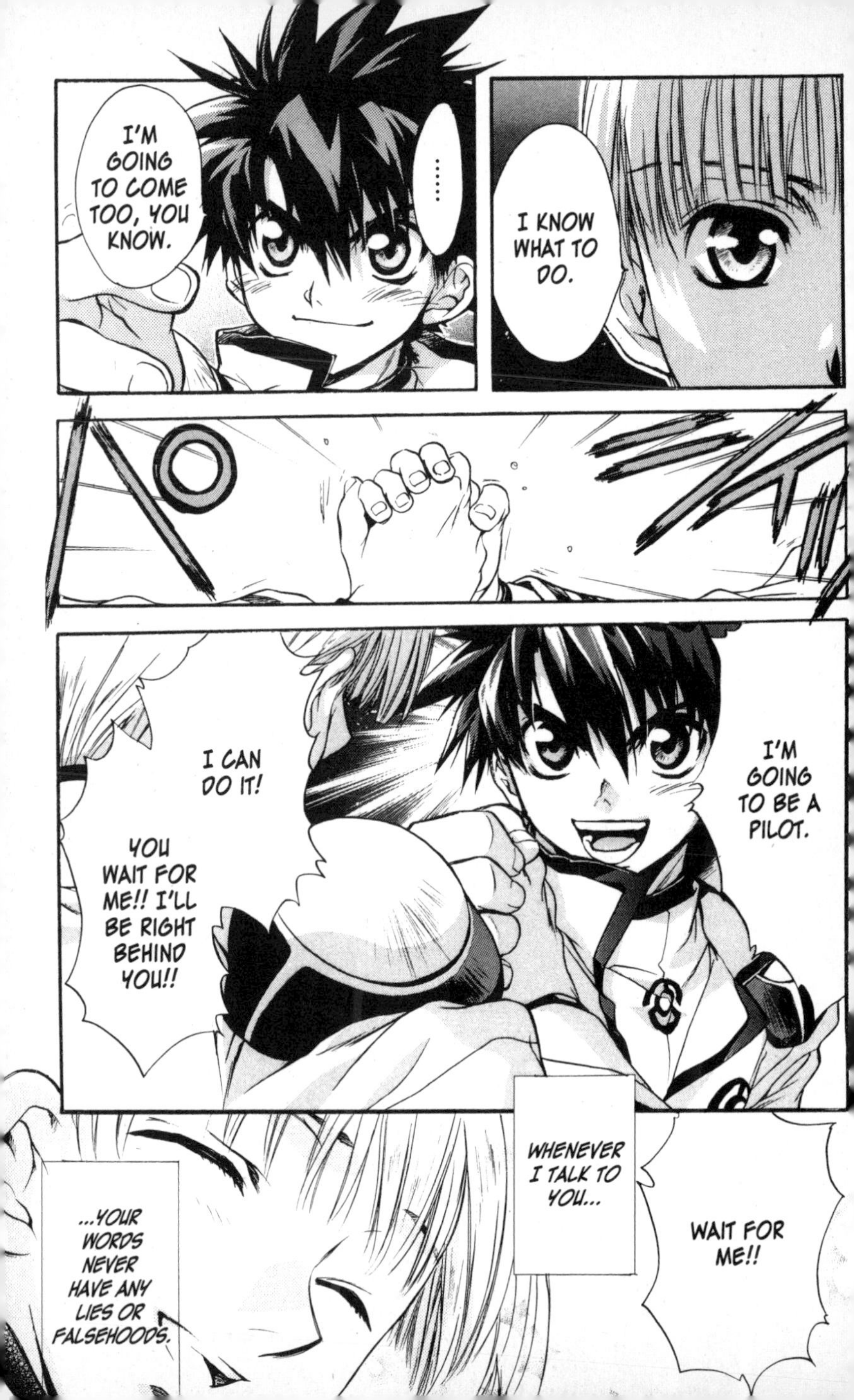
I KNOW WHAT TO DO.
......
I'M GOING TO COME TOO, YOU KNOW.
I'M GOING TO BE A PILOT.
I CAN DO IT!
YOU WAIT FOR ME!! I'LL BE RIGHT BEHIND YOU!!
WAIT FOR ME!!
WHENEVER I TALK TO YOU...
...YOUR WORDS NEVER HAVE ANY LIES OR FALSEHOODS.

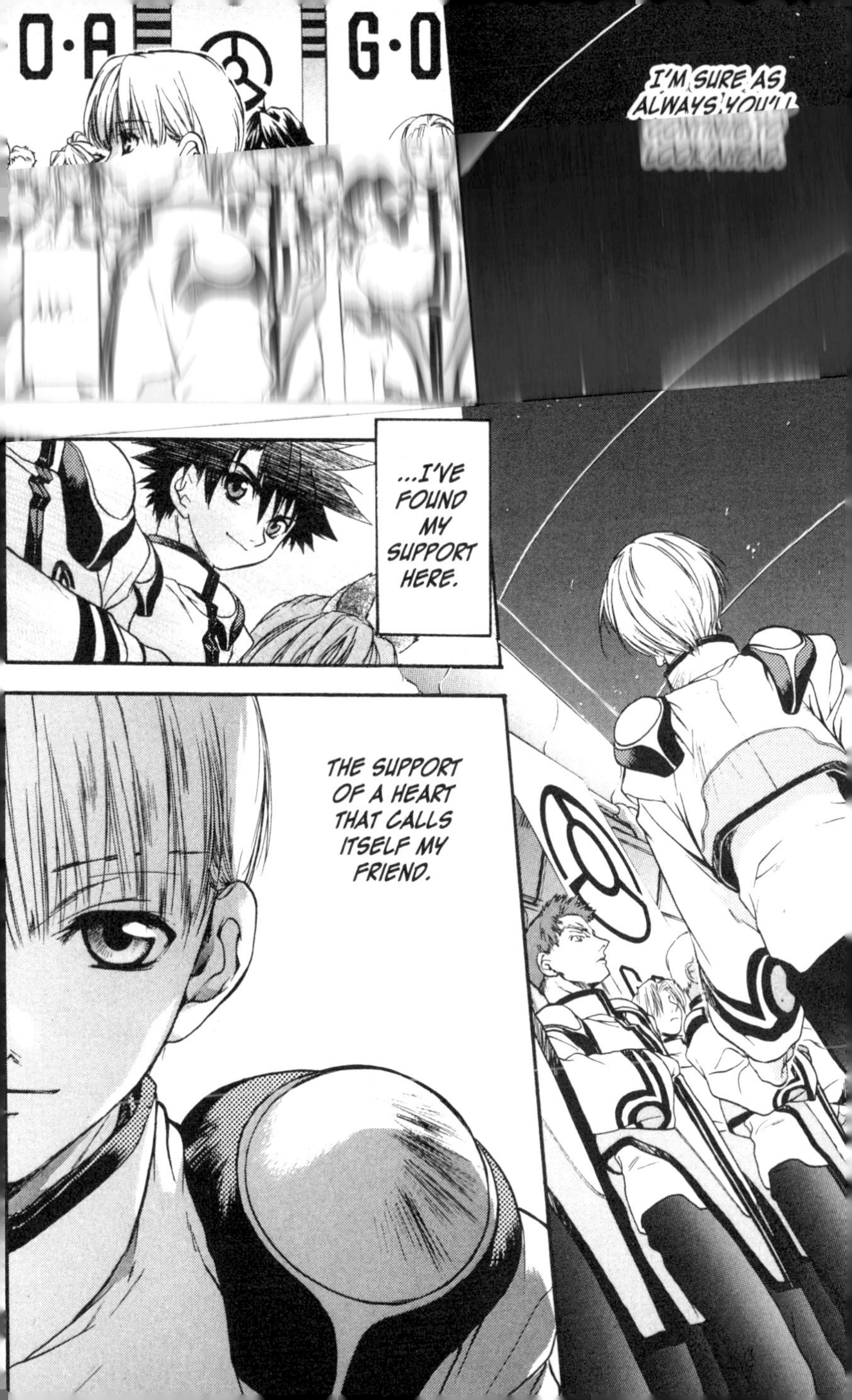
I'M SURE AS ALWAYS YOU'LL
...I'VE FOUND MY SUPPORT HERE.
THE SUPPORT OF A HEART THAT CALLS ITSELF MY FRIEND.

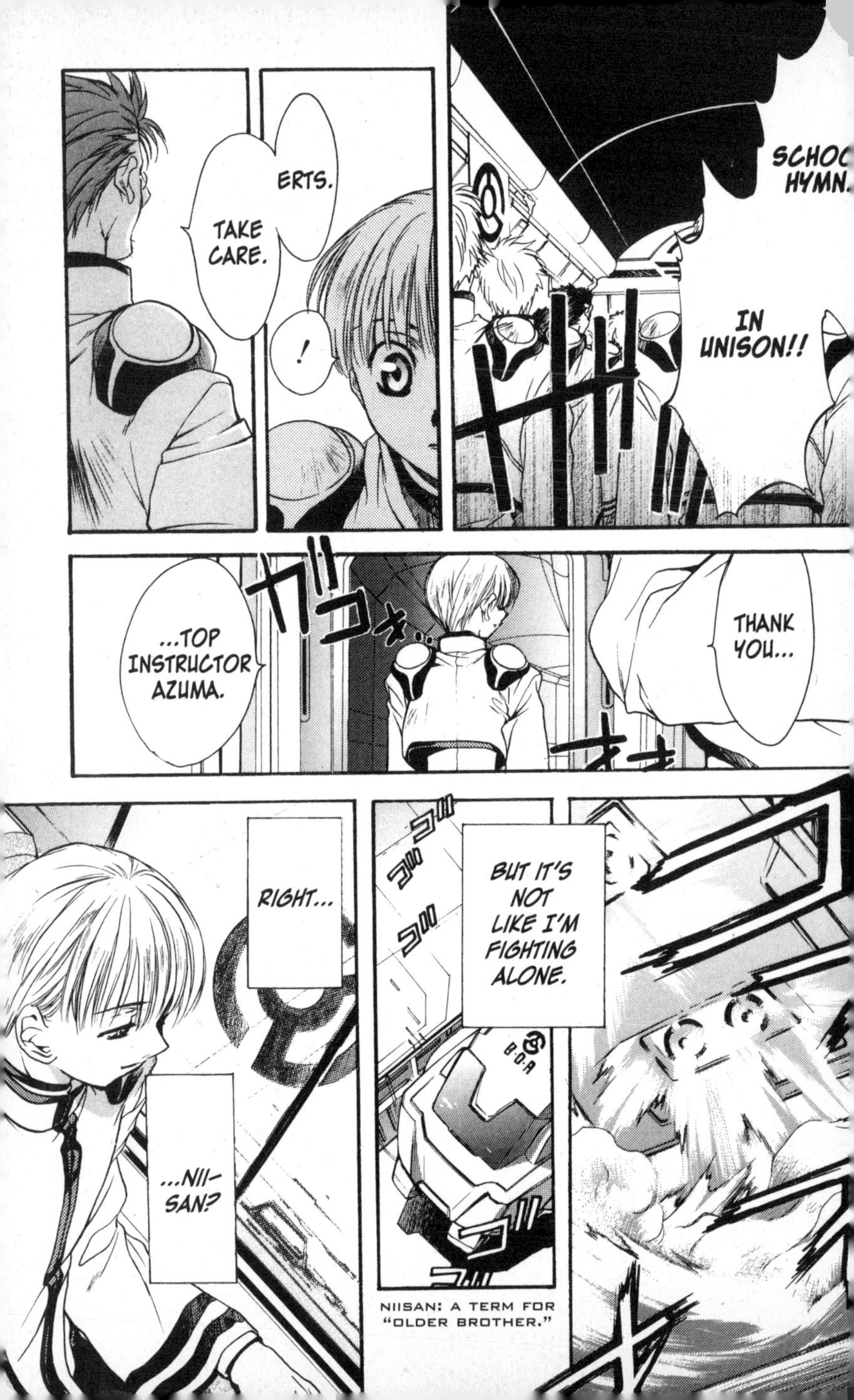
SCHOC HYMN.
IN UNISON!!
ERTS.
TAKE CARE.
!
THANK YOU...
...TOP INSTRUCTOR AZUMA.
BUT IT'S NOT LIKE I'M FIGHTING ALONE.
RIGHT...
...NII-SAN?
NIISAN: A TERM FOR "OLDER BROTHER."

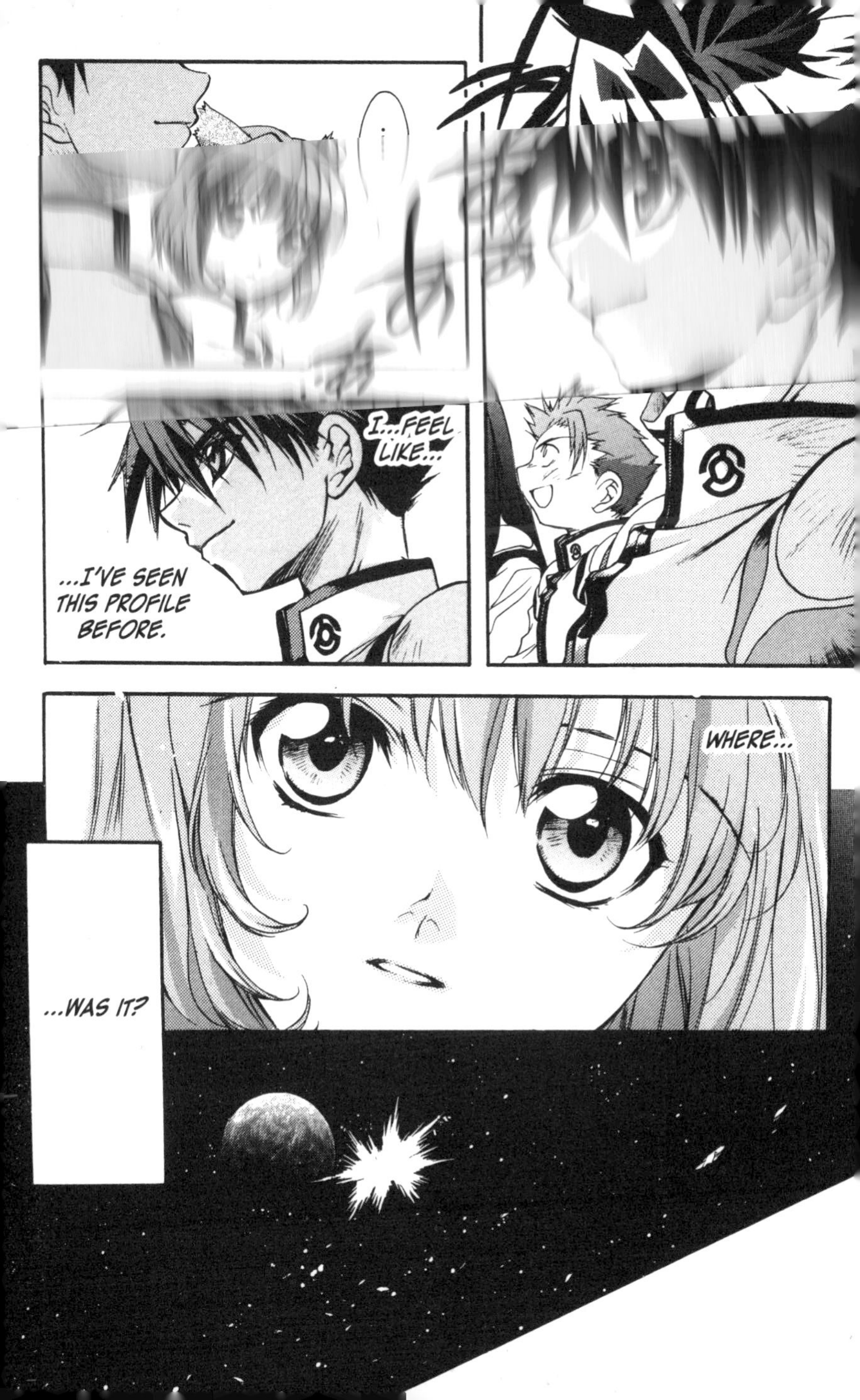
I...FEEL LIKE...
...I'VE SEEN THIS PROFILE BEFORE.
WHERE...
...WAS IT?

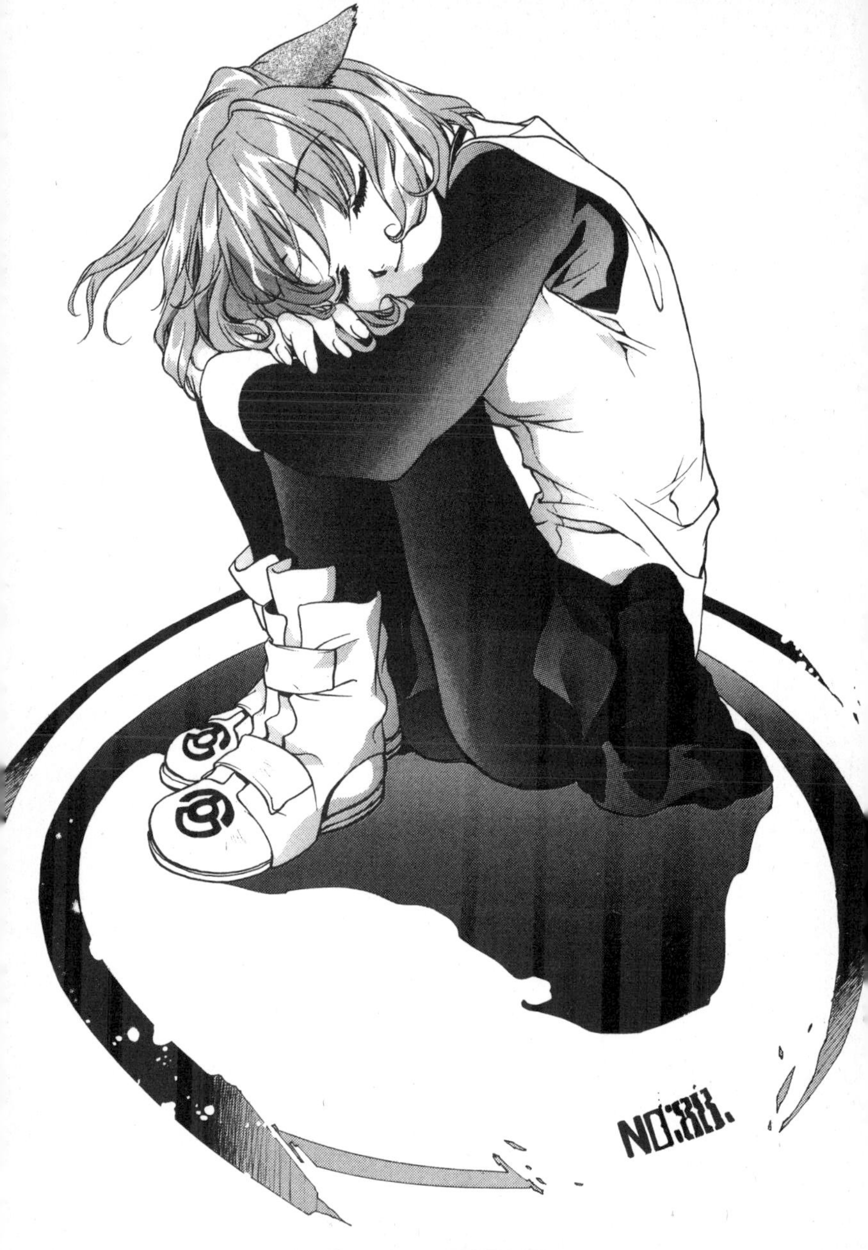
NO.38.

MyTH 21 REQUIEM

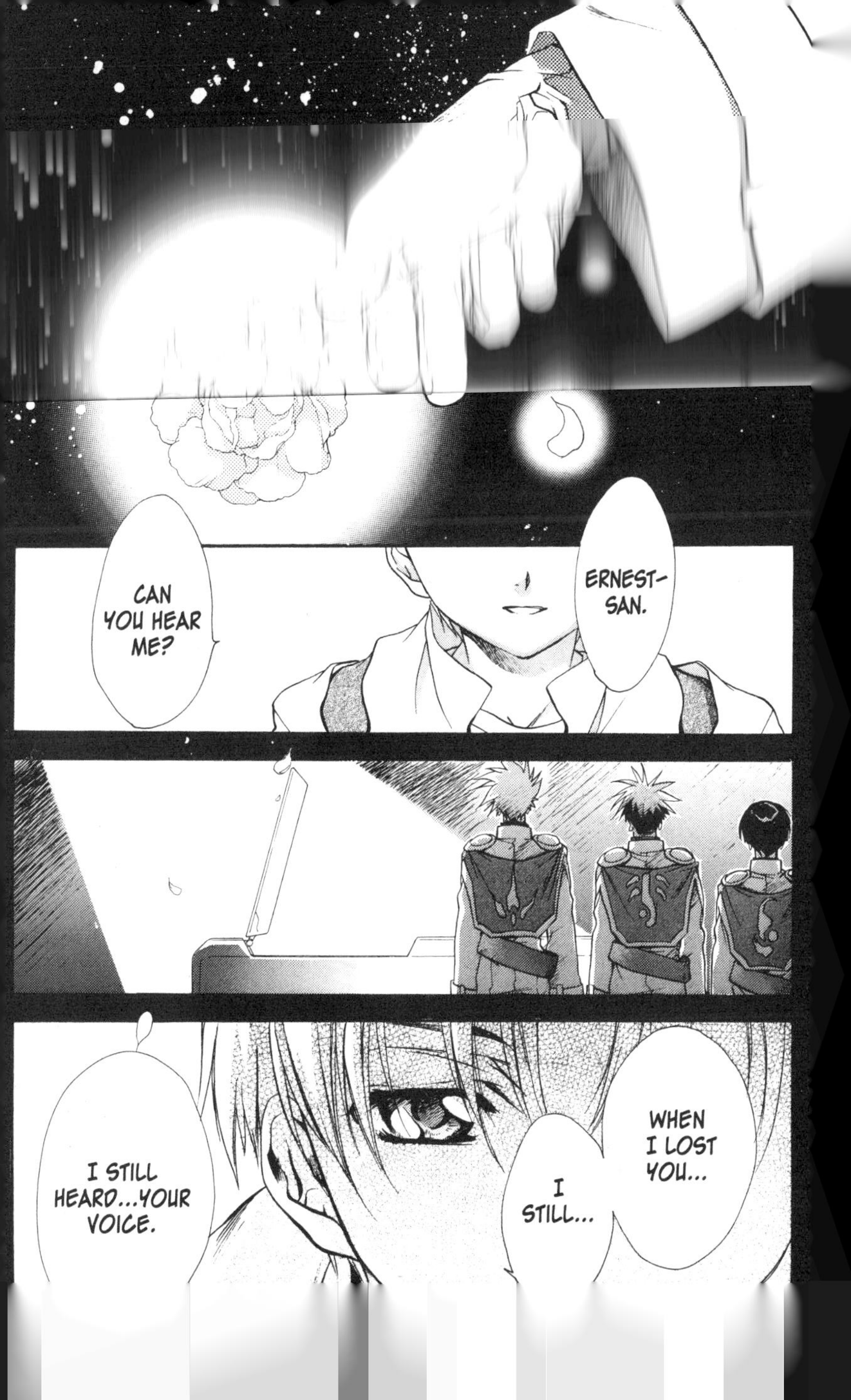
ERNEST-SAN.
CAN YOU HEAR ME?
WHEN I LOST YOU...
I STILL...
I STILL HEARD...YOUR VOICE.

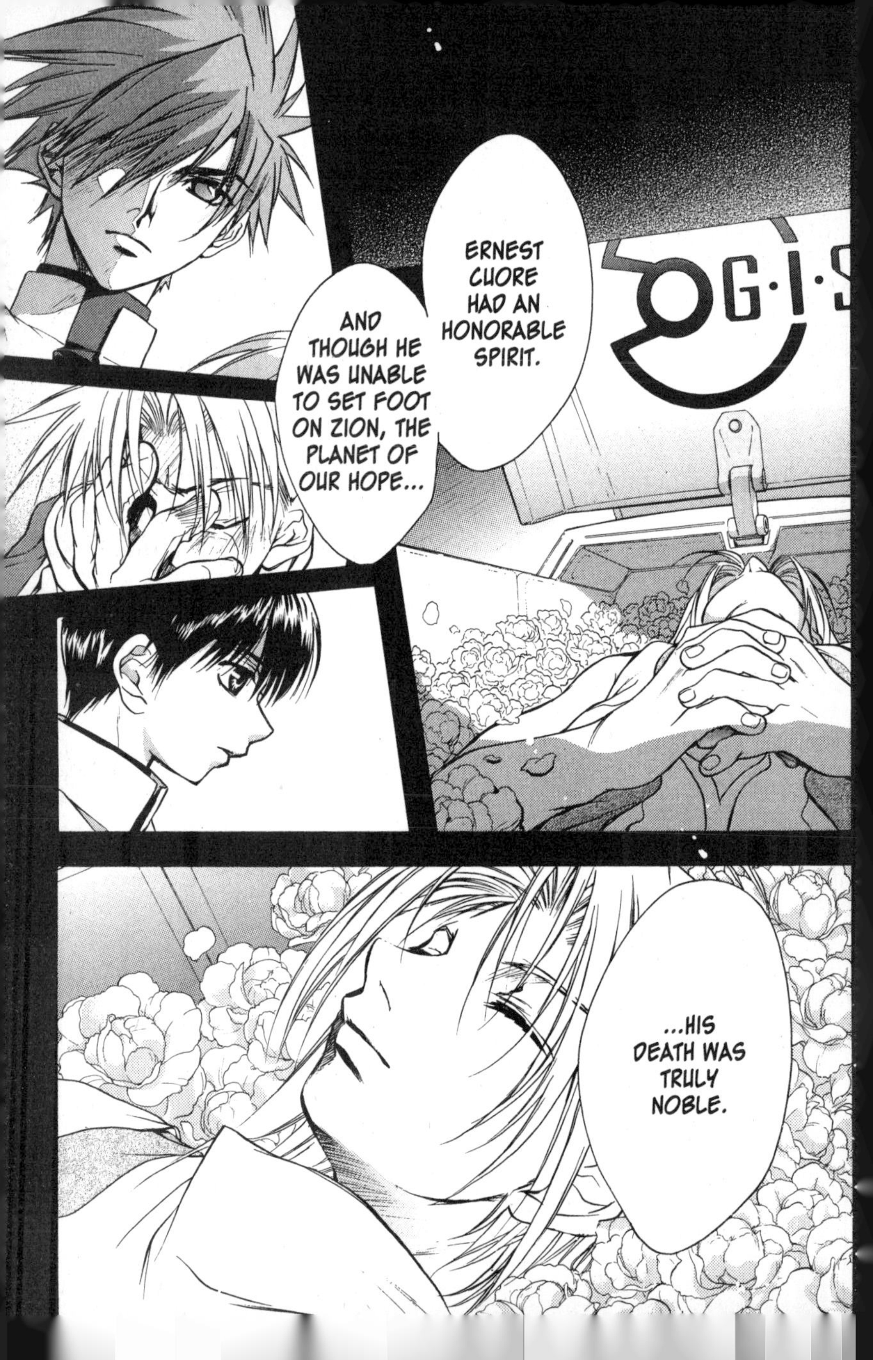
ERNEST CUORE HAD AN HONORABLE SPIRIT.
AND THOUGH HE WAS UNABLE TO SET FOOT ON ZION, THE PLANET OF OUR HOPE...
...HIS DEATH WAS TRULY NOBLE.

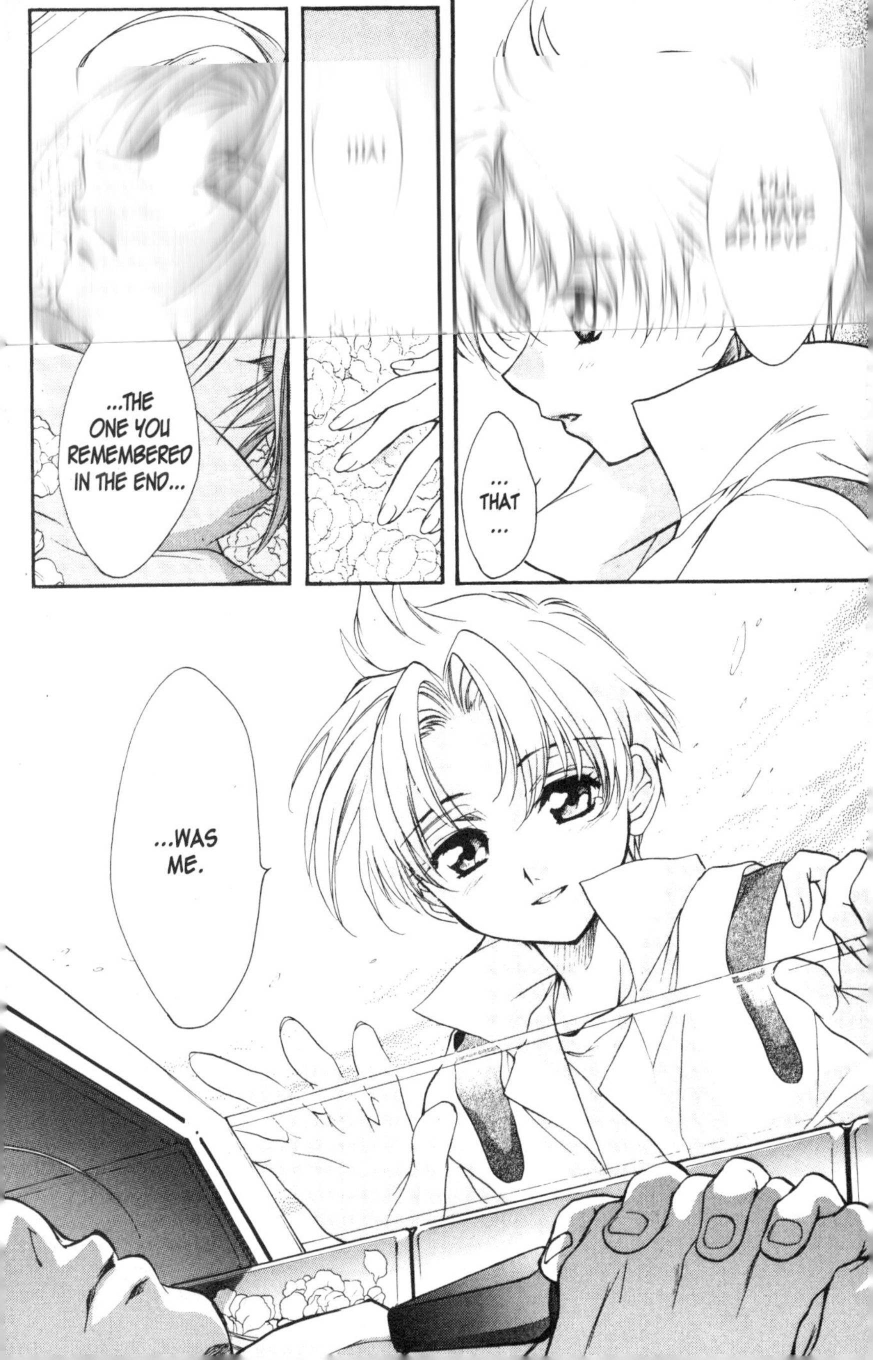
...THAT...
...THE ONE YOU REMEMBERED IN THE END...
...WAS ME.

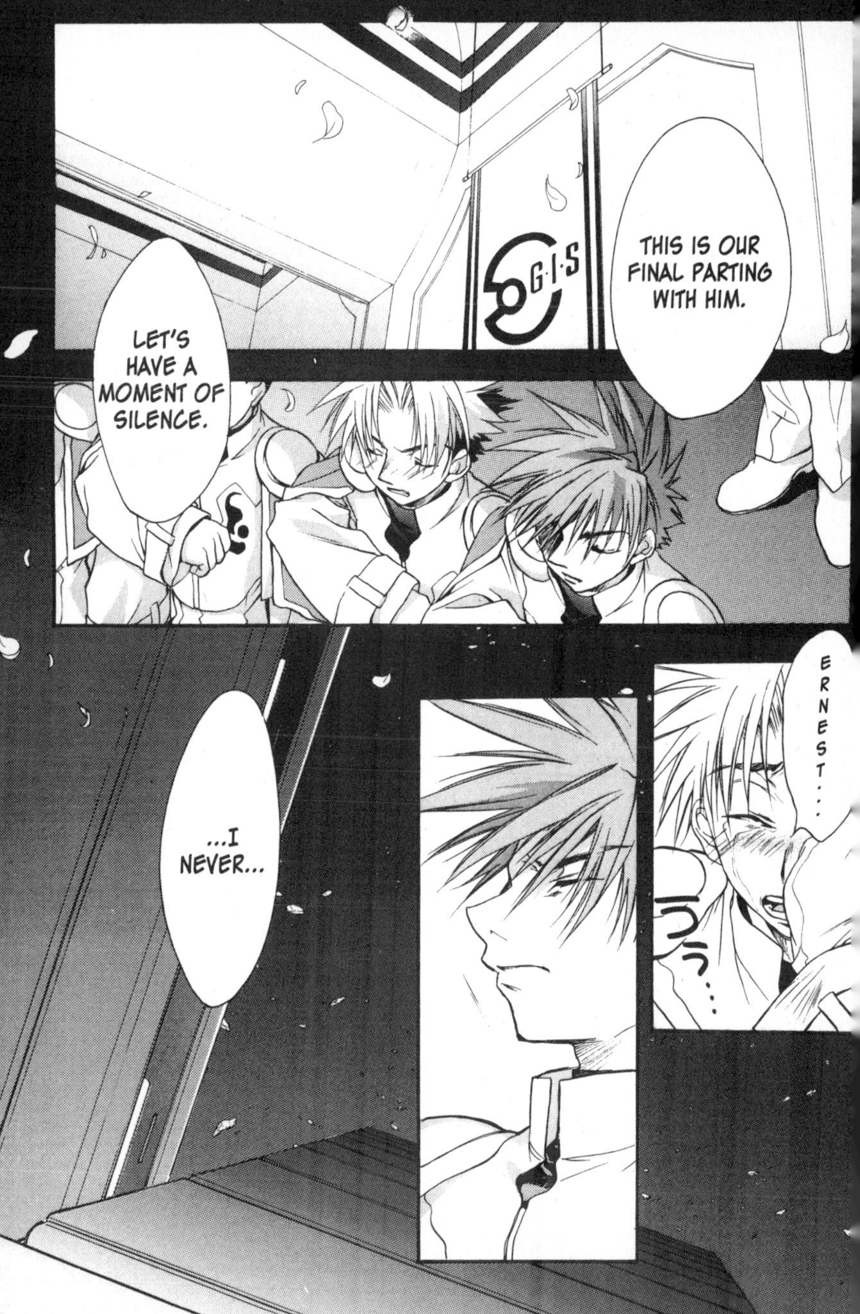
THIS IS OUR FINAL PARTING WITH HIM.
LET'S HAVE A MOMENT OF SILENCE.
G·I·S
ERNEST...
...I NEVER...

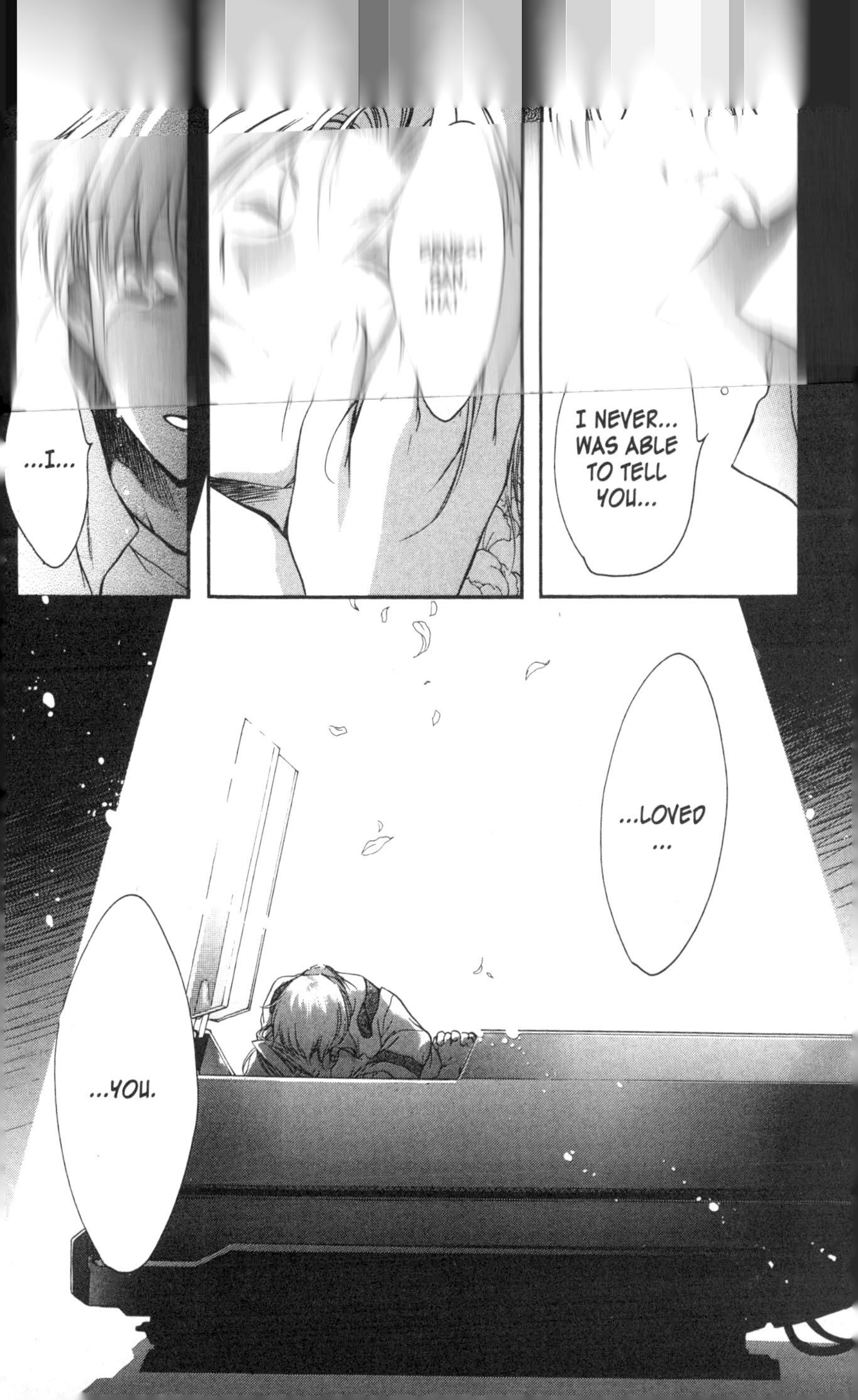
I NEVER... WAS ABLE TO TELL YOU...
...I...
...LOVED ...
...YOU.

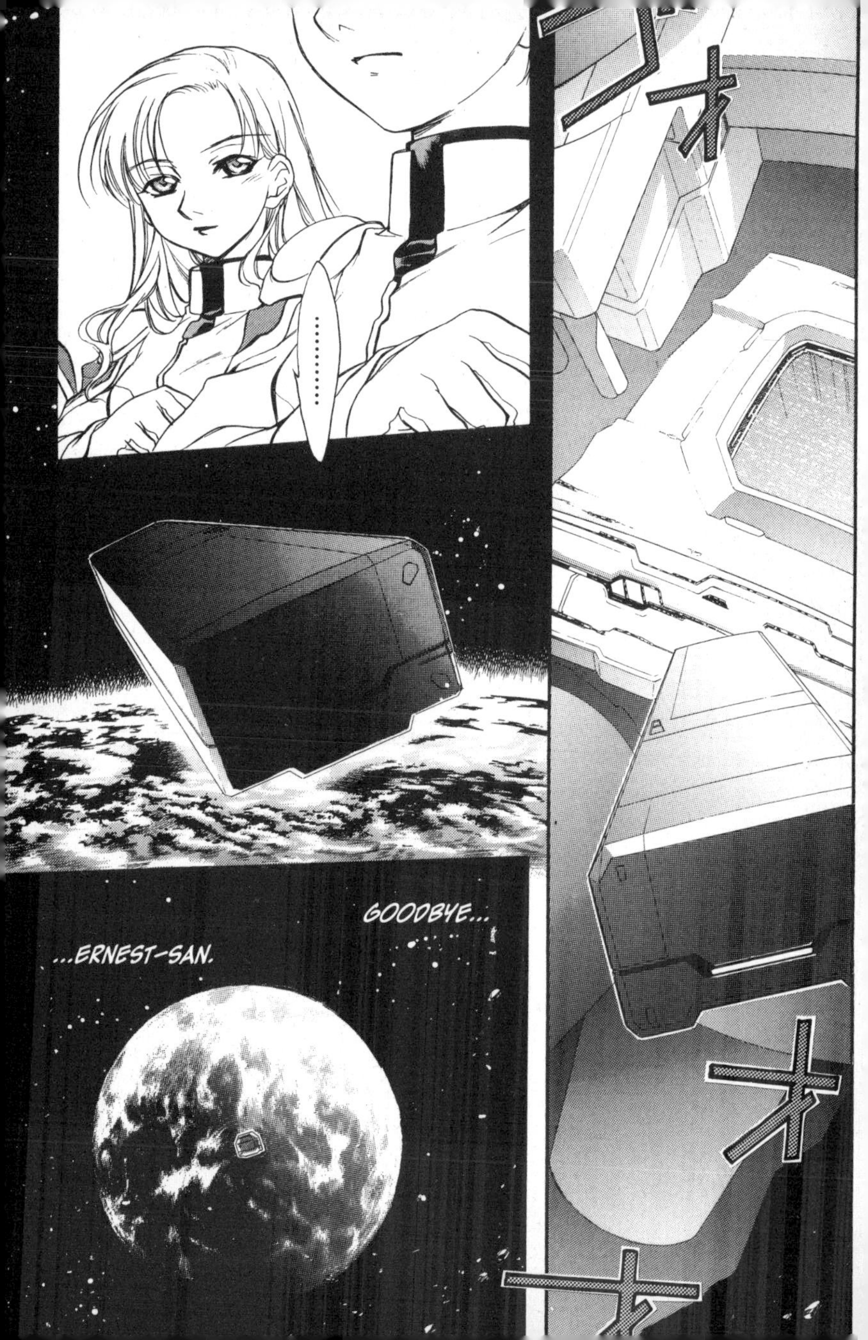
ゴオオオ
……
GOODBYE...
...ERNEST-SAN.

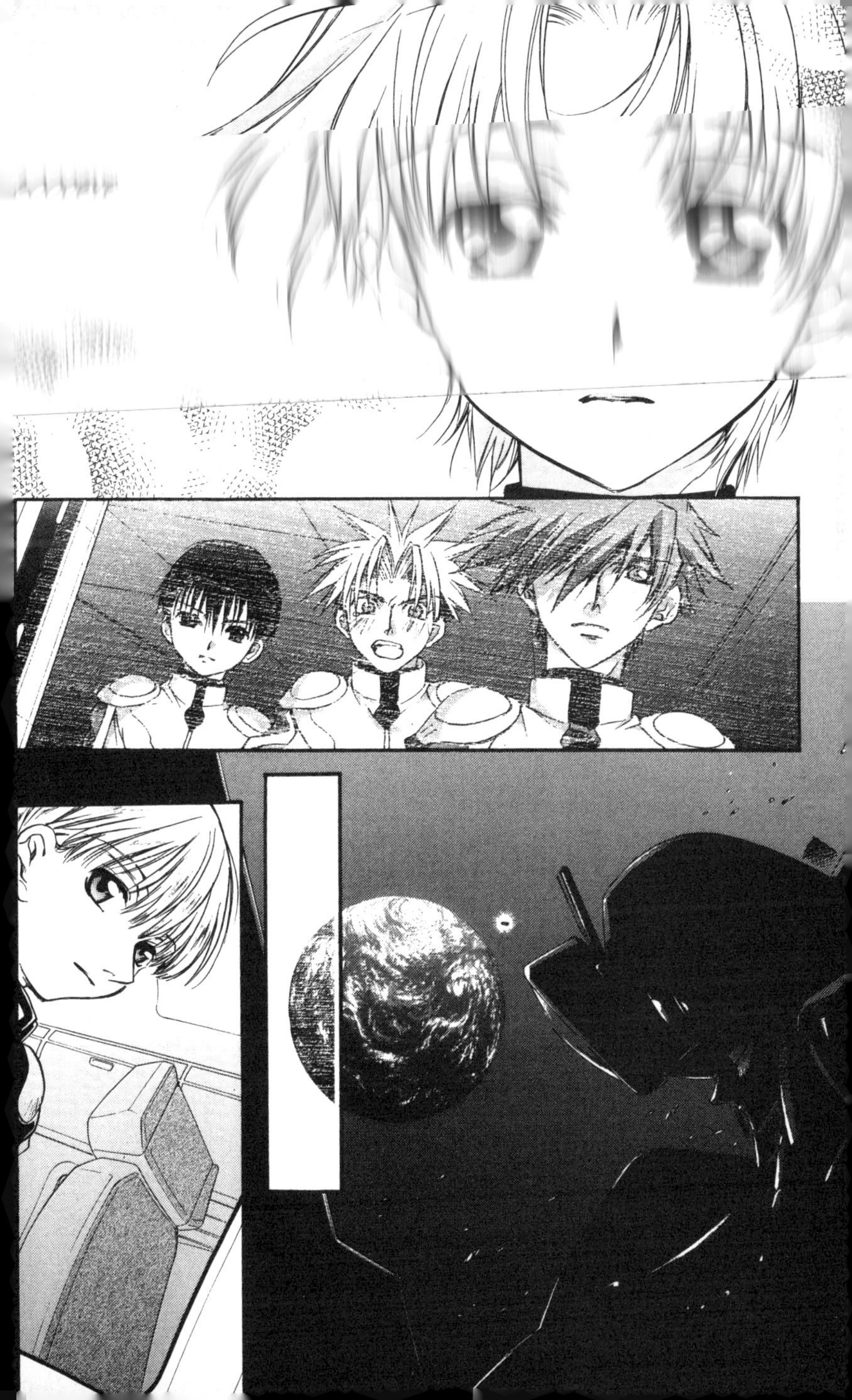

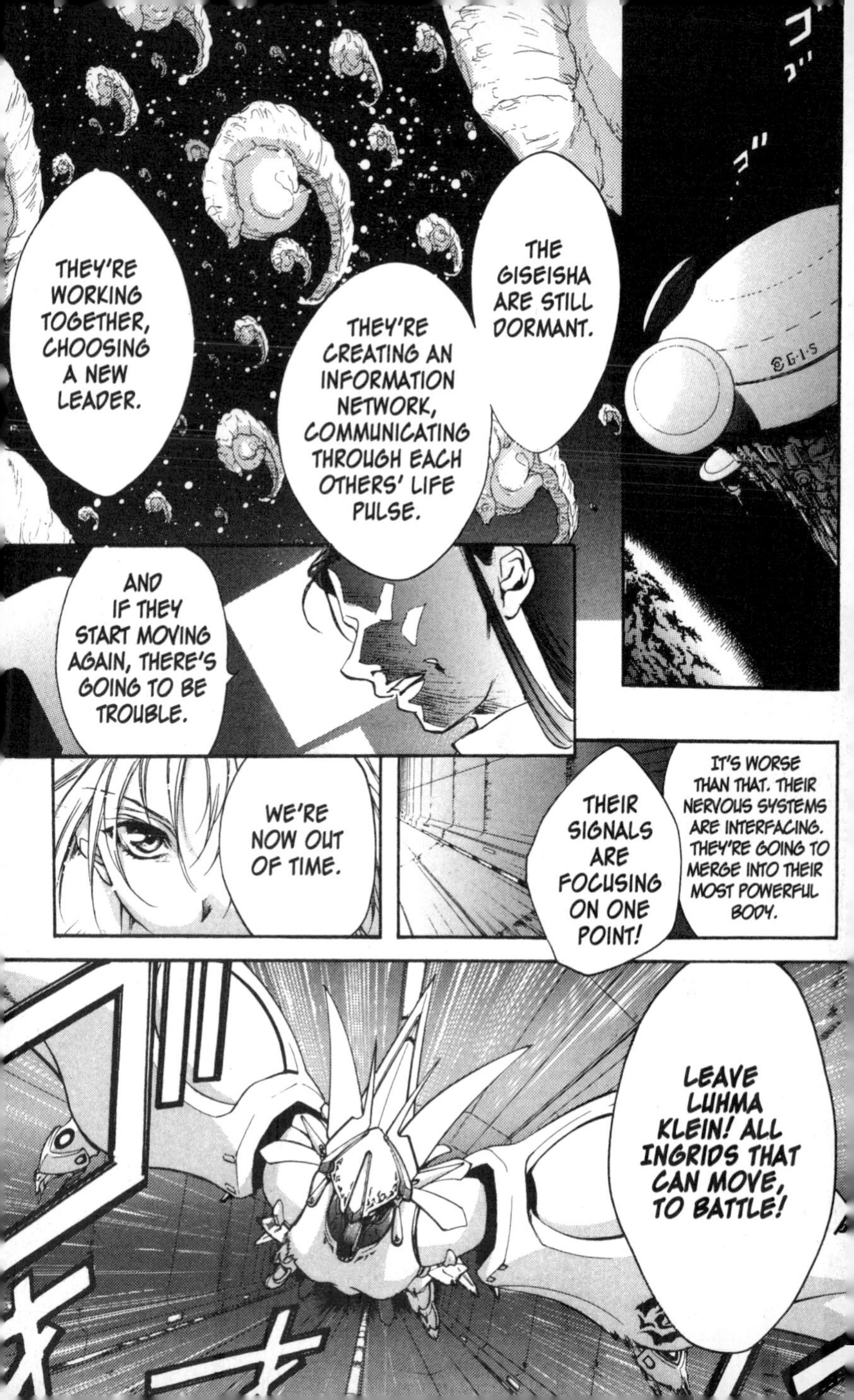
THE GISEISHA ARE STILL DORMANT.
THEY'RE CREATING AN INFORMATION NETWORK, COMMUNICATING THROUGH EACH OTHERS' LIFE PULSE.
THEY'RE WORKING TOGETHER, CHOOSING A NEW LEADER.
AND IF THEY START MOVING AGAIN, THERE'S GOING TO BE TROUBLE.
IT'S WORSE THAN THAT. THEIR NERVOUS SYSTEMS ARE INTERFACING. THEY'RE GOING TO MERGE INTO THEIR MOST POWERFUL BODY.
THEIR SIGNALS ARE FOCUSING ON ONE POINT!
WE'RE NOW OUT OF TIME.
LEAVE LUHMA KLEIN! ALL INGRIDS THAT CAN MOVE, TO BATTLE!

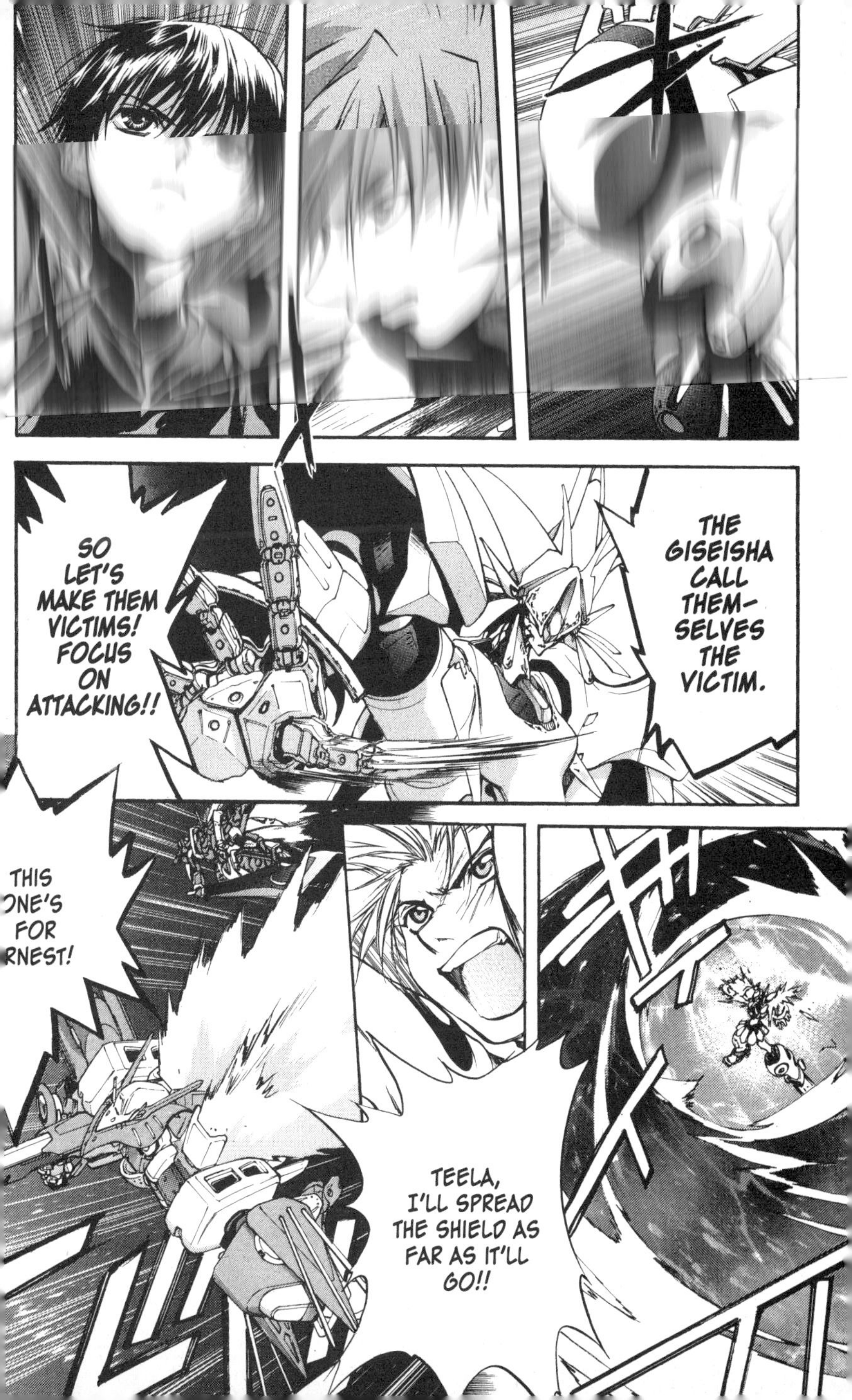
THE GISEISHA CALL THEMSELVES THE VICTIM.
SO LET'S MAKE THEM VICTIMS! FOCUS ON ATTACKING!!
TEELA, I'LL SPREAD THE SHIELD AS FAR AS IT'LL GO!!
THIS ONE'S FOR RNEST!

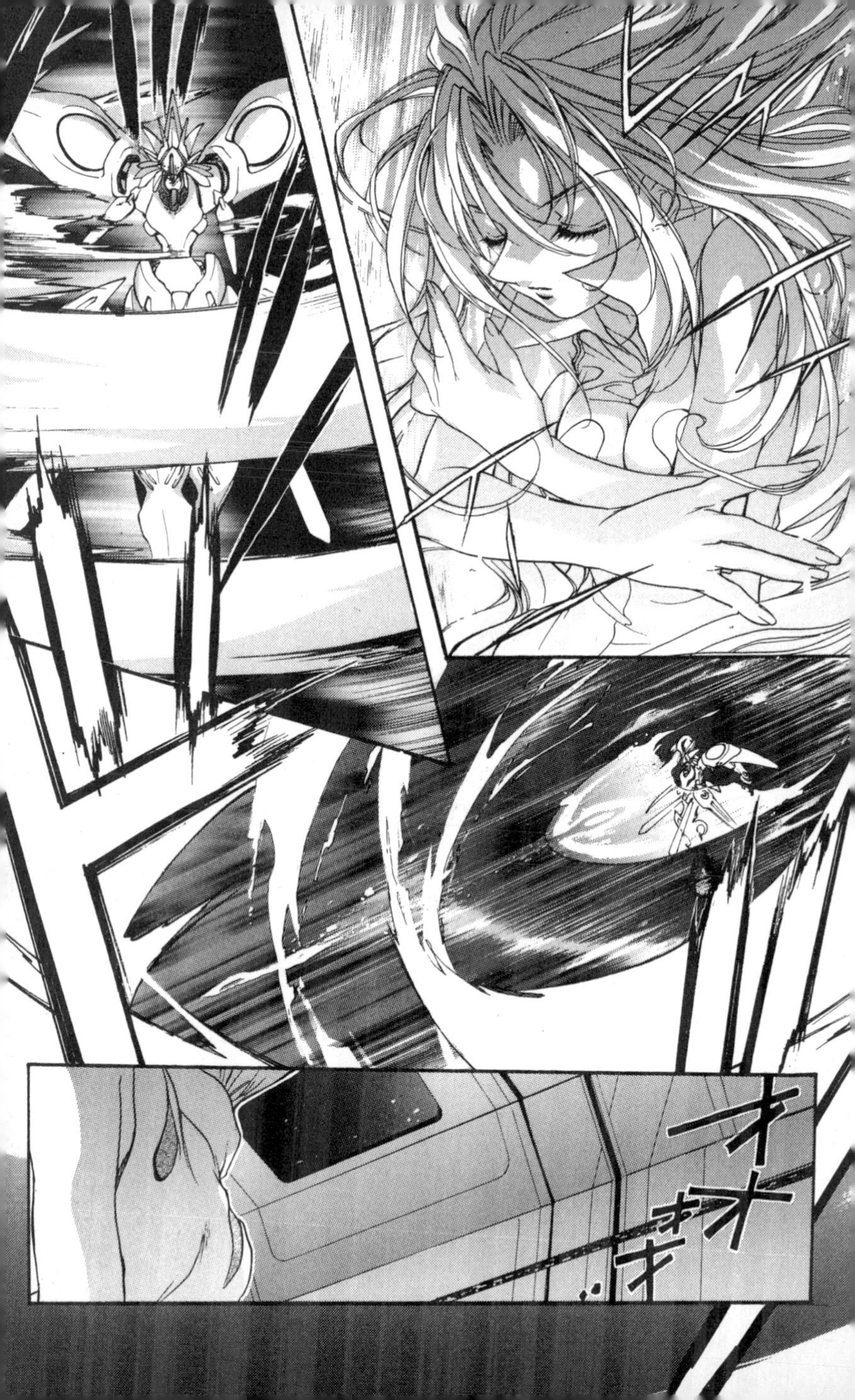
オオォオ

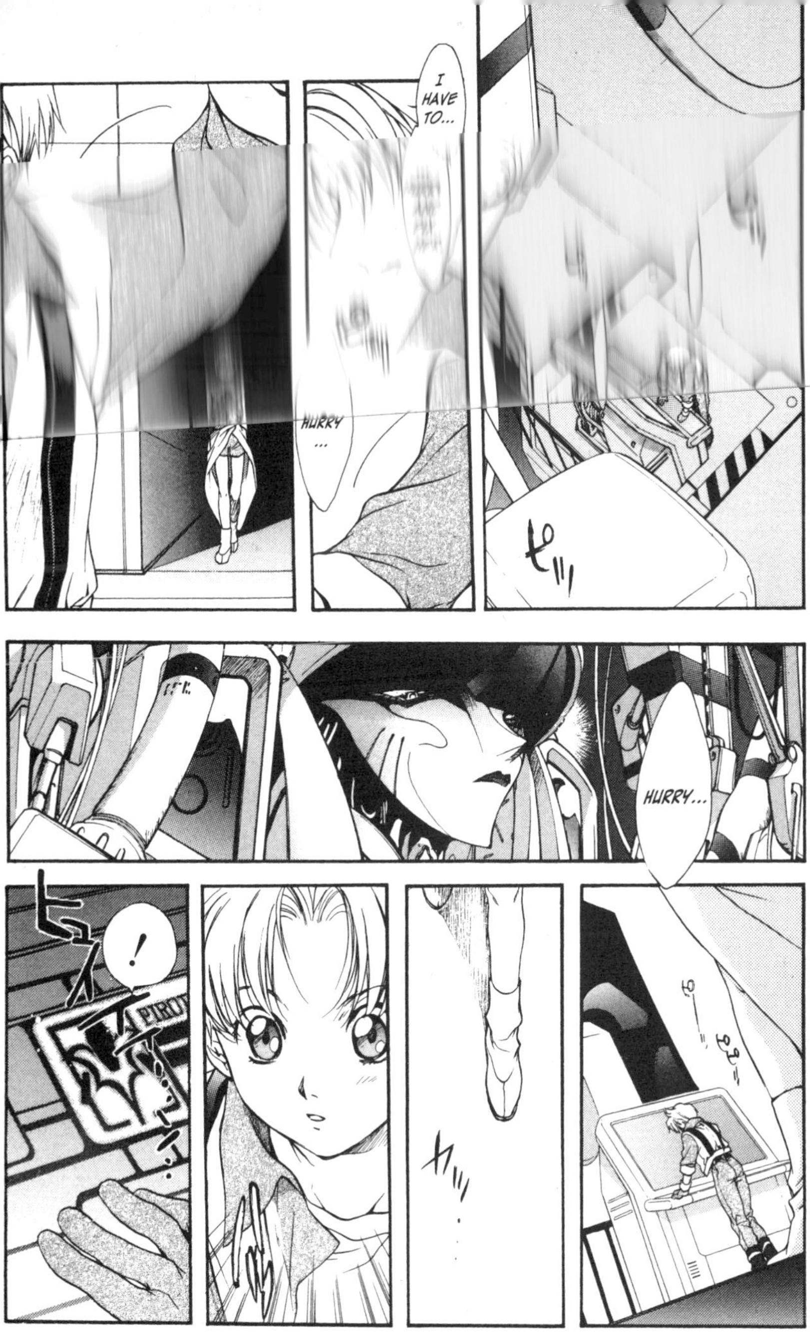
I HAVE TO...
HURRY ...
HURRY...
!

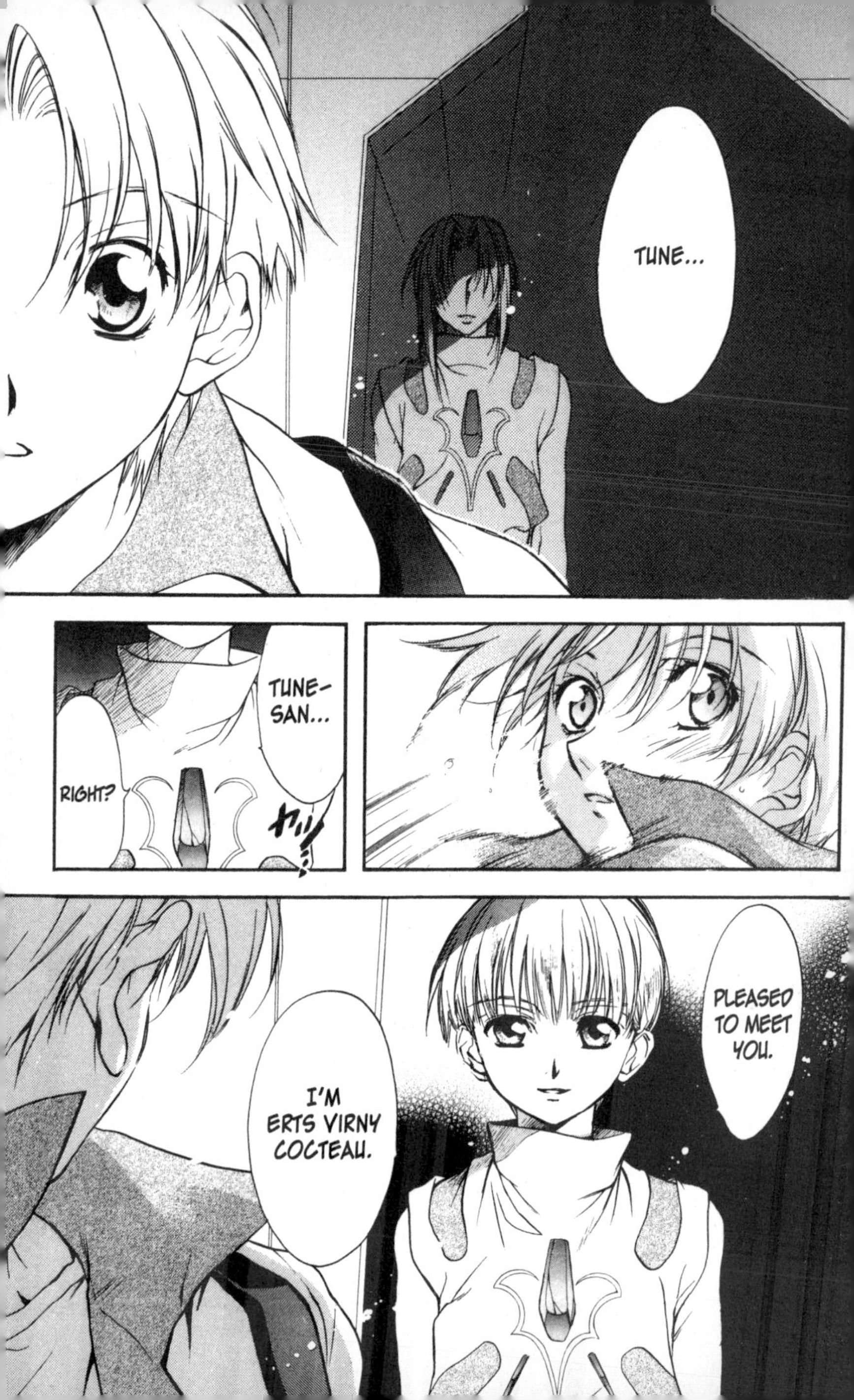
TUNE...
TUNE-SAN...
RIGHT?
PLEASED TO MEET YOU.
I'M ERTS VIRNY COCTEAU.

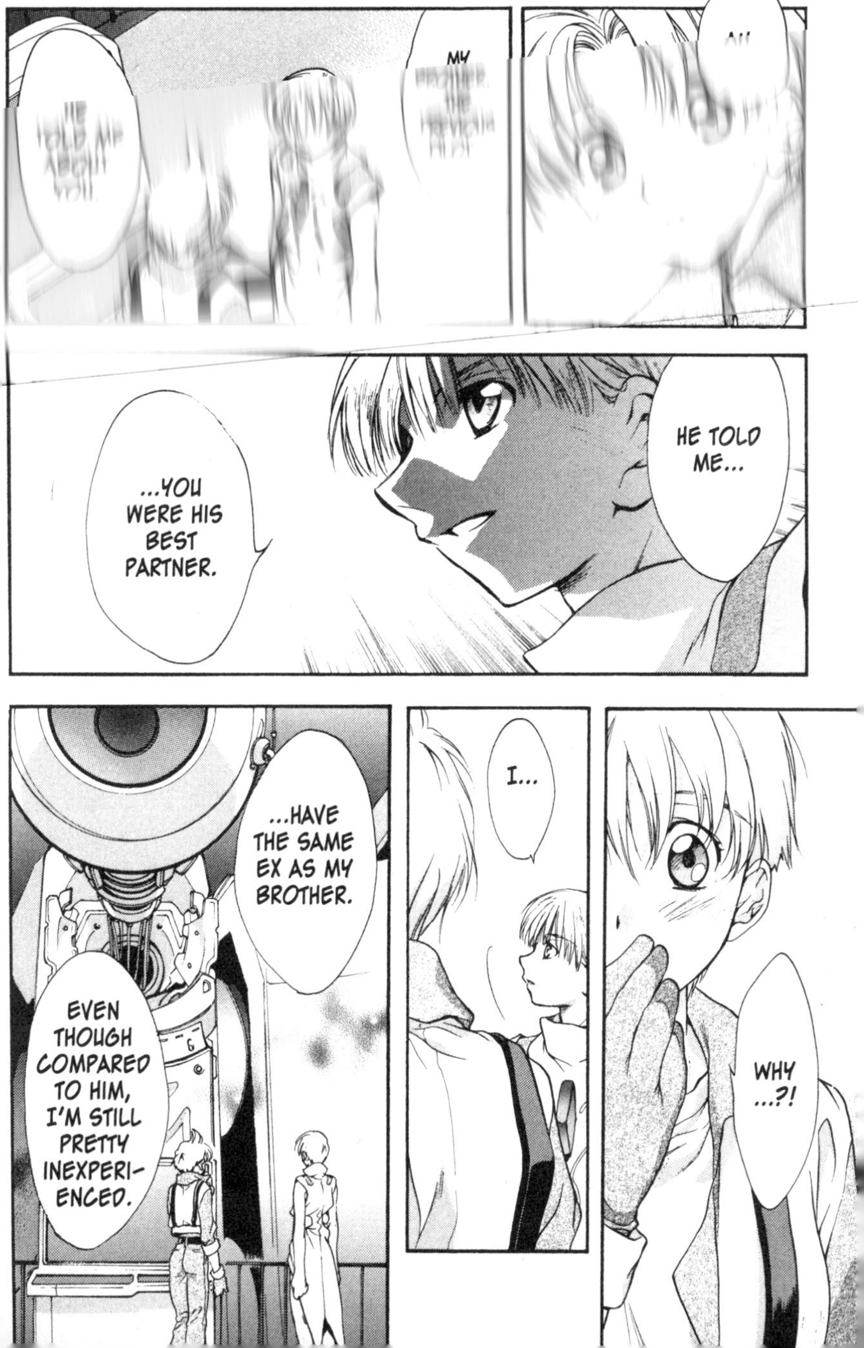
MY
HE TOLD ME...
...YOU WERE HIS BEST PARTNER.
WHY ...?!
I...
...HAVE THE SAME EX AS MY BROTHER.
EVEN THOUGH COMPARED TO HIM, I'M STILL PRETTY INEXPERIENCED.

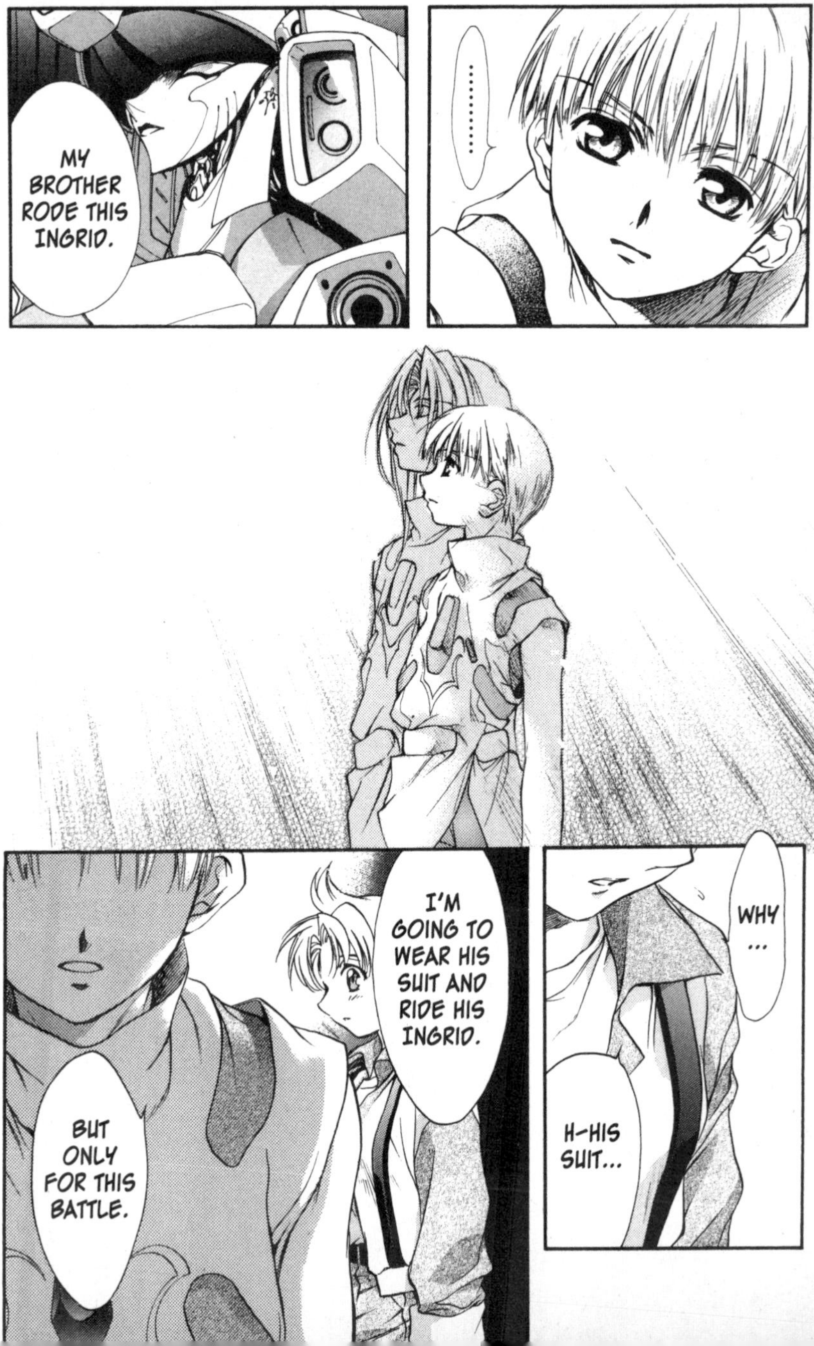
……
MY BROTHER RODE THIS INGRID.
WHY ...
H-HIS SUIT...
I'M GOING TO WEAR HIS SUIT AND RIDE HIS INGRID.
BUT ONLY FOR THIS BATTLE.

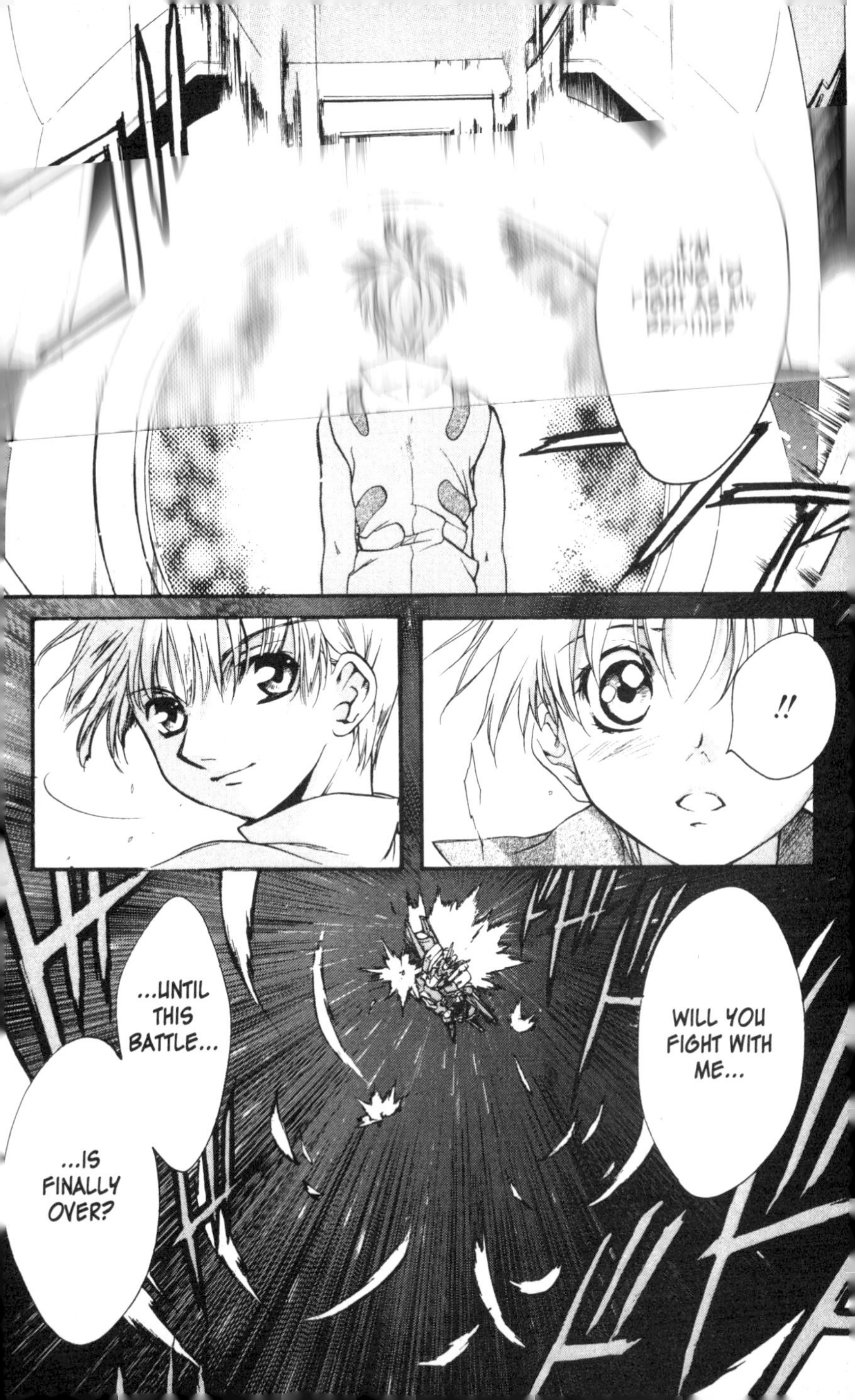
!!
WILL YOU FIGHT WITH ME...
...UNTIL THIS BATTLE...
...IS FINALLY OVER?

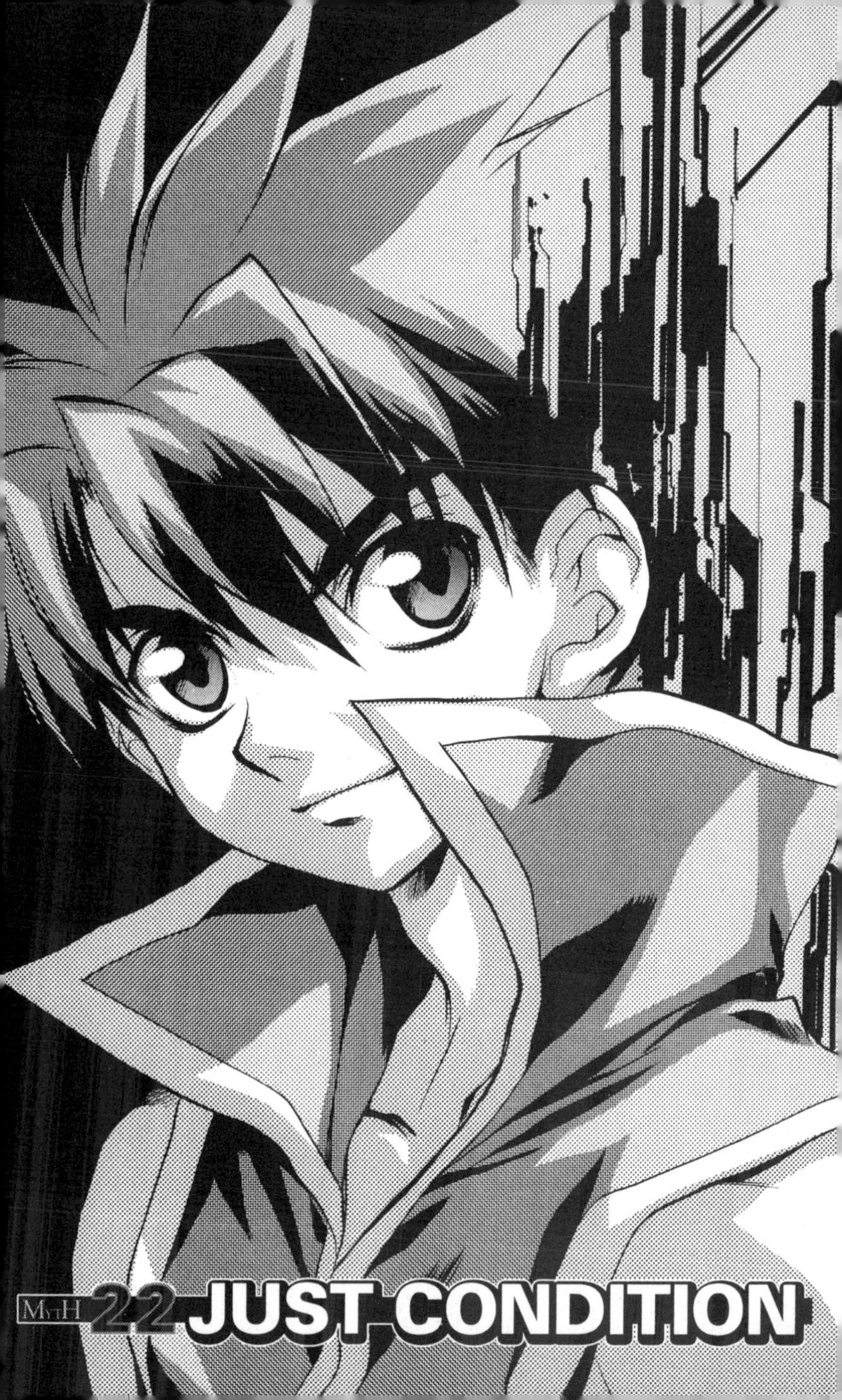
MyTH 22 JUST CONDITION

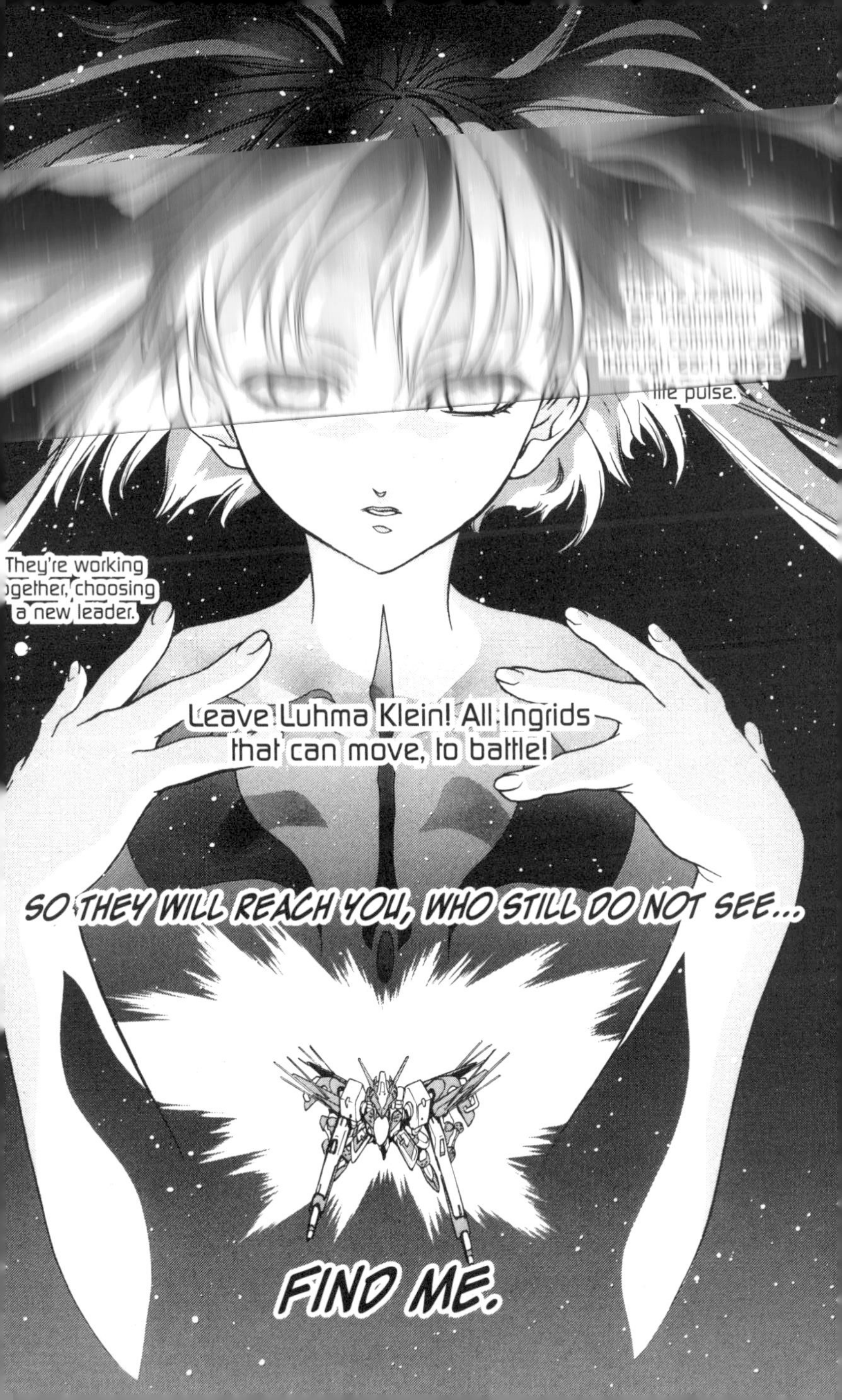
life pulse.
They're working
gether, choosing
a new leader.
Leave Luhma Klein! All Ingrids that can move, to battle!
SO THEY WILL REACH YOU, WHO STILL DO NOT SEE...
FIND ME.

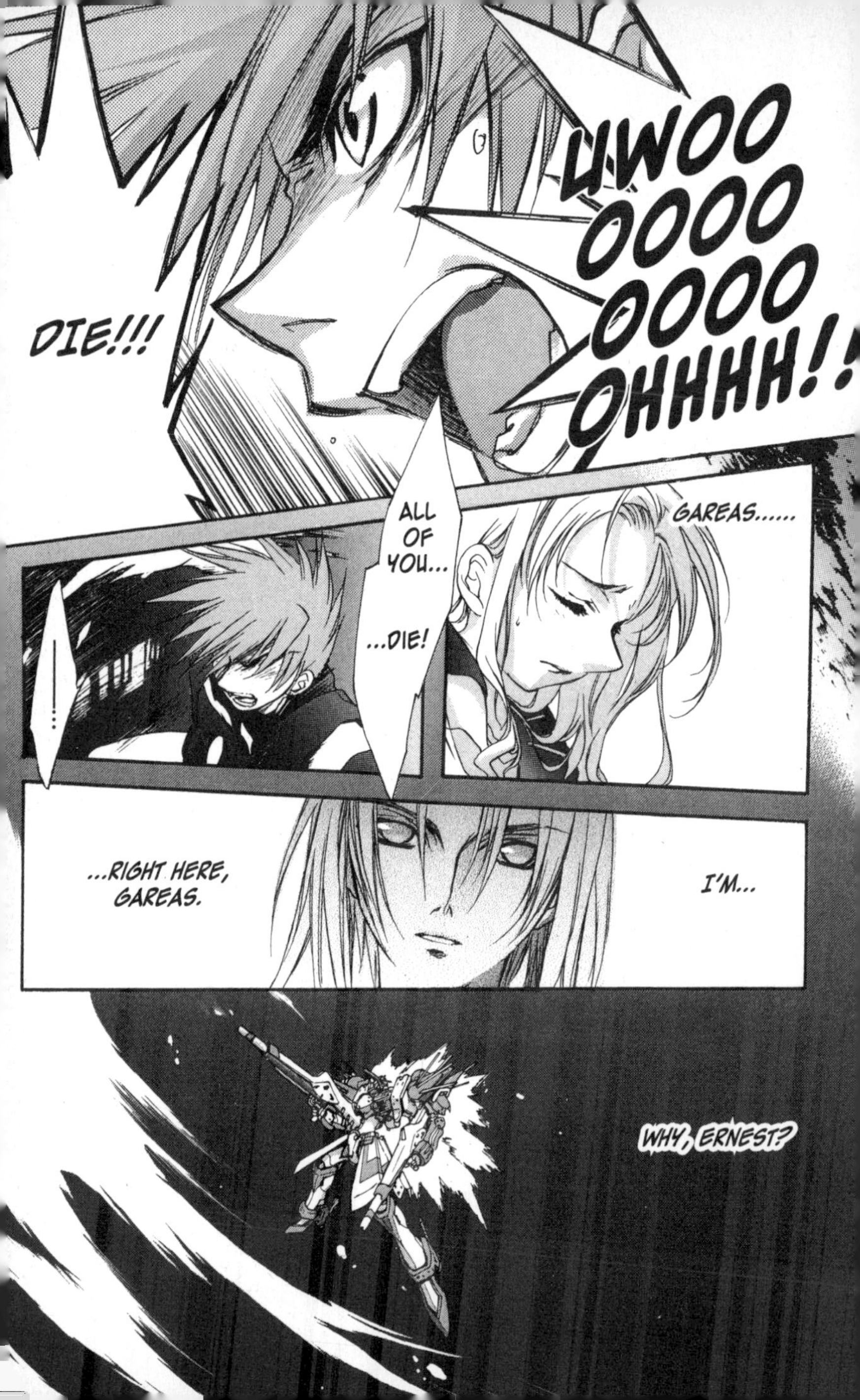
UWOO
OOOO
OOOO
OHHHH!!
DIE!!!
GAREAS......
ALL OF YOU...
...DIE!
......!
I'M...
...RIGHT HERE, GAREAS.
WHY, ERNEST?

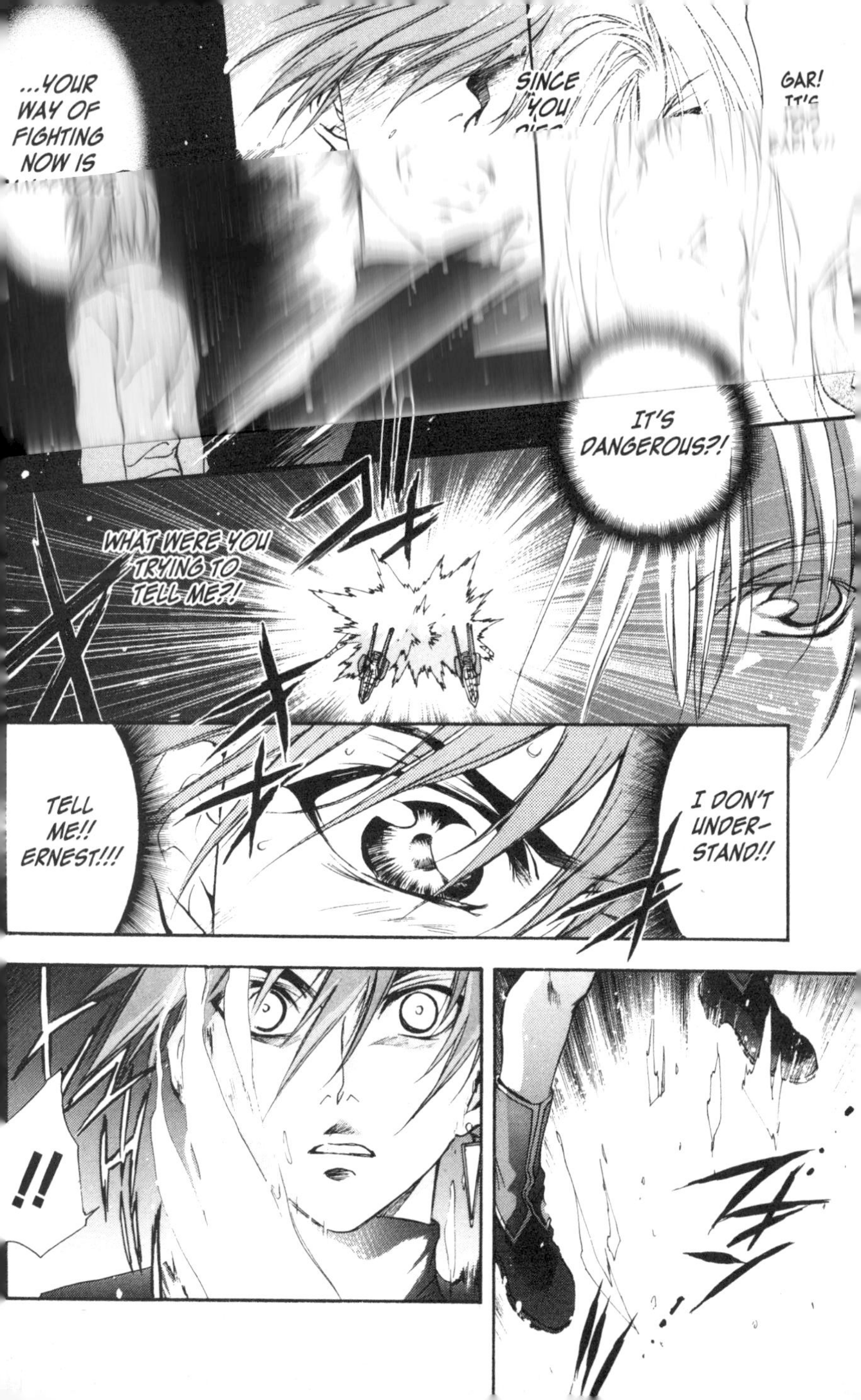
GAR!
SINCE YOU
...YOUR WAY OF FIGHTING NOW IS
IT'S DANGEROUS?!
WHAT WERE YOU TRYING TO TELL ME?!
I DON'T UNDER-STAND!!
TELL ME!! ERNEST!!!
!!

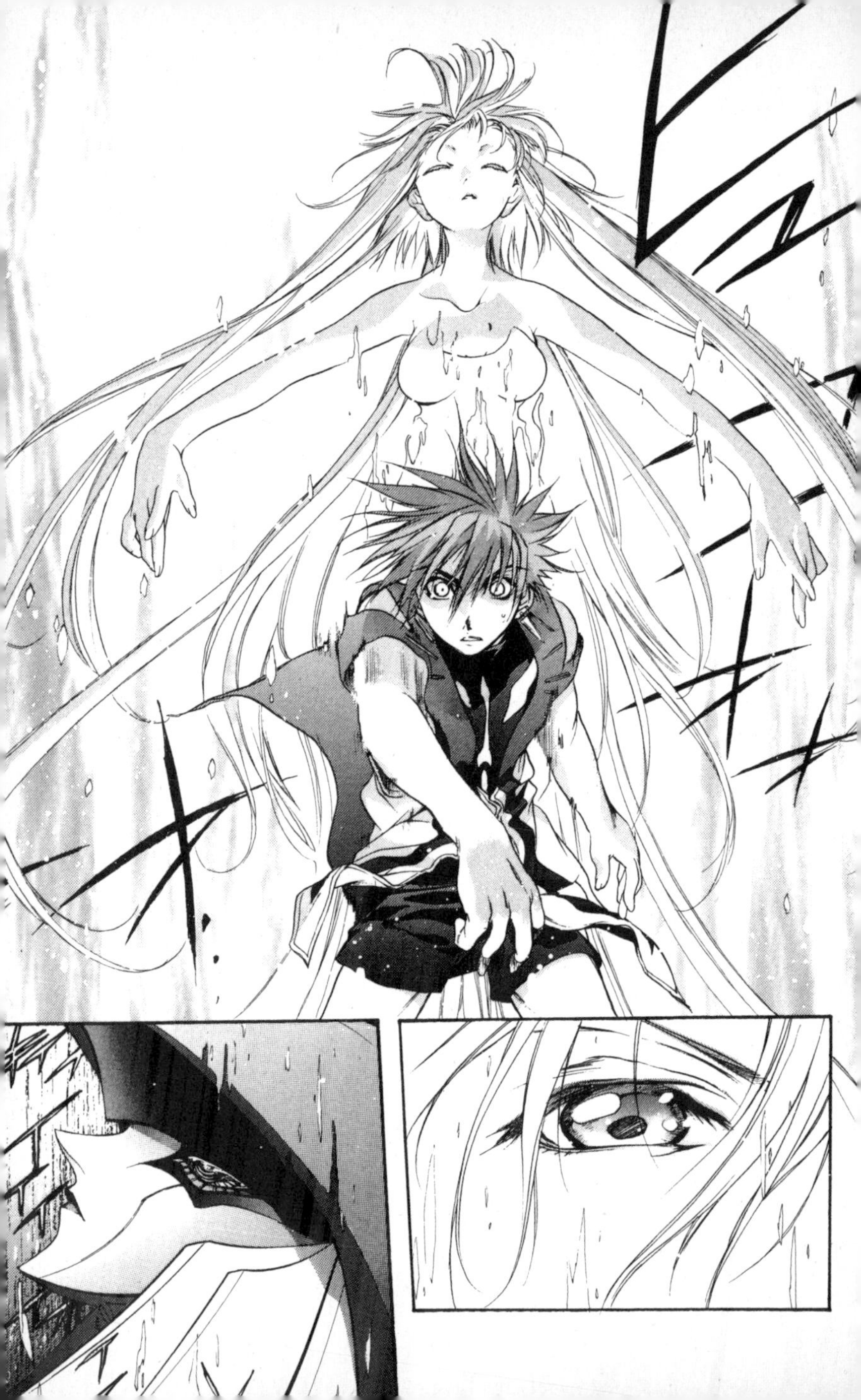

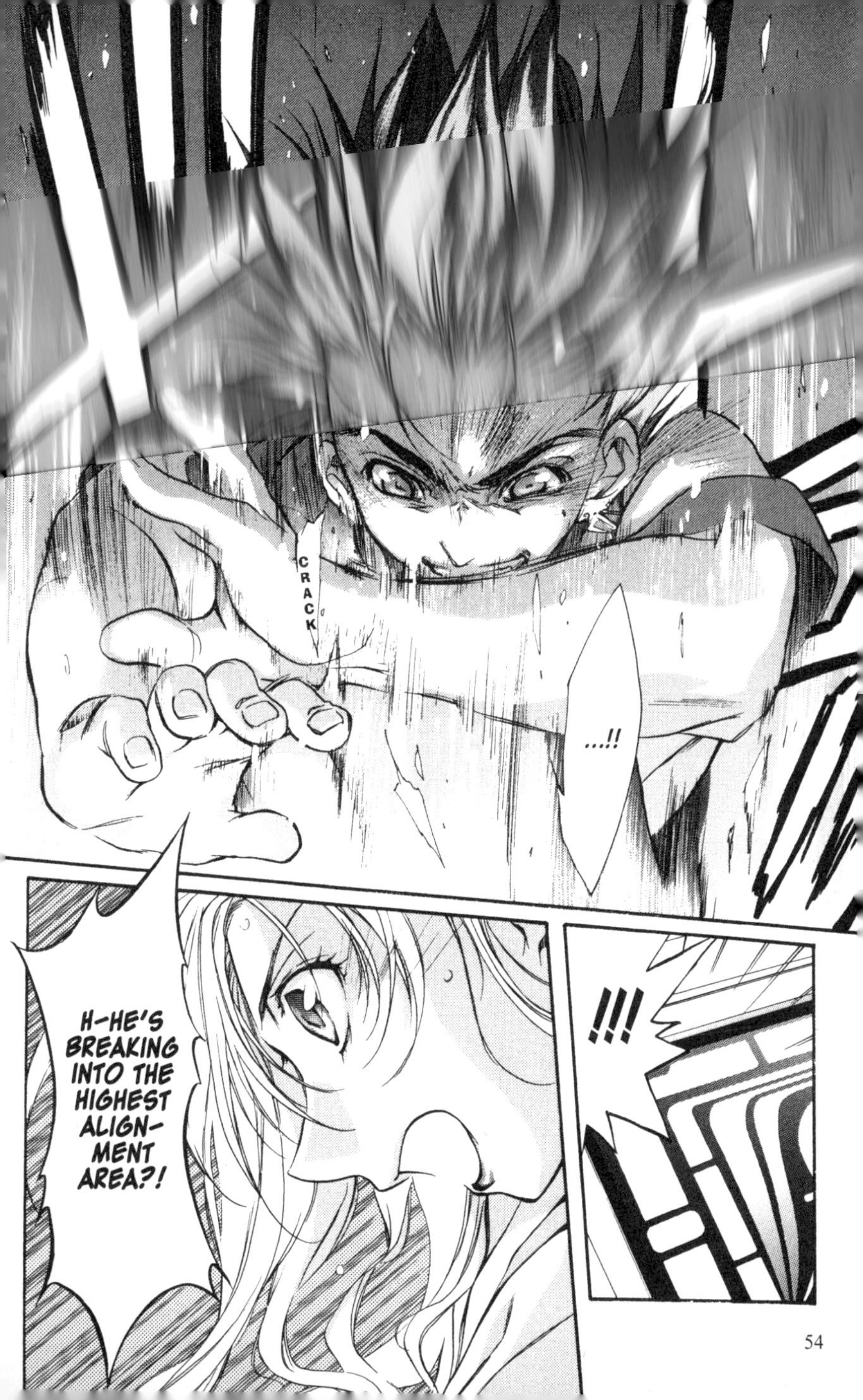
CRACK
...!!
!!!
H-HE'S BREAKING INTO THE HIGHEST ALIGN-MENT AREA?!

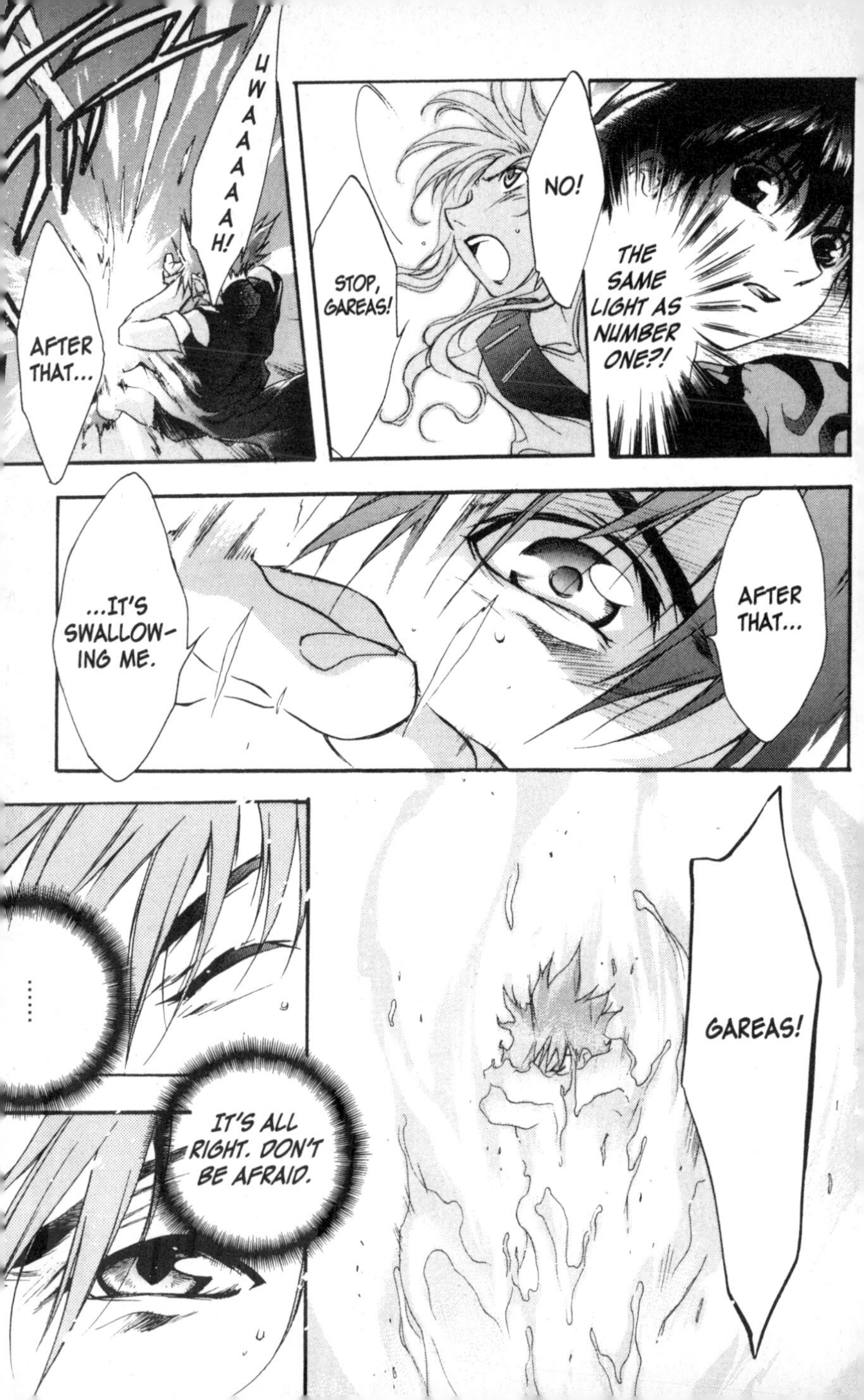
THE SAME LIGHT AS NUMBER ONE?!
NO!
STOP, GAREAS!
UWAAAAAAH!
AFTER THAT...
AFTER THAT...
...IT'S SWALLOWING ME.
GAREAS!
......
IT'S ALL RIGHT. DON'T BE AFRAID.

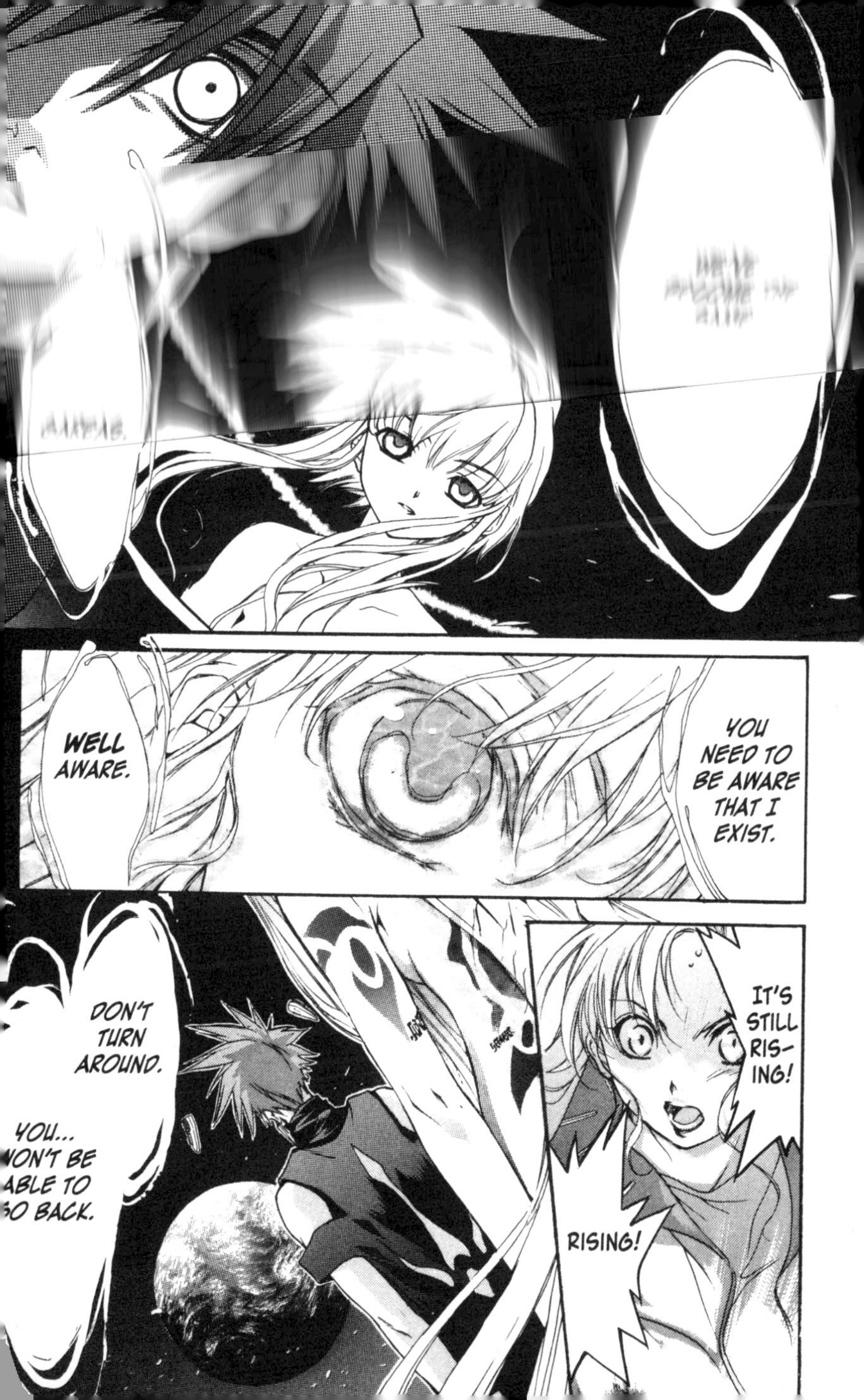
YOU NEED TO BE AWARE THAT I EXIST.
WELL AWARE.
IT'S STILL RIS-ING!
RISING!
DON'T TURN AROUND.
YOU... WON'T BE ABLE TO GO BACK.

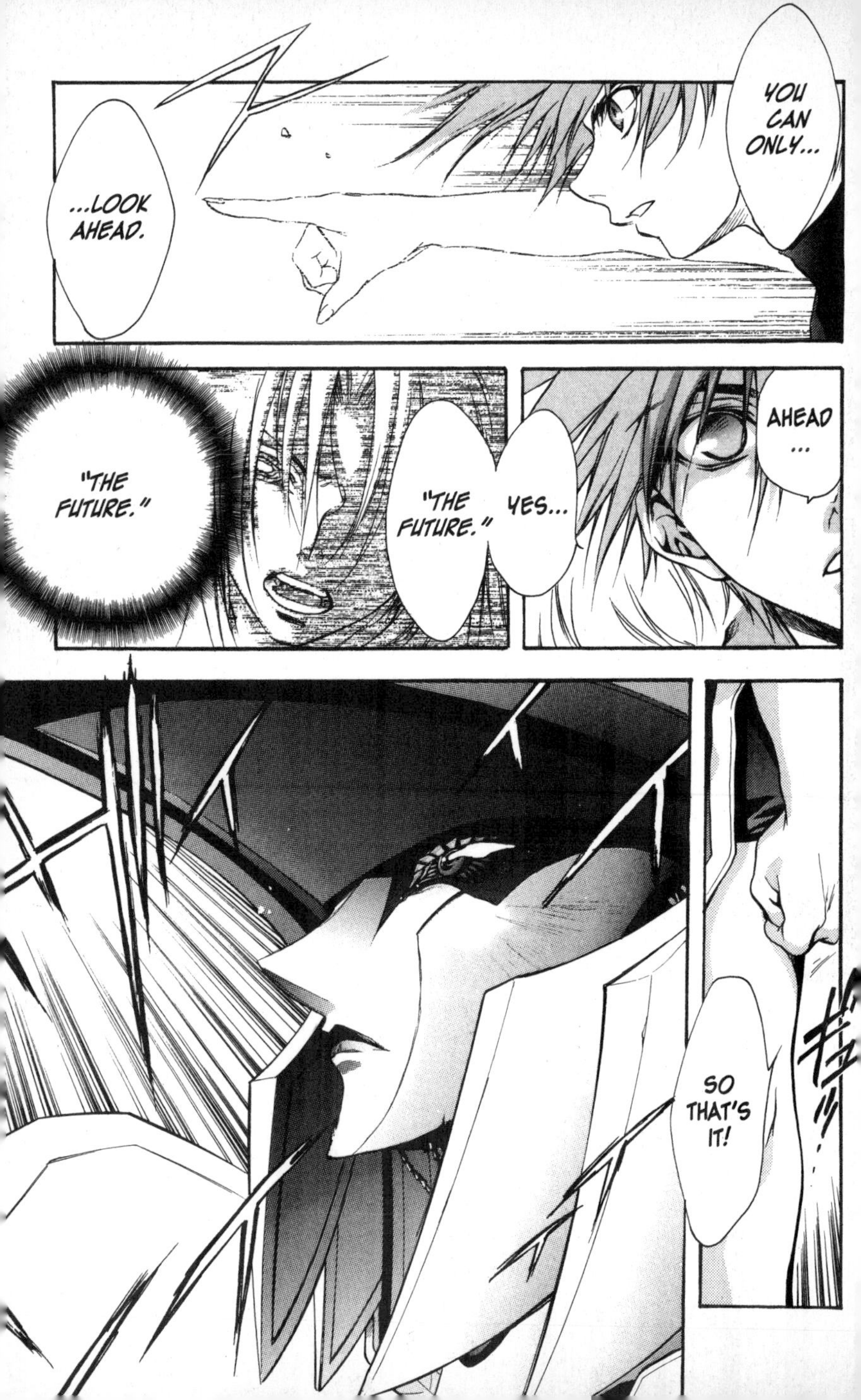
YOU CAN ONLY...
...LOOK AHEAD.
AHEAD ...
YES...
"THE FUTURE."
"THE FUTURE."
SO THAT'S IT!

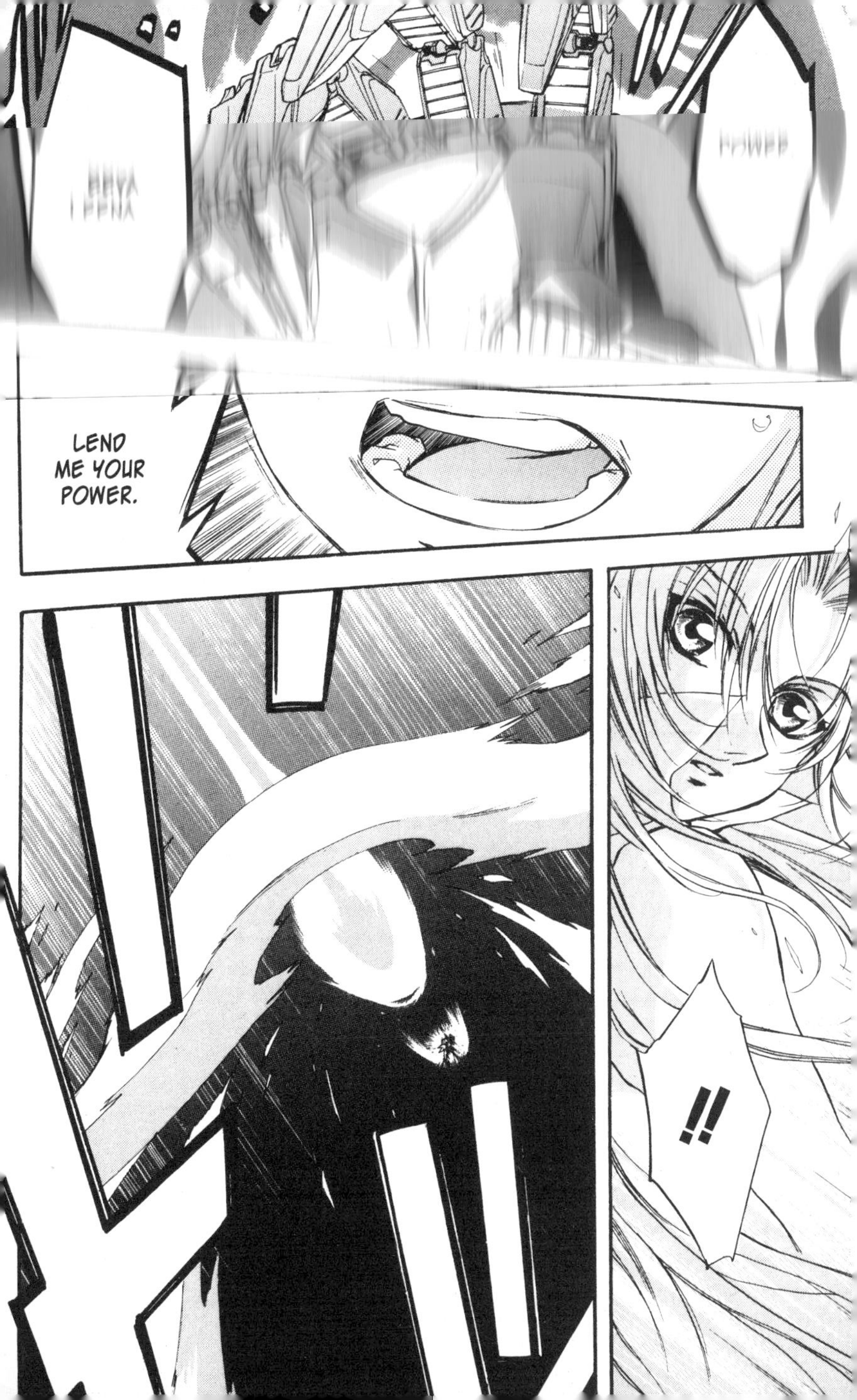
LEND ME YOUR POWER.
!!

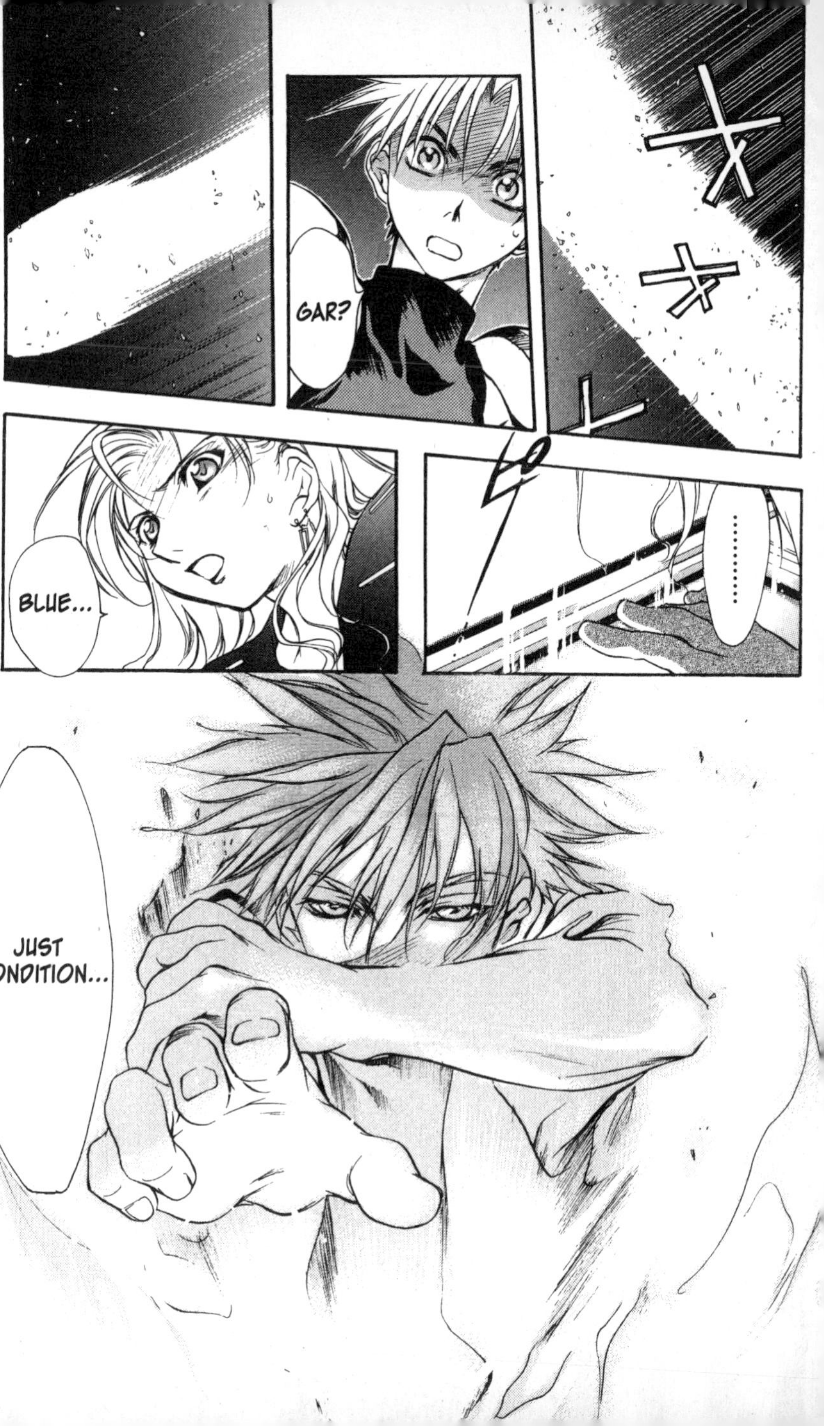
GAR?
......
BLUE...
JUST CONDITION...

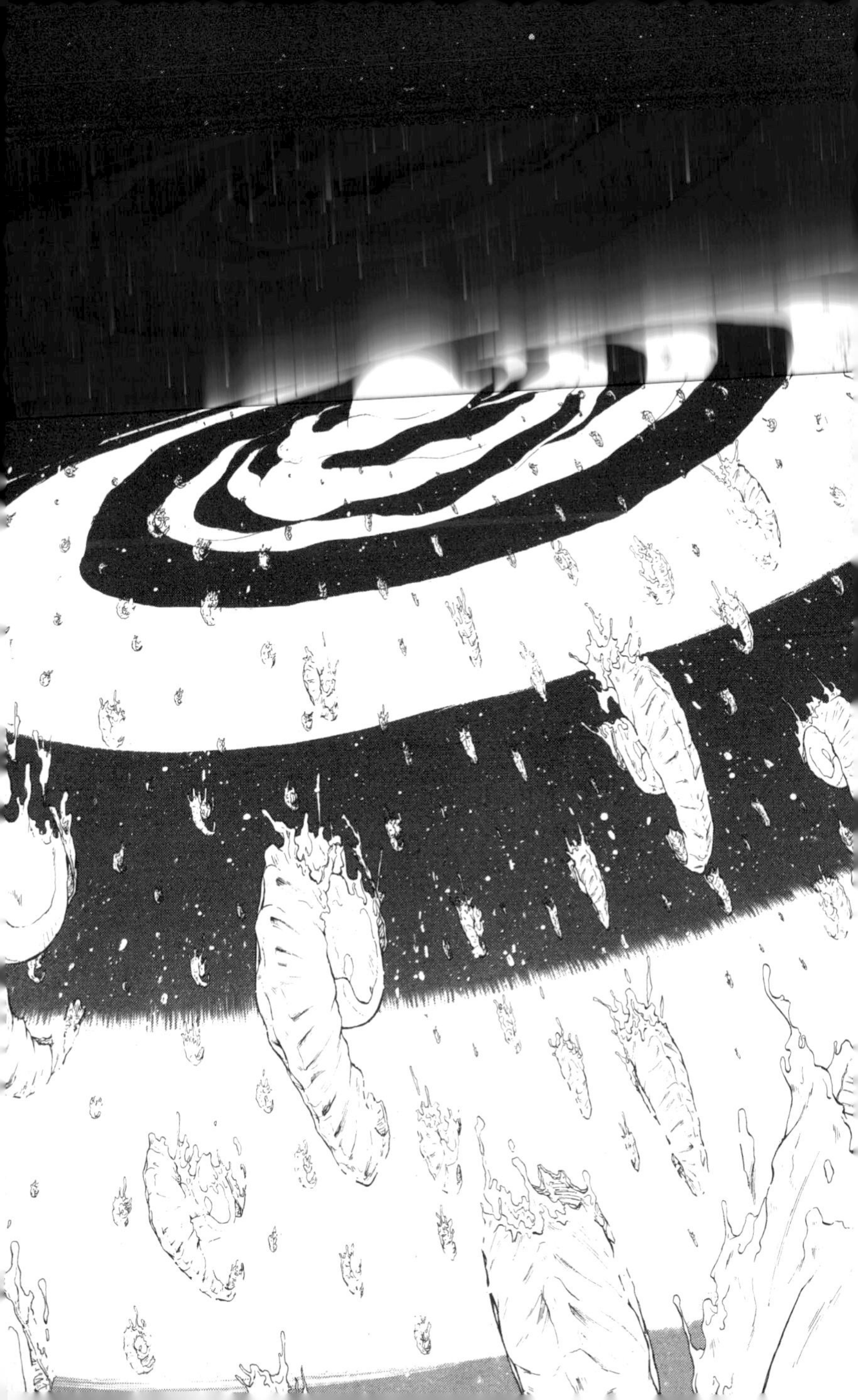

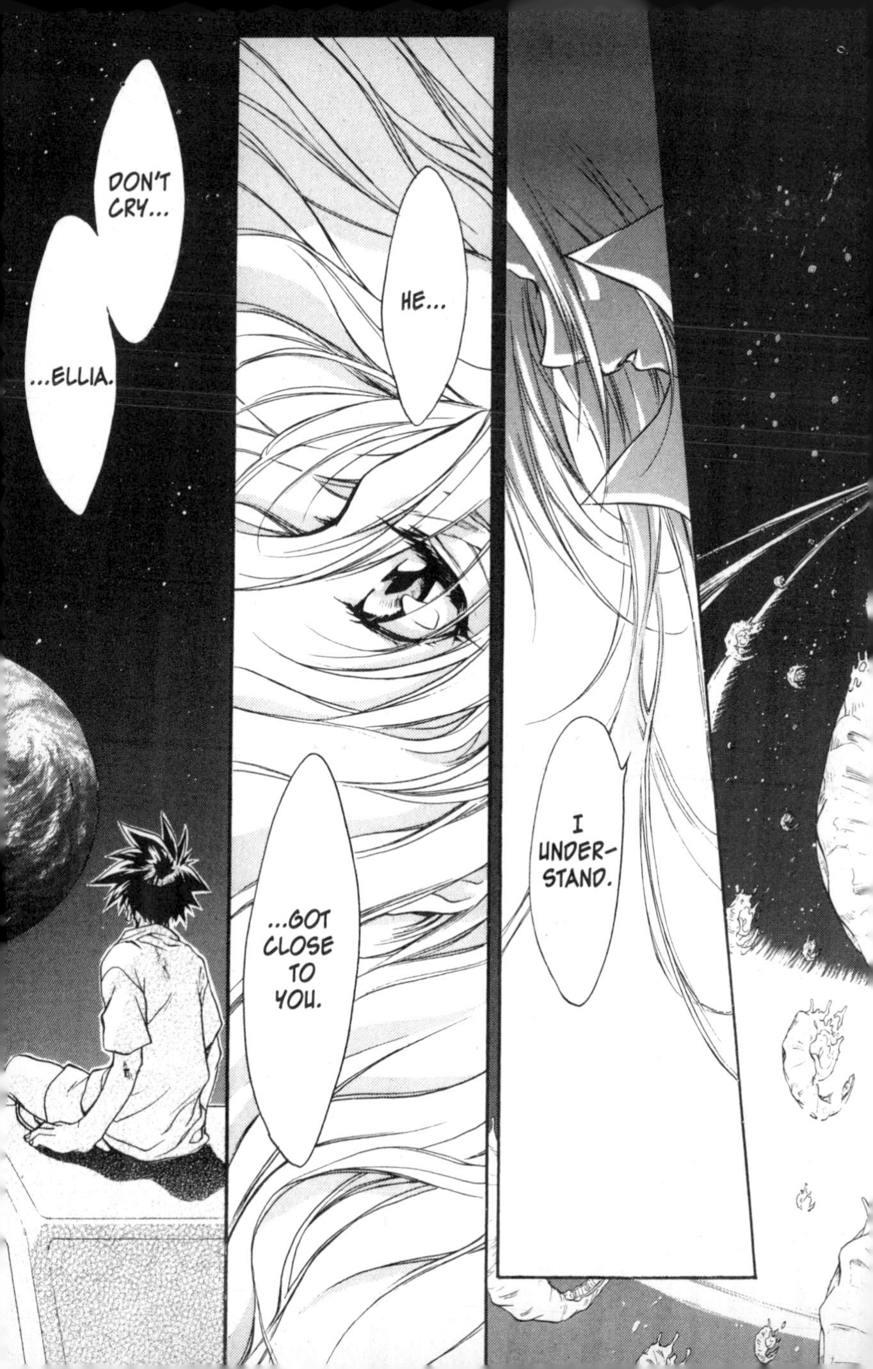
I UNDERSTAND.
HE...
...GOT CLOSE TO YOU.
DON'T CRY...
...ELLIA.

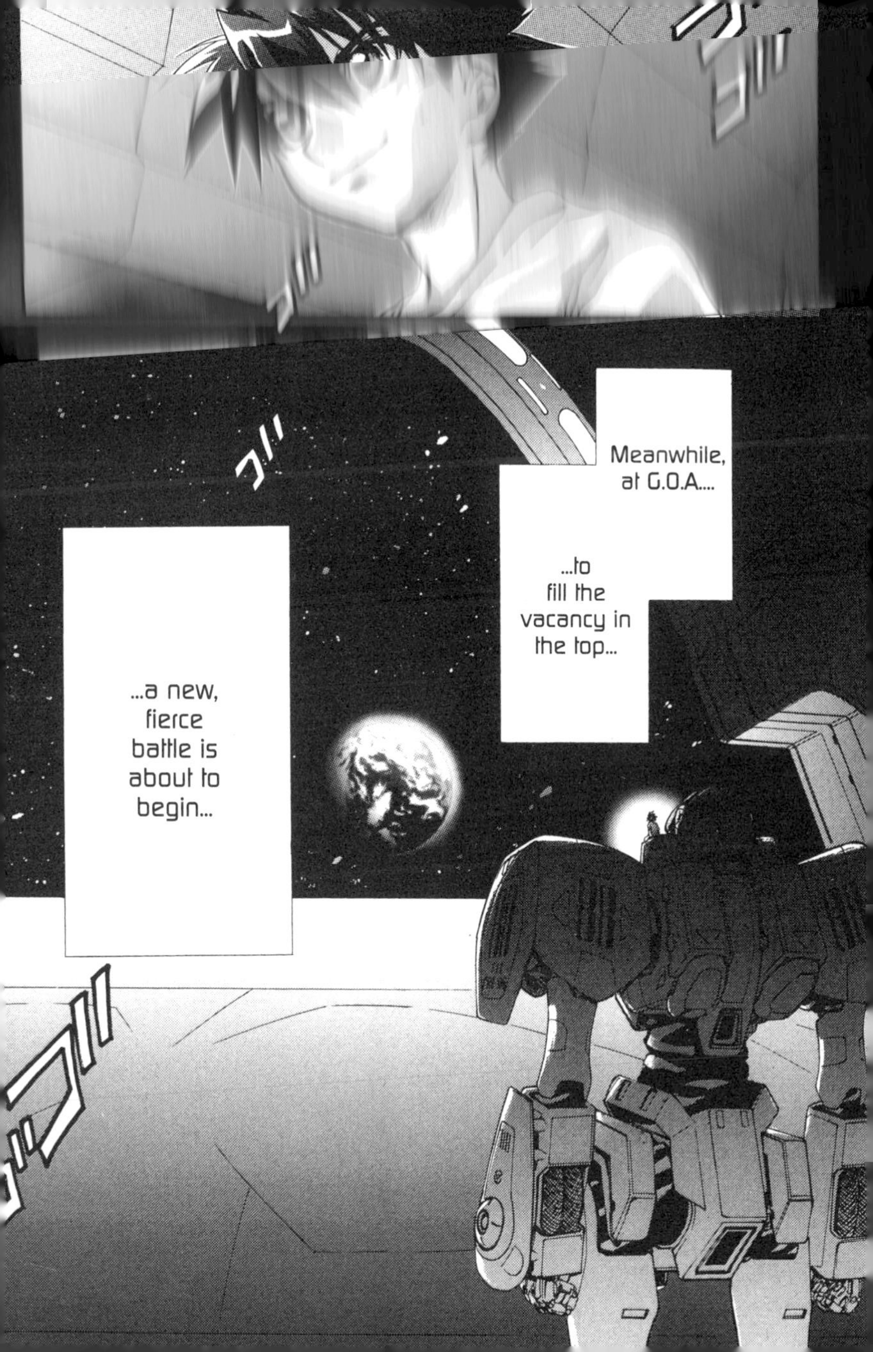
Meanwhile, at G.O.A....
...to fill the vacancy in the top...
...a new, fierce battle is about to begin...

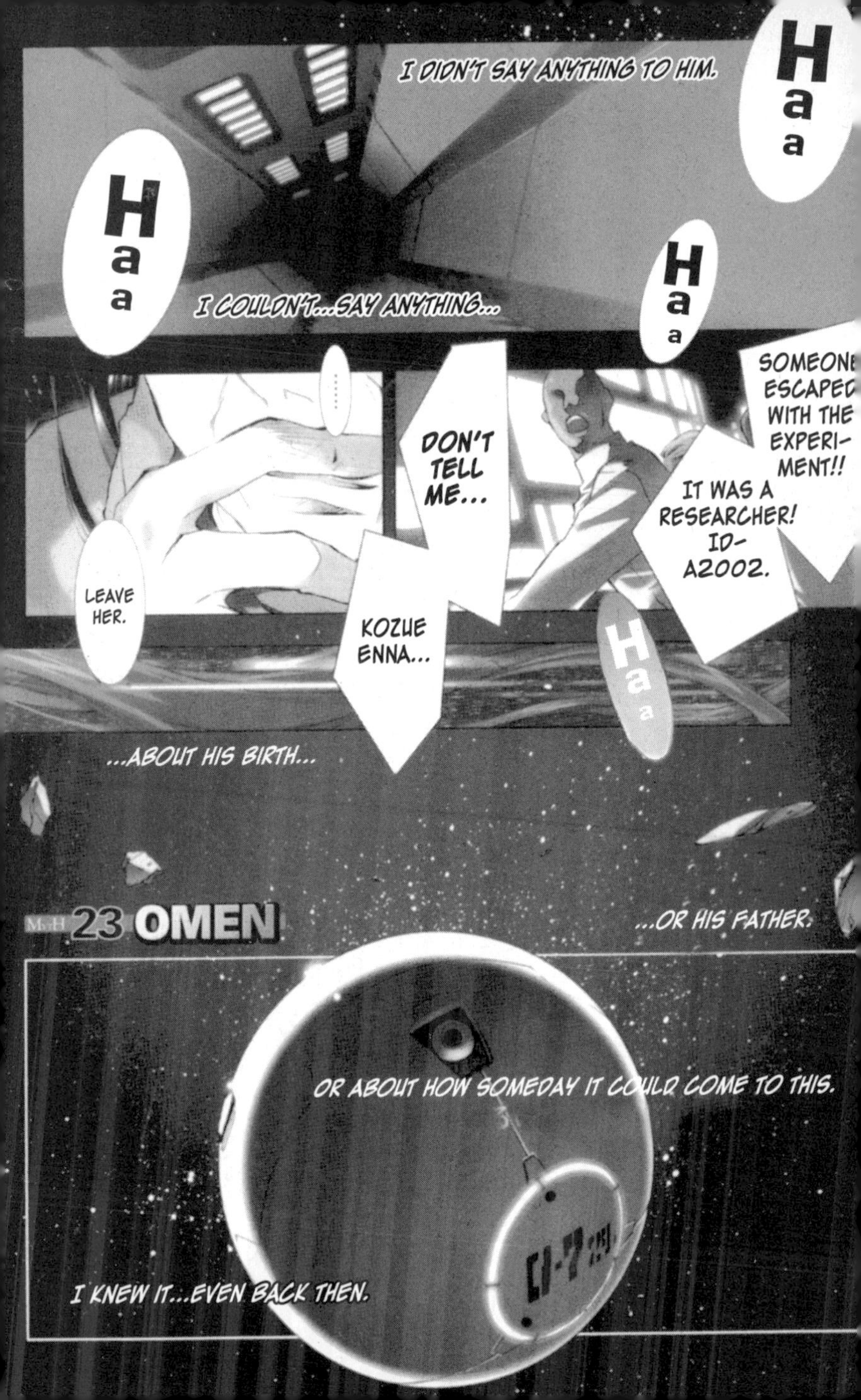
I DIDN'T SAY ANYTHING TO HIM.
Haa
Haa
I COULDN'T...SAY ANYTHING...
Haa
SOMEONE ESCAPED WITH THE EXPERIMENT!!
IT WAS A RESEARCHER! ID-A2002.
DON'T TELL ME...
KOZUE ENNA...
......
LEAVE HER.
Haa
...ABOUT HIS BIRTH...
23 OMEN
...OR HIS FATHER.
OR ABOUT HOW SOMEDAY IT COULD COME TO THIS.
I KNEW IT...EVEN BACK THEN.

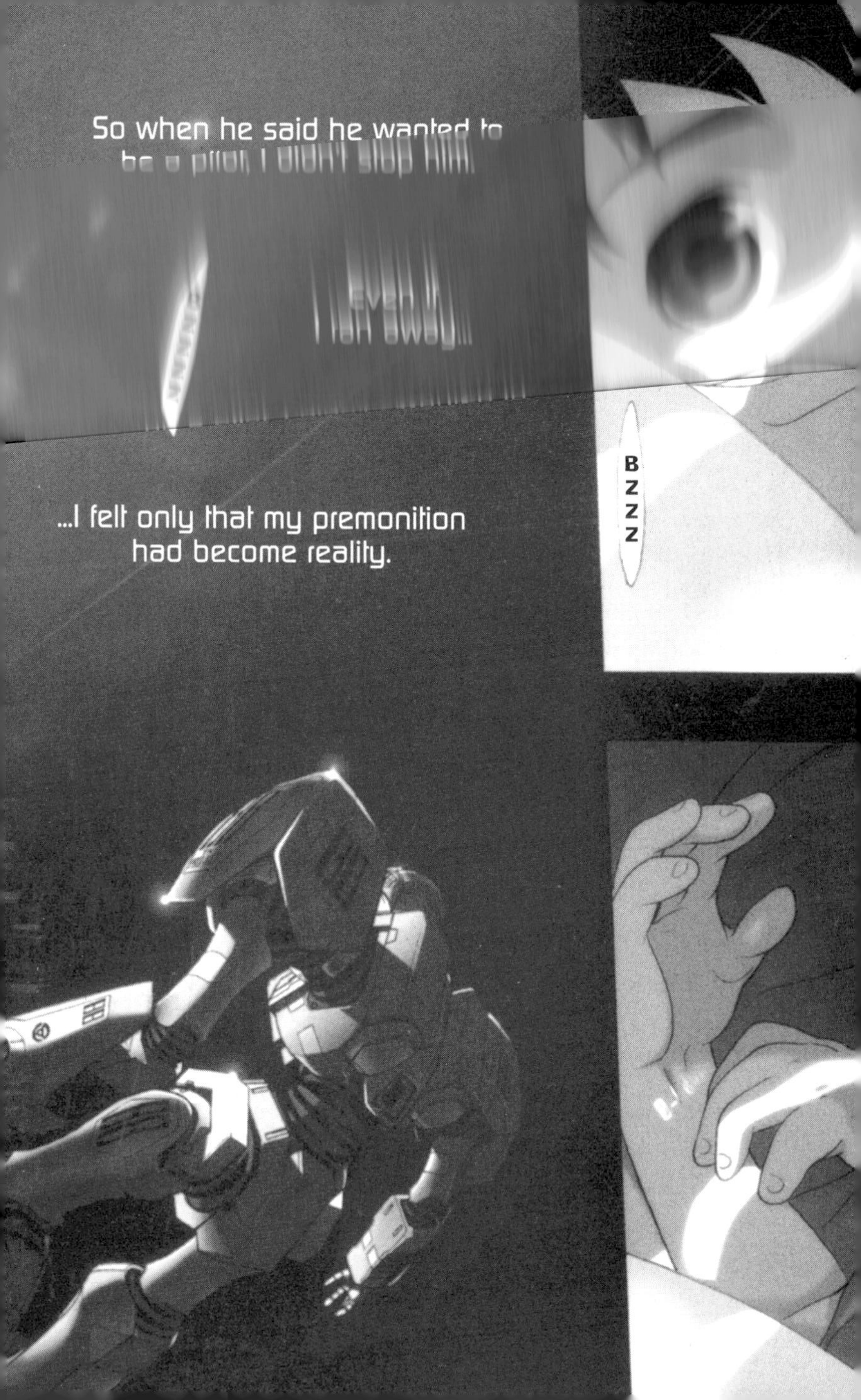
So when he said he wanted to be a pilot, I didn't stop him.
BZZZ
...I felt only that my premonition had become reality.

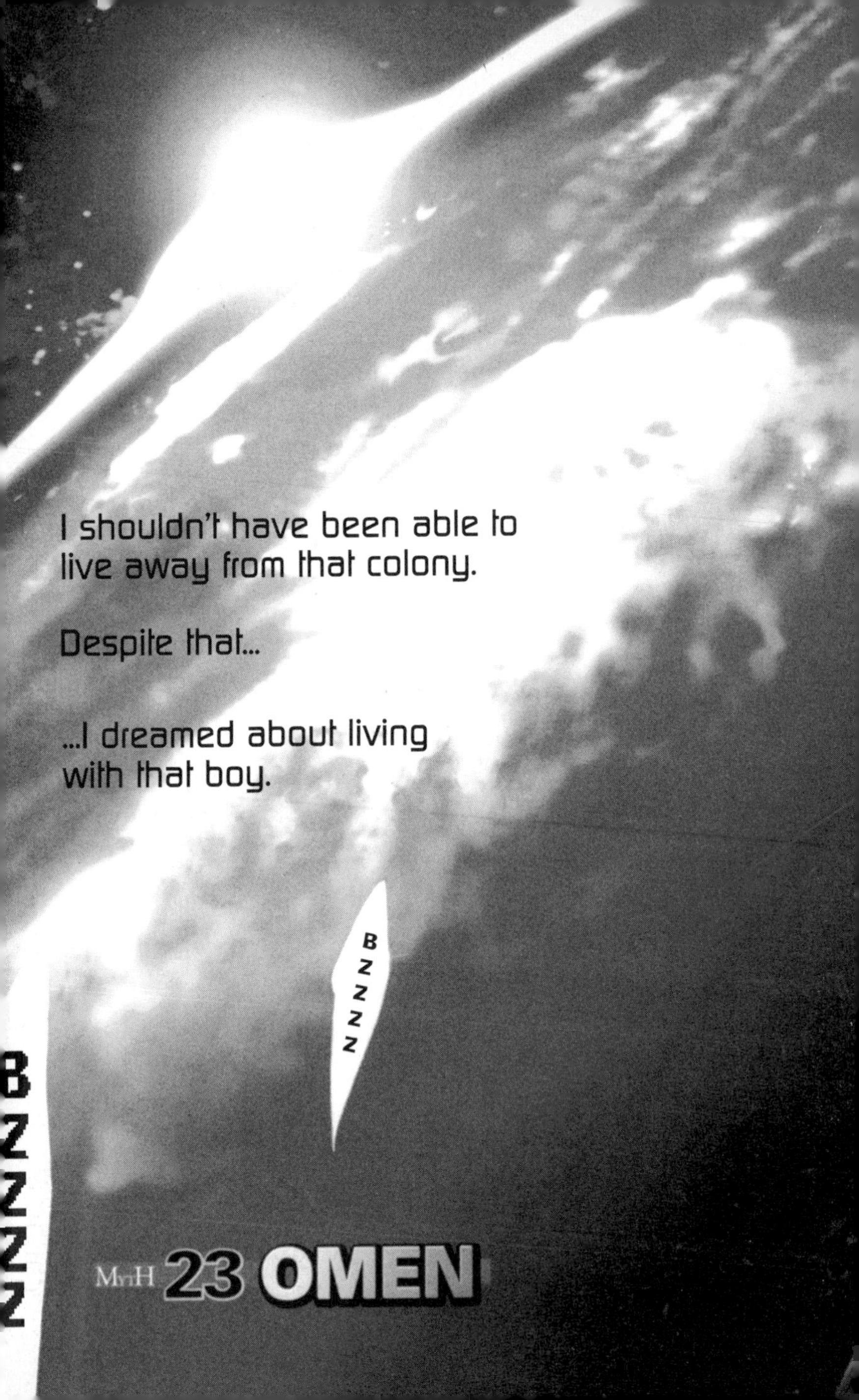
I shouldn't have been able to live away from that colony.
Despite that...
...I dreamed about living with that boy.
BZZZZ
BZZZZ
MyTH 23 OMEN

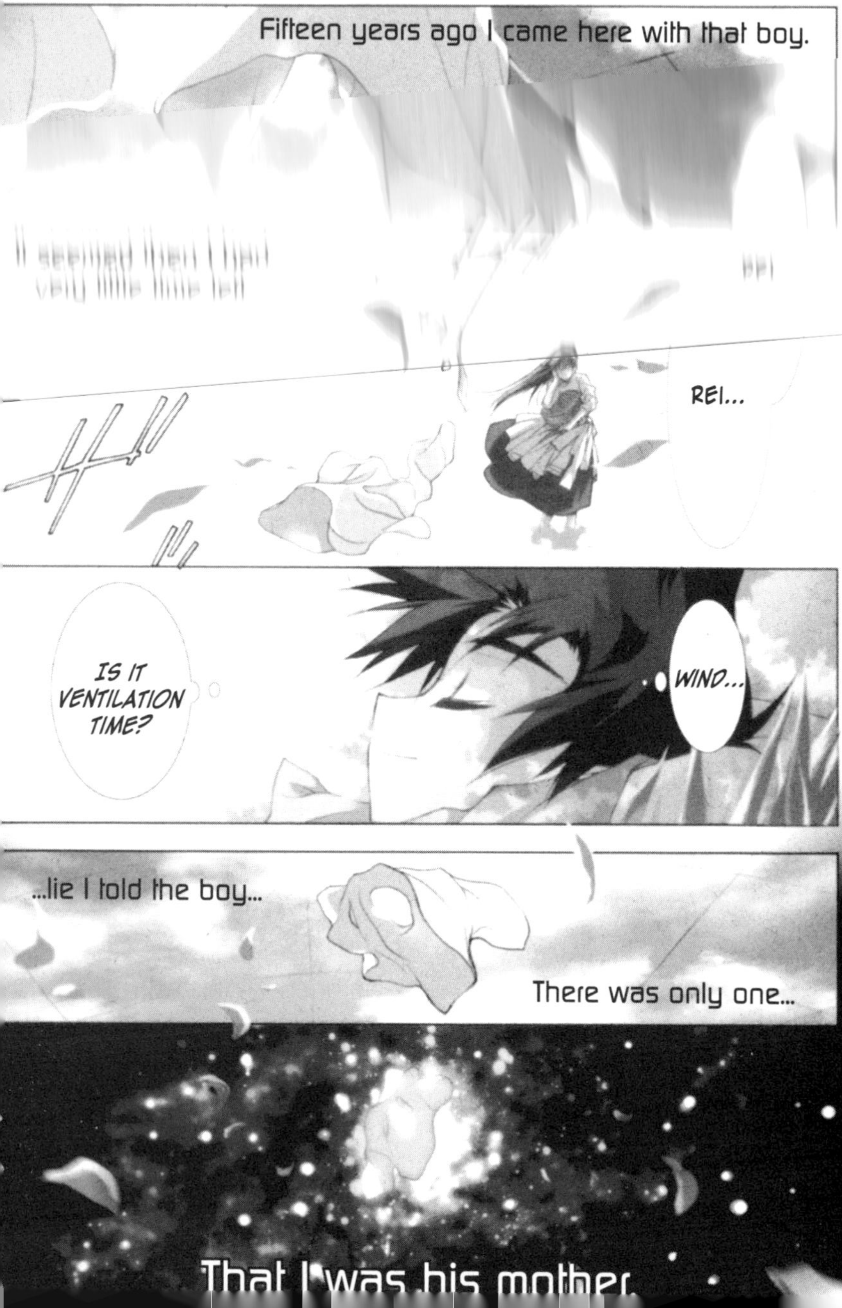
Fifteen years ago I came here with that boy.
REI...
WIND...
IS IT VENTILATION TIME?
There was only one...
...lie I told the boy...
That I was his mother.

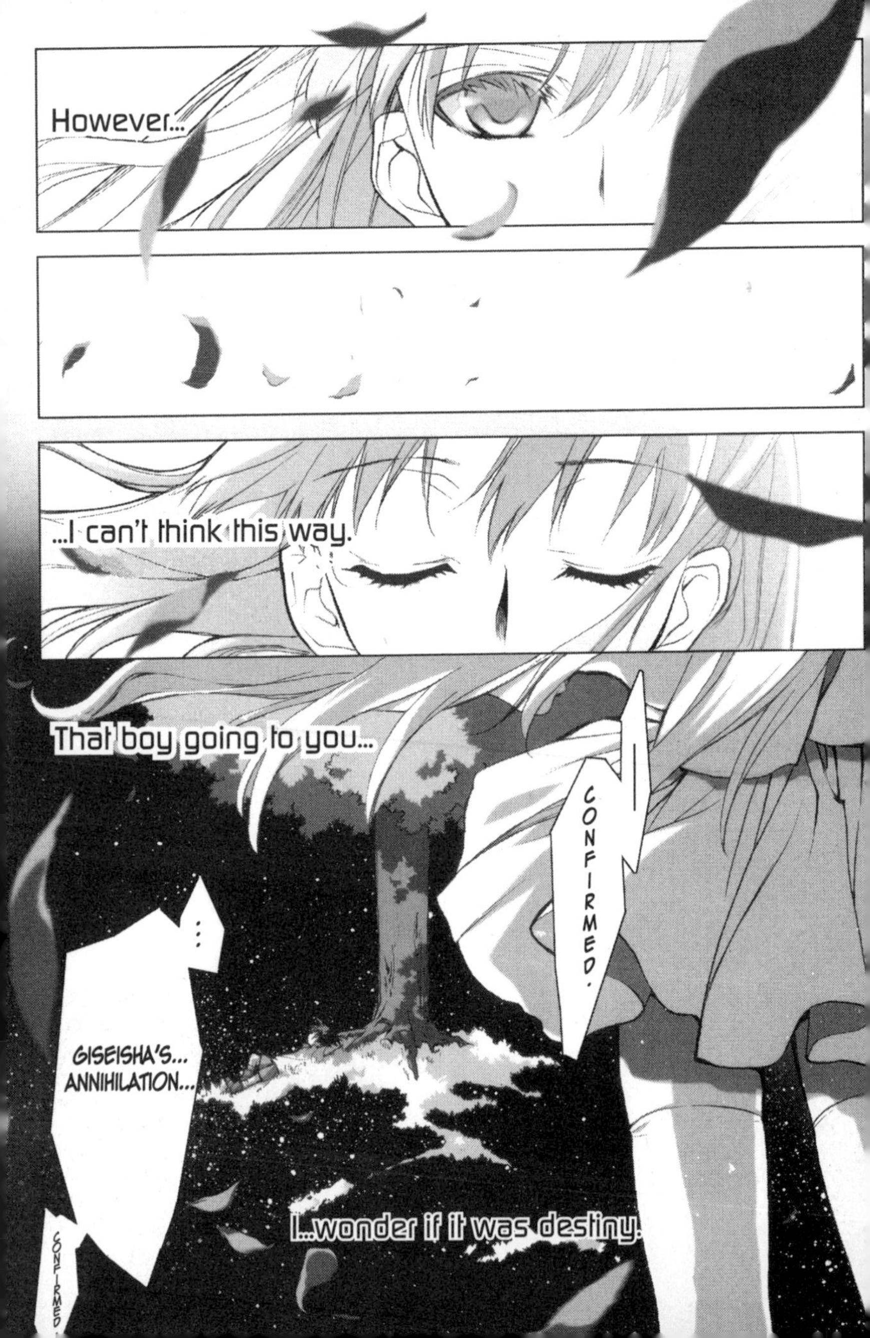
However...
...I can't think this way.
CONFIRMED.
That boy going to you...
...
GISEISHA'S... ANNIHILATION...
I...wonder if it was destiny.
CONFIRMED

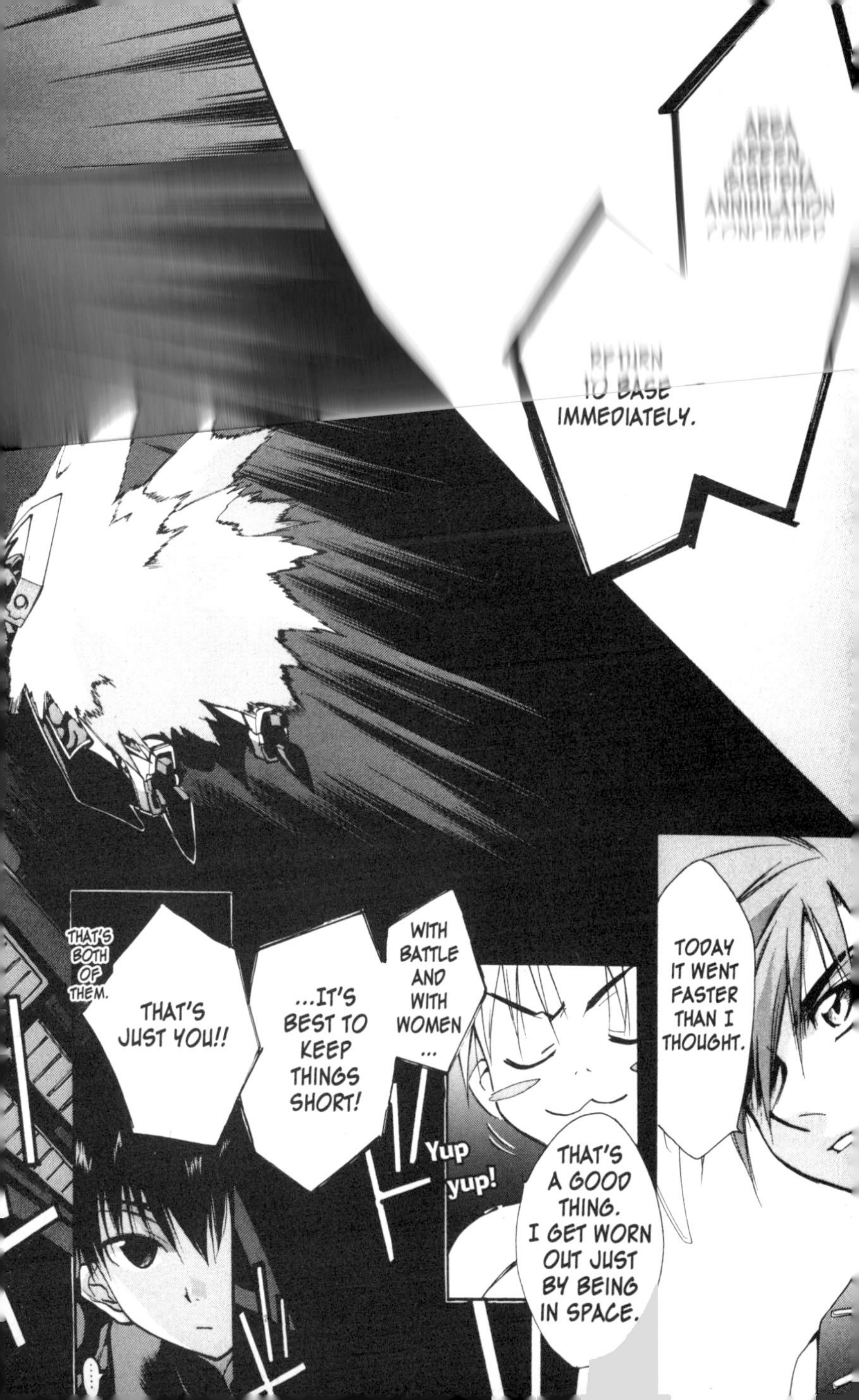

IMMEDIATELY.
TODAY IT WENT FASTER THAN I THOUGHT.
THAT'S A GOOD THING. I GET WORN OUT JUST BY BEING IN SPACE.
Yup yup!
WITH BATTLE AND WITH WOMEN ...
...IT'S BEST TO KEEP THINGS SHORT!
THAT'S JUST YOU!!
THAT'S BOTH OF THEM.
...

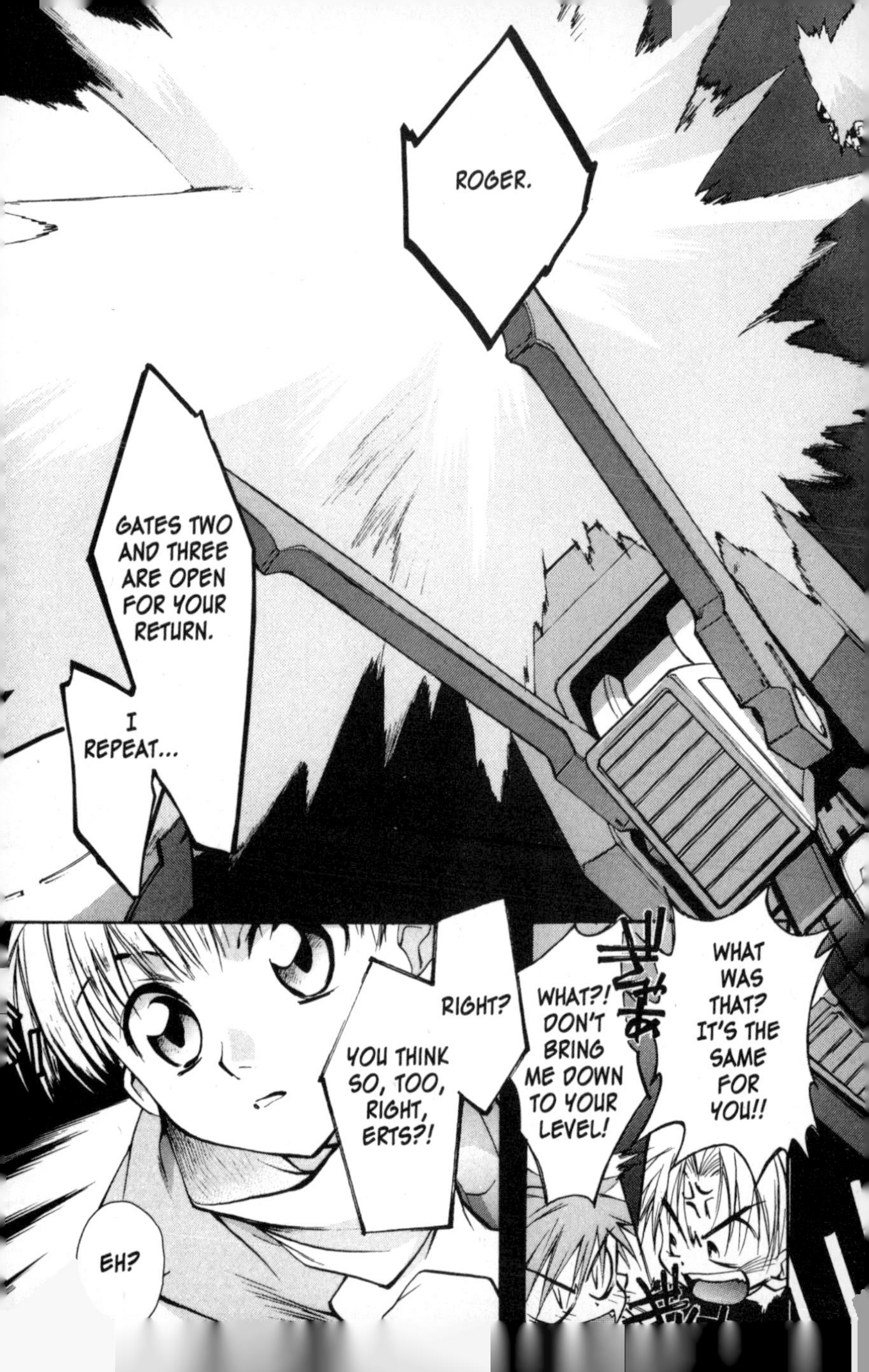
ROGER.
GATES TWO AND THREE ARE OPEN FOR YOUR RETURN.
I REPEAT...
WHAT WAS THAT? IT'S THE SAME FOR YOU!!
WHAT?! DON'T BRING ME DOWN TO YOUR LEVEL!
RIGHT?
YOU THINK SO, TOO, RIGHT, ERTS?!
EH?

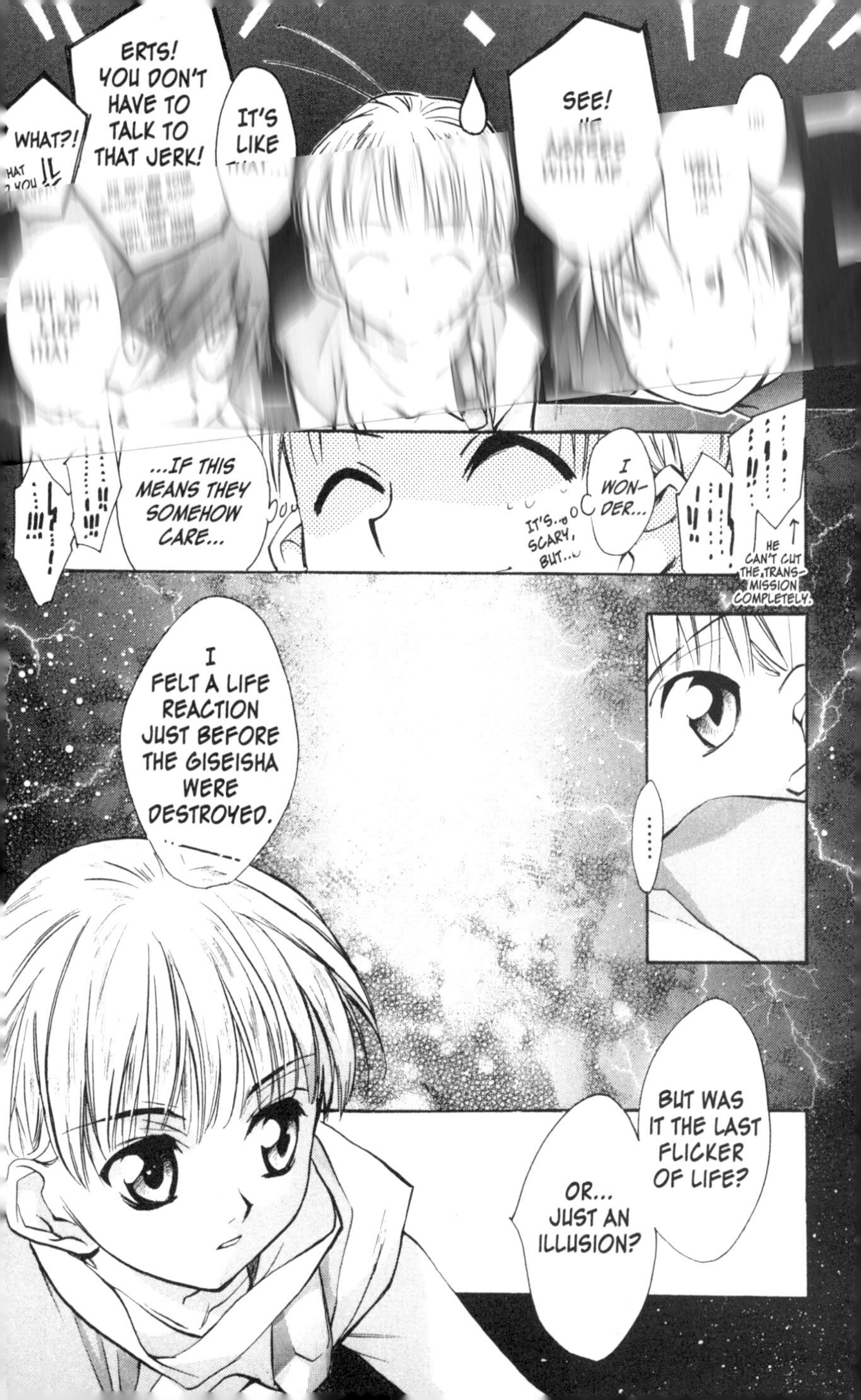
SEE!
IT'S LIKE
ERTS! YOU DON'T HAVE TO TALK TO THAT JERK!
WHAT?!
HE CAN'T CUT THE TRANS-MISSION COMPLETELY.
I WON-DER...
IT'S... SCARY, BUT...
...IF THIS MEANS THEY SOMEHOW CARE...
I FELT A LIFE REACTION JUST BEFORE THE GISEISHA WERE DESTROYED.
BUT WAS IT THE LAST FLICKER OF LIFE?
OR... JUST AN ILLUSION?

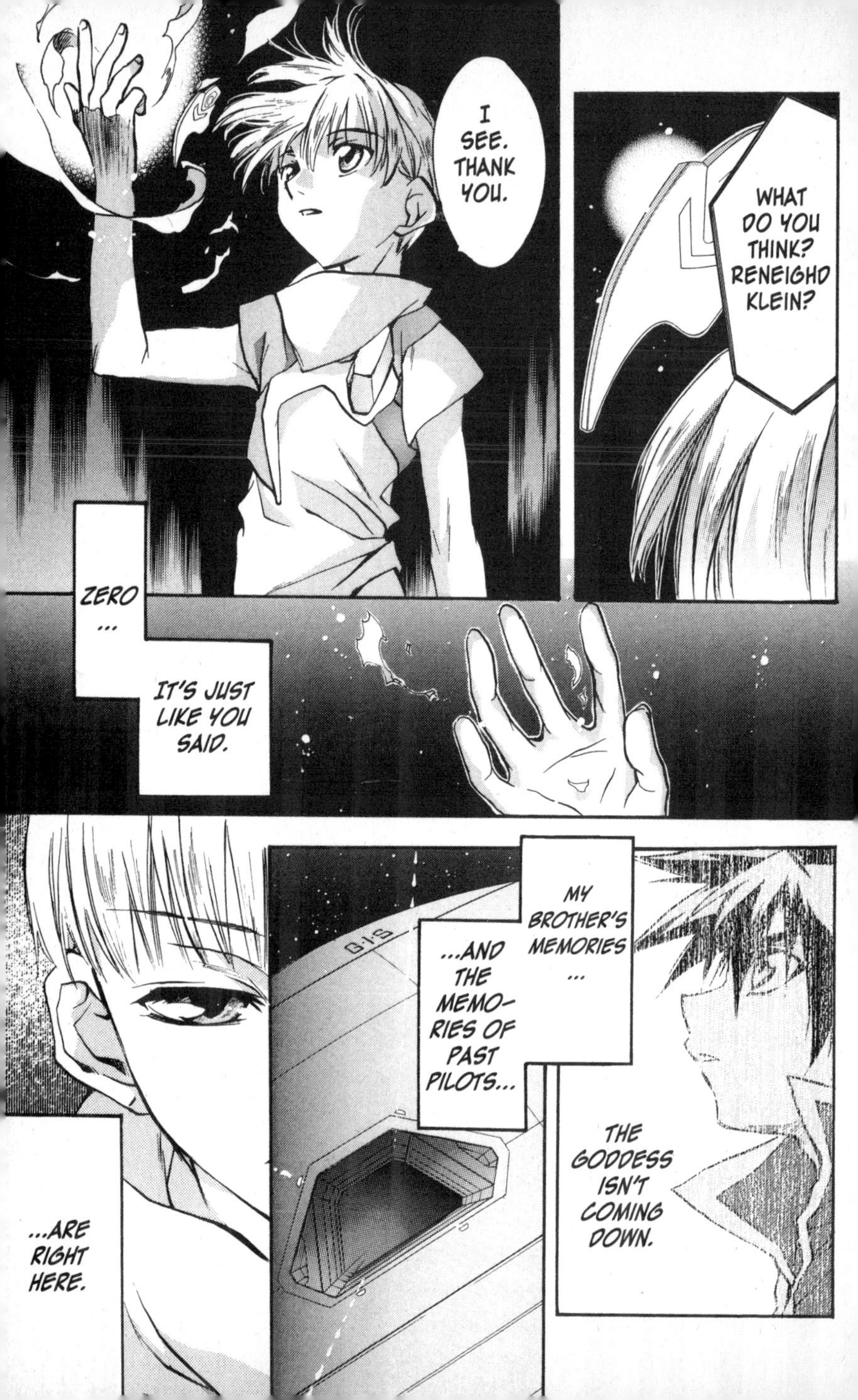
WHAT DO YOU THINK? RENEIGHD KLEIN?
I SEE. THANK YOU.
ZERO ...
IT'S JUST LIKE YOU SAID.
MY BROTHER'S MEMORIES ...
THE GODDESS ISN'T COMING DOWN.
...AND THE MEMO-RIES OF PAST PILOTS...
...ARE RIGHT HERE.

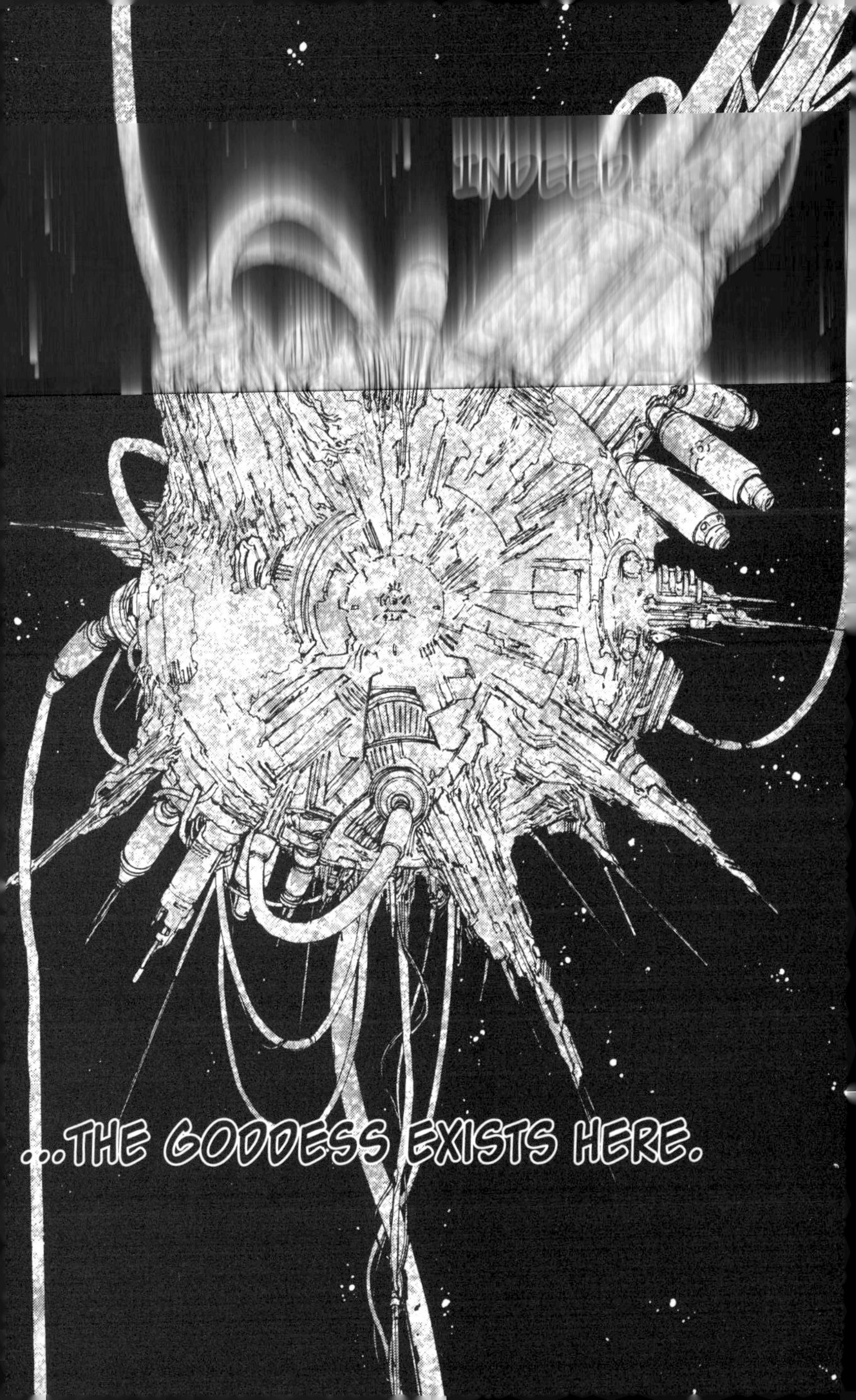
INDEED...
...THE GODDESS EXISTS HERE.

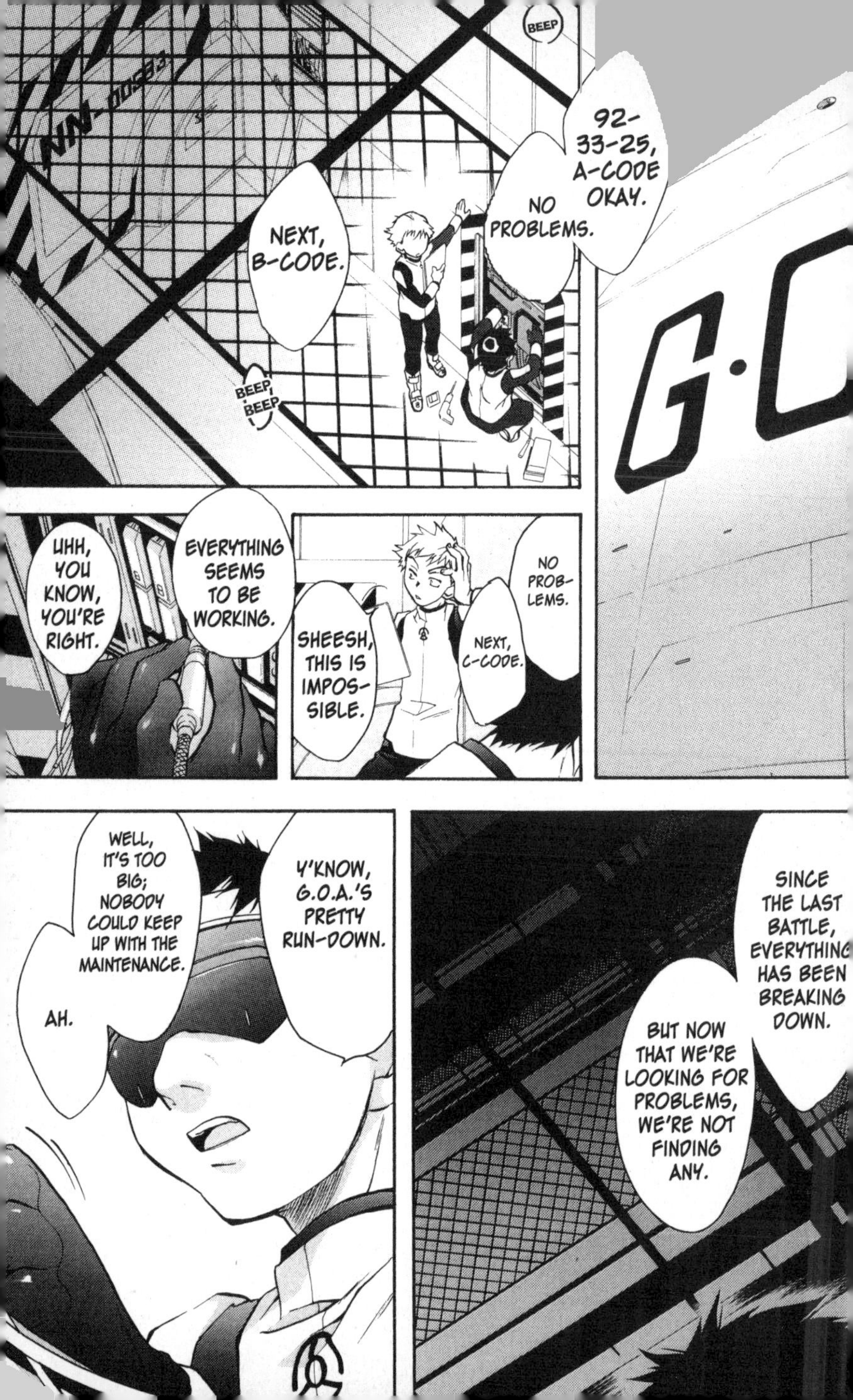
BEEP
92-33-25, A-CODE OKAY.
NO PROBLEMS.
NEXT, B-CODE.
BEEP, BEEP
NO PROB-LEMS.
NEXT, C-CODE.
SHEESH, THIS IS IMPOS-SIBLE.
EVERYTHING SEEMS TO BE WORKING.
UHH, YOU KNOW, YOU'RE RIGHT.
SINCE THE LAST BATTLE, EVERYTHING HAS BEEN BREAKING DOWN.
BUT NOW THAT WE'RE LOOKING FOR PROBLEMS, WE'RE NOT FINDING ANY.
Y'KNOW, G.O.A.'S PRETTY RUN-DOWN.
WELL, IT'S TOO BIG; NOBODY COULD KEEP UP WITH THE MAINTENANCE.
AH.

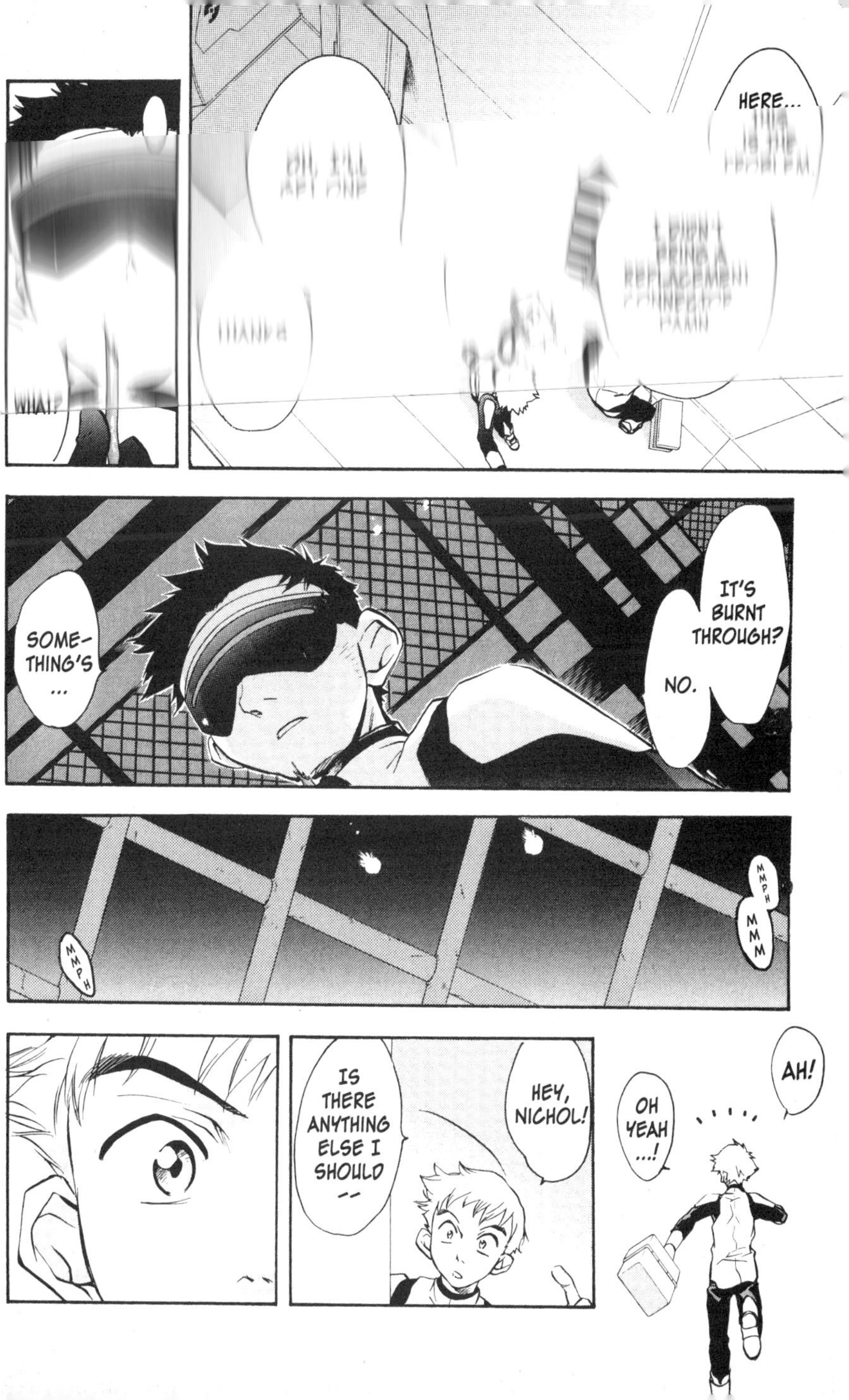
HERE...
WHAT!?
IT'S BURNT THROUGH?
NO.
SOME-THING'S...
MMPH
MMM
MMPH
AH!
OH YEAH...!
HEY, NICHOL!
IS THERE ANYTHING ELSE I SHOULD --

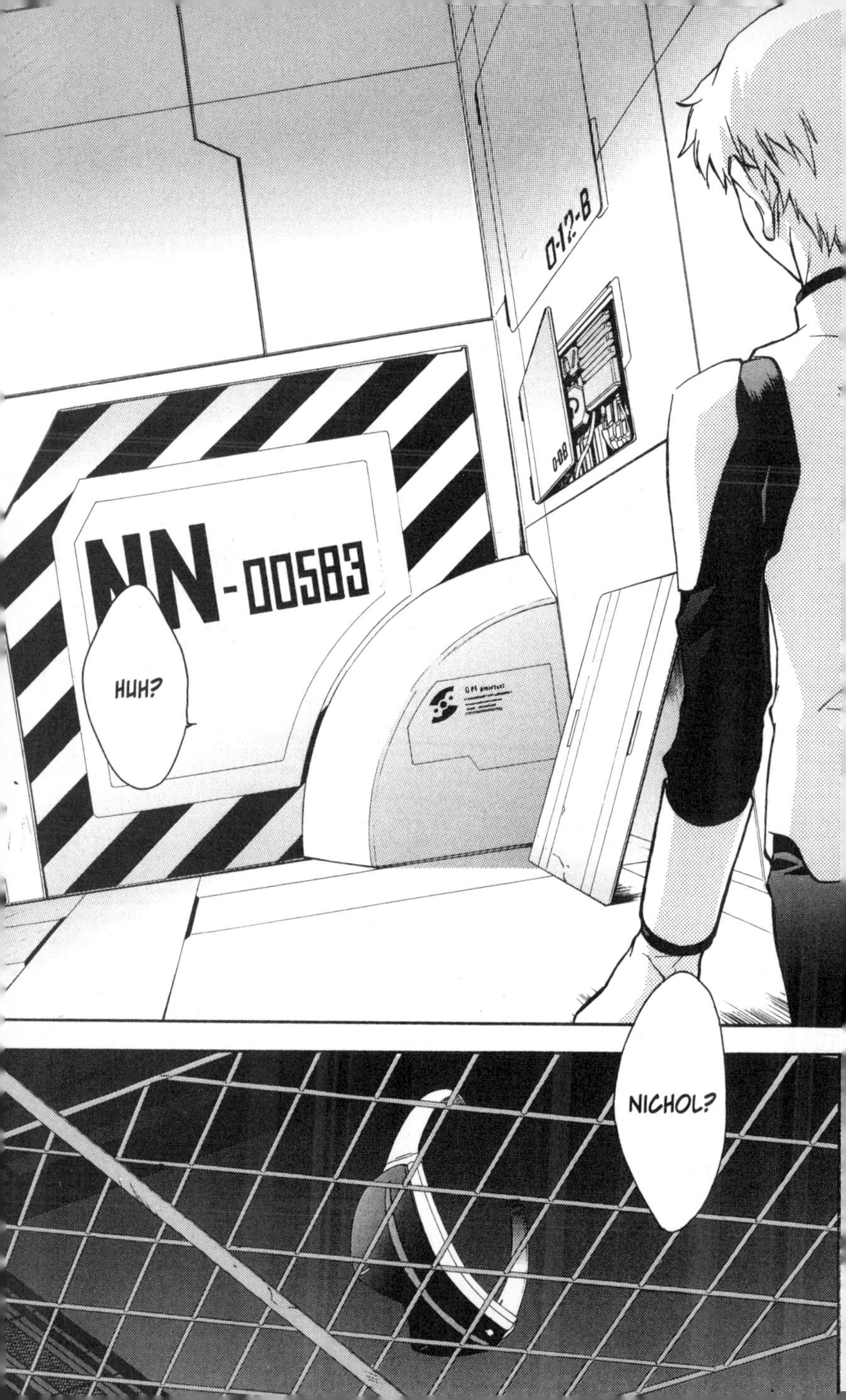
0-12-B
NN-00583
HUH?
NICHOL?

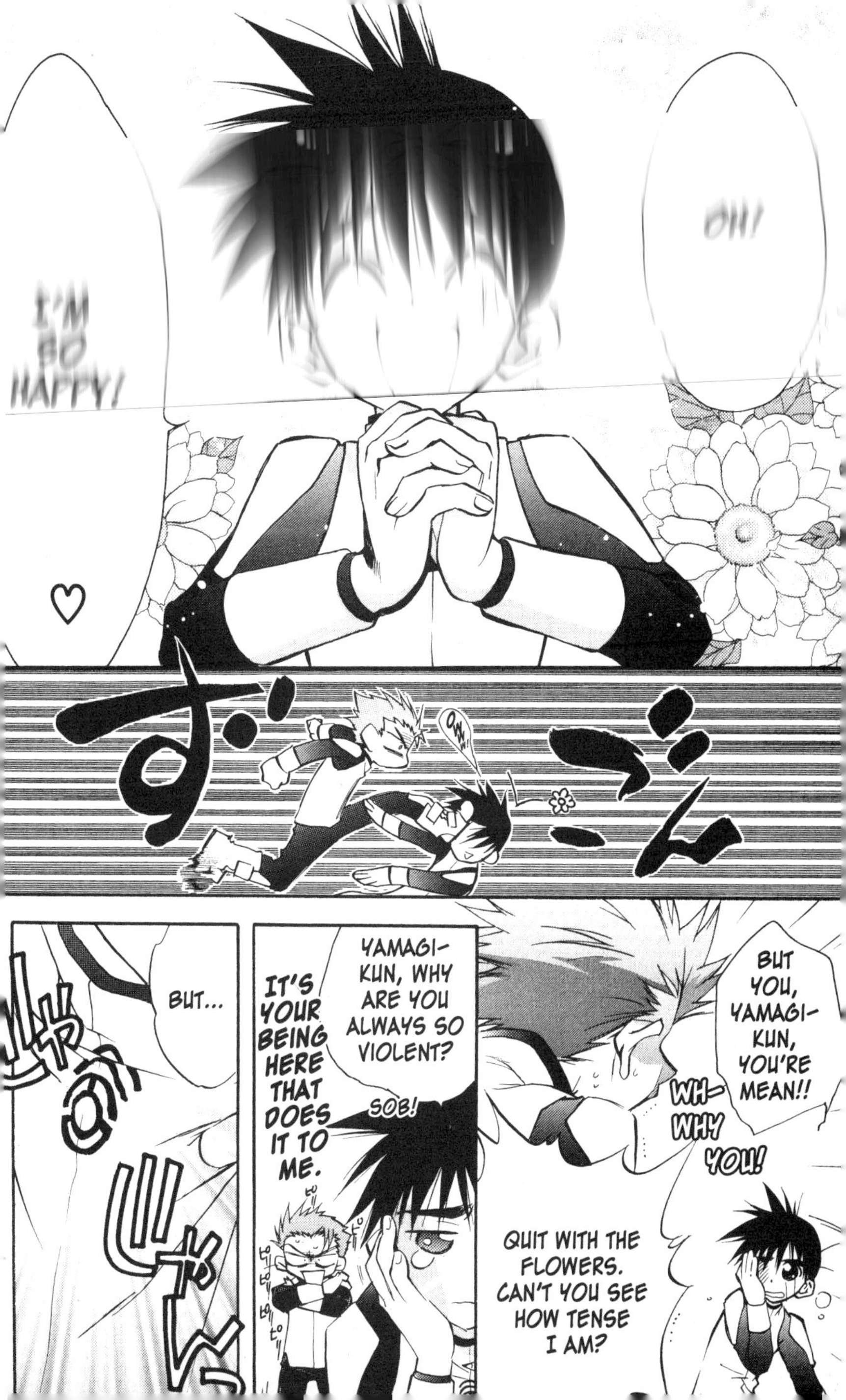
OH!
I'M SO HAPPY!
♥
ずごーん
OWW!
BUT YOU, YAMAGI-KUN, YOU'RE MEAN!!
WH-WHY YOU!
QUIT WITH THE FLOWERS. CAN'T YOU SEE HOW TENSE I AM?
YAMAGI-KUN, WHY ARE YOU ALWAYS SO VIOLENT?
SOB!
IT'S YOUR BEING HERE THAT DOES IT TO ME.
BUT...

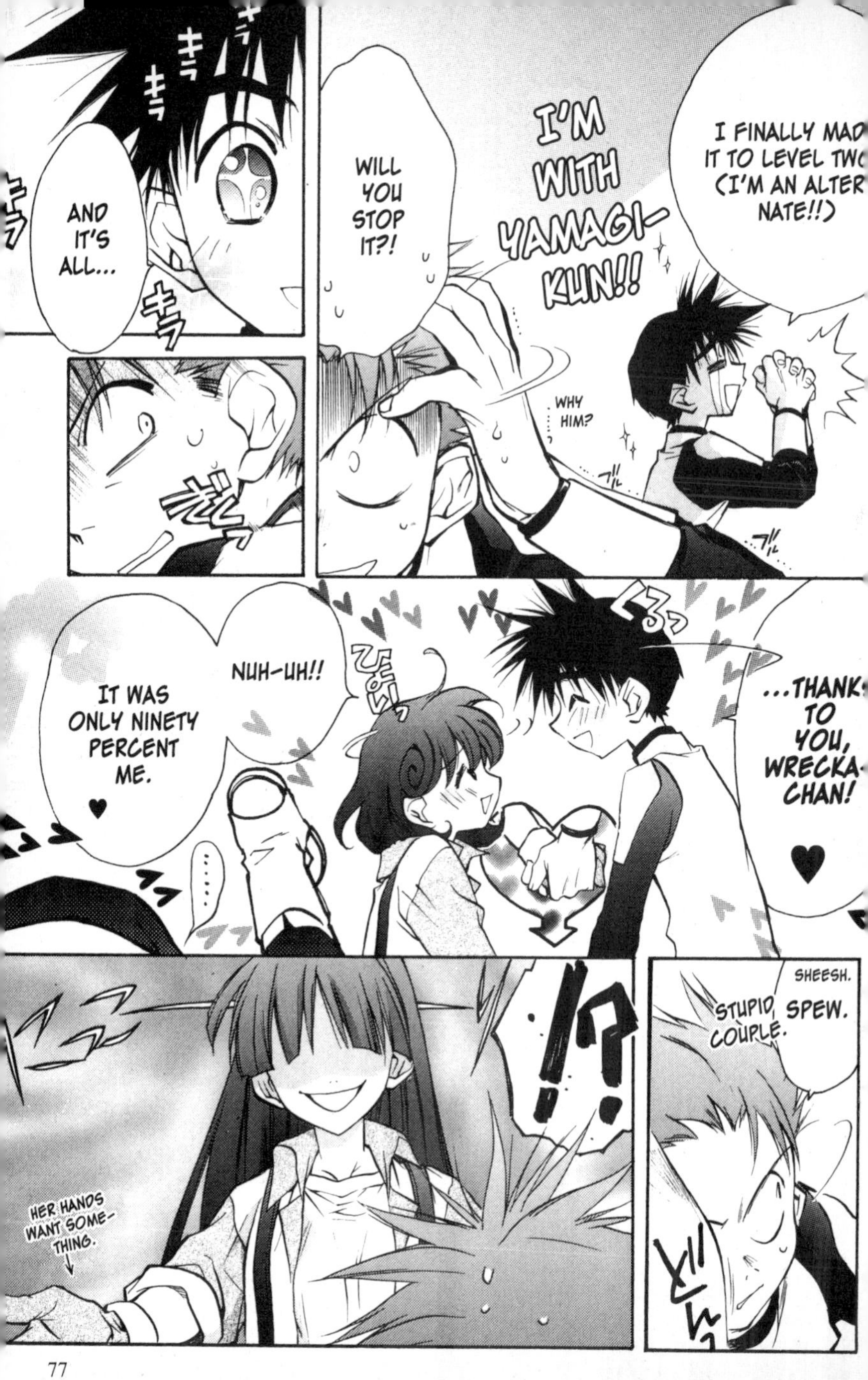
I FINALLY MAD IT TO LEVEL TWO (I'M AN ALTER NATE!!)
I'M WITH YAMAGI-KUN!!
WILL YOU STOP IT?!
WHY HIM?
AND IT'S ALL...
...THANK TO YOU, WRECKA-CHAN! ♥
NUH-UH!!
IT WAS ONLY NINETY PERCENT ME. ♥
......
SHEESH.
STUPID COUPLE.
SPEW.
HER HANDS WANT SOME-THING.

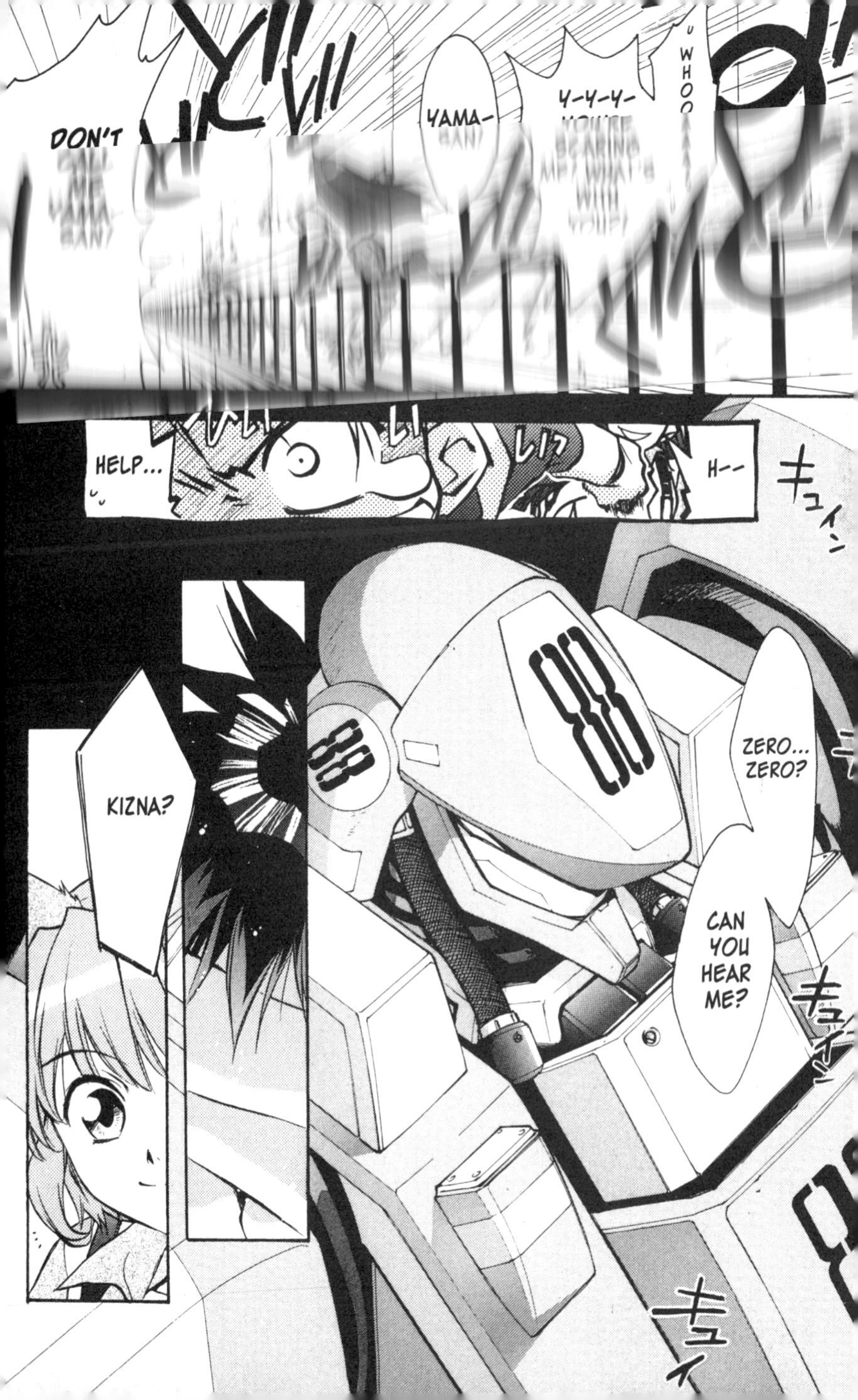
WHOO
Y-Y-Y-
YAMA-
DON'T
H--
HELP...
キュイン
ZERO... ZERO?
CAN YOU HEAR ME?
キュイン
キュイ
KIZNA?

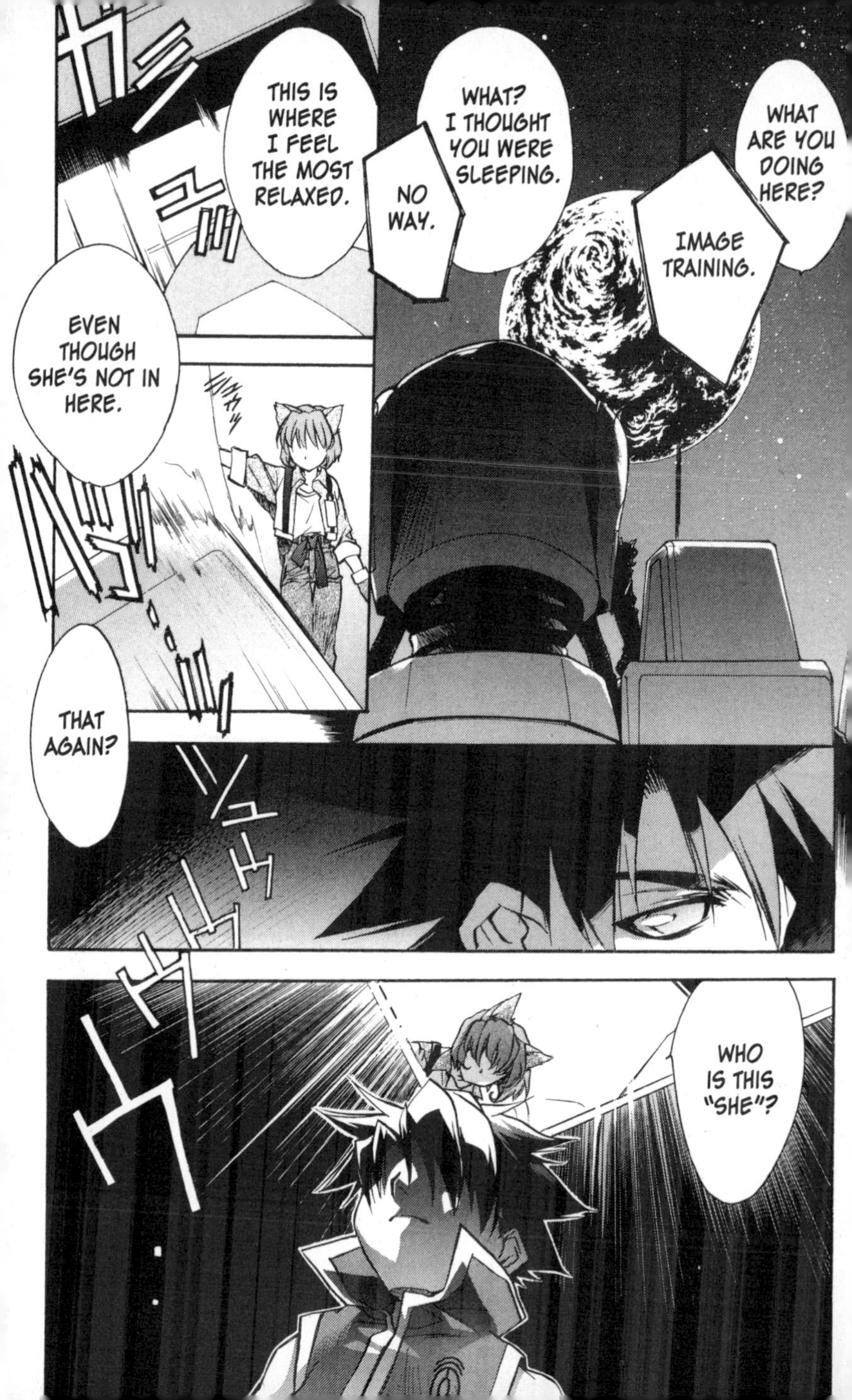
WHAT ARE YOU DOING HERE?
IMAGE TRAINING.
WHAT? I THOUGHT YOU WERE SLEEPING.
NO WAY.
THIS IS WHERE I FEEL THE MOST RELAXED.
EVEN THOUGH SHE'S NOT IN HERE.
THAT AGAIN?
WHO IS THIS "SHE"?

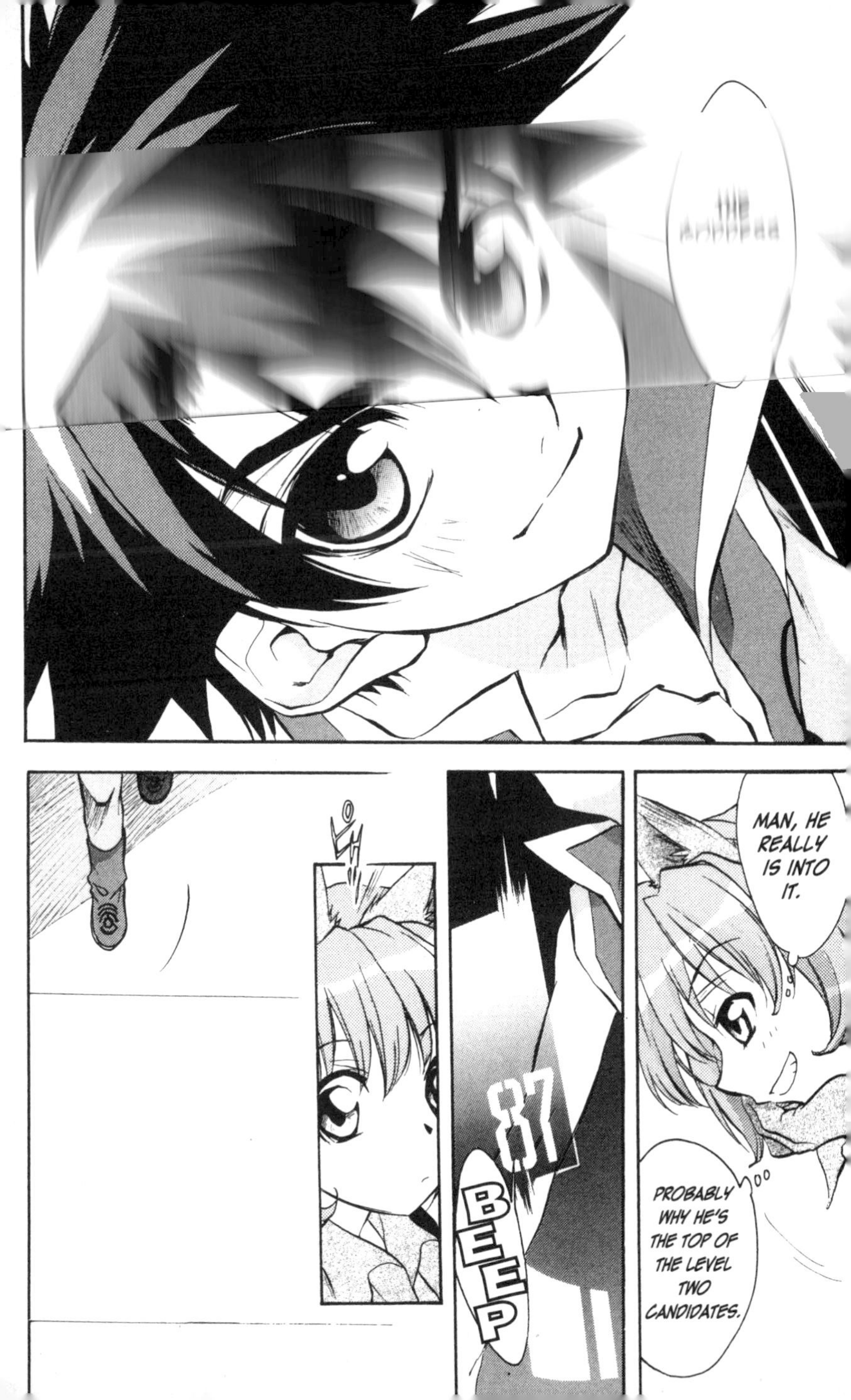
MAN, HE REALLY IS INTO IT.
PROBABLY WHY HE'S THE TOP OF THE LEVEL TWO CANDIDATES.
87
BEEP

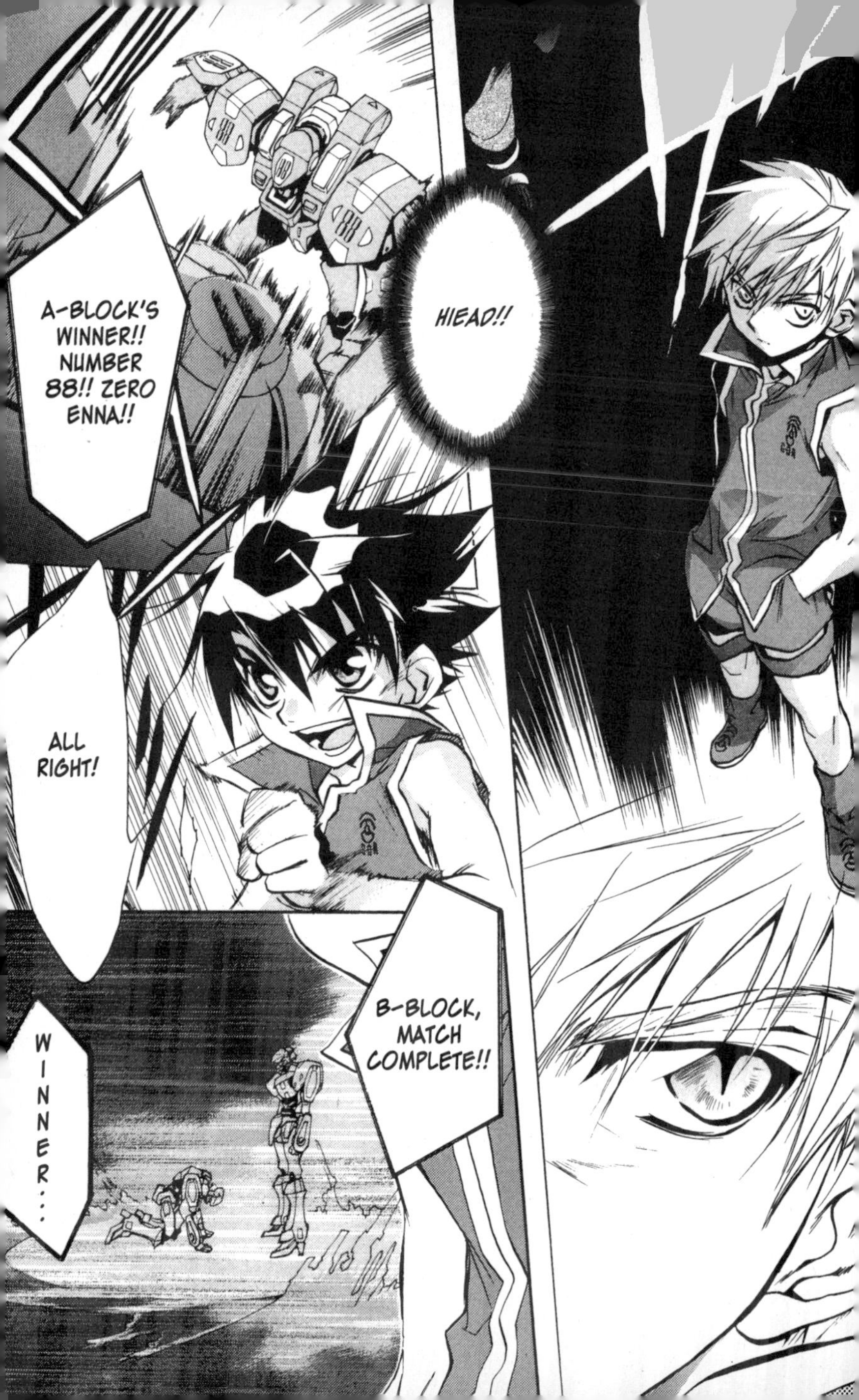
A-BLOCK'S WINNER!! NUMBER 88!! ZERO ENNA!!
ALL RIGHT!
B-BLOCK, MATCH COMPLETE!!
WINNER...
HIEAD!!

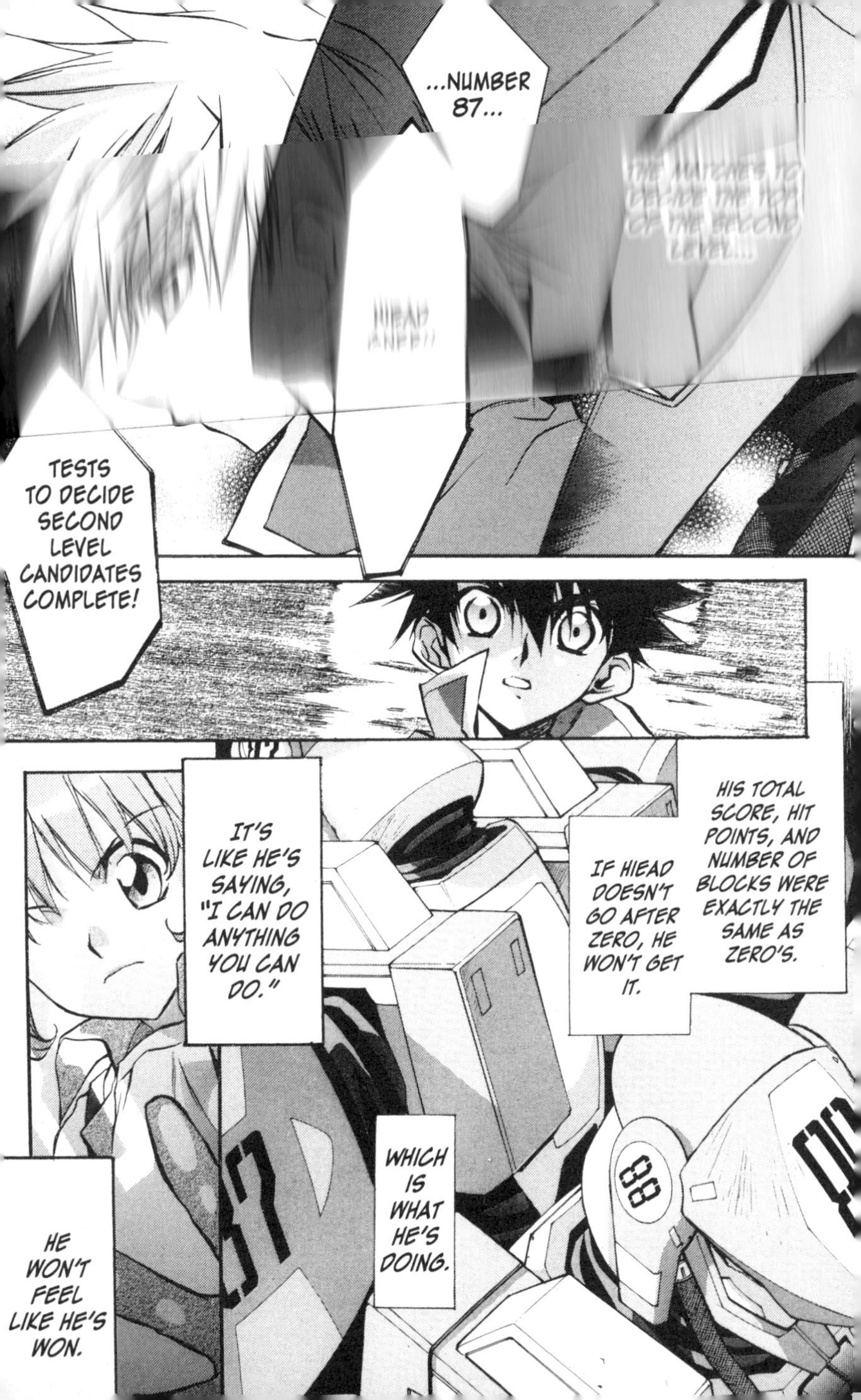
...NUMBER 87...
TESTS TO DECIDE SECOND LEVEL CANDIDATES COMPLETE!
HIS TOTAL SCORE, HIT POINTS, AND NUMBER OF BLOCKS WERE EXACTLY THE SAME AS ZERO'S.
IF HIEAD DOESN'T GO AFTER ZERO, HE WON'T GET IT.
IT'S LIKE HE'S SAYING, "I CAN DO ANYTHING YOU CAN DO."
WHICH IS WHAT HE'S DOING.
HE WON'T FEEL LIKE HE'S WON.
88

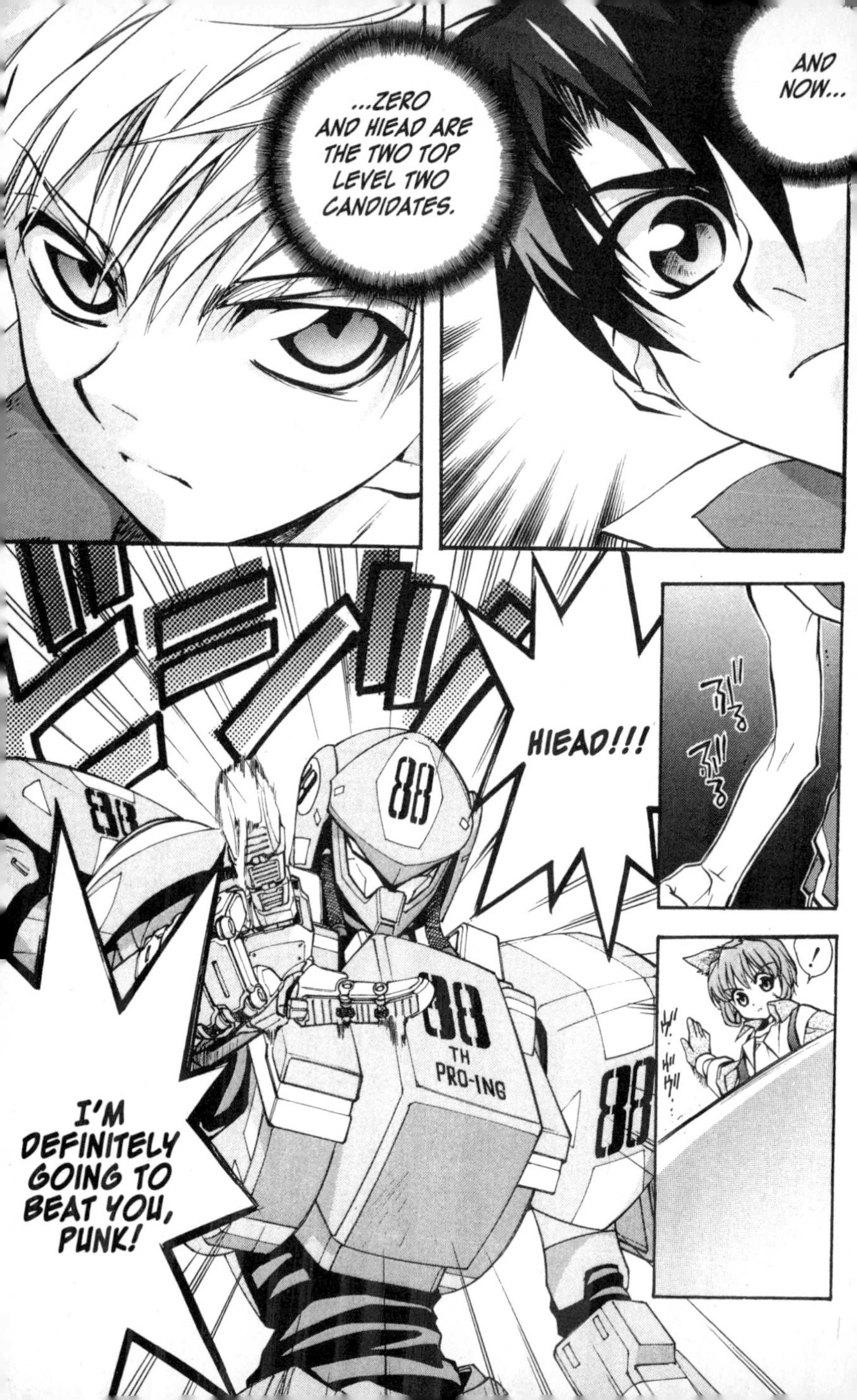
AND NOW...
...ZERO AND HIEAD ARE THE TWO TOP LEVEL TWO CANDIDATES.
!
HIEAD!!!
88 TH PRO-ING
I'M DEFINITELY GOING TO BEAT YOU, PUNK!

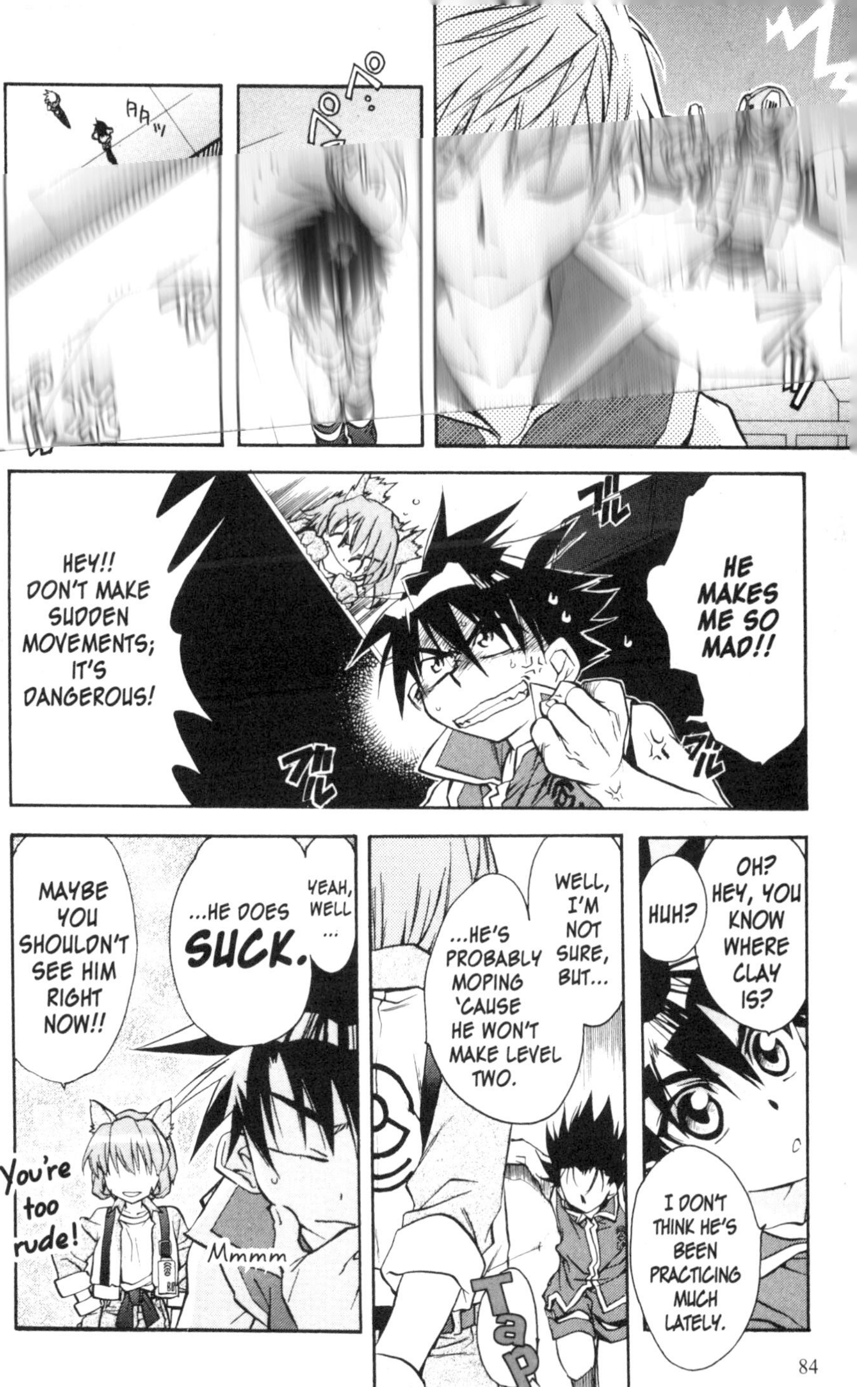
HE MAKES ME SO MAD!!
HEY!! DON'T MAKE SUDDEN MOVEMENTS; IT'S DANGEROUS!
OH? HEY, YOU KNOW WHERE CLAY IS?
HUH?
I DON'T THINK HE'S BEEN PRACTICING MUCH LATELY.
WELL, I'M NOT SURE, BUT...
...HE'S PROBABLY MOPING 'CAUSE HE WON'T MAKE LEVEL TWO.
Tap
YEAH, WELL ...
...HE DOES SUCK.
MAYBE YOU SHOULDN'T SEE HIM RIGHT NOW!!
Mmmm
You're too rude!

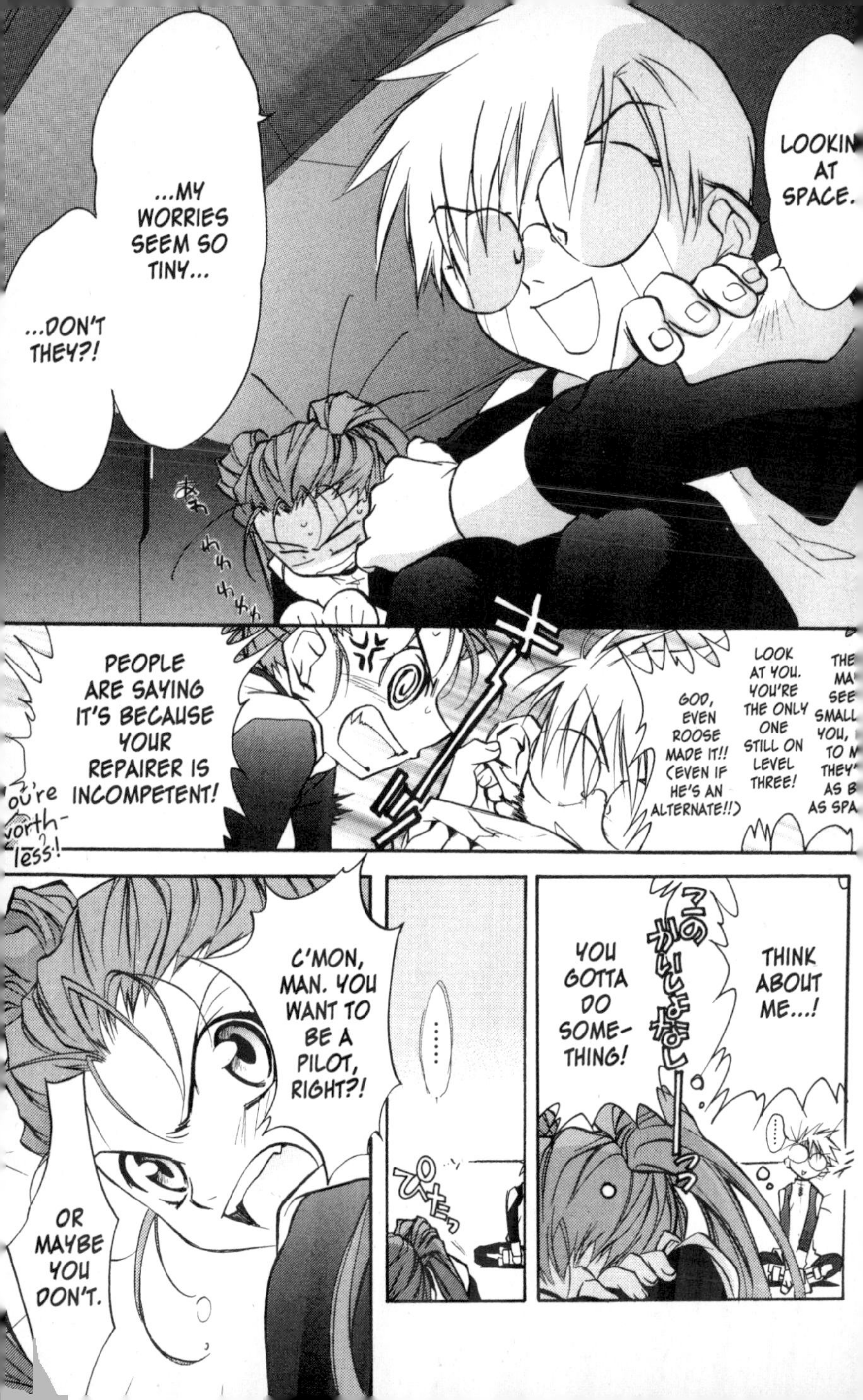
LOOKIN AT SPACE.
...MY WORRIES SEEM SO TINY...
...DON'T THEY?!
THE MA SEE SMALL YOU, TO M THEY' AS B AS SPA
LOOK AT YOU. YOU'RE THE ONLY ONE STILL ON LEVEL THREE!
GOD, EVEN ROOSE MADE IT!! (EVEN IF HE'S AN ALTERNATE!!)
PEOPLE ARE SAYING IT'S BECAUSE YOUR REPAIRER IS INCOMPETENT!
ou're worth-less!
THINK ABOUT ME...!
YOU GOTTA DO SOME-THING!
このかいしょなしーっっ
...
......
ぴたっ
C'MON, MAN. YOU WANT TO BE A PILOT, RIGHT?!
OR MAYBE YOU DON'T.

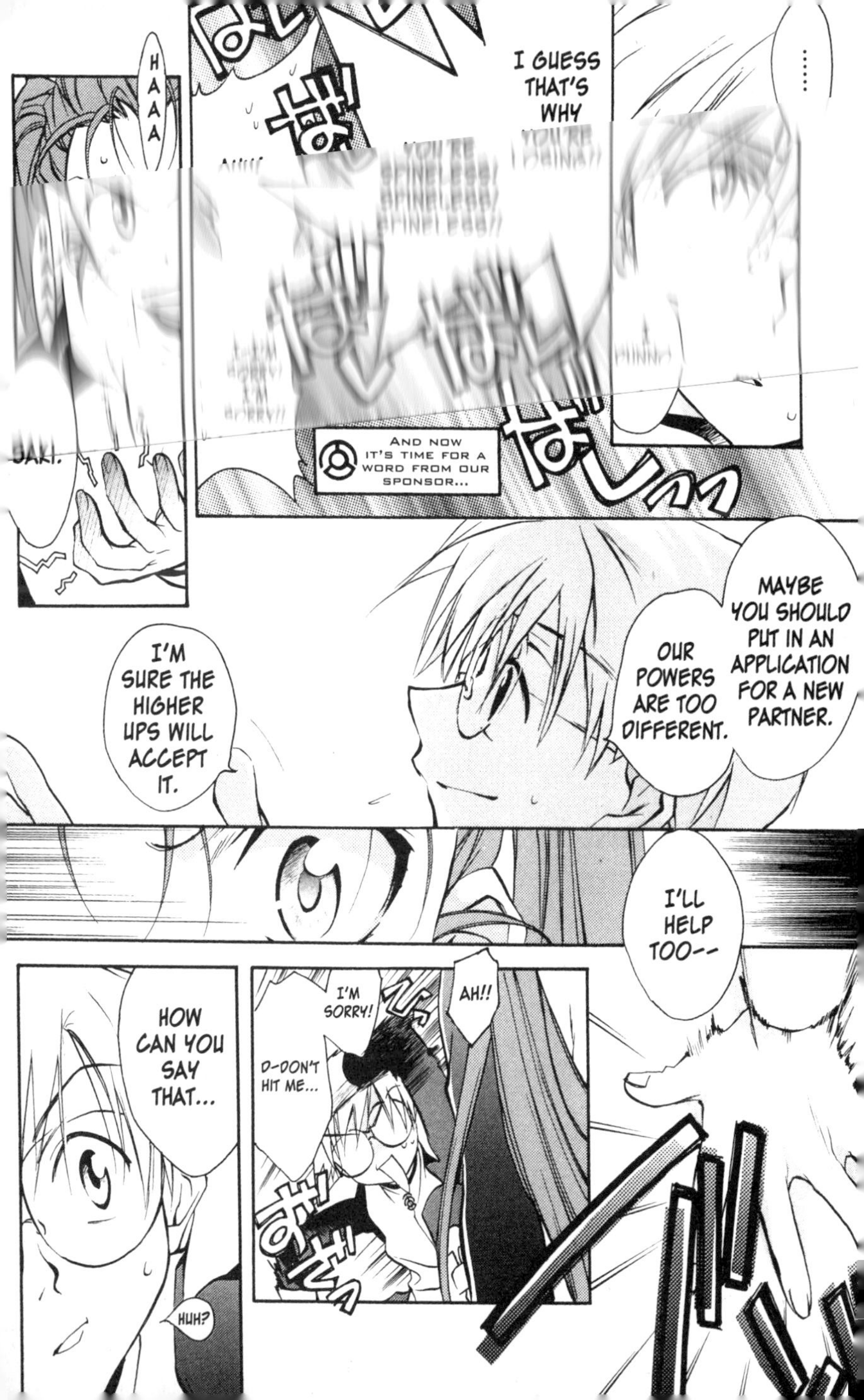
......
I GUESS THAT'S WHY
AND NOW IT'S TIME FOR A WORD FROM OUR SPONSOR...
HAAA
MAYBE YOU SHOULD PUT IN AN APPLICATION FOR A NEW PARTNER.
OUR POWERS ARE TOO DIFFERENT.
I'M SURE THE HIGHER UPS WILL ACCEPT IT.
I'LL HELP TOO--
AH!!
I'M SORRY!
D-DON'T HIT ME...
HOW CAN YOU SAY THAT...
HUH?

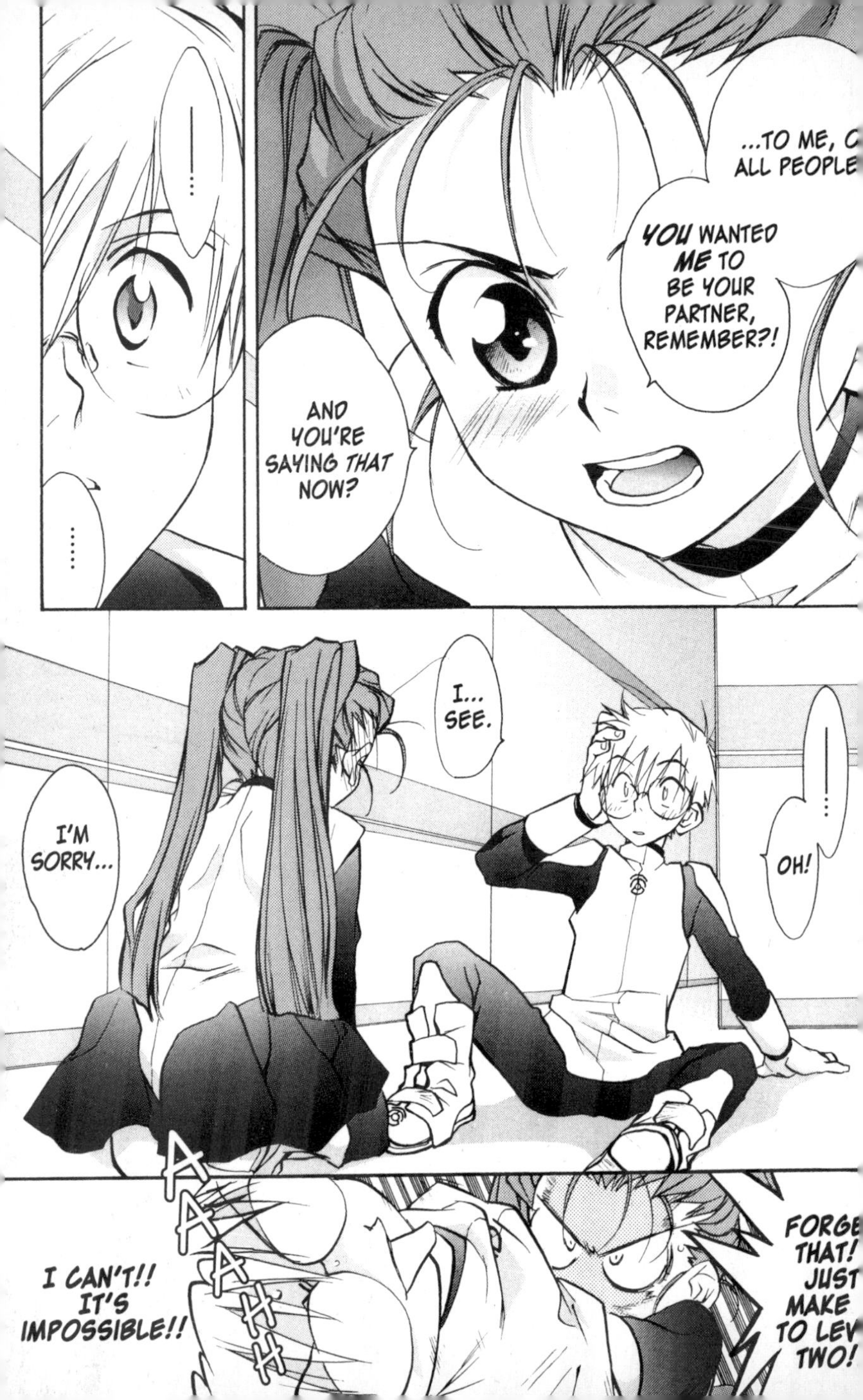
...TO ME, ALL PEOPLE
YOU WANTED ME TO BE YOUR PARTNER, REMEMBER?!
AND YOU'RE SAYING THAT NOW?
......
......
......
OH!
I... SEE.
I'M SORRY...
FORGE THAT! JUST MAKE TO LEV TWO!
AAAHH
I CAN'T!! IT'S IMPOSSIBLE!!

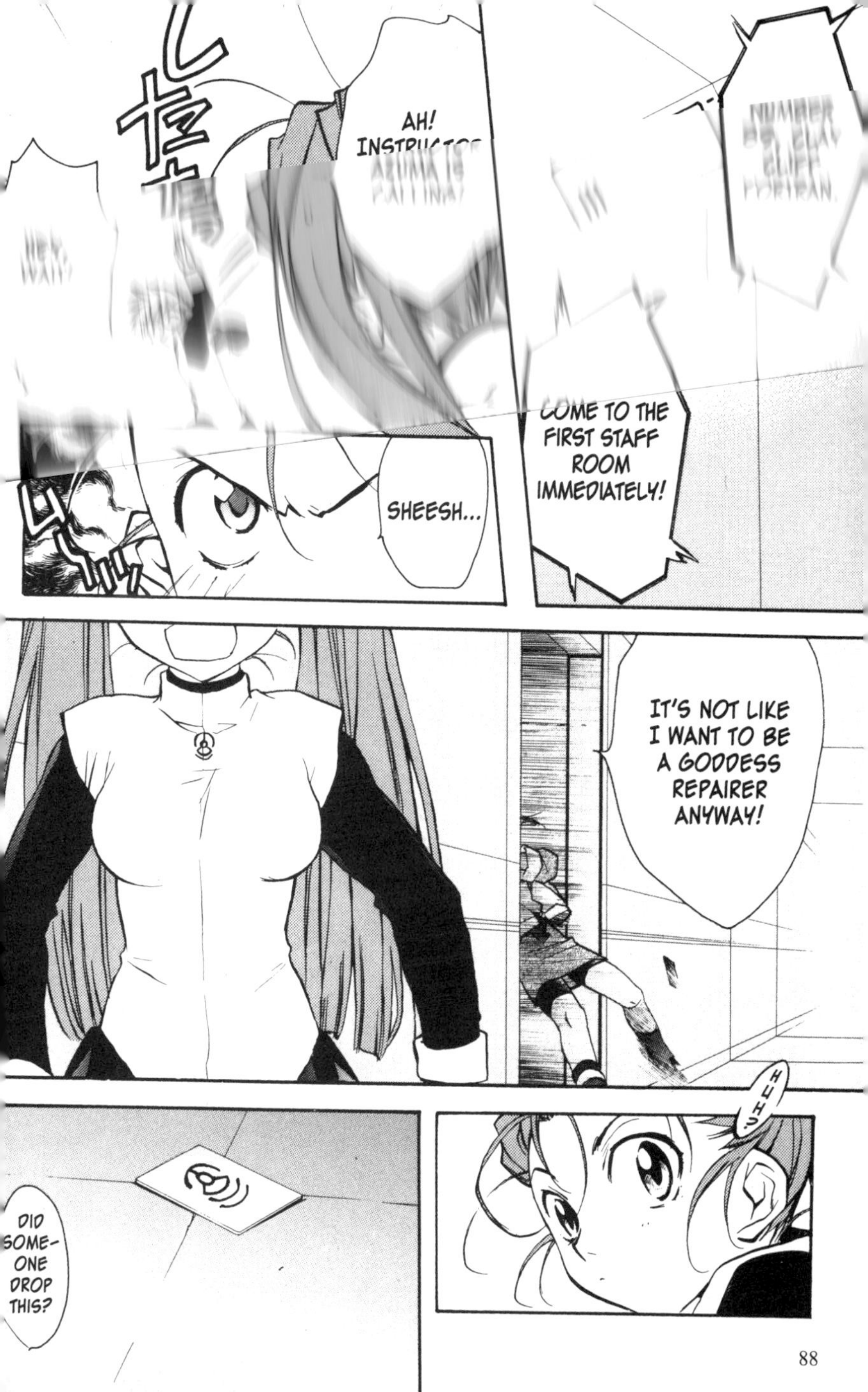
COME TO THE FIRST STAFF ROOM IMMEDIATELY!
AH!
SHEESH...
IT'S NOT LIKE I WANT TO BE A GODDESS REPAIRER ANYWAY!
HUH?
DID SOME-ONE DROP THIS?

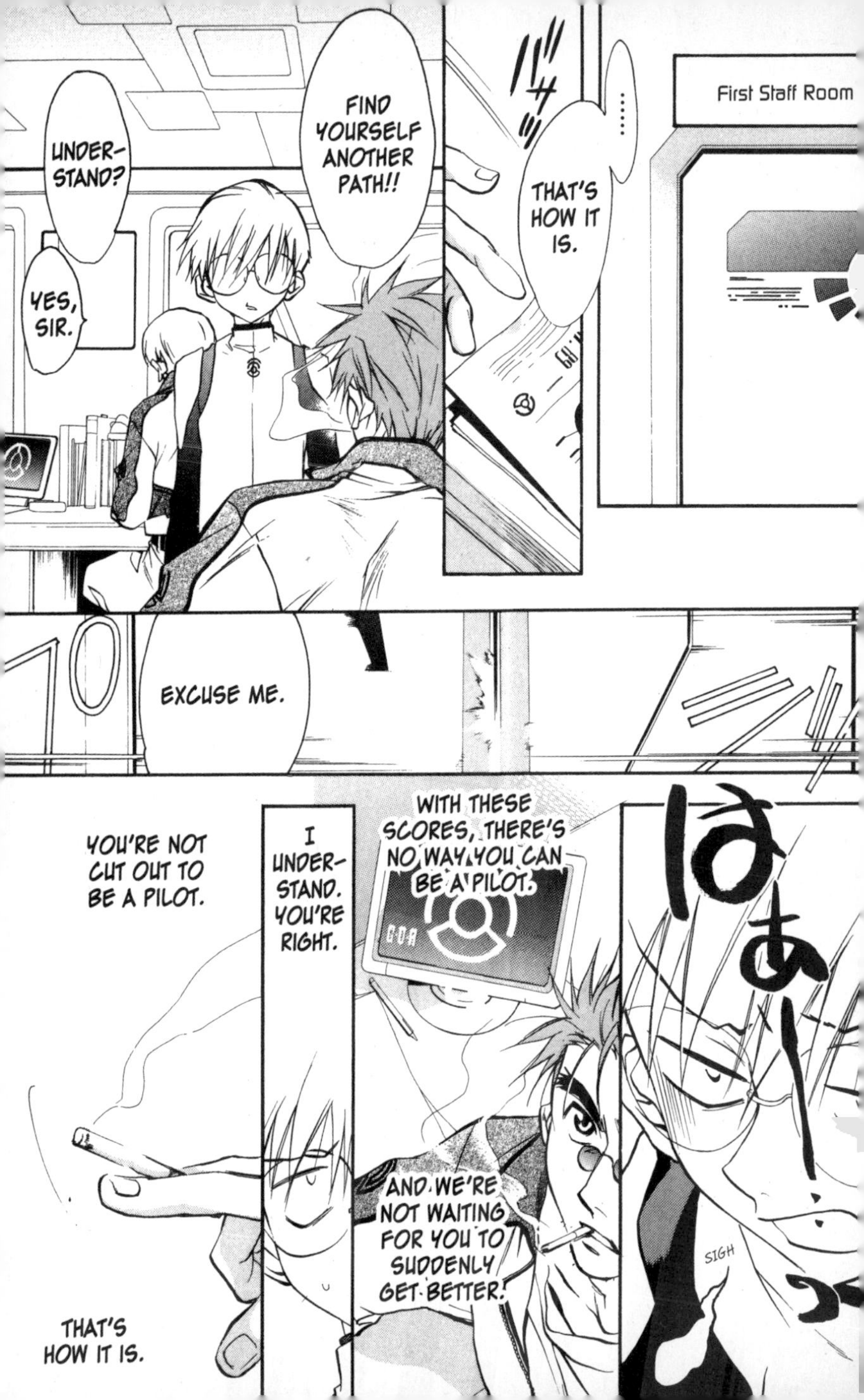
First Staff Room
......
THAT'S HOW IT IS.
FIND YOURSELF ANOTHER PATH!!
UNDER-STAND?
YES, SIR.
EXCUSE ME.
はぁ
SIGH
WITH THESE SCORES, THERE'S NO WAY YOU CAN BE A PILOT.
I UNDER-STAND. YOU'RE RIGHT.
YOU'RE NOT CUT OUT TO BE A PILOT.
AND WE'RE NOT WAITING FOR YOU TO SUDDENLY GET BETTER.
THAT'S HOW IT IS.

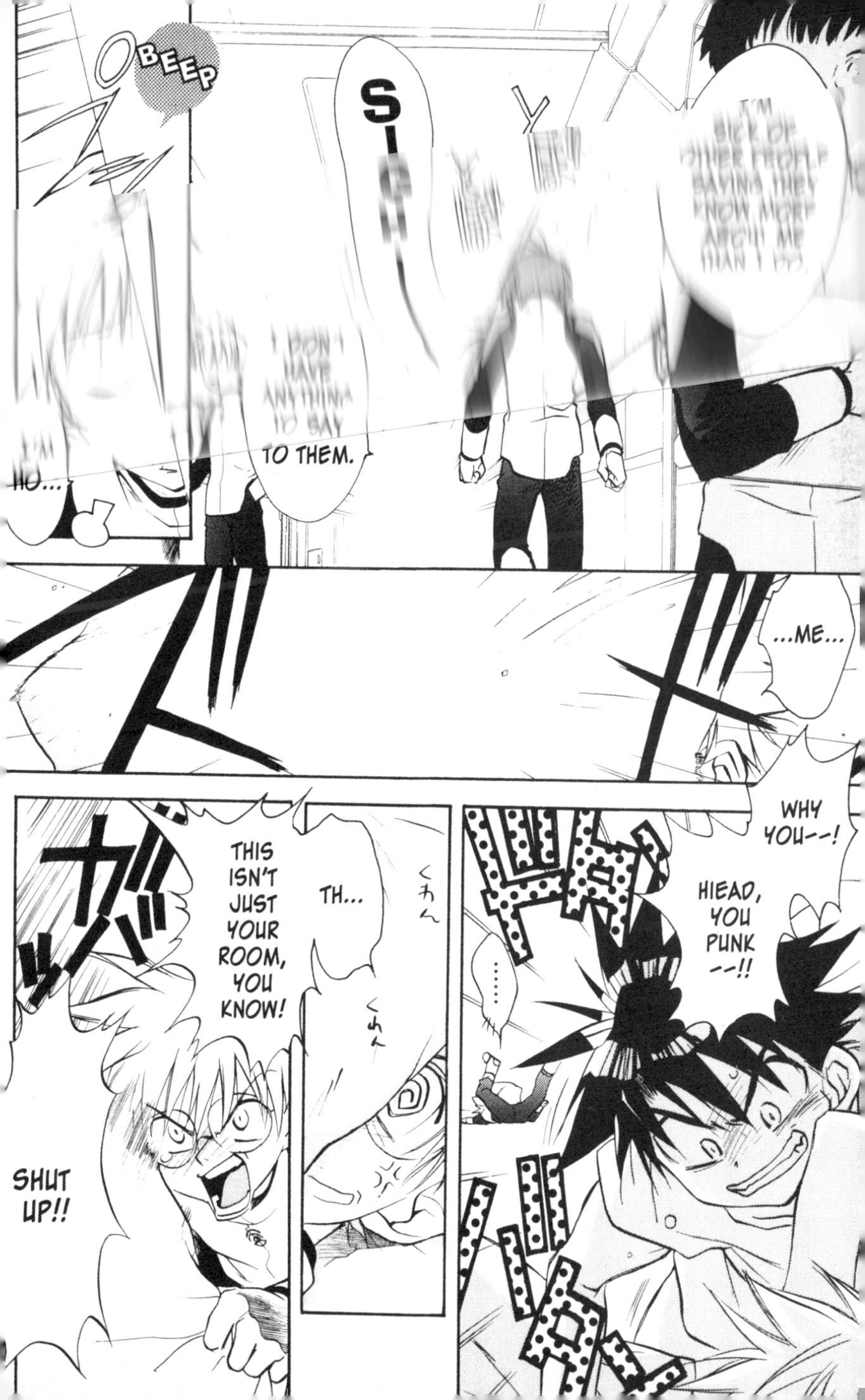
I'M SICK OF OTHER PEOPLE SAYING THEY KNOW MORE ABOUT ME THAN I DO.
I DON'T HAVE ANYTHING TO SAY TO THEM.
BEEP
...ME...
WHY YOU--!
HIEAD, YOU PUNK--!!
......
TH...
くわん
くわん
THIS ISN'T JUST YOUR ROOM, YOU KNOW!
SHUT UP!!

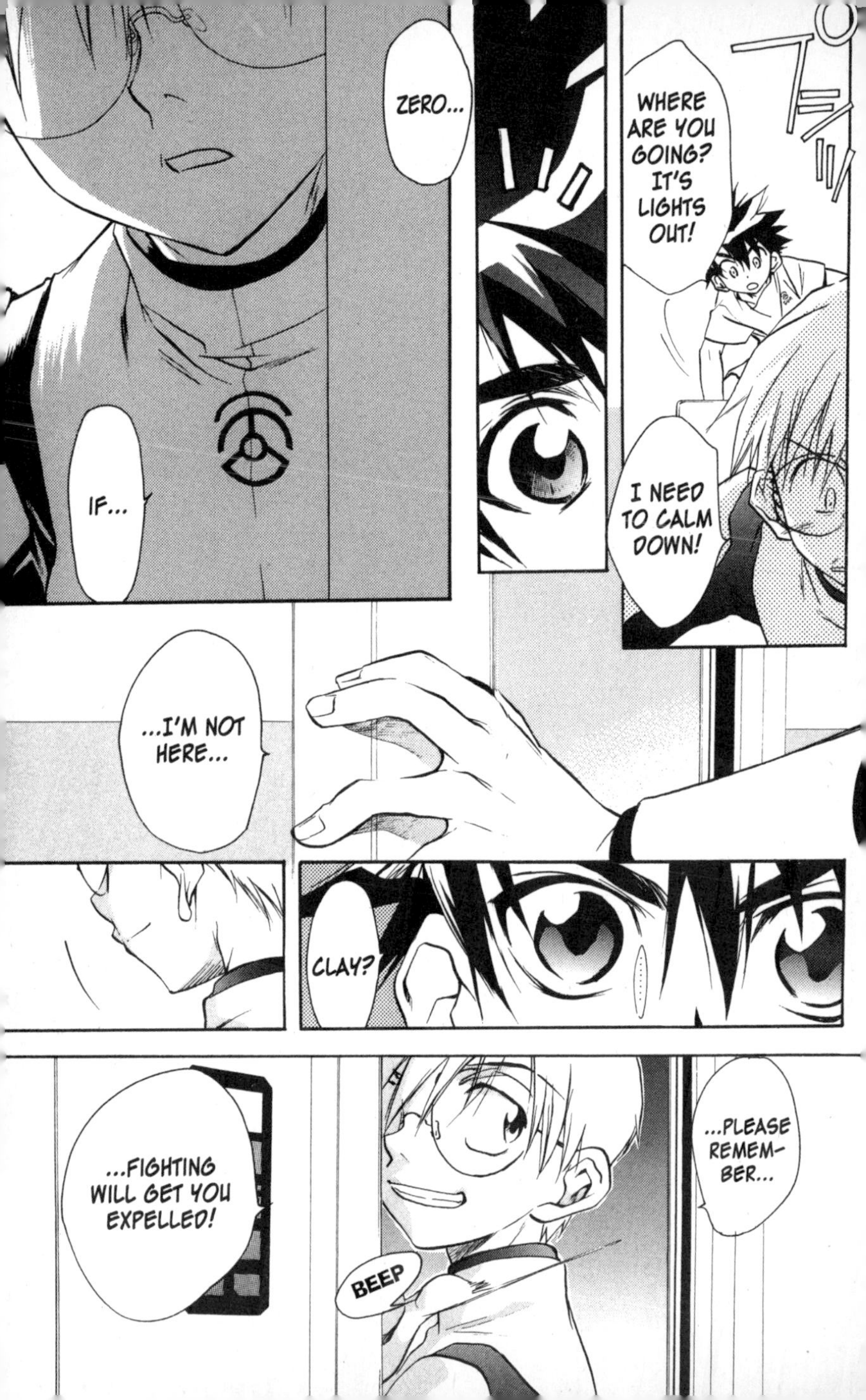
WHERE ARE YOU GOING? IT'S LIGHTS OUT!
I NEED TO CALM DOWN!
ZERO...
IF...
...I'M NOT HERE...
CLAY?
...PLEASE REMEMBER...
BEEP
...FIGHTING WILL GET YOU EXPELLED!

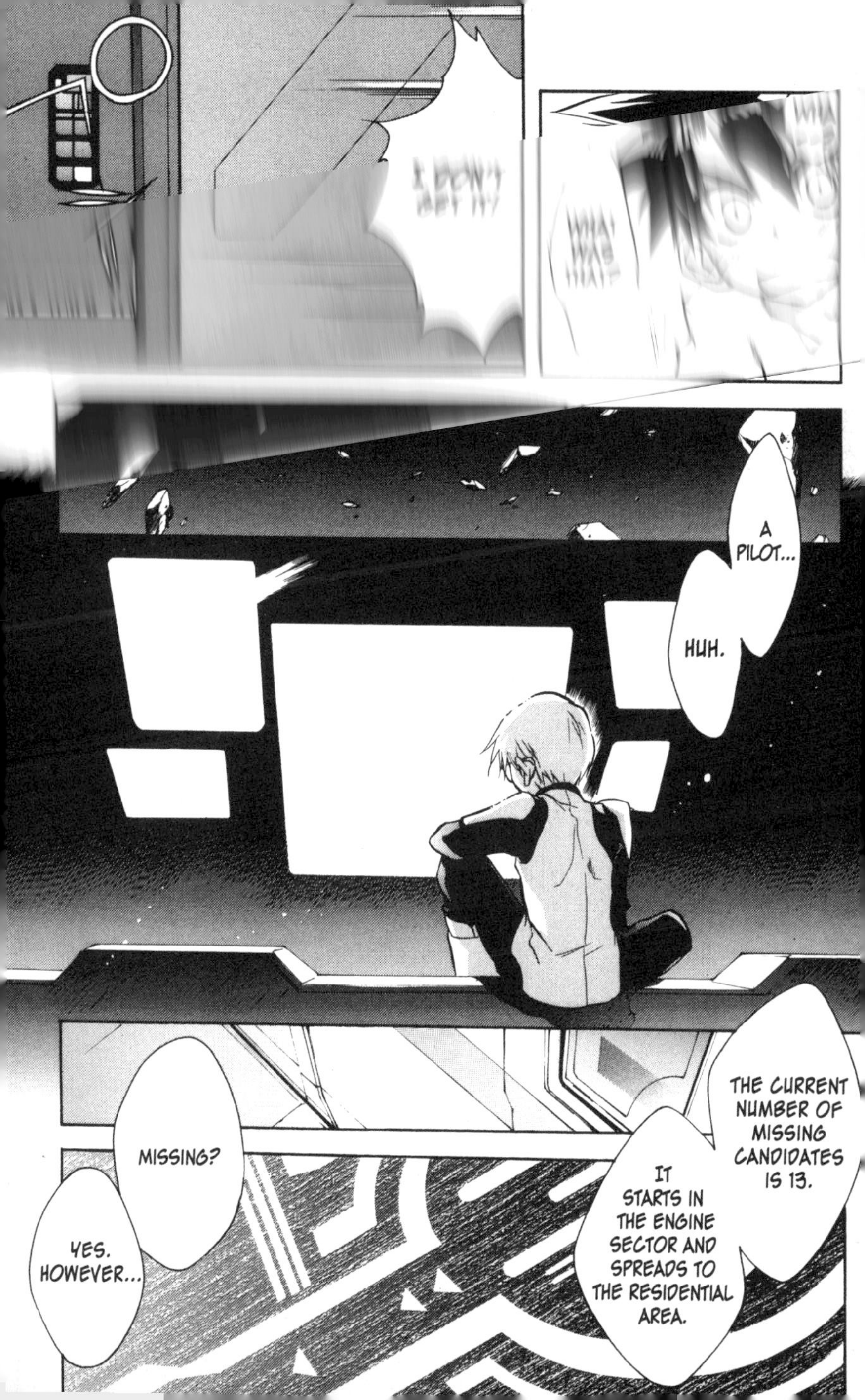
A PILOT...
HUH.
THE CURRENT NUMBER OF MISSING CANDIDATES IS 13.
IT STARTS IN THE ENGINE SECTOR AND SPREADS TO THE RESIDENTIAL AREA.
MISSING?
YES. HOWEVER...

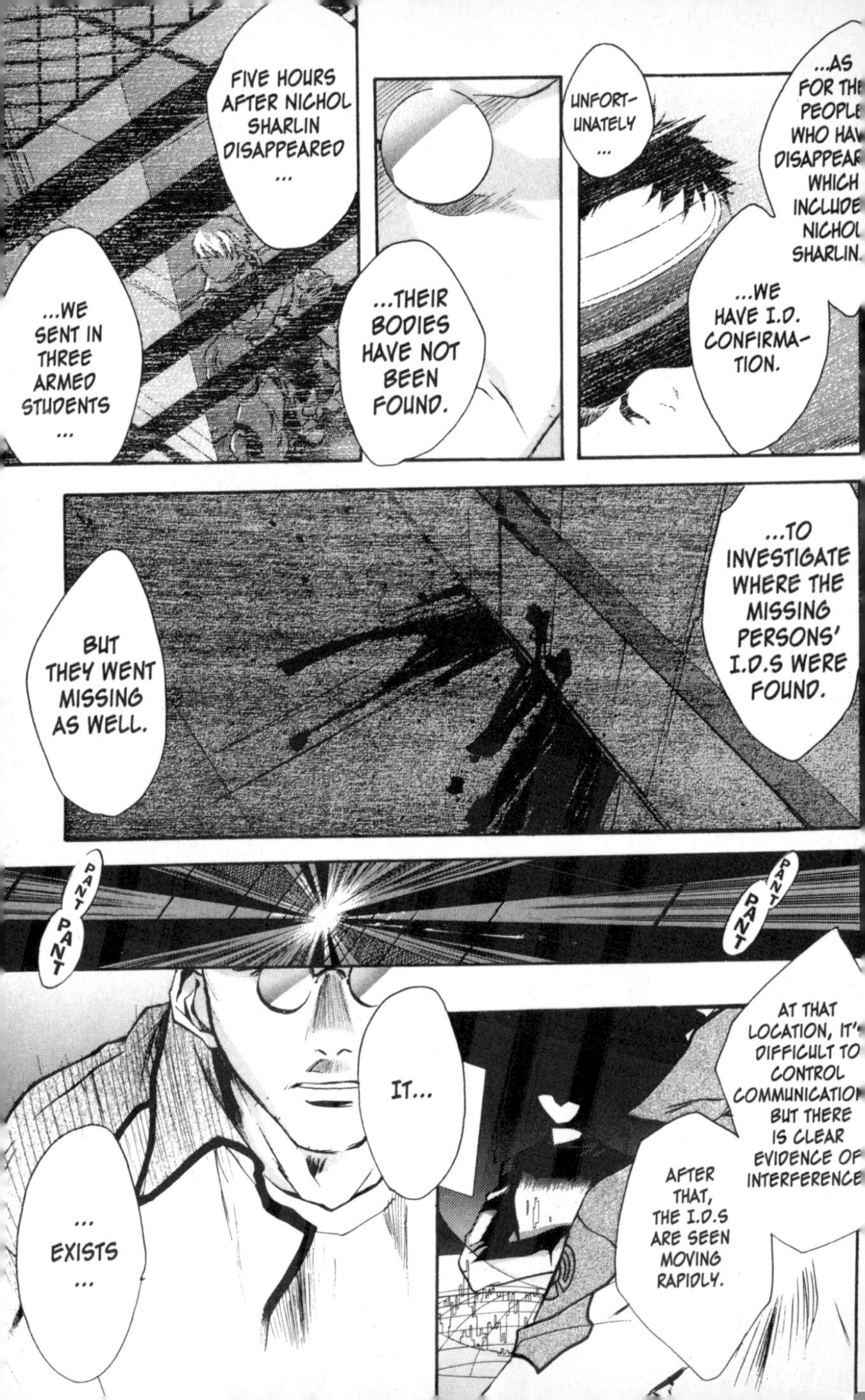
...AS FOR TH PEOPLE WHO HAV DISAPPEAR WHICH INCLUDE NICHOL SHARLIN.
UNFORT-UNATELY ...
...WE HAVE I.D. CONFIRMA-TION.
...THEIR BODIES HAVE NOT BEEN FOUND.
FIVE HOURS AFTER NICHOL SHARLIN DISAPPEARED ...
...WE SENT IN THREE ARMED STUDENTS ...
...TO INVESTIGATE WHERE THE MISSING PERSONS' I.D.S WERE FOUND.
BUT THEY WENT MISSING AS WELL.
PANT PANT
PANT PANT
AT THAT LOCATION, IT' DIFFICULT TO CONTROL COMMUNICATIO BUT THERE IS CLEAR EVIDENCE OF INTERFERENCE
AFTER THAT, THE I.D.S ARE SEEN MOVING RAPIDLY.
IT...
... EXISTS ...

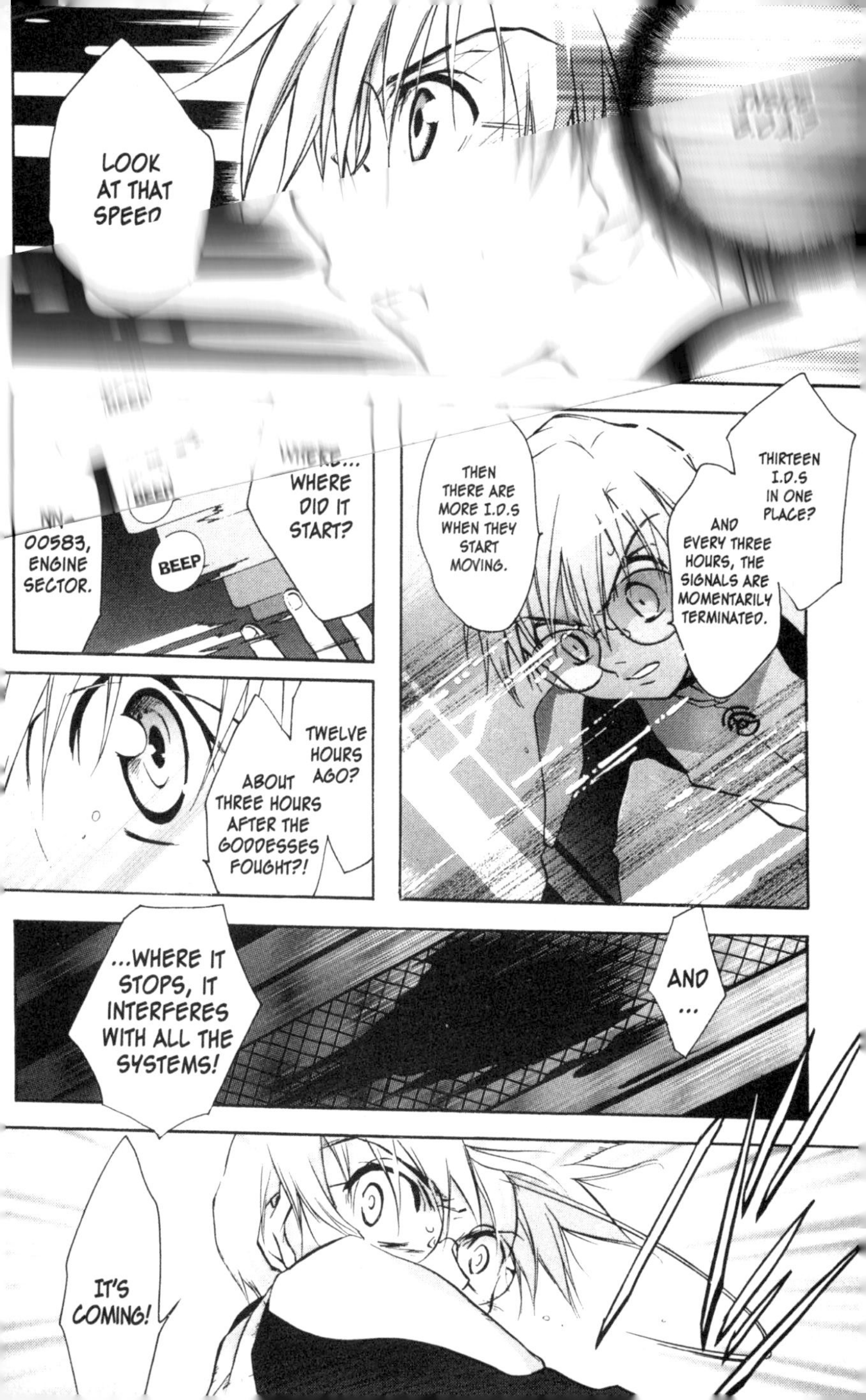
LOOK AT THAT SPEED
THIRTEEN I.D.S IN ONE PLACE?
AND EVERY THREE HOURS, THE SIGNALS ARE MOMENTARILY TERMINATED.
THEN THERE ARE MORE I.D.S WHEN THEY START MOVING.
WHERE... WHERE DID IT START?
BEEP
NN... 00583, ENGINE SECTOR.
TWELVE HOURS AGO?
ABOUT THREE HOURS AFTER THE GODDESSES FOUGHT?!
AND ...
...WHERE IT STOPS, IT INTERFERES WITH ALL THE SYSTEMS!
IT'S COMING!

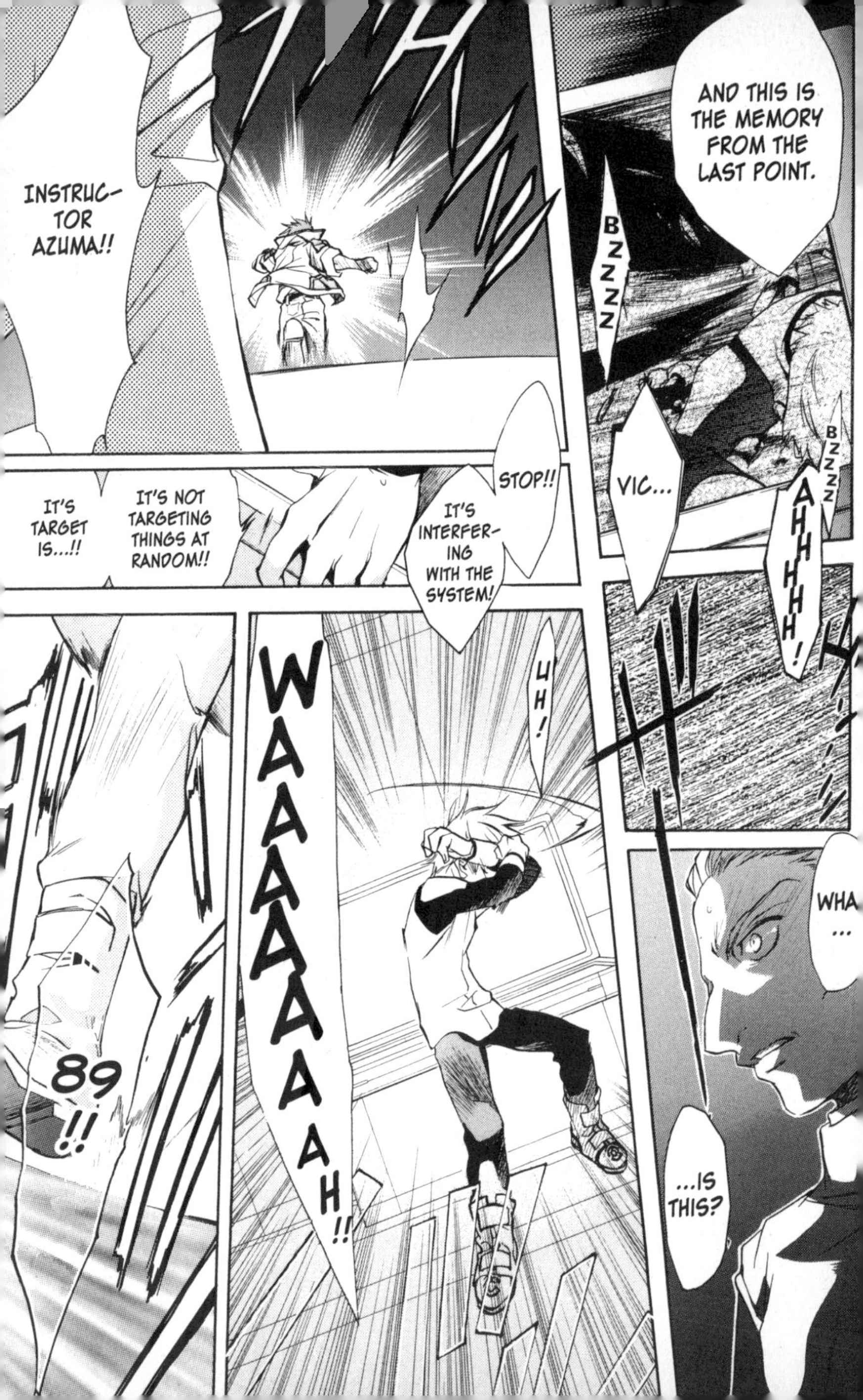
AND THIS IS THE MEMORY FROM THE LAST POINT.
BZZZZ
VIC...
BZZZ
AHHHHHH!
INSTRUC-TOR AZUMA!!
STOP!!
IT'S INTERFER-ING WITH THE SYSTEM!
IT'S NOT TARGETING THINGS AT RANDOM!!
IT'S TARGET IS...!!
WHA...
...IS THIS?
UH!
WAAAAAAAH!!
89!!

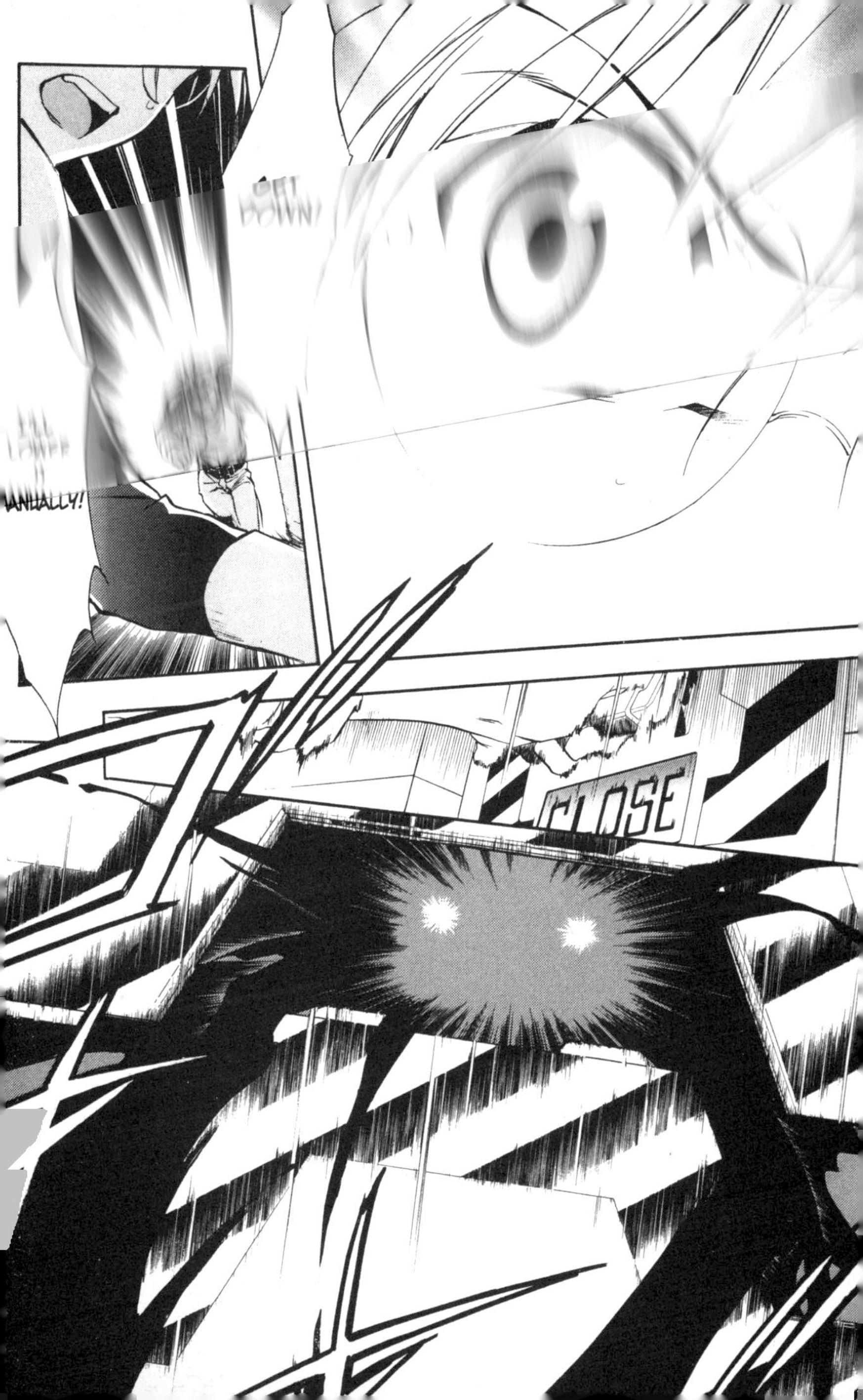
GET DOWN!
CLOSE

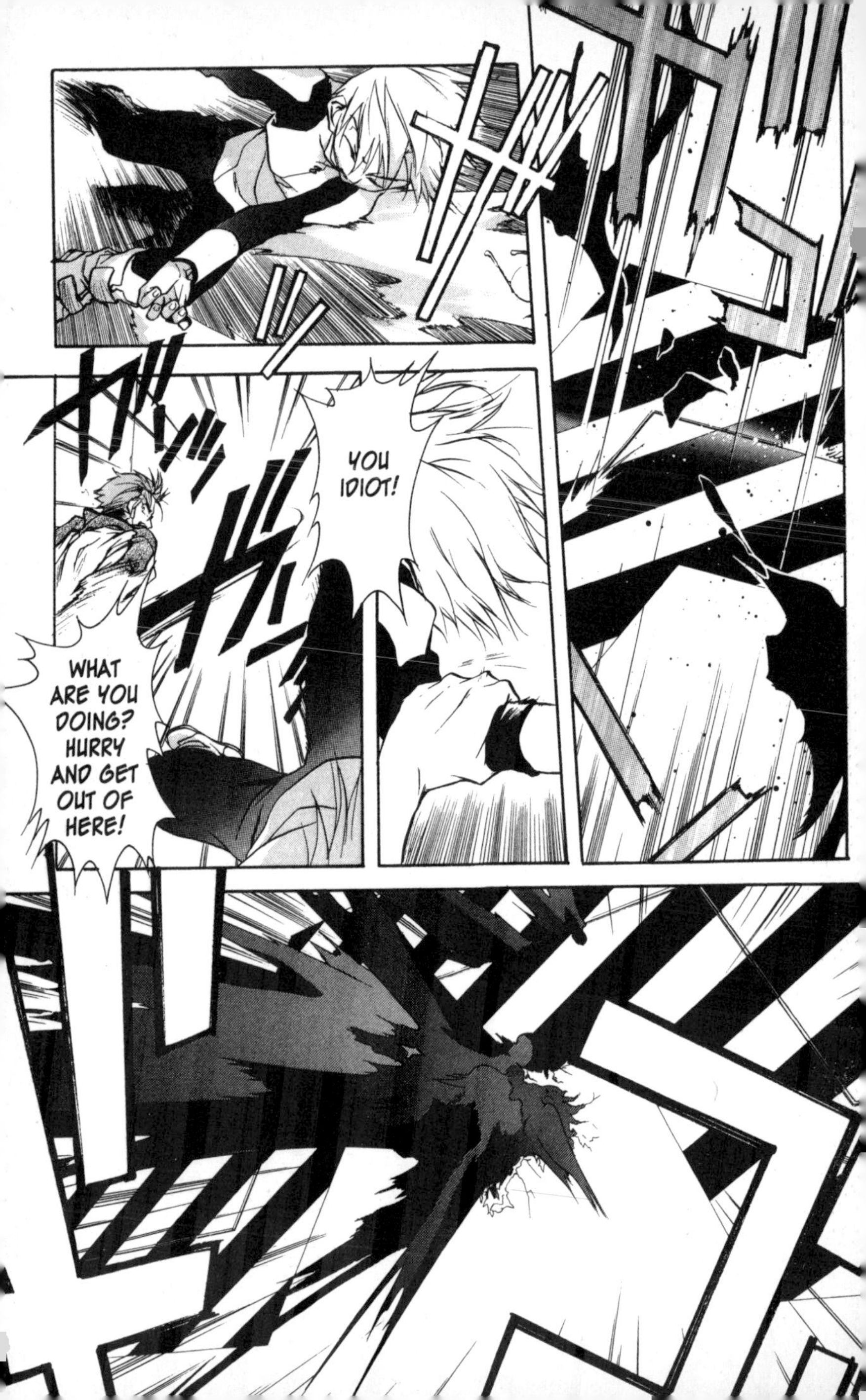
YOU IDIOT!
WHAT ARE YOU DOING? HURRY AND GET OUT OF HERE!

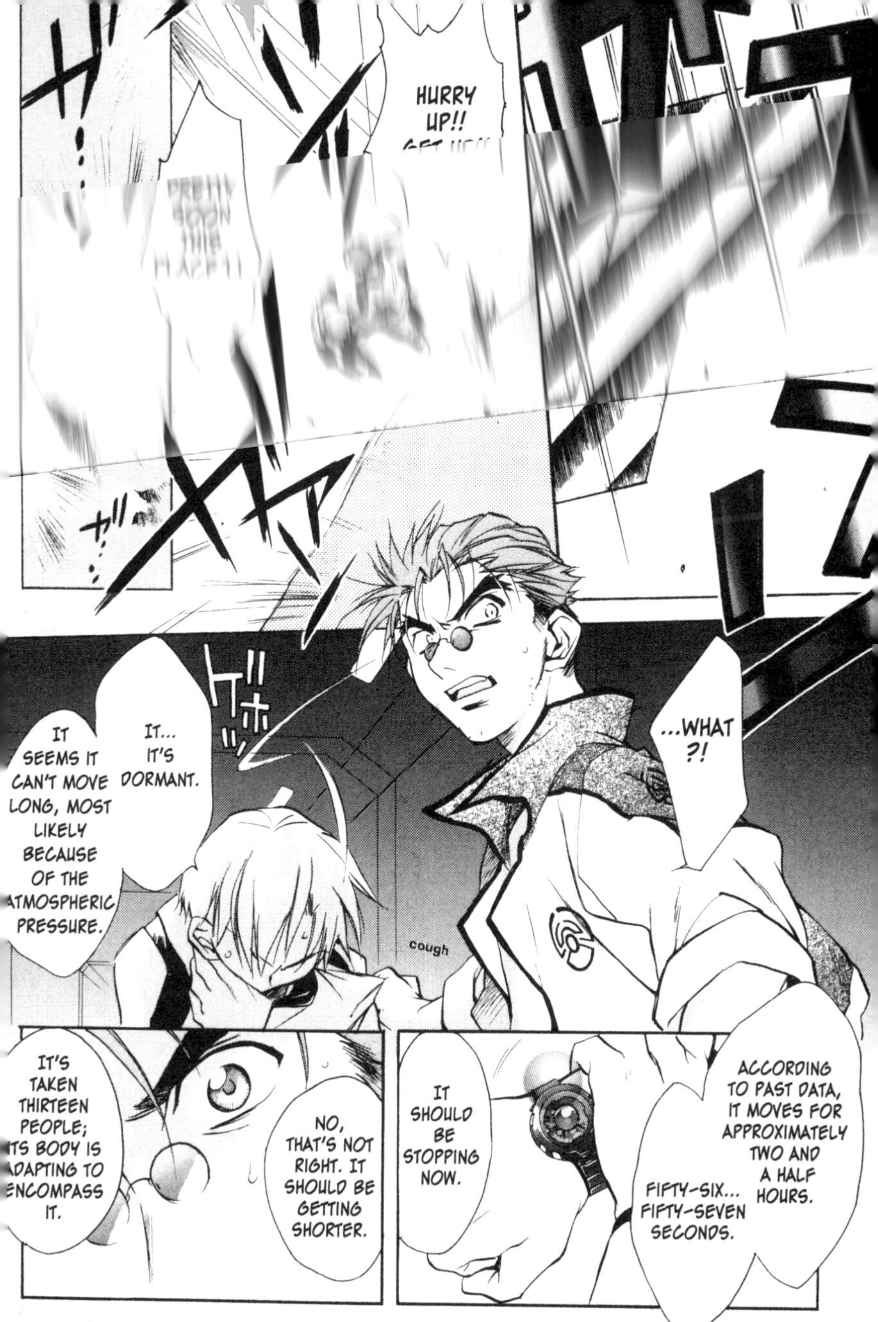
HURRY UP!!
...WHAT ?!
cough
IT... IT'S DORMANT.
IT SEEMS IT CAN'T MOVE LONG, MOST LIKELY BECAUSE OF THE ATMOSPHERIC PRESSURE.
ACCORDING TO PAST DATA, IT MOVES FOR APPROXIMATELY TWO AND A HALF HOURS.
FIFTY-SIX... FIFTY-SEVEN SECONDS.
IT SHOULD BE STOPPING NOW.
NO, THAT'S NOT RIGHT. IT SHOULD BE GETTING SHORTER.
IT'S TAKEN THIRTEEN PEOPLE; ITS BODY IS ADAPTING TO ENCOMPASS IT.

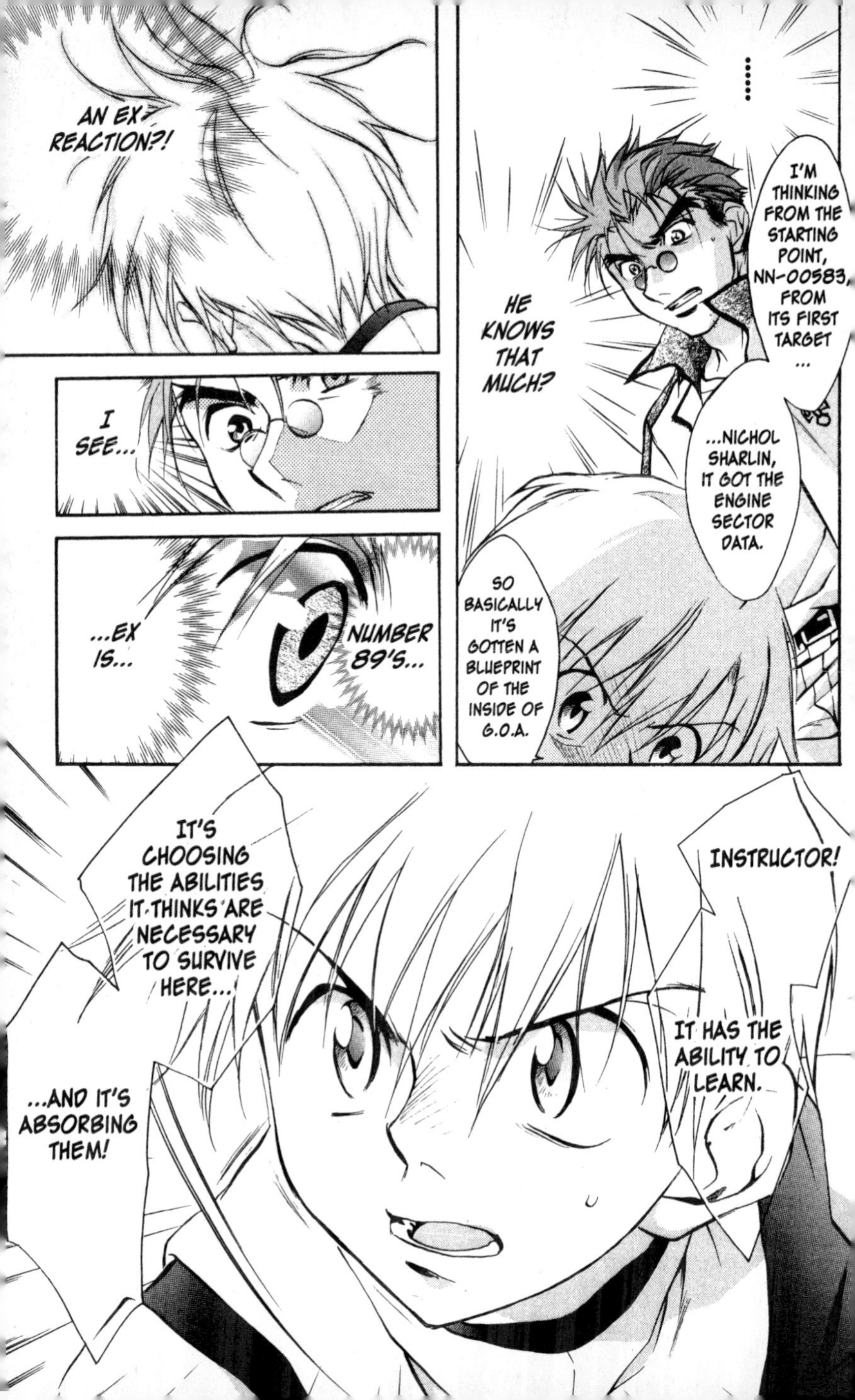
......
I'M THINKING FROM THE STARTING POINT, NN-00583, FROM ITS FIRST TARGET ...
HE KNOWS THAT MUCH?
...NICHOL SHARLIN, IT GOT THE ENGINE SECTOR DATA.
SO BASICALLY IT'S GOTTEN A BLUEPRINT OF THE INSIDE OF G.O.A.
AN EX-REACTION?!
I SEE...
NUMBER 89'S...
...EX IS...
INSTRUCTOR!
IT HAS THE ABILITY TO LEARN.
IT'S CHOOSING THE ABILITIES IT THINKS ARE NECESSARY TO SURVIVE HERE...
...AND IT'S ABSORBING THEM!

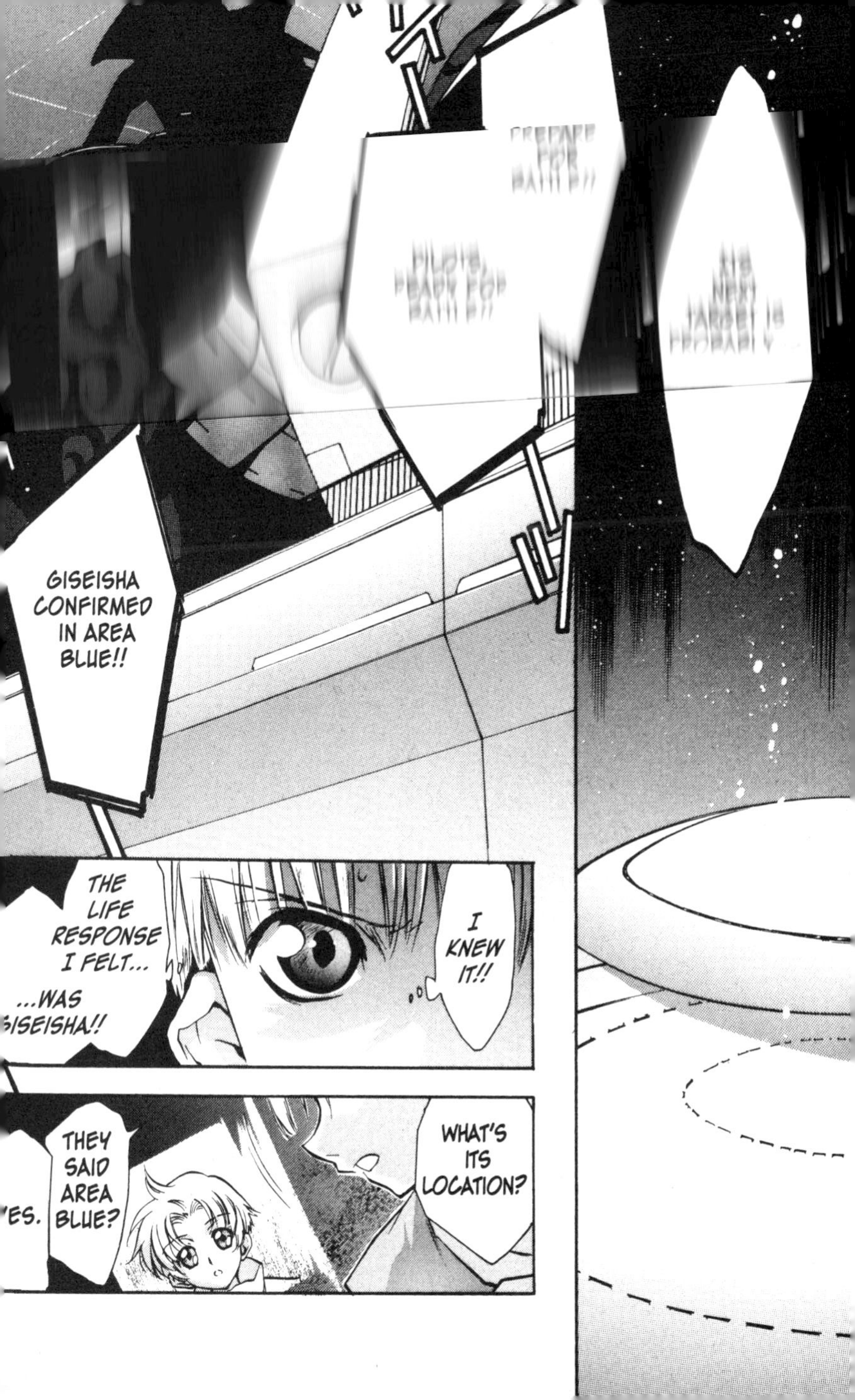
GISEISHA CONFIRMED IN AREA BLUE!!
I KNEW IT!!
THE LIFE RESPONSE I FELT...
...WAS ISEISHA!!
WHAT'S ITS LOCATION?
THEY SAID AREA BLUE?
ES.

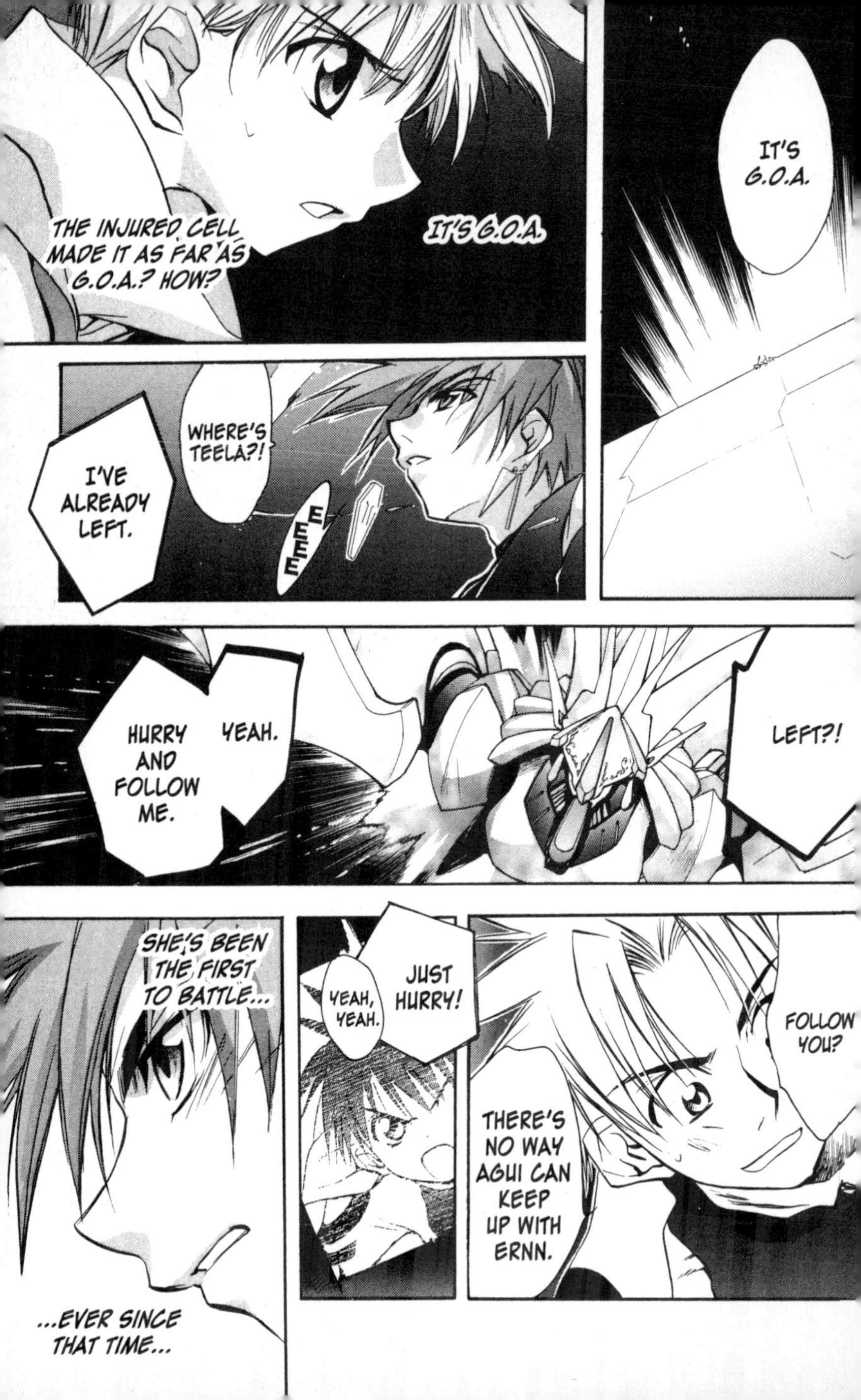
IT'S G.O.A.
IT'S G.O.A.
THE INJURED CELL MADE IT AS FAR AS G.O.A.? HOW?
WHERE'S TEELA?!
EEEE
I'VE ALREADY LEFT.
LEFT?!
YEAH.
HURRY AND FOLLOW ME.
FOLLOW YOU?
THERE'S NO WAY AGUI CAN KEEP UP WITH ERNN.
JUST HURRY!
YEAH, YEAH.
SHE'S BEEN THE FIRST TO BATTLE...
...EVER SINCE THAT TIME...

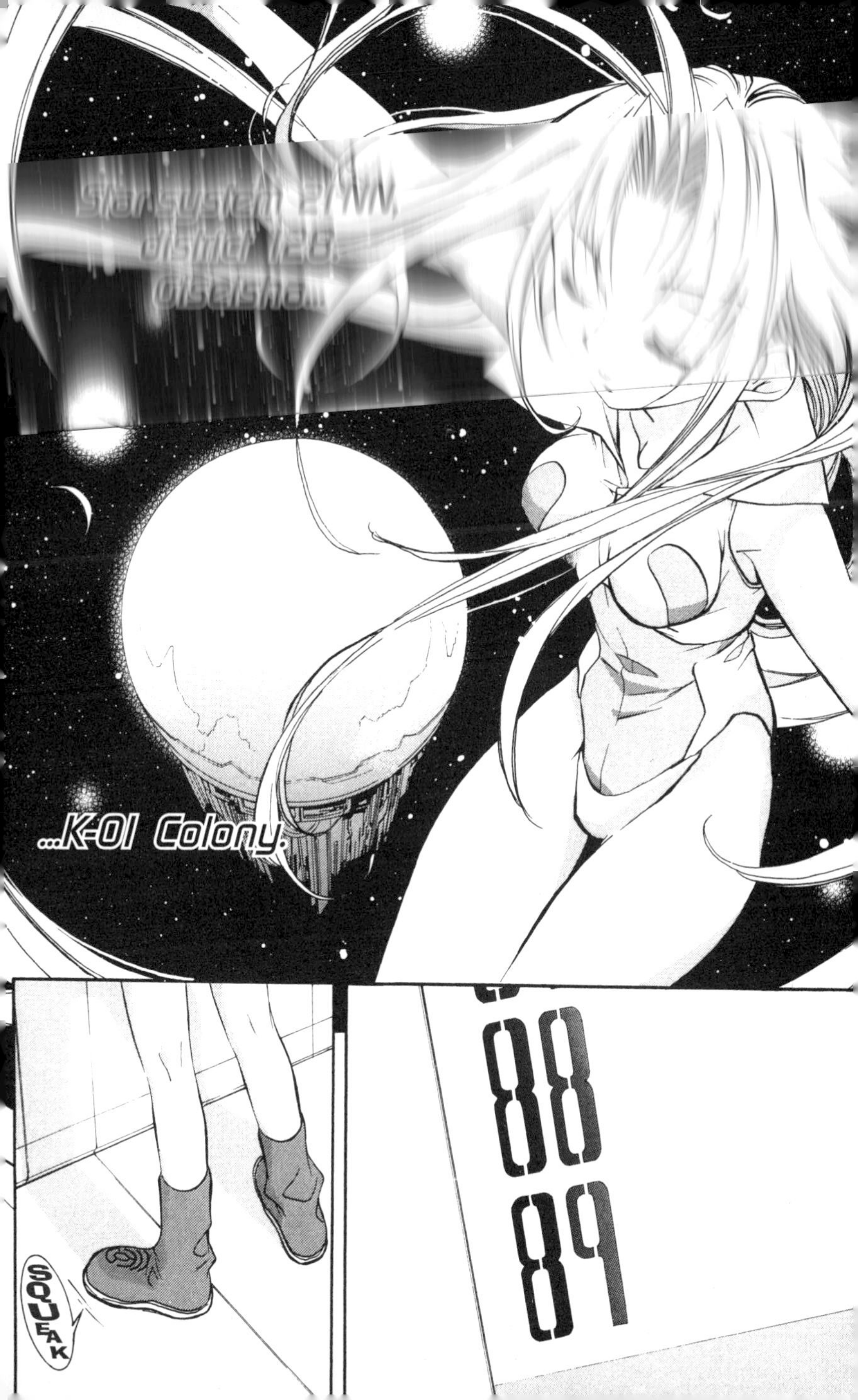
...K-01 Colony.
88
89
SQUEAK

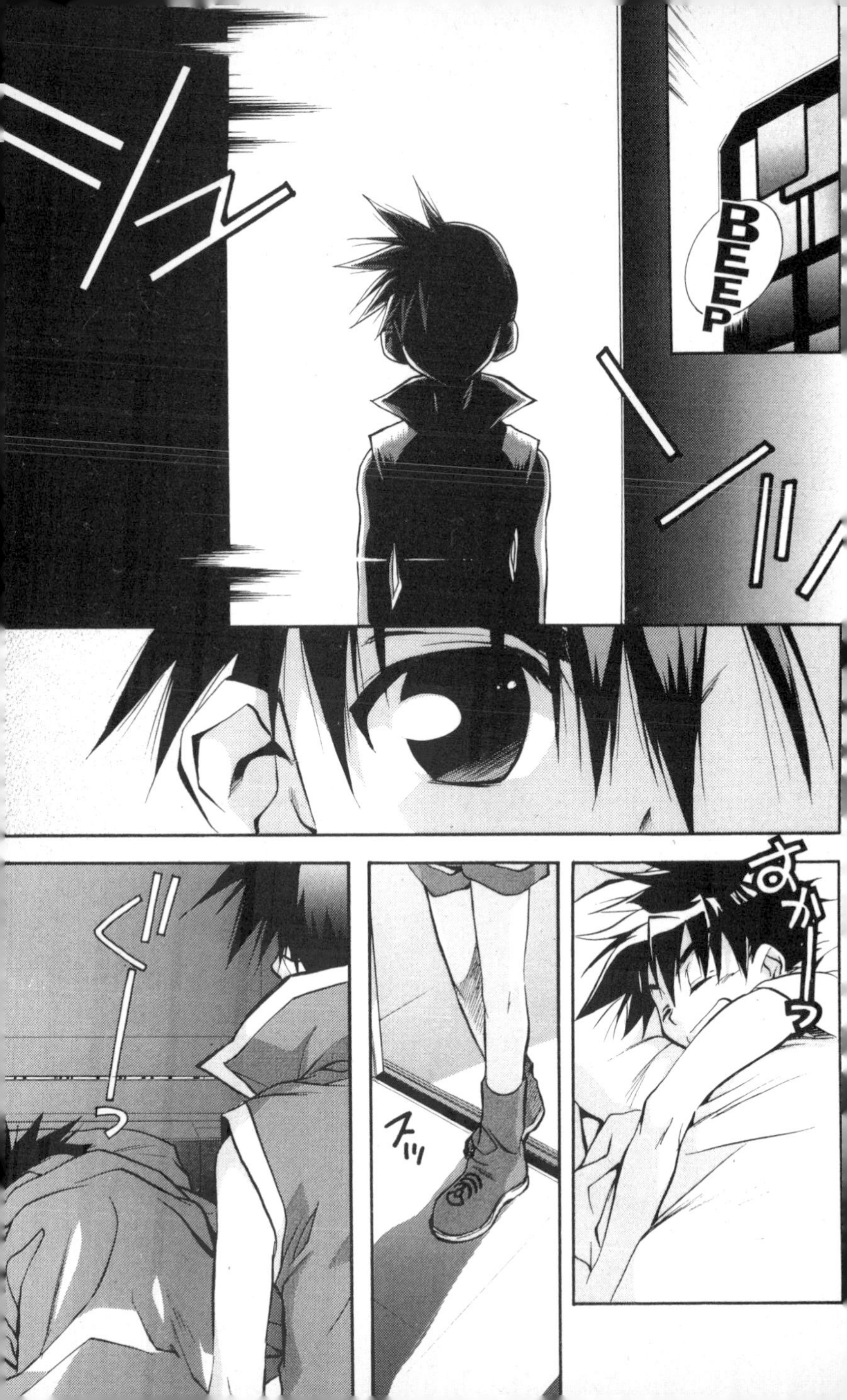
BEEP
すかーっ
スッ
ぐーっ

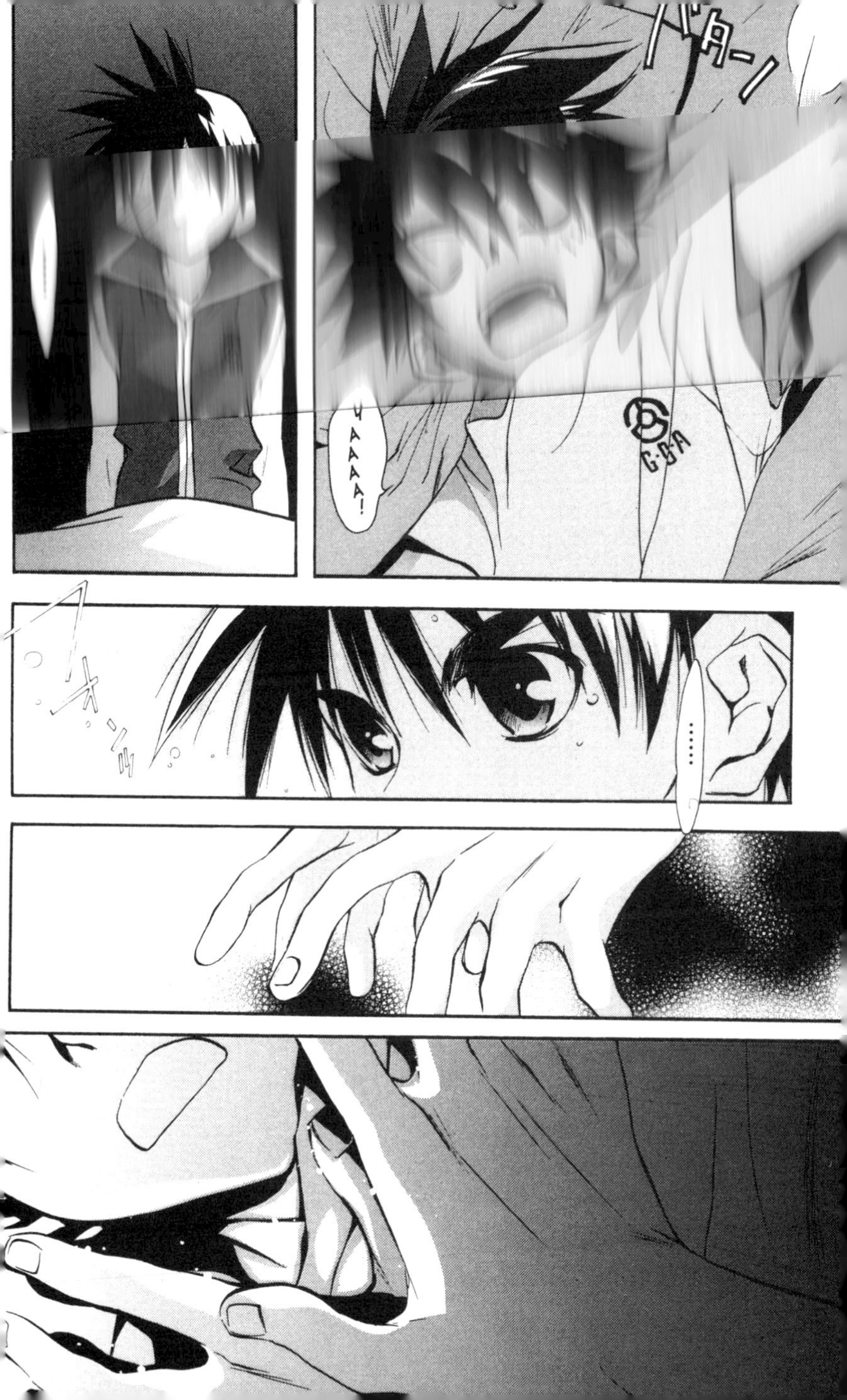
バターン
UAAAA!
G.S.A
......

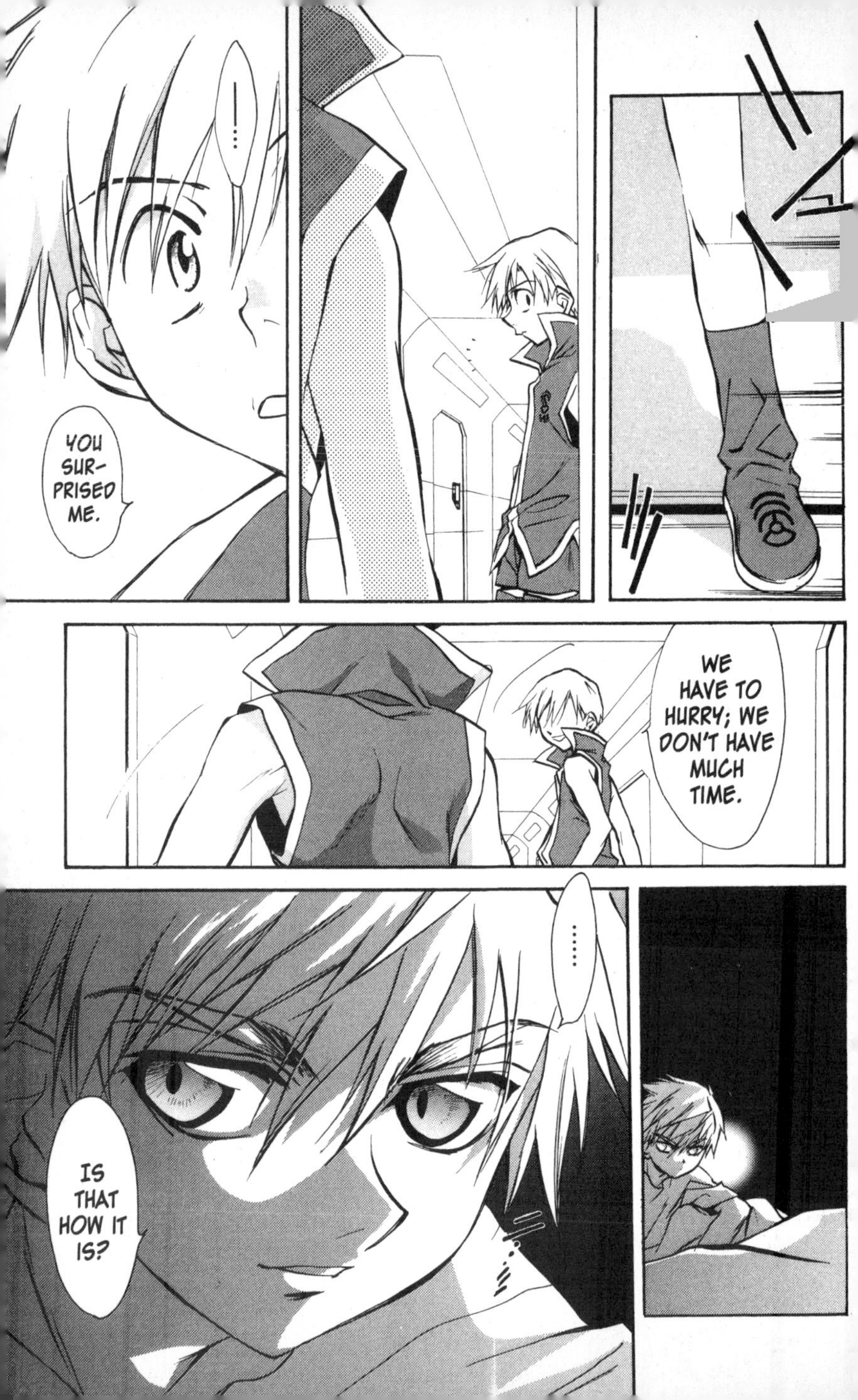

!...
YOU SUR-PRISED ME.
WE HAVE TO HURRY; WE DON'T HAVE MUCH TIME.
......
IS THAT HOW IT IS?

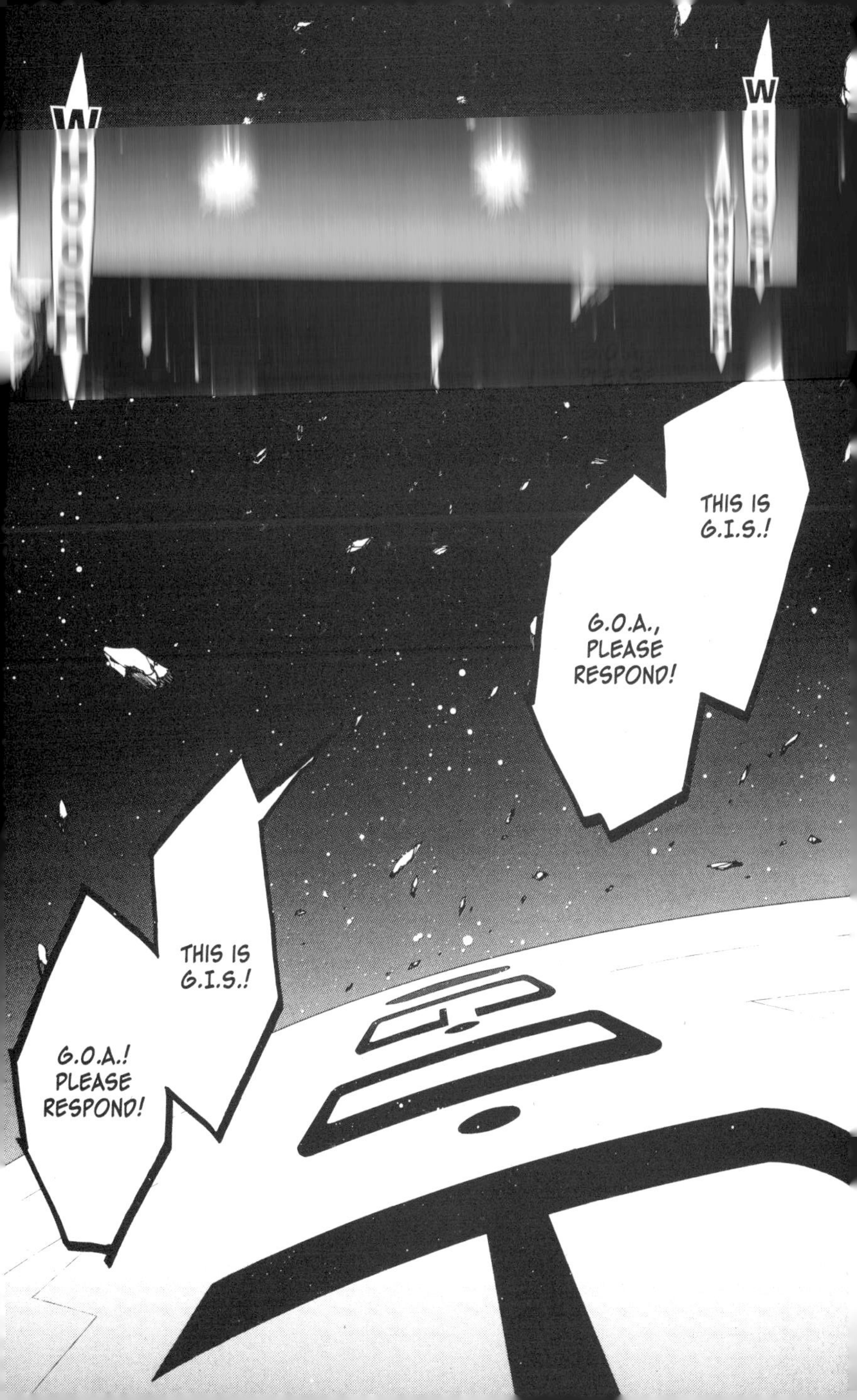
THIS IS G.I.S.!
G.O.A., PLEASE RESPOND!
THIS IS G.I.S.!
G.O.A.! PLEASE RESPOND!

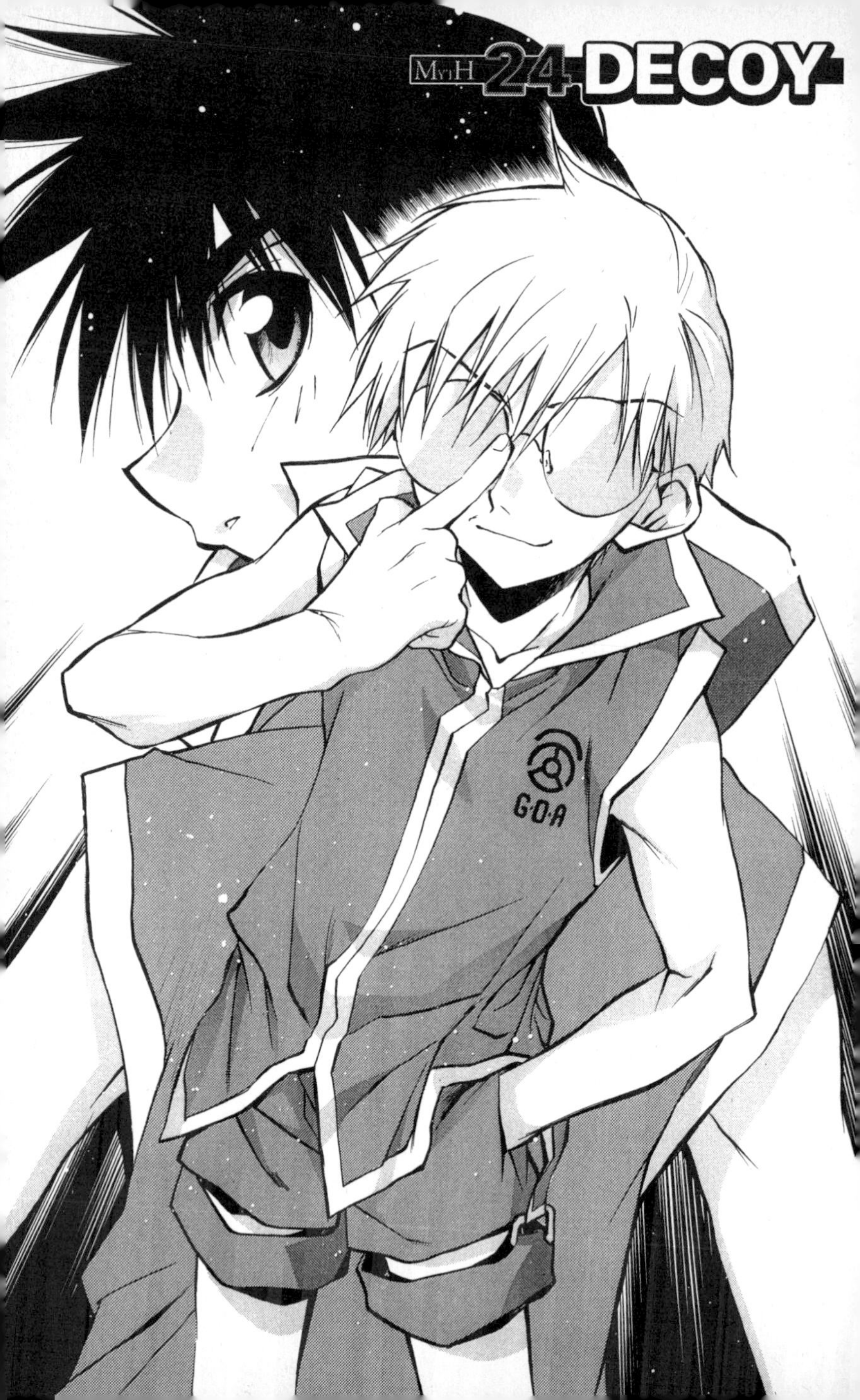
MYTH 24 DECOY
G·O·A

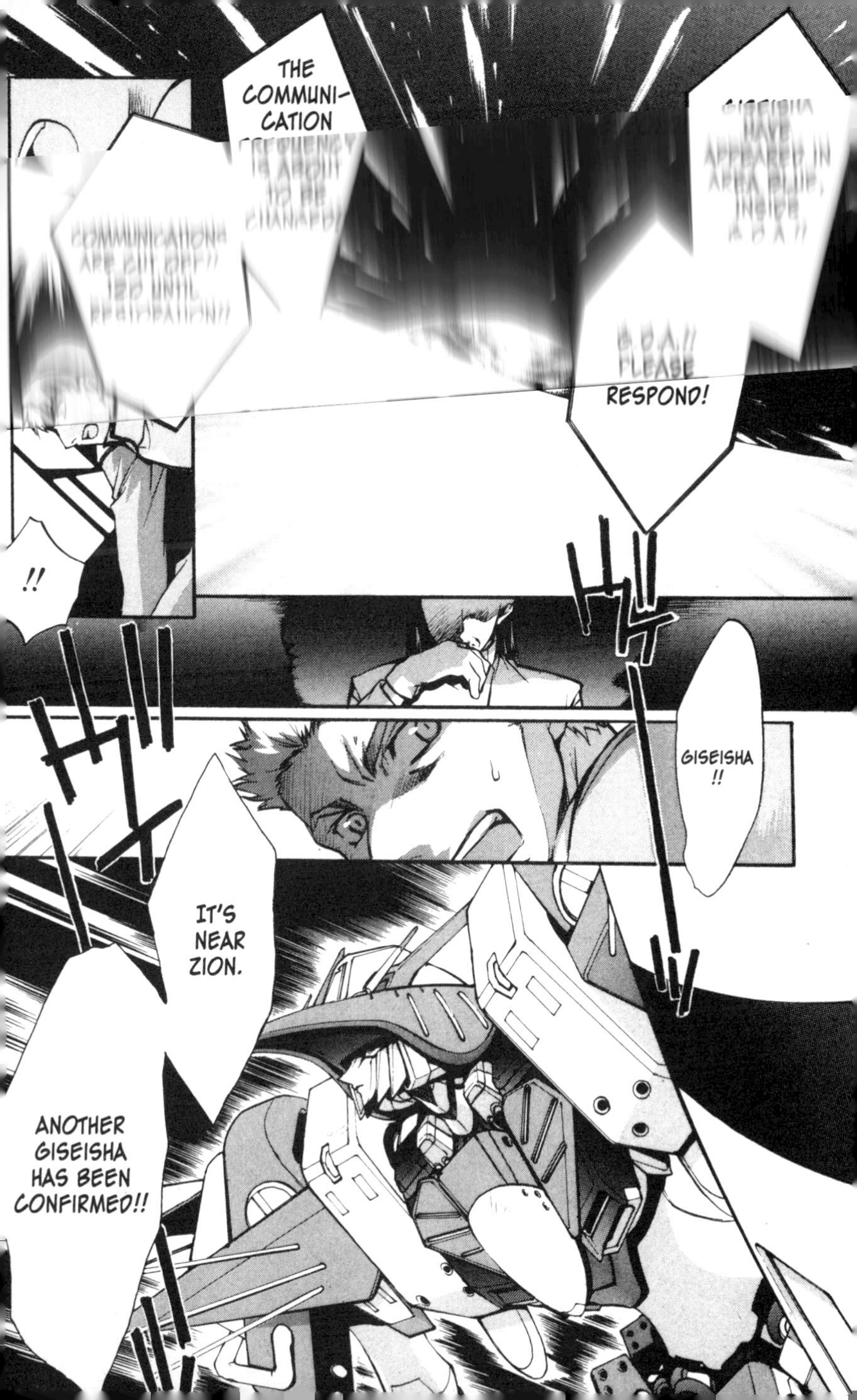
RESPOND!
THE COMMUNI-
CATION
!!
GISEISHA !!
IT'S NEAR ZION.
ANOTHER GISEISHA HAS BEEN CONFIRMED!!

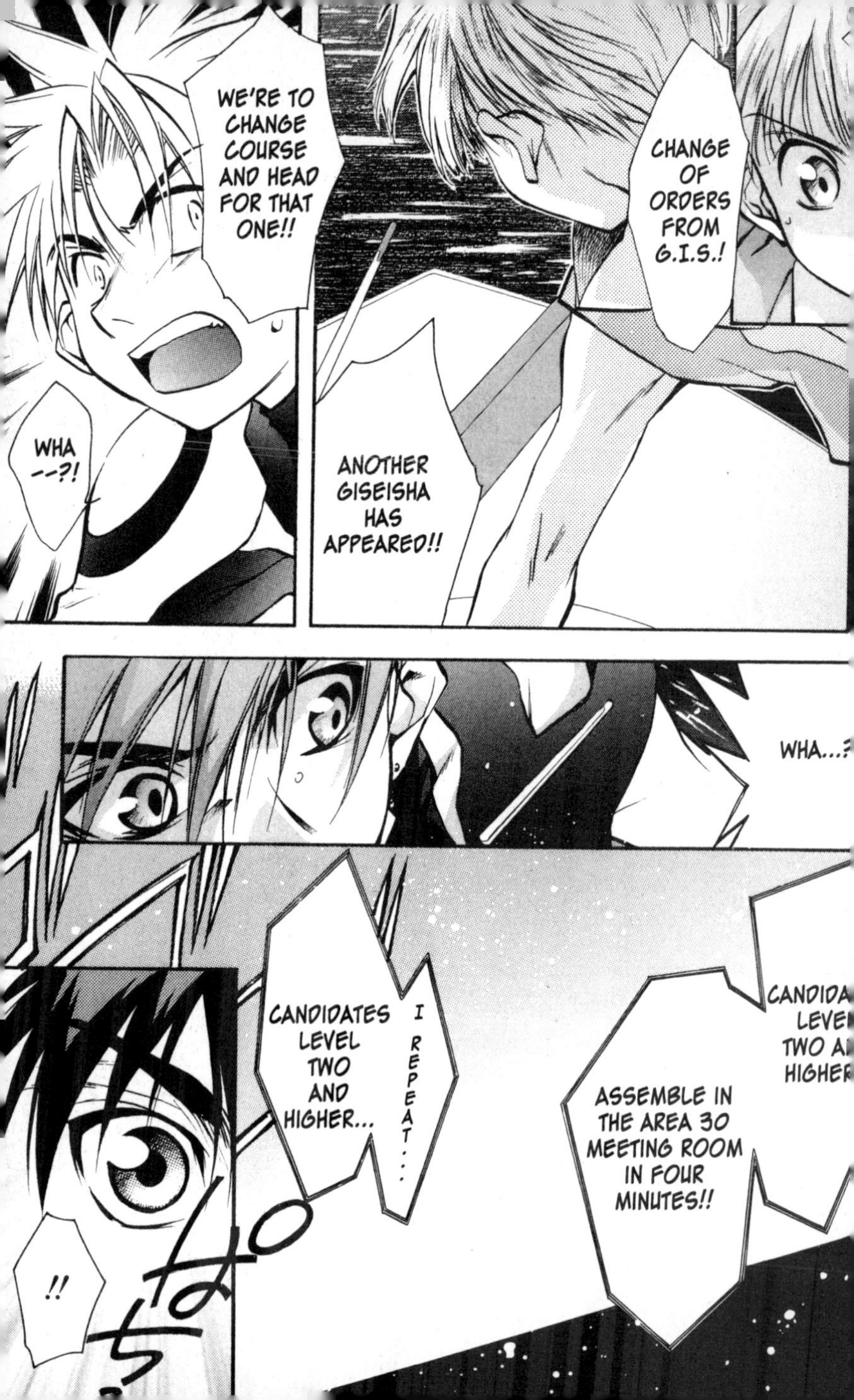
CHANGE OF ORDERS FROM G.I.S.!
ANOTHER GISEISHA HAS APPEARED!!
WE'RE TO CHANGE COURSE AND HEAD FOR THAT ONE!!
WHA--?!
WHA...?!
CANDIDA LEVE TWO A HIGHER
ASSEMBLE IN THE AREA 30 MEETING ROOM IN FOUR MINUTES!!
I REPEAT...
CANDIDATES LEVEL TWO AND HIGHER...
!!

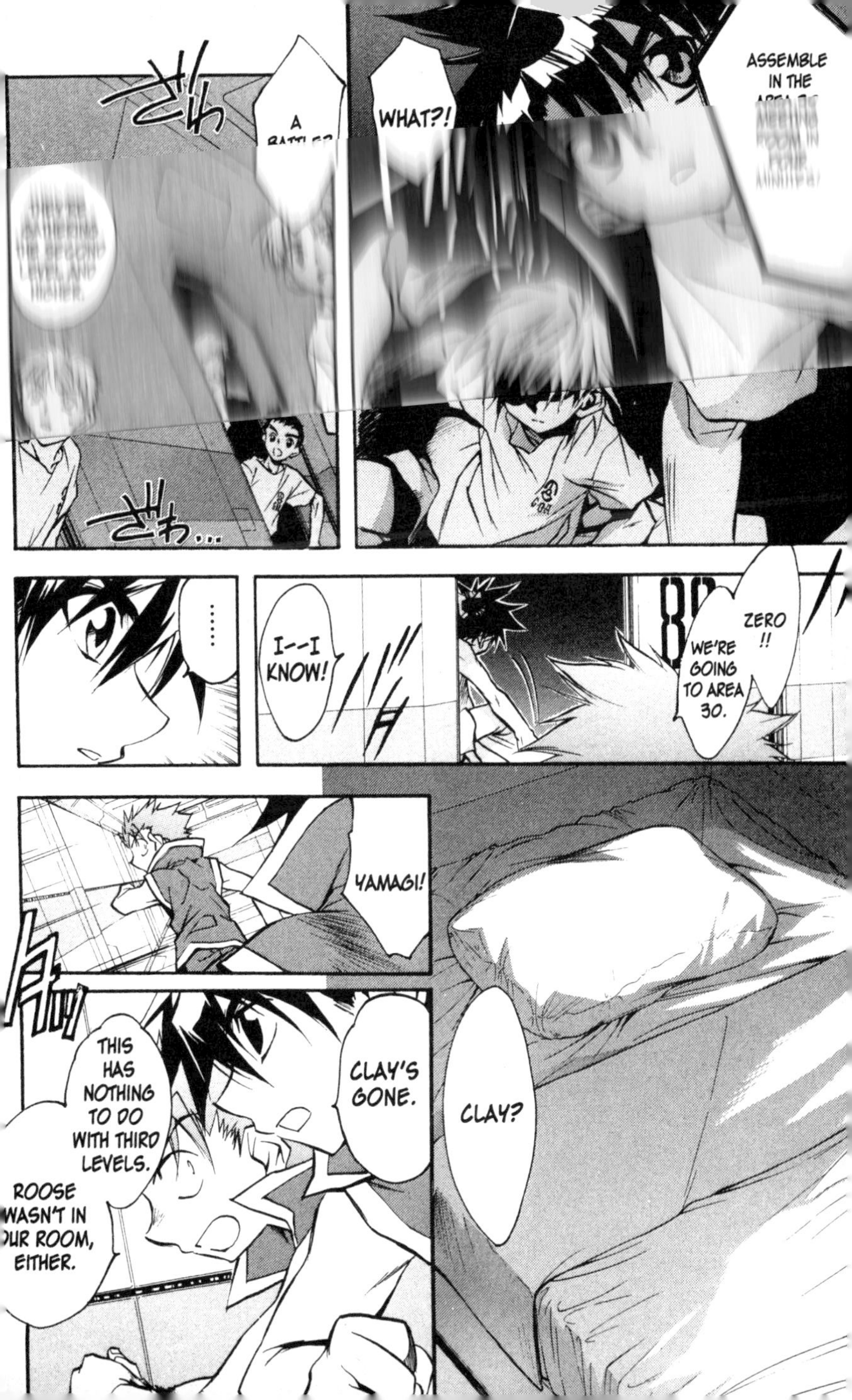
ASSEMBLE IN THE
WHAT?!
A
ざわ
ざわ...
ZERO !!
WE'RE GOING TO AREA 30.
I--I KNOW!
......
CLAY?
YAMAGI!
CLAY'S GONE.
THIS HAS NOTHING TO DO WITH THIRD LEVELS.
ROOSE WASN'T IN UR ROOM, EITHER.

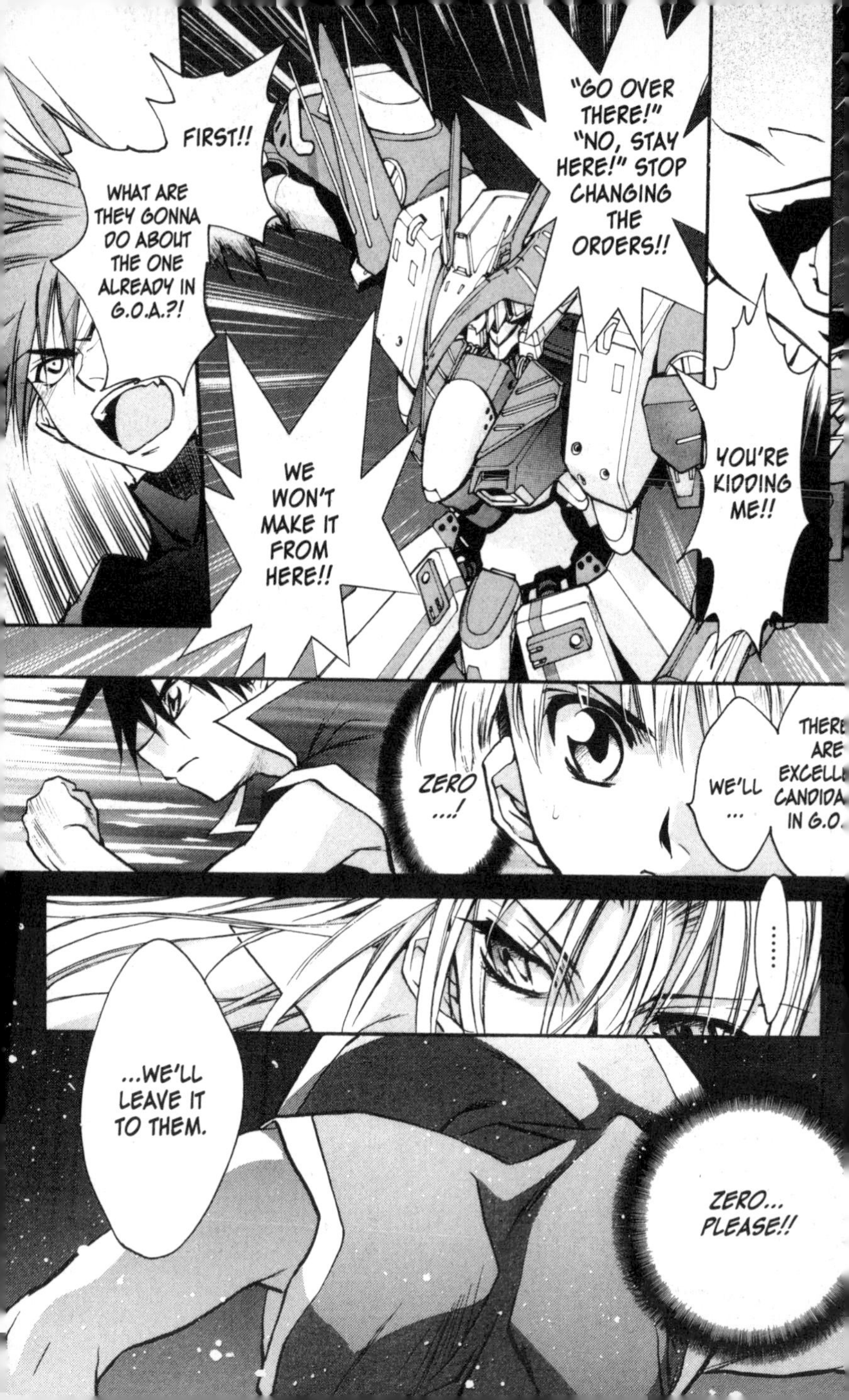
YOU'RE KIDDING ME!!
"GO OVER THERE!" "NO, STAY HERE!" STOP CHANGING THE ORDERS!!
FIRST!!
WHAT ARE THEY GONNA DO ABOUT THE ONE ALREADY IN G.O.A.?!
WE WON'T MAKE IT FROM HERE!!
THERE ARE EXCELL CANDIDA IN G.O.
WE'LL ...
ZERO ...!
......
...WE'LL LEAVE IT TO THEM.
ZERO... PLEASE!!

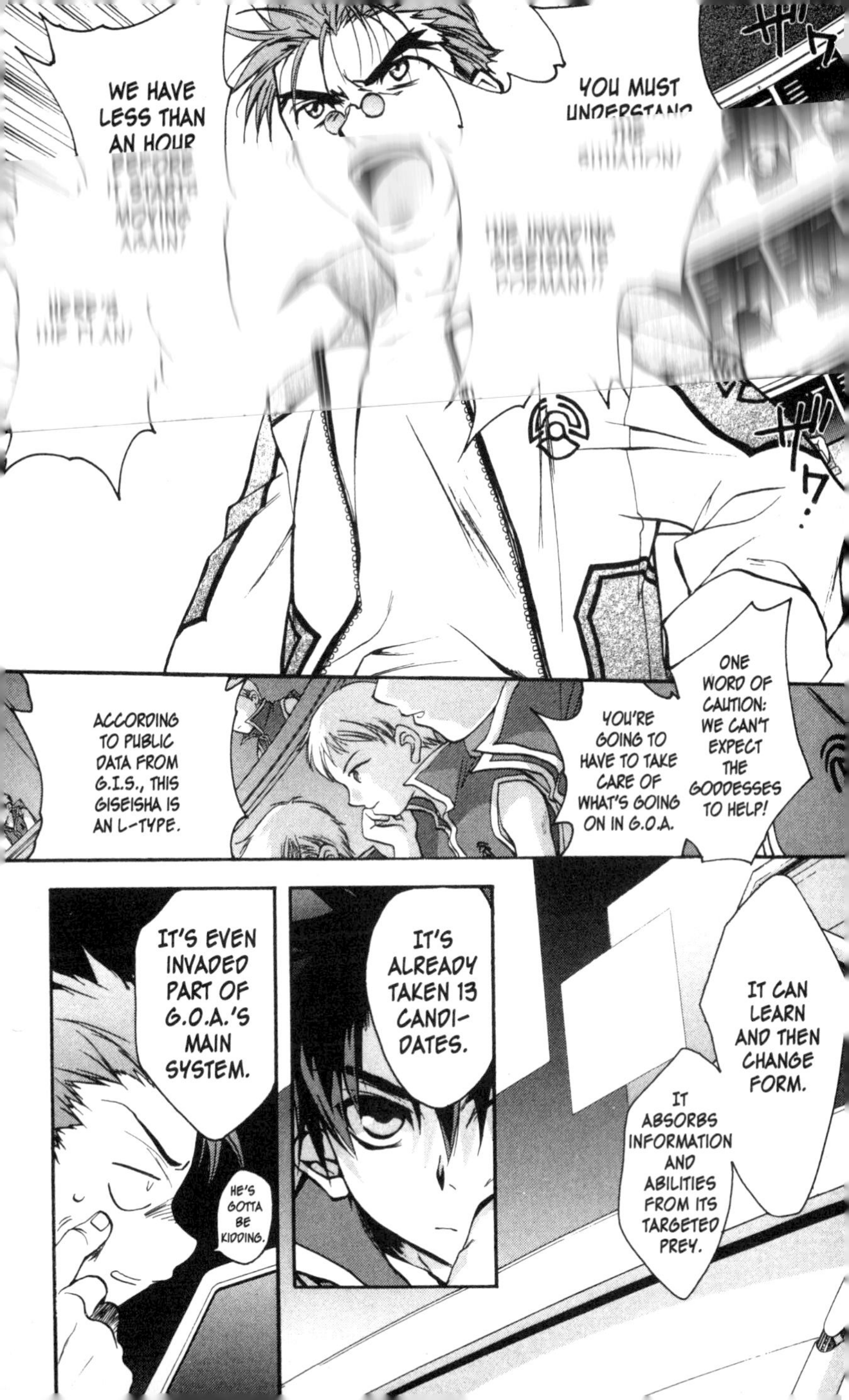
YOU MUST
WE HAVE LESS THAN AN HOUR
ONE WORD OF CAUTION: WE CAN'T EXPECT THE GODDESSES TO HELP!
YOU'RE GOING TO HAVE TO TAKE CARE OF WHAT'S GOING ON IN G.O.A.
ACCORDING TO PUBLIC DATA FROM G.I.S., THIS GISEISHA IS AN L-TYPE.
IT CAN LEARN AND THEN CHANGE FORM.
IT ABSORBS INFORMATION AND ABILITIES FROM ITS TARGETED PREY.
IT'S ALREADY TAKEN 13 CANDI-DATES.
IT'S EVEN INVADED PART OF G.O.A.'S MAIN SYSTEM.
HE'S GOTTA BE KIDDING.

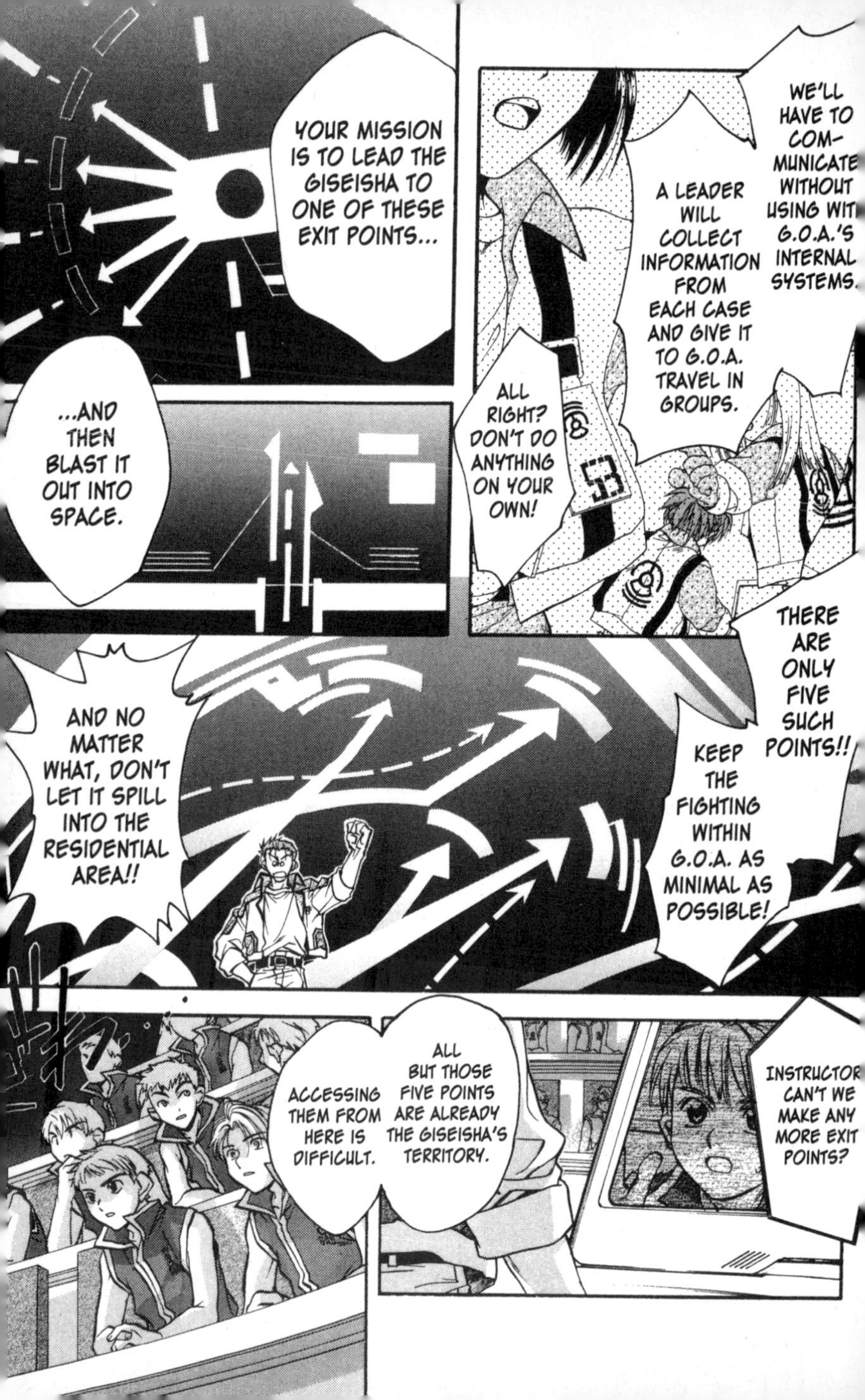
WE'LL HAVE TO COM-MUNICATE WITHOUT USING WIT G.O.A.'S INTERNAL SYSTEMS.
A LEADER WILL COLLECT INFORMATION FROM EACH CASE AND GIVE IT TO G.O.A. TRAVEL IN GROUPS.
ALL RIGHT? DON'T DO ANYTHING ON YOUR OWN!
YOUR MISSION IS TO LEAD THE GISEISHA TO ONE OF THESE EXIT POINTS...
...AND THEN BLAST IT OUT INTO SPACE.
THERE ARE ONLY FIVE SUCH POINTS!!
KEEP THE FIGHTING WITHIN G.O.A. AS MINIMAL AS POSSIBLE!
AND NO MATTER WHAT, DON'T LET IT SPILL INTO THE RESIDENTIAL AREA!!
INSTRUCTOR CAN'T WE MAKE ANY MORE EXIT POINTS?
ALL BUT THOSE FIVE POINTS ARE ALREADY THE GISEISHA'S TERRITORY.
ACCESSING THEM FROM HERE IS DIFFICULT.

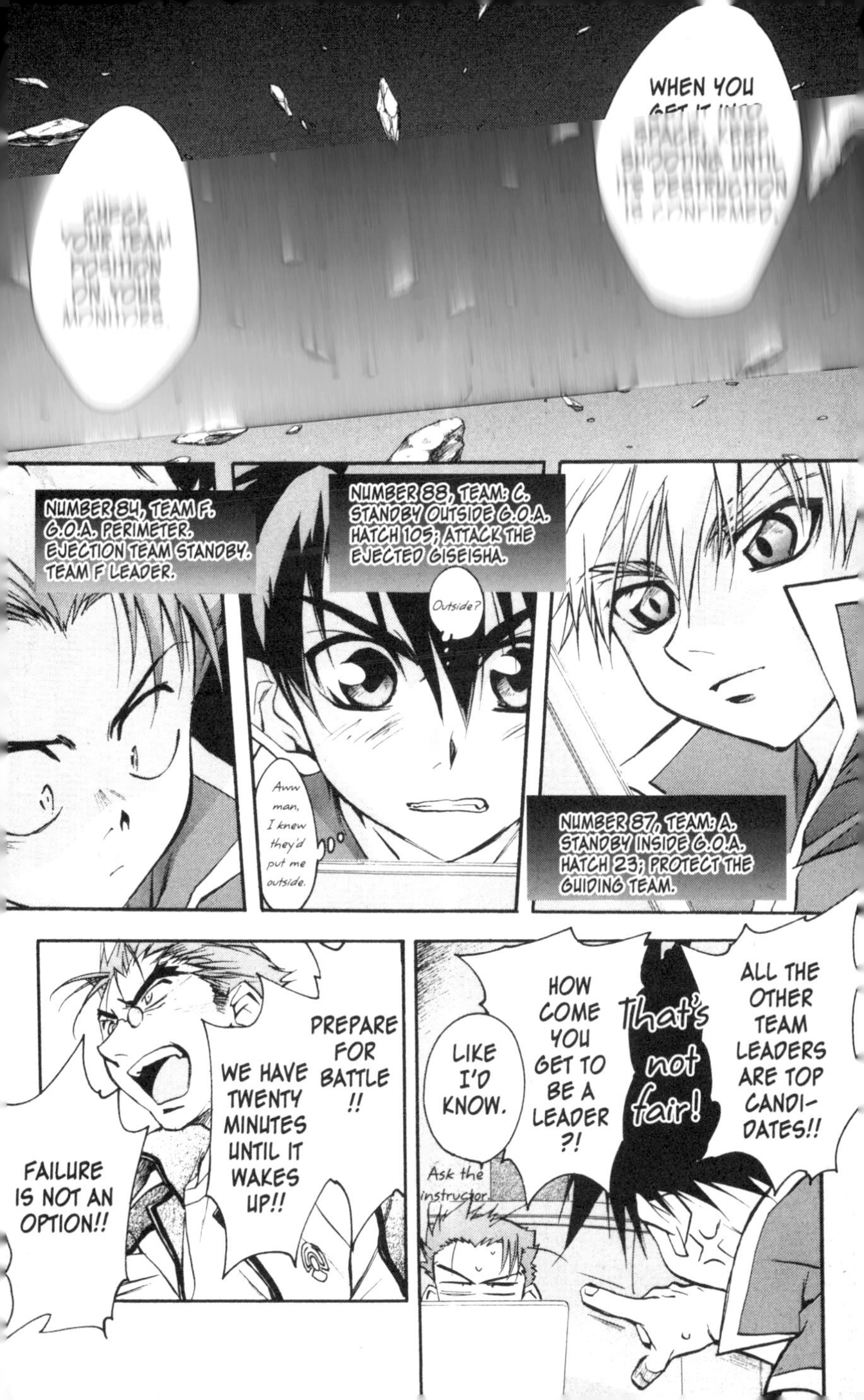
WHEN YOU GET IT INTO SPACE, KEEP SHOOTING UNTIL ITS DESTRUCTION IS CONFIRMED.
CHECK YOUR TEAM POSITION ON YOUR MONITORS.
NUMBER 87, TEAM: A. STANDBY INSIDE G.O.A. HATCH 23; PROTECT THE GUIDING TEAM.
NUMBER 88, TEAM: C. STANDBY OUTSIDE G.O.A. HATCH 105; ATTACK THE EJECTED GISEISHA.
Outside?
Aww man, I knew they'd put me outside.
NUMBER 84, TEAM F. G.O.A. PERIMETER. EJECTION TEAM STANDBY. TEAM F LEADER.
ALL THE OTHER TEAM LEADERS ARE TOP CANDI-DATES!!
That's not fair!
HOW COME YOU GET TO BE A LEADER?!
LIKE I'D KNOW.
Ask the instructor.
PREPARE FOR BATTLE!!
WE HAVE TWENTY MINUTES UNTIL IT WAKES UP!!
FAILURE IS NOT AN OPTION!!

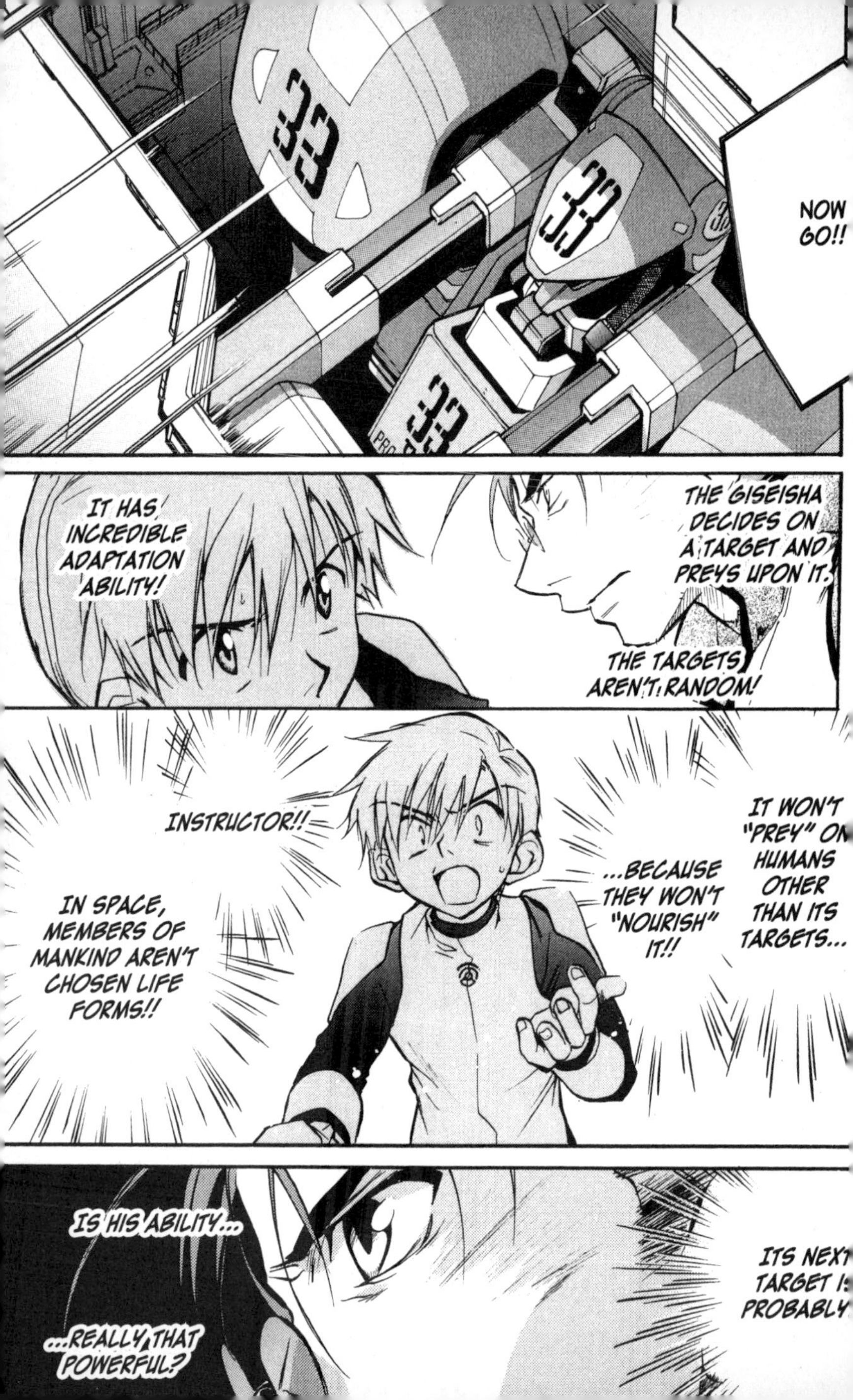
NOW GO!!
THE GISEISHA DECIDES ON A TARGET AND PREYS UPON IT.
THE TARGETS AREN'T RANDOM!
IT HAS INCREDIBLE ADAPTATION ABILITY!
IT WON'T "PREY" ON HUMANS OTHER THAN ITS TARGETS...
...BECAUSE THEY WON'T "NOURISH" IT!!
INSTRUCTOR!!
IN SPACE, MEMBERS OF MANKIND AREN'T CHOSEN LIFE FORMS!!
ITS NEXT TARGET IS PROBABLY
IS HIS ABILITY...
...REALLY THAT POWERFUL?

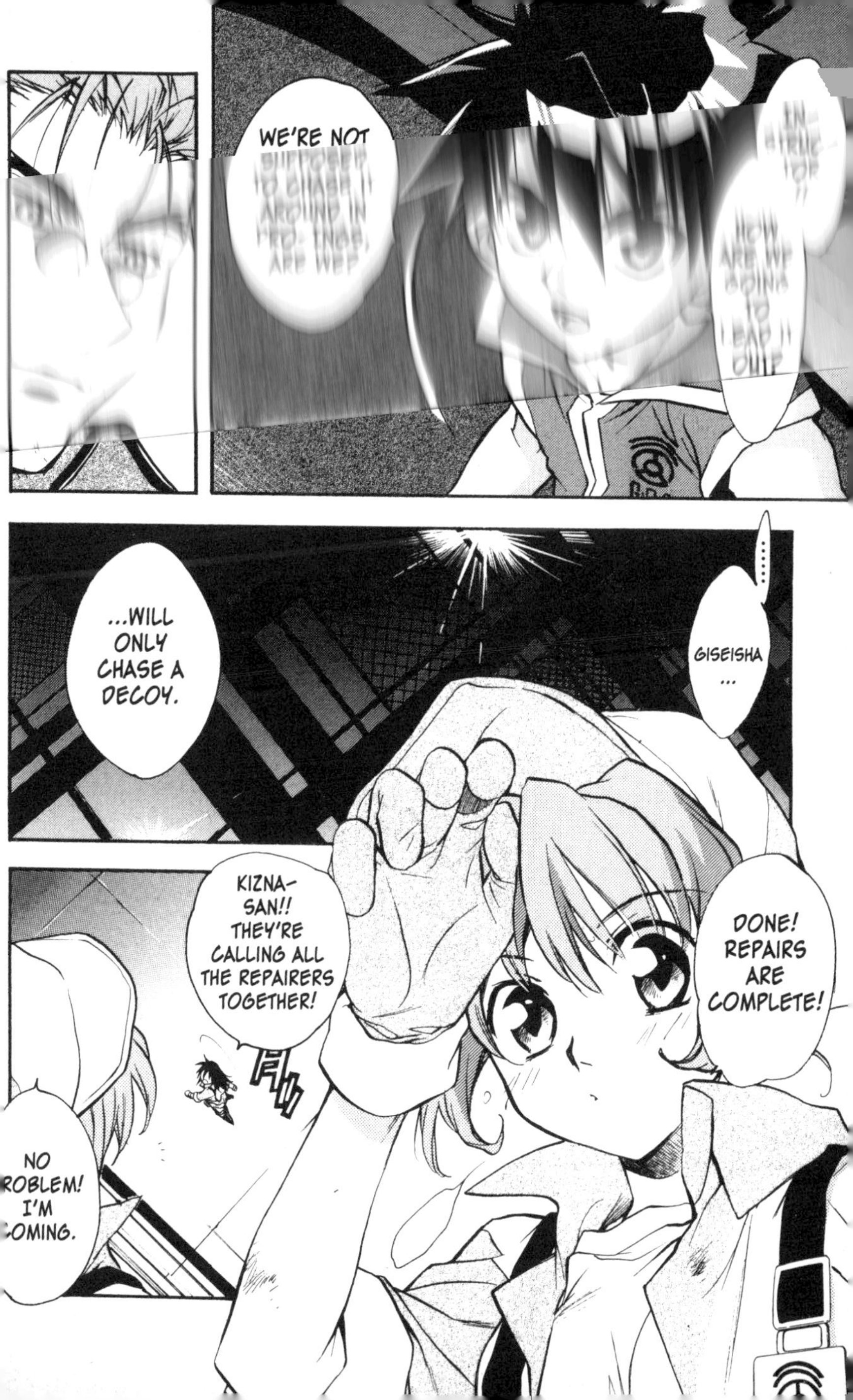
WE'RE NOT
...
GISEISHA ...
...WILL ONLY CHASE A DECOY.
DONE! REPAIRS ARE COMPLETE!
KIZNA-SAN!! THEY'RE CALLING ALL THE REPAIRERS TOGETHER!
NO ROBLEM! I'M OMING.

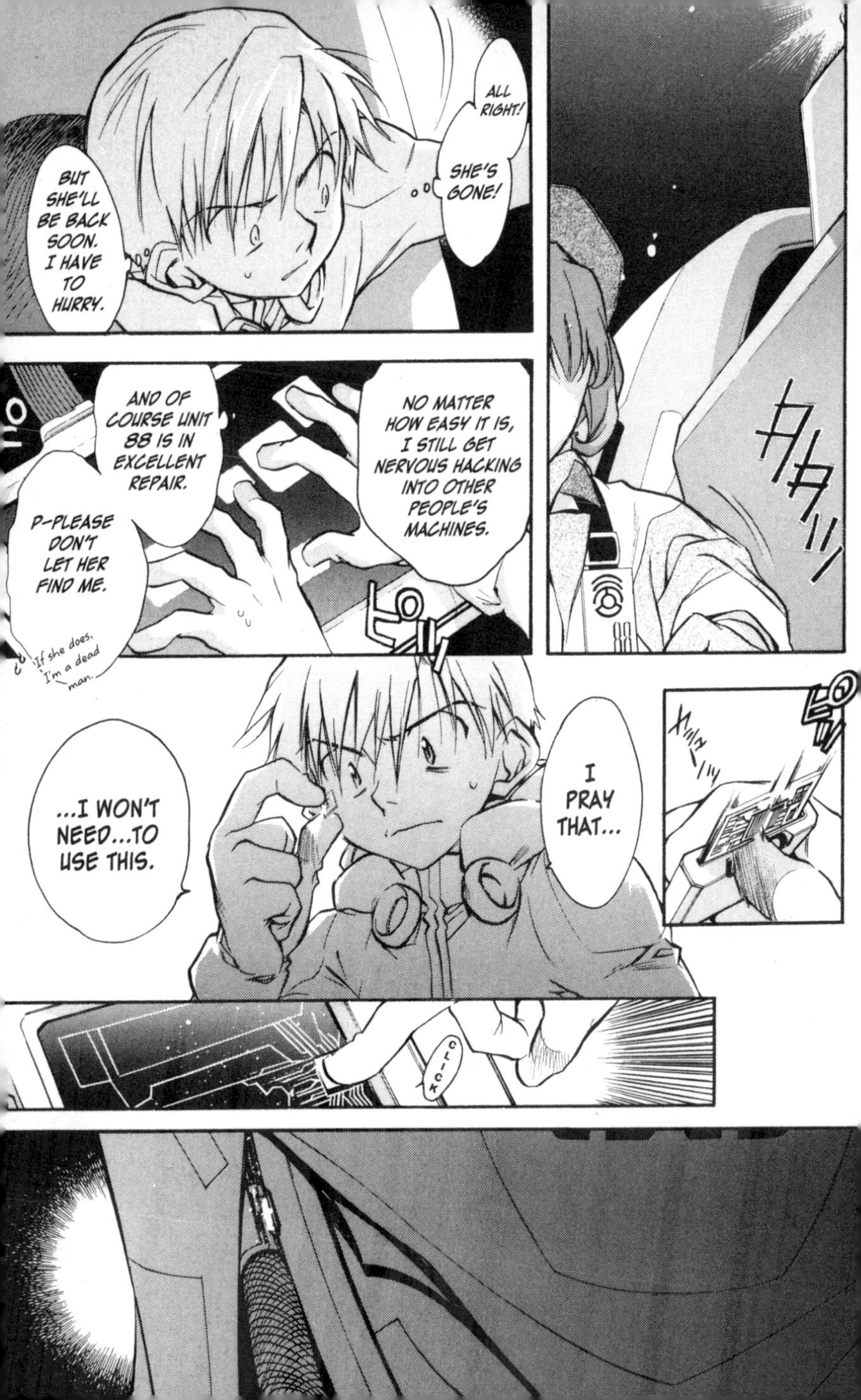
ALL RIGHT!
SHE'S GONE!
BUT SHE'LL BE BACK SOON. I HAVE TO HURRY.
NO MATTER HOW EASY IT IS, I STILL GET NERVOUS HACKING INTO OTHER PEOPLE'S MACHINES.
AND OF COURSE UNIT 88 IS IN EXCELLENT REPAIR.
P-PLEASE DON'T LET HER FIND ME.
If she does, I'm a dead man.
I PRAY THAT...
...I WON'T NEED...TO USE THIS.
CLICK

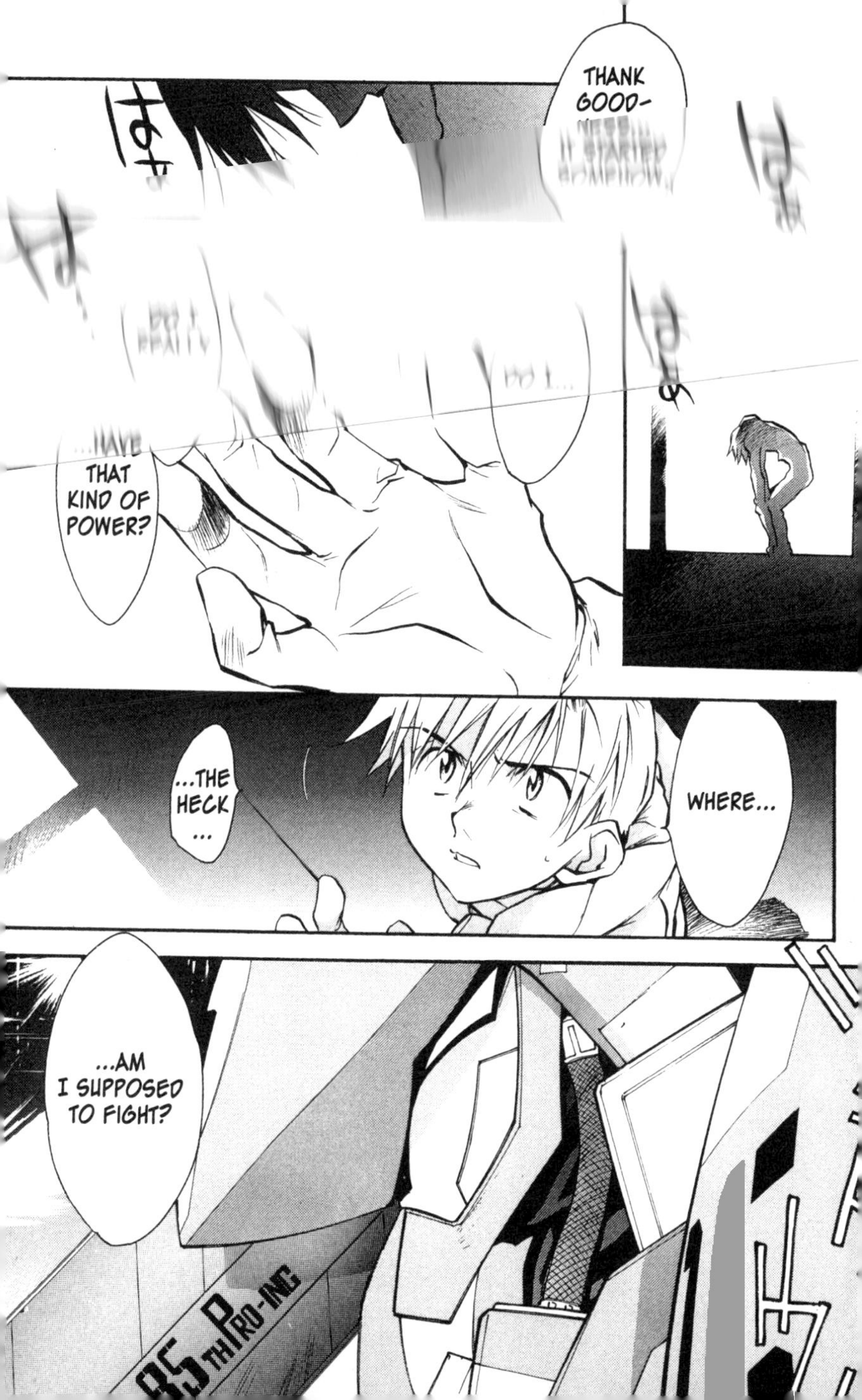
THANK GOOD-
THAT KIND OF POWER?
WHERE...
...THE HECK ...
...AM I SUPPOSED TO FIGHT?
85TH PRO-ING

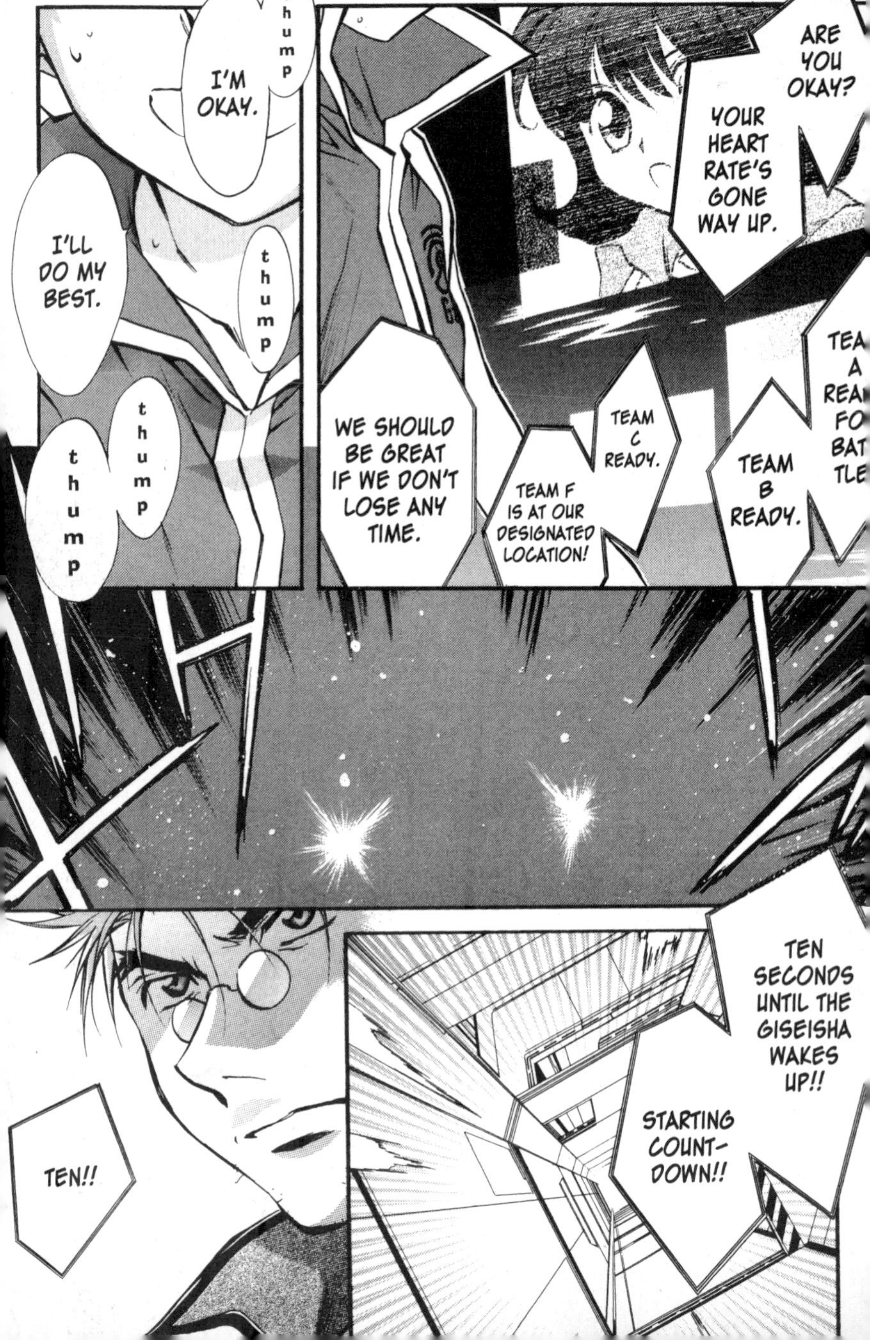
ARE YOU OKAY?
YOUR HEART RATE'S GONE WAY UP.
TEA A REA FO BAT TLE
TEAM B READY.
TEAM C READY.
TEAM F IS AT OUR DESIGNATED LOCATION!
WE SHOULD BE GREAT IF WE DON'T LOSE ANY TIME.
thump
I'M OKAY.
thump
I'LL DO MY BEST.
thump
thump
TEN SECONDS UNTIL THE GISEISHA WAKES UP!!
STARTING COUNT-DOWN!!
TEN!!

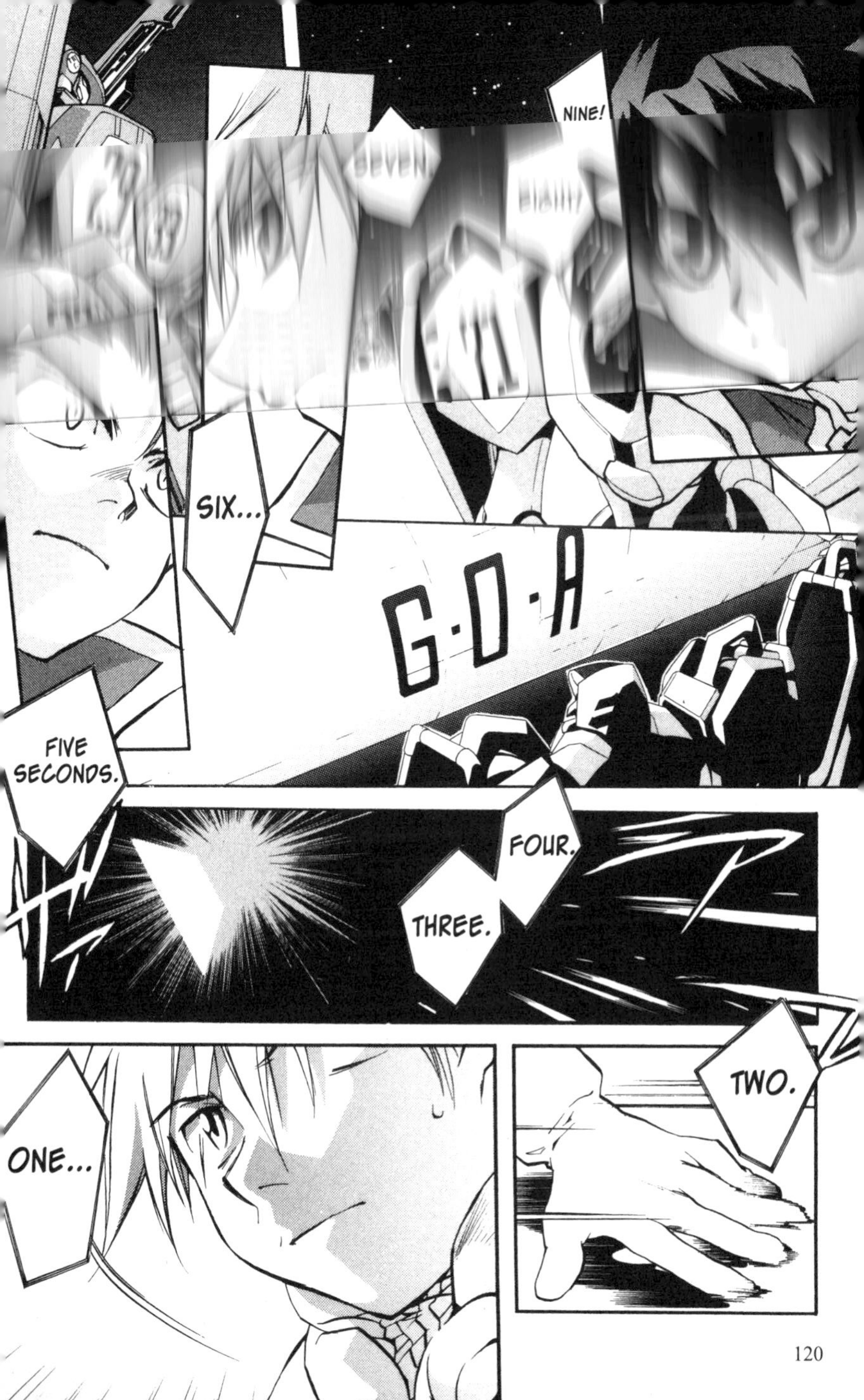
NINE!
SEVEN
SIX...
G-D-A
FIVE SECONDS.
FOUR.
THREE.
TWO.
ONE...

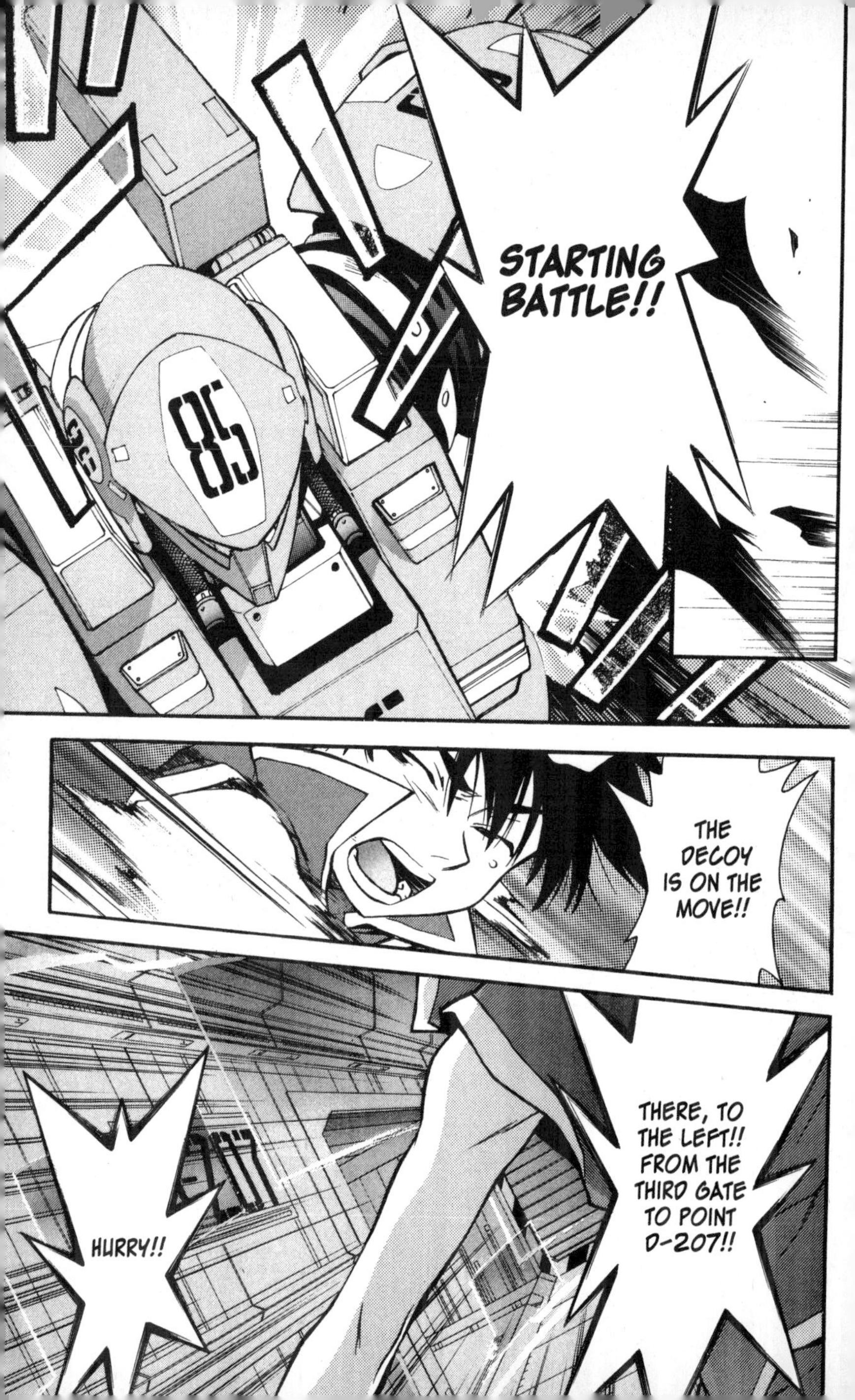
STARTING BATTLE!!
THE DECOY IS ON THE MOVE!!
THERE, TO THE LEFT!! FROM THE THIRD GATE TO POINT D-207!!
HURRY!!

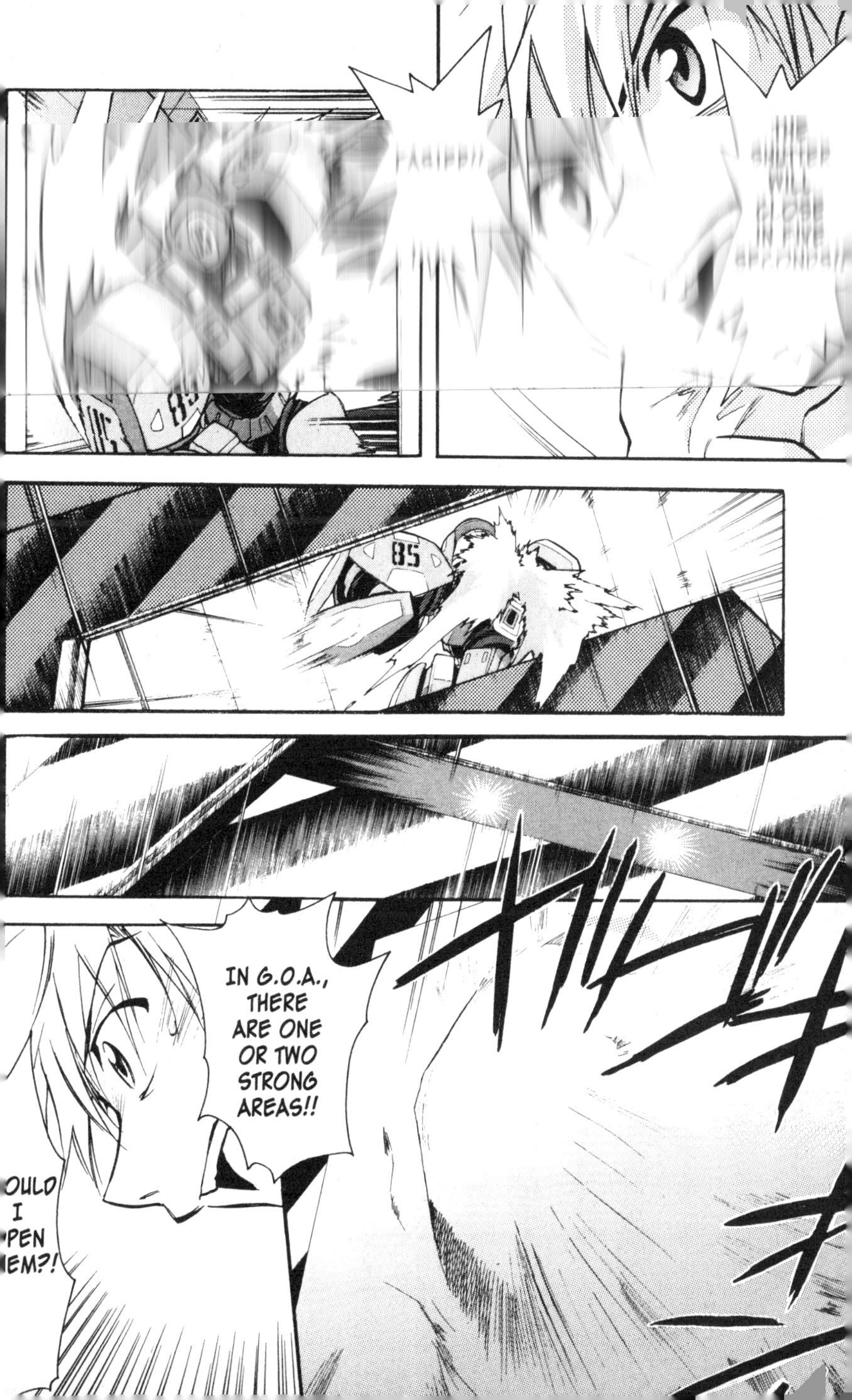
IN G.O.A., THERE ARE ONE OR TWO STRONG AREAS!!
OULD I PEN EM?!

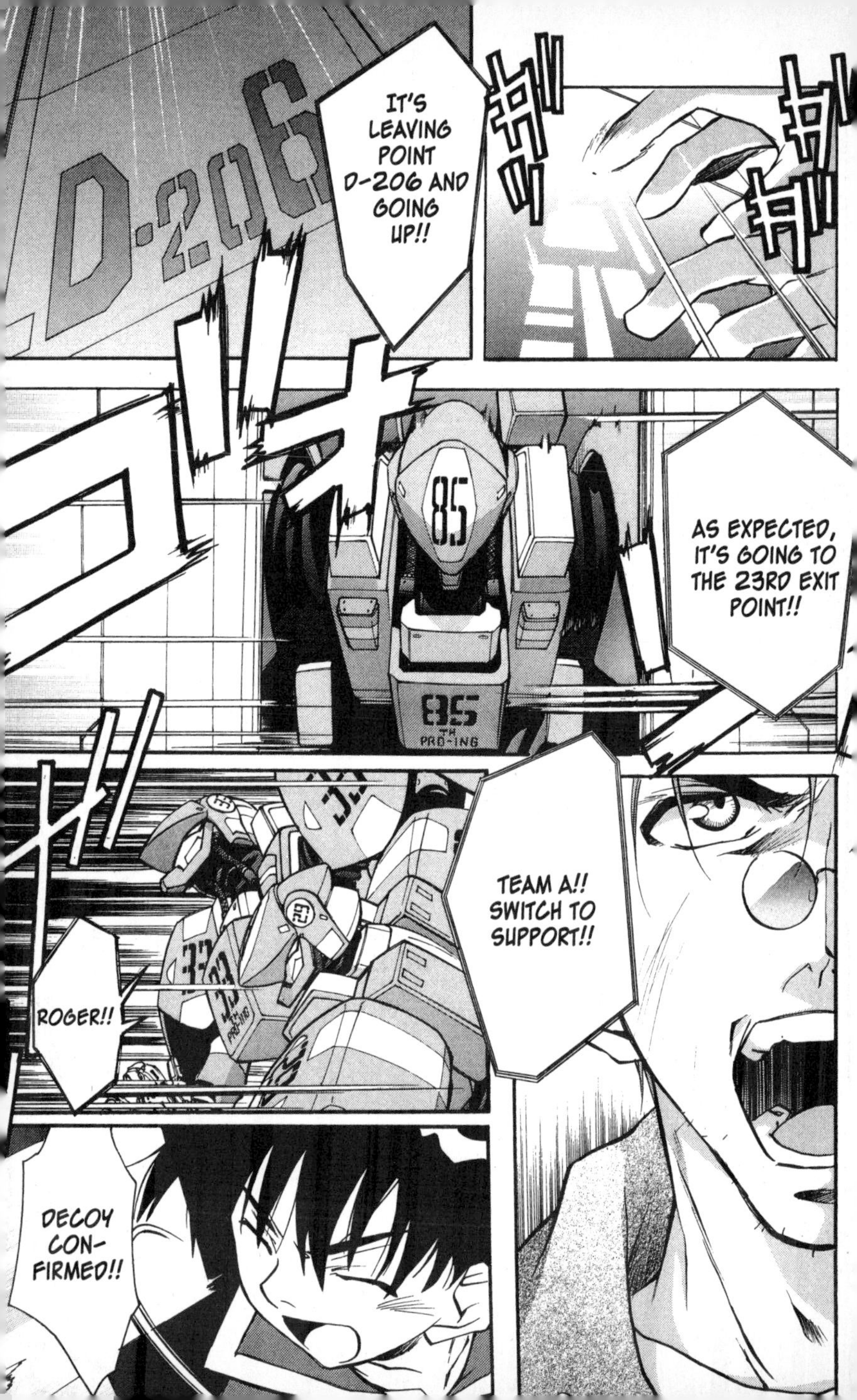
IT'S LEAVING POINT D-206 AND GOING UP!!
AS EXPECTED, IT'S GOING TO THE 23RD EXIT POINT!!
TEAM A!! SWITCH TO SUPPORT!!
ROGER!!
DECOY CON-FIRMED!!

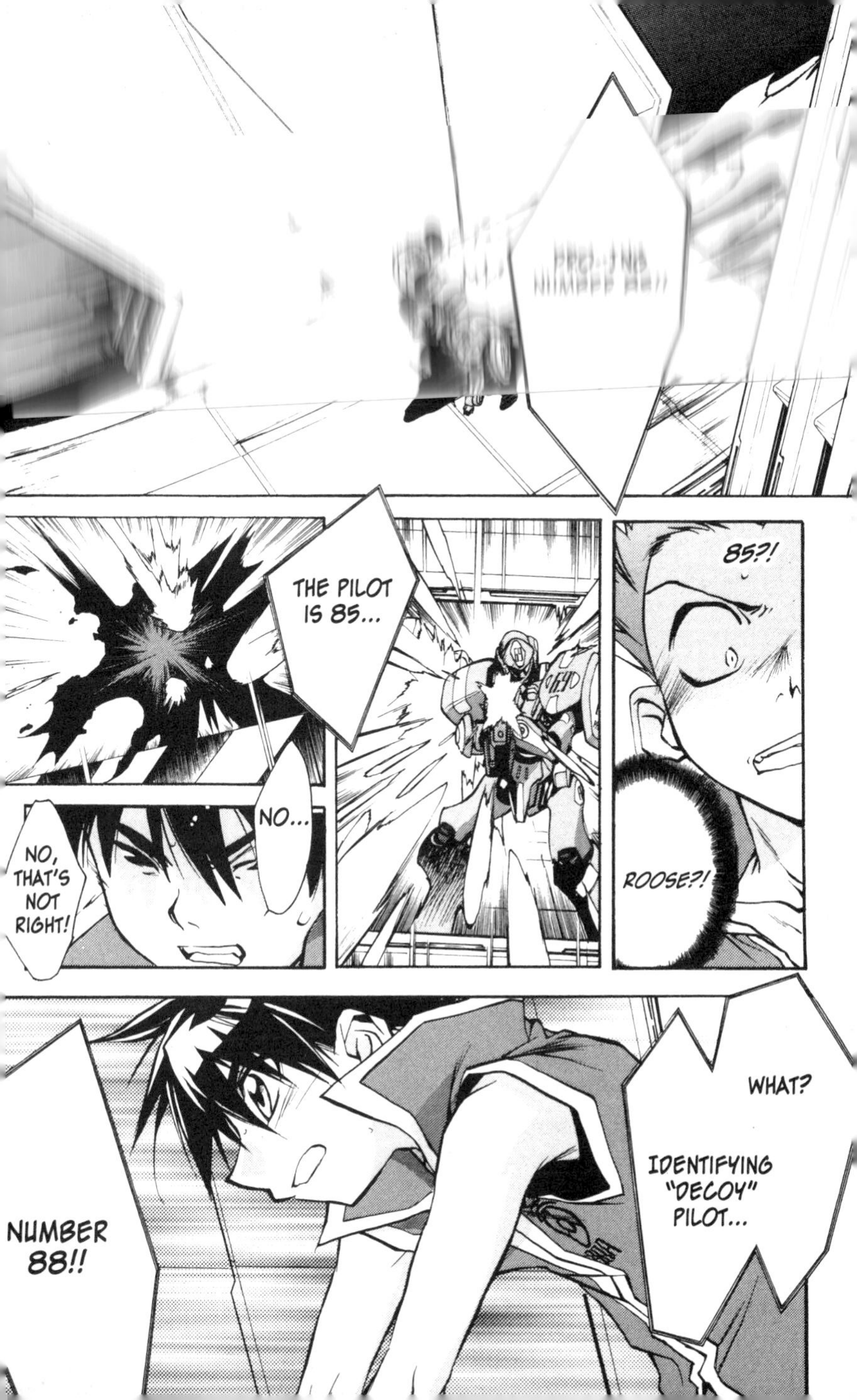
THE PILOT IS 85...
85?!
ROOSE?!
NO...
NO, THAT'S NOT RIGHT!
WHAT?
IDENTIFYING "DECOY" PILOT...
NUMBER 88!!

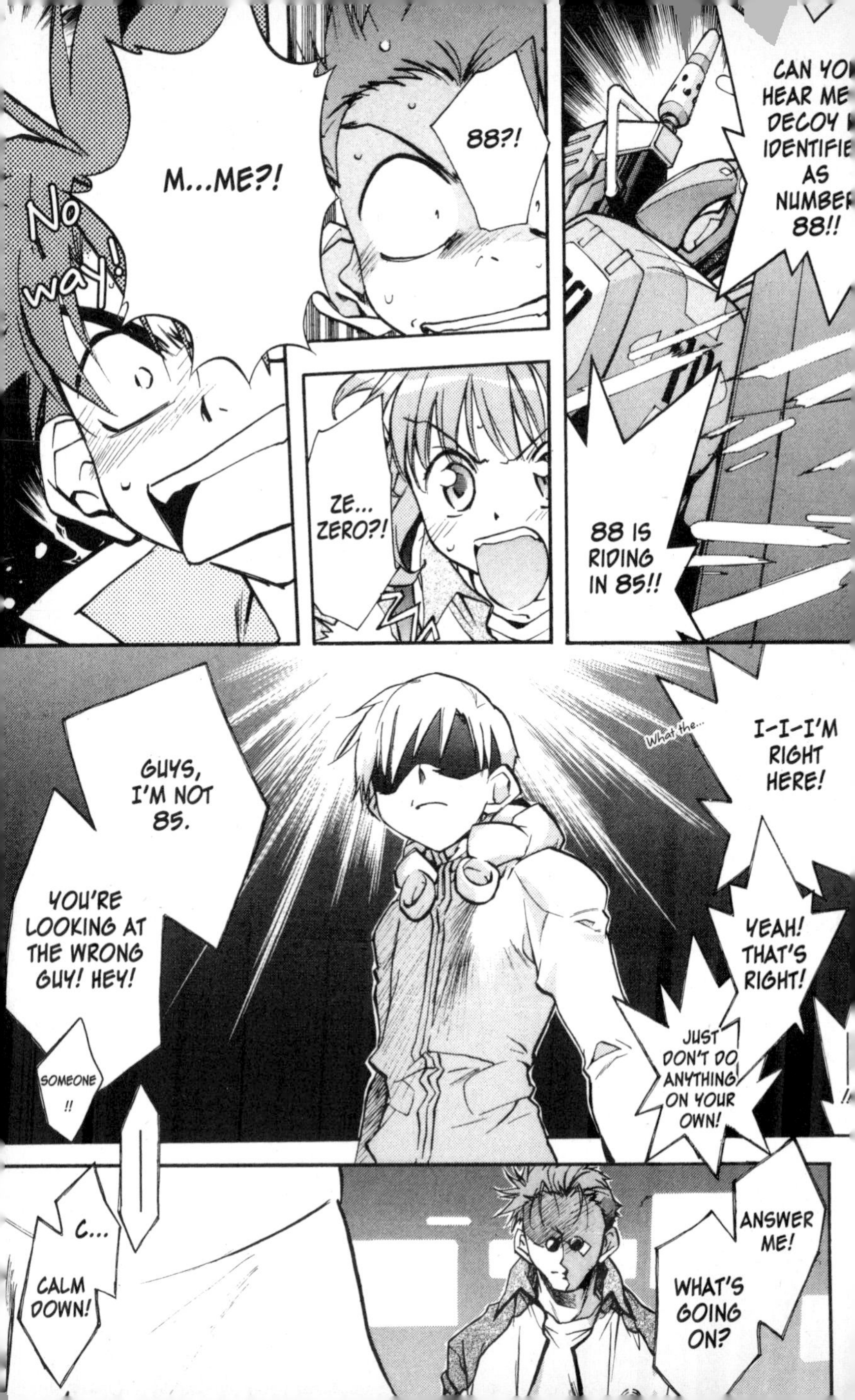
CAN YO HEAR ME DECOY IDENTIFIE AS NUMBER 88!!
88 IS RIDING IN 85!!
88?!
ZE... ZERO?!
M...ME?!
No way!
I-I-I'M RIGHT HERE!
What the...
YEAH! THAT'S RIGHT!
JUST DON'T DO ANYTHING ON YOUR OWN!
GUYS, I'M NOT 85.
YOU'RE LOOKING AT THE WRONG GUY! HEY!
SOMEONE !!
ANSWER ME!
WHAT'S GOING ON?
C...
CALM DOWN!

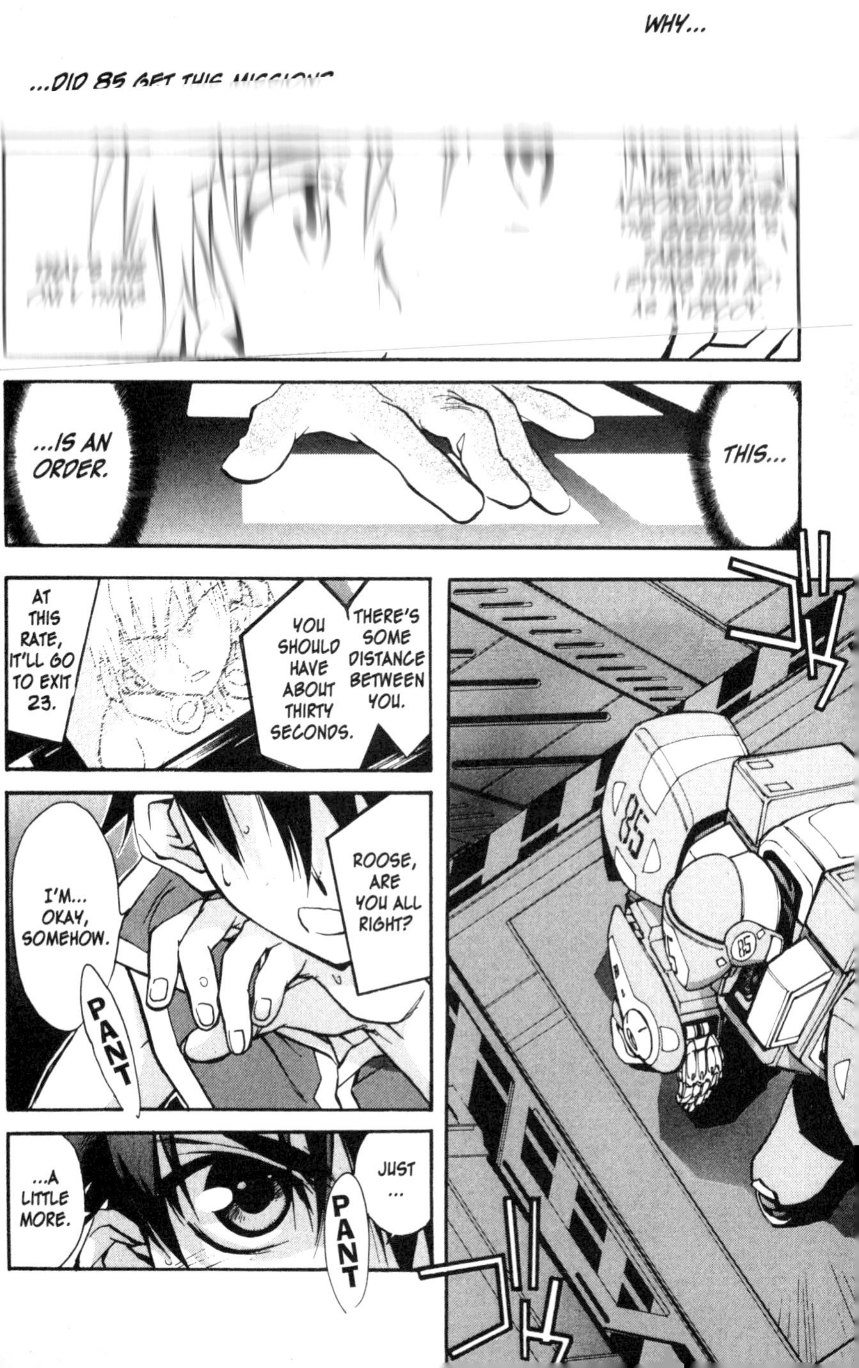
WHY...
...DID 85 GET THIS MISSION
THIS...
...IS AN ORDER.
THERE'S SOME DISTANCE BETWEEN YOU.
YOU SHOULD HAVE ABOUT THIRTY SECONDS.
AT THIS RATE, IT'LL GO TO EXIT 23.
ROOSE, ARE YOU ALL RIGHT?
I'M... OKAY, SOMEHOW.
PANT
JUST...
PANT
...A LITTLE MORE.

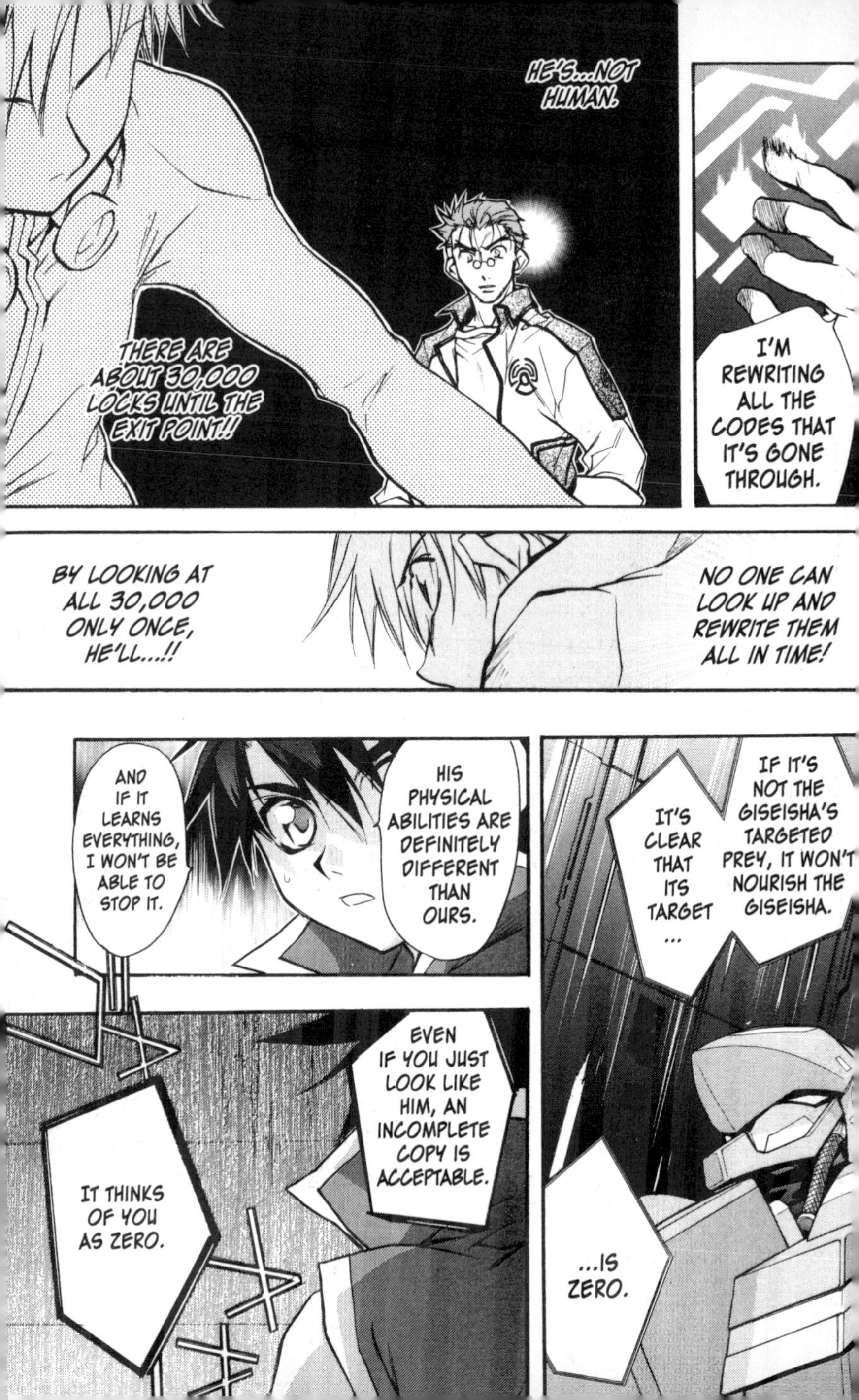
I'M REWRITING ALL THE CODES THAT IT'S GONE THROUGH.
HE'S...NOT HUMAN.
THERE ARE ABOUT 30,000 LOCKS UNTIL THE EXIT POINT!!
NO ONE CAN LOOK UP AND REWRITE THEM ALL IN TIME!
BY LOOKING AT ALL 30,000 ONLY ONCE, HE'LL...!!
IF IT'S NOT THE GISEISHA'S TARGETED PREY, IT WON'T NOURISH THE GISEISHA.
IT'S CLEAR THAT ITS TARGET...
...IS ZERO.
HIS PHYSICAL ABILITIES ARE DEFINITELY DIFFERENT THAN OURS.
AND IF IT LEARNS EVERYTHING, I WON'T BE ABLE TO STOP IT.
EVEN IF YOU JUST LOOK LIKE HIM, AN INCOMPLETE COPY IS ACCEPTABLE.
IT THINKS OF YOU AS ZERO.

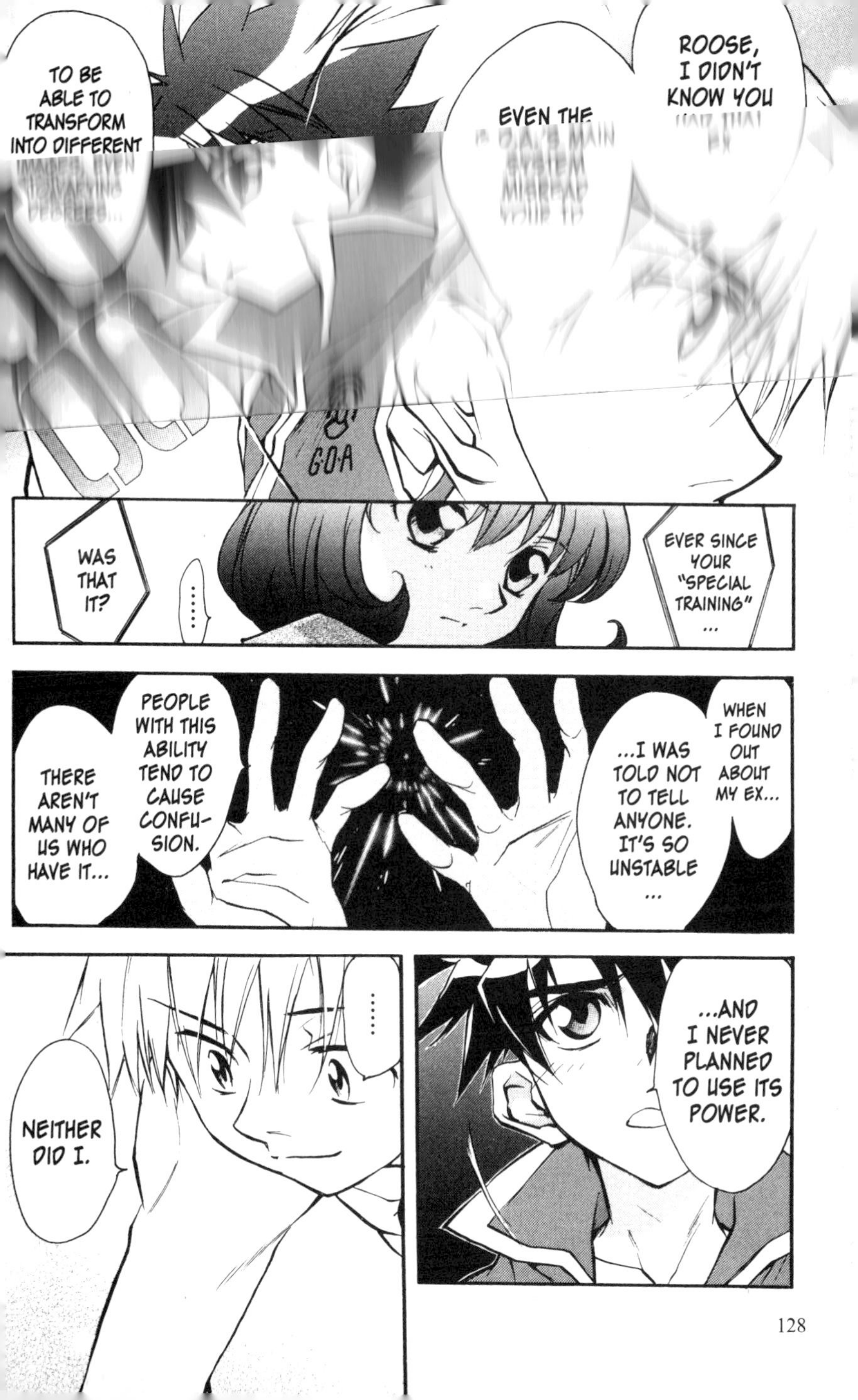
ROOSE, I DIDN'T KNOW YOU
EVEN THE
TO BE ABLE TO TRANSFORM INTO DIFFERENT
EVER SINCE YOUR "SPECIAL TRAINING" ...
......
WAS THAT IT?
G·O·A
WHEN I FOUND OUT ABOUT MY EX...
...I WAS TOLD NOT TO TELL ANYONE. IT'S SO UNSTABLE ...
PEOPLE WITH THIS ABILITY TEND TO CAUSE CONFU-SION.
THERE AREN'T MANY OF US WHO HAVE IT...
...AND I NEVER PLANNED TO USE ITS POWER.
......
NEITHER DID I.

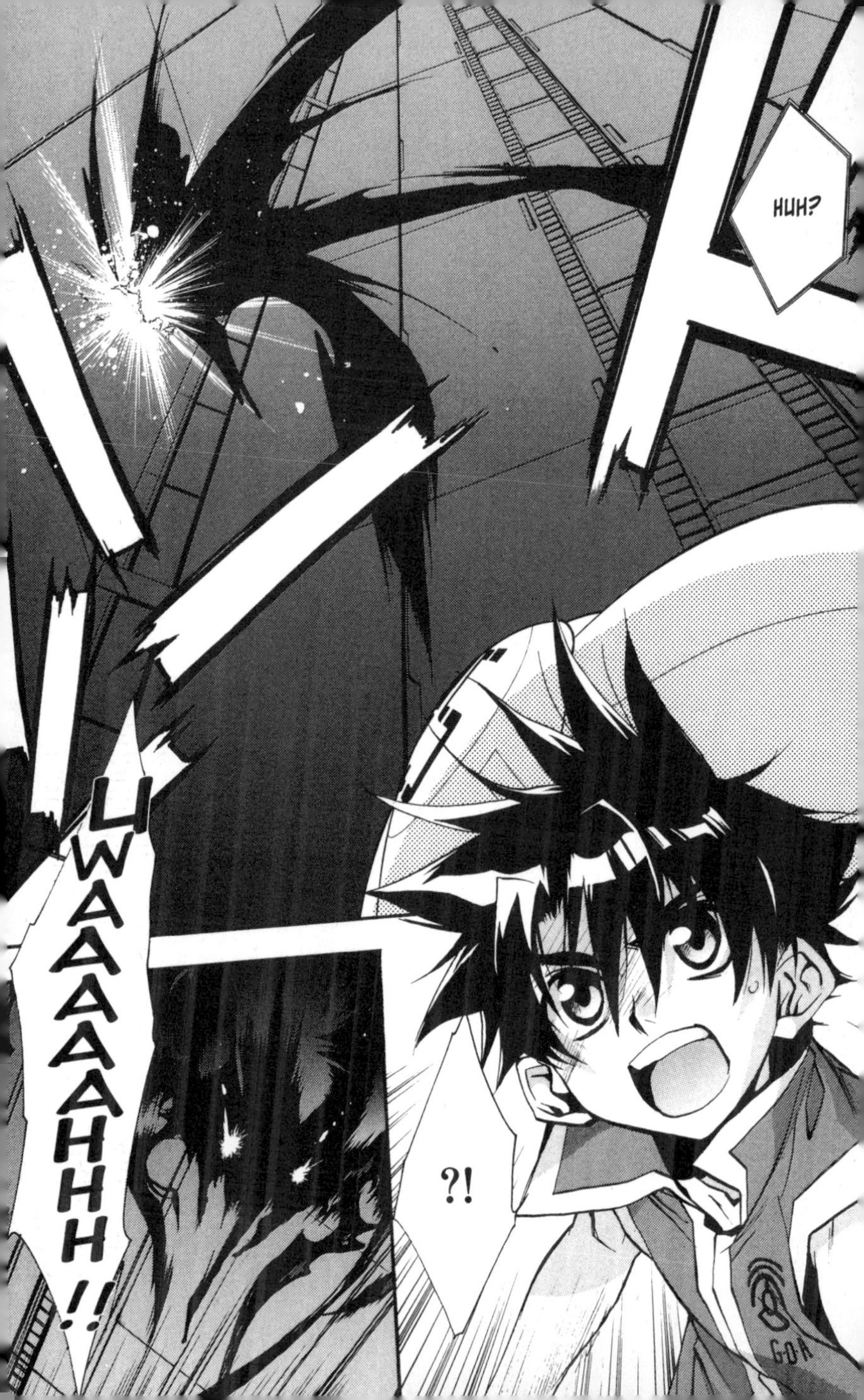
HUH?
UWAAAAAHHH!!
?!

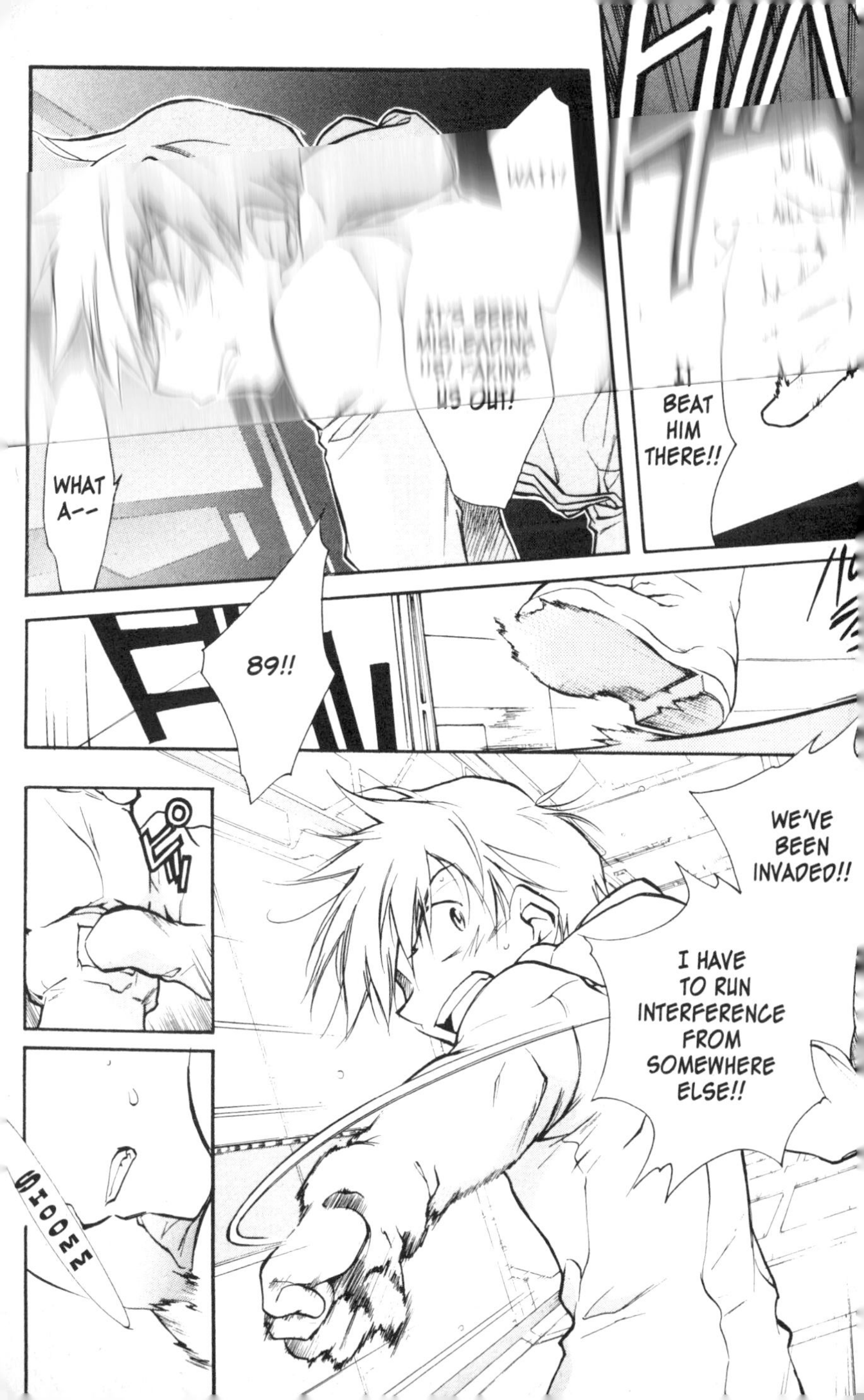
BEAT HIM THERE!!
WHAT A--
89!!
WE'VE BEEN INVADED!!
I HAVE TO RUN INTERFERENCE FROM SOMEWHERE ELSE!!

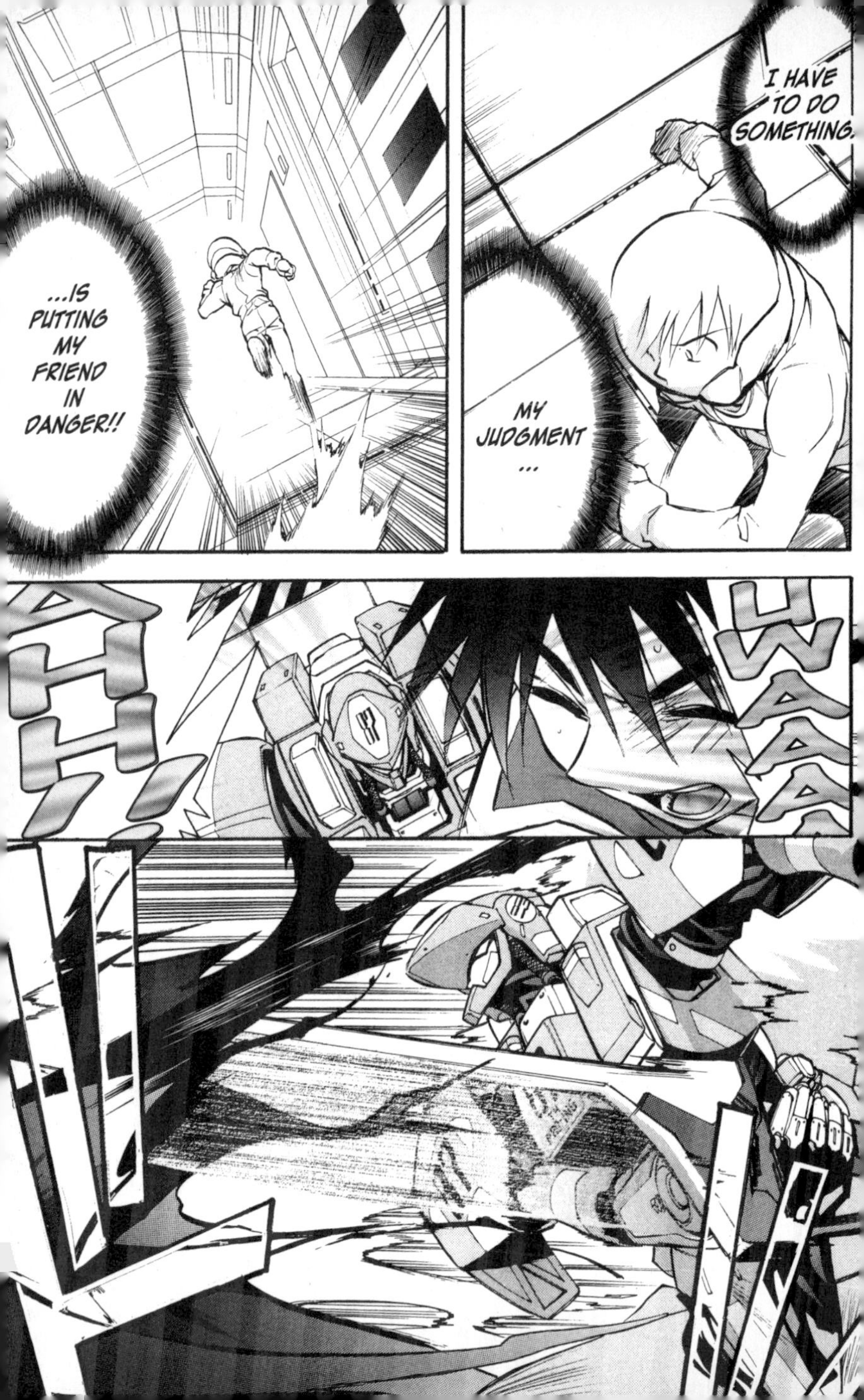
I HAVE TO DO SOMETHING.
MY JUDGMENT ...
...IS PUTTING MY FRIEND IN DANGER!!
UWAAAA
AHH!!

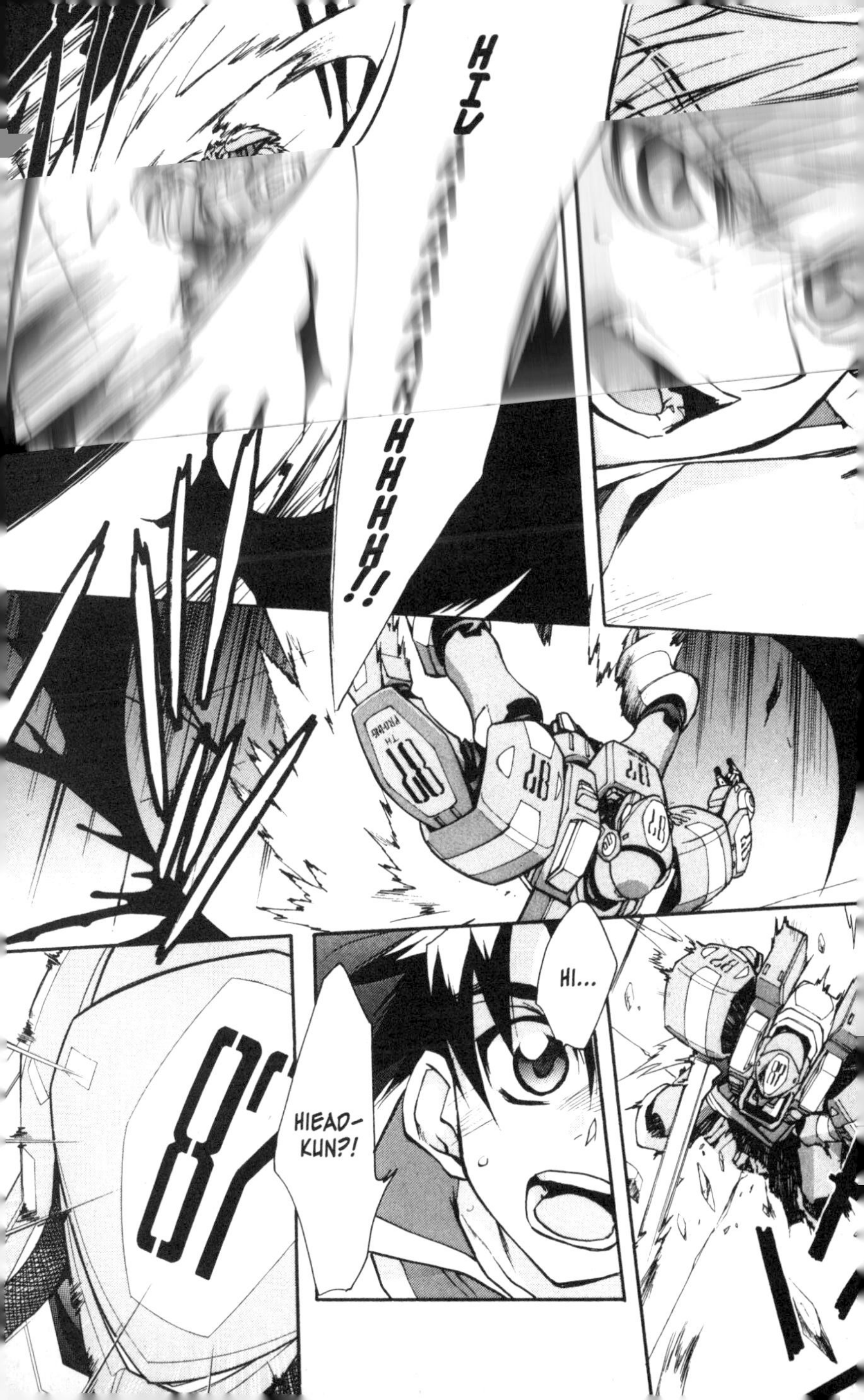
HIVVHHHHHH?!!
HI...
HIEAD-KUN?!

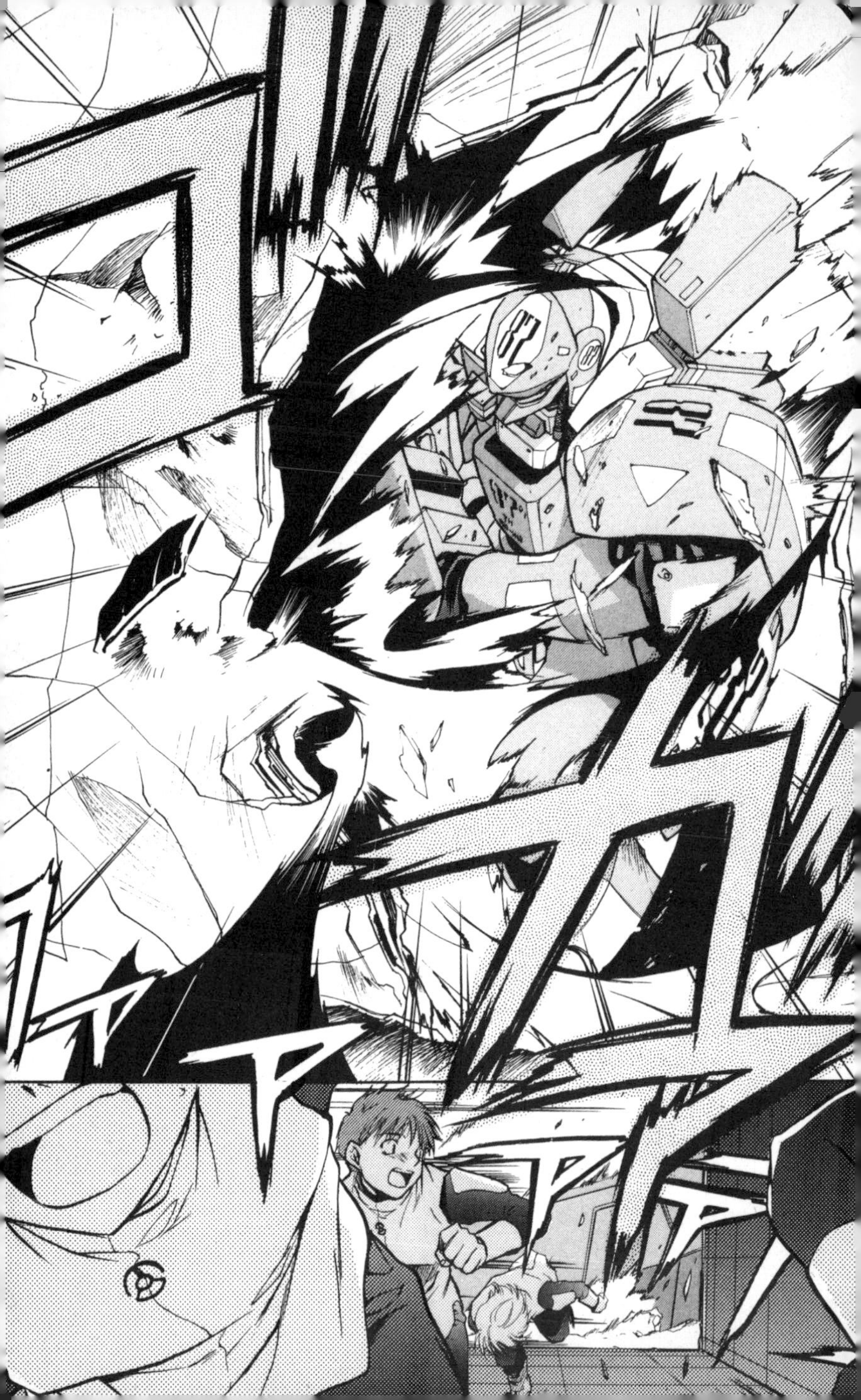

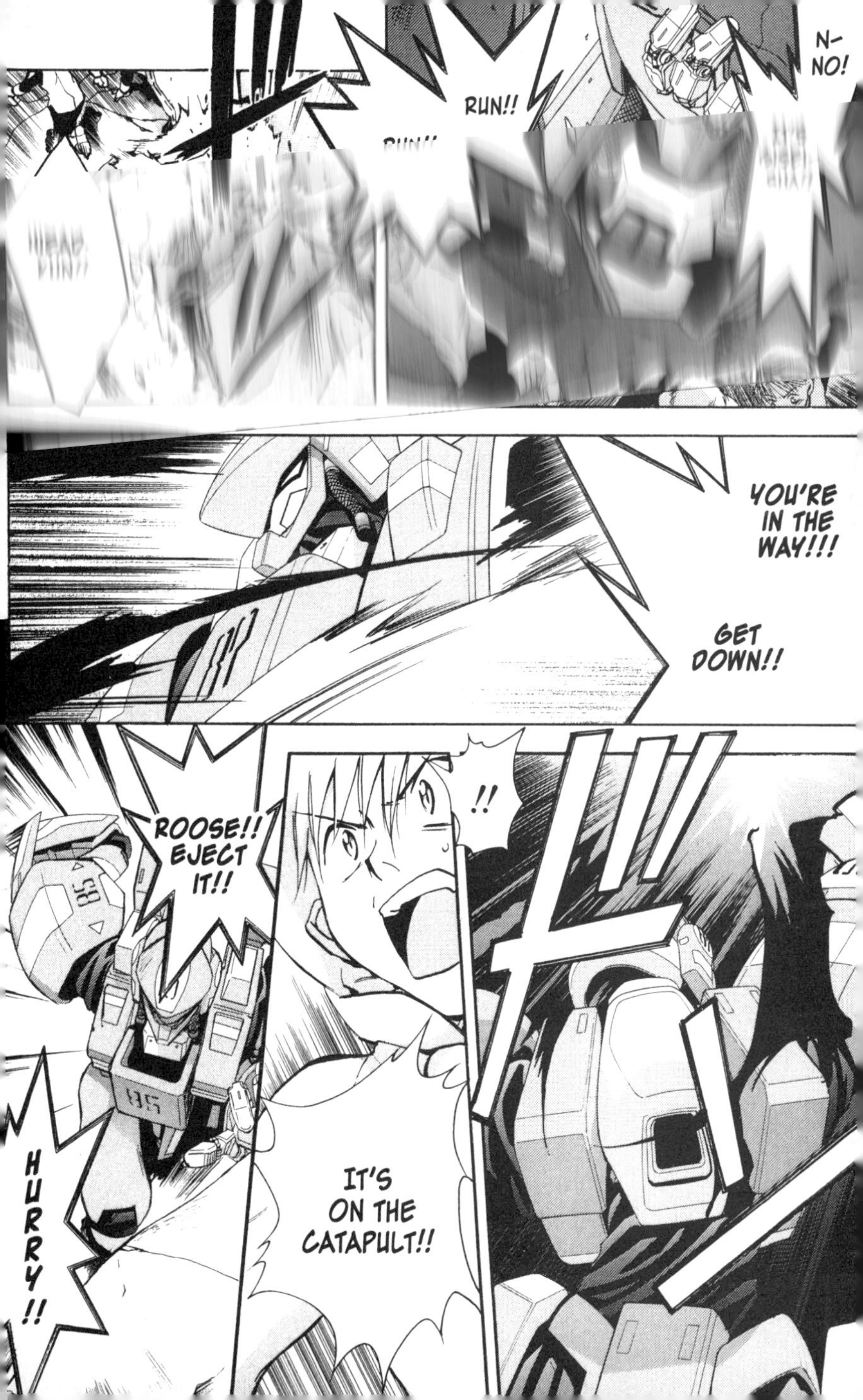
N- NO!
RUN!!
YOU'RE IN THE WAY!!!
GET DOWN!!
!!
IT'S ON THE CATAPULT!!
ROOSE!! EJECT IT!!
HURRY!!

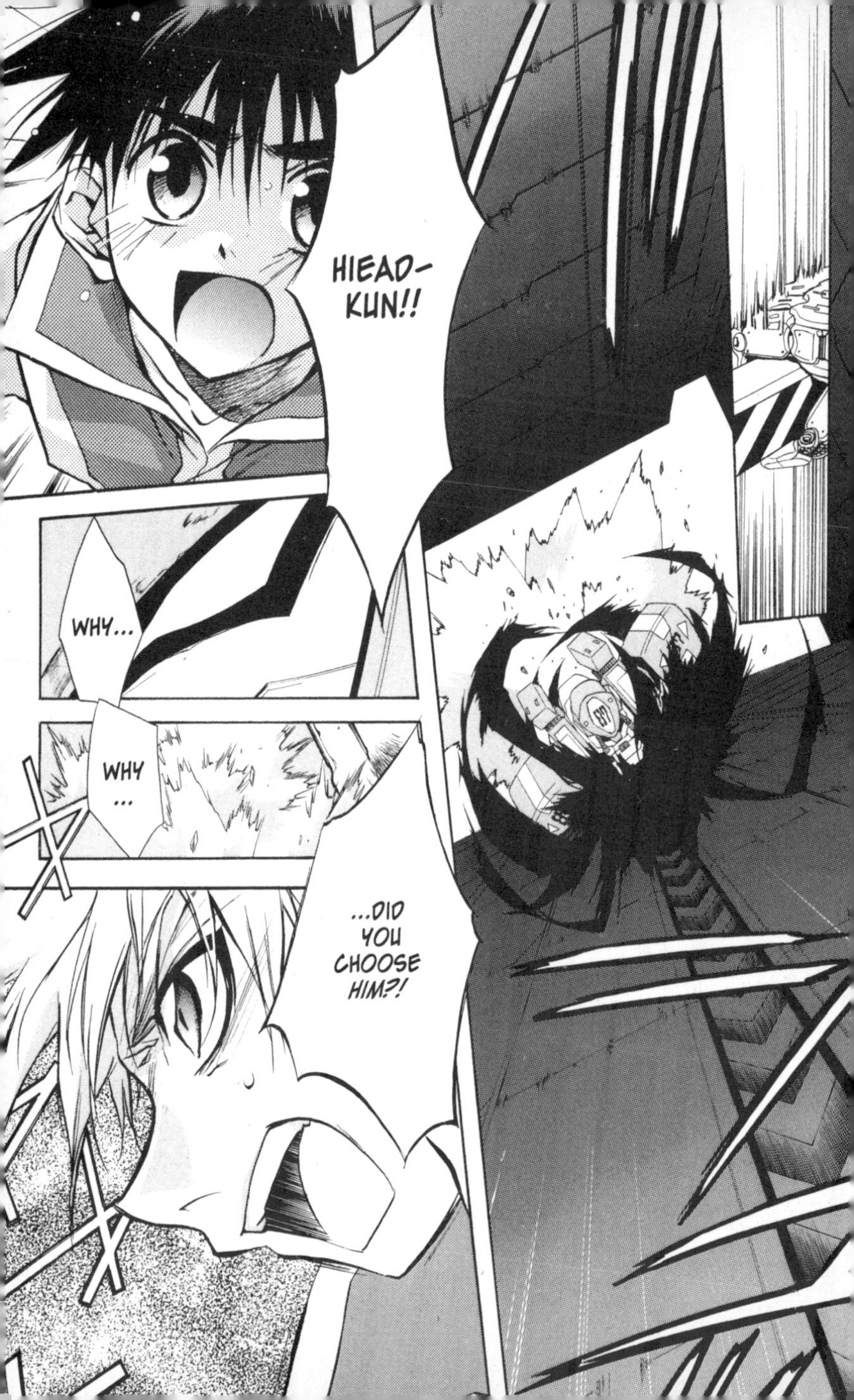
HIEAD-KUN!!
WHY...
WHY ...
...DID YOU CHOOSE HIM?!

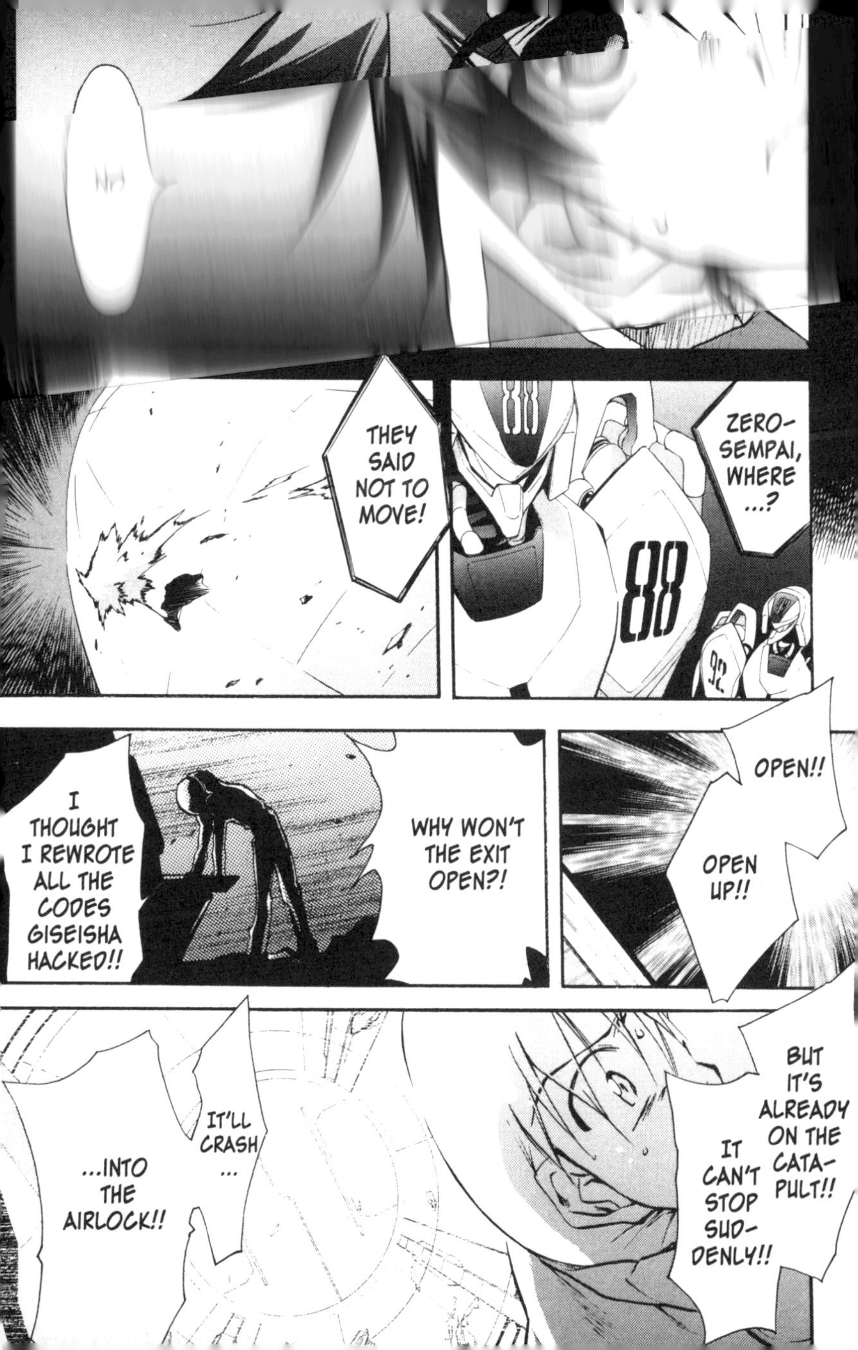
ZERO-SEMPAI, WHERE ...?
THEY SAID NOT TO MOVE!
OPEN!!
OPEN UP!!
WHY WON'T THE EXIT OPEN?!
I THOUGHT I REWROTE ALL THE CODES GISEISHA HACKED!!
BUT IT'S ALREADY ON THE CATA-PULT!!
IT CAN'T STOP SUD-DENLY!!
IT'LL CRASH ...
...INTO THE AIRLOCK!!

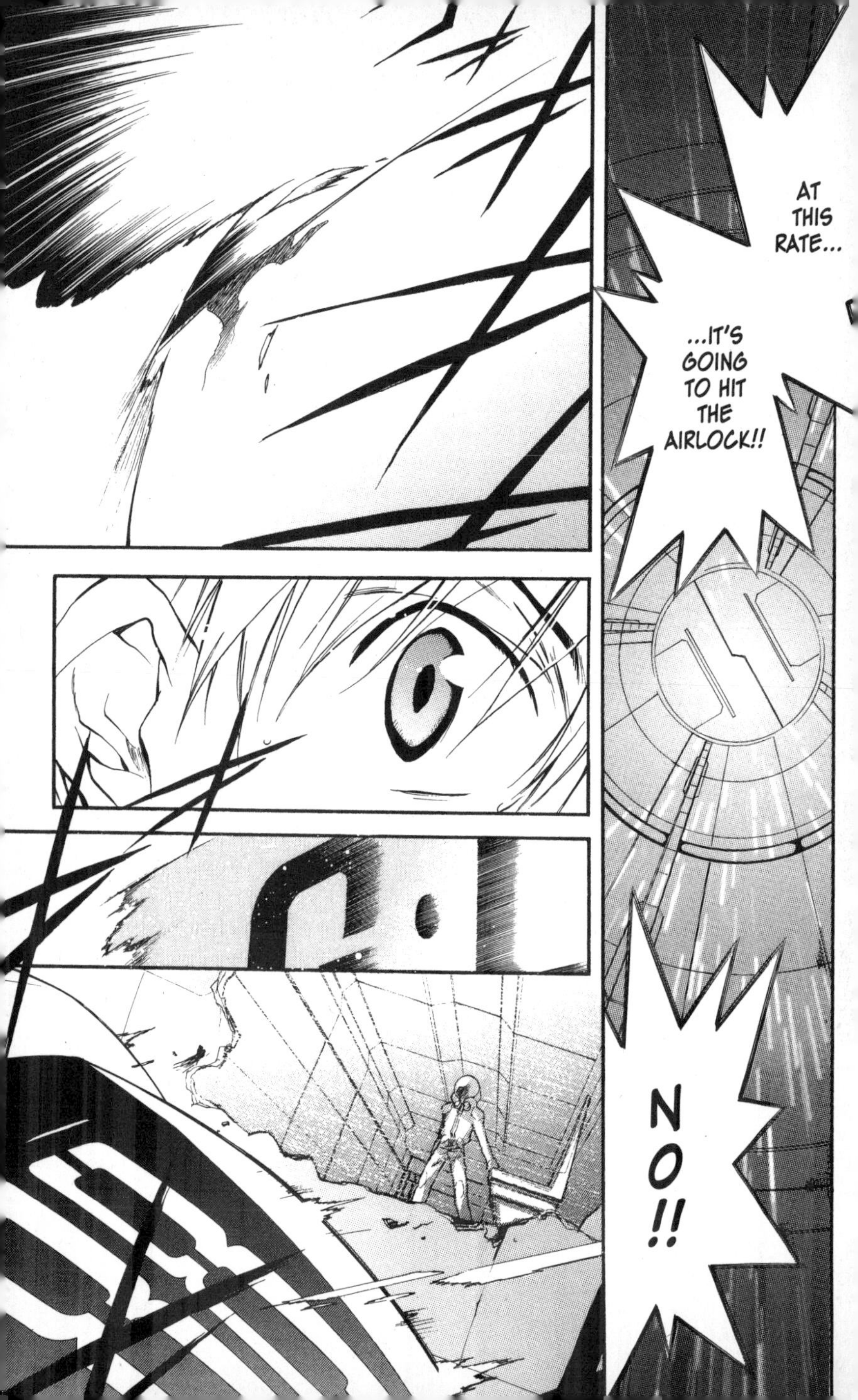
AT THIS RATE...
...IT'S GOING TO HIT THE AIRLOCK!!
NO!!

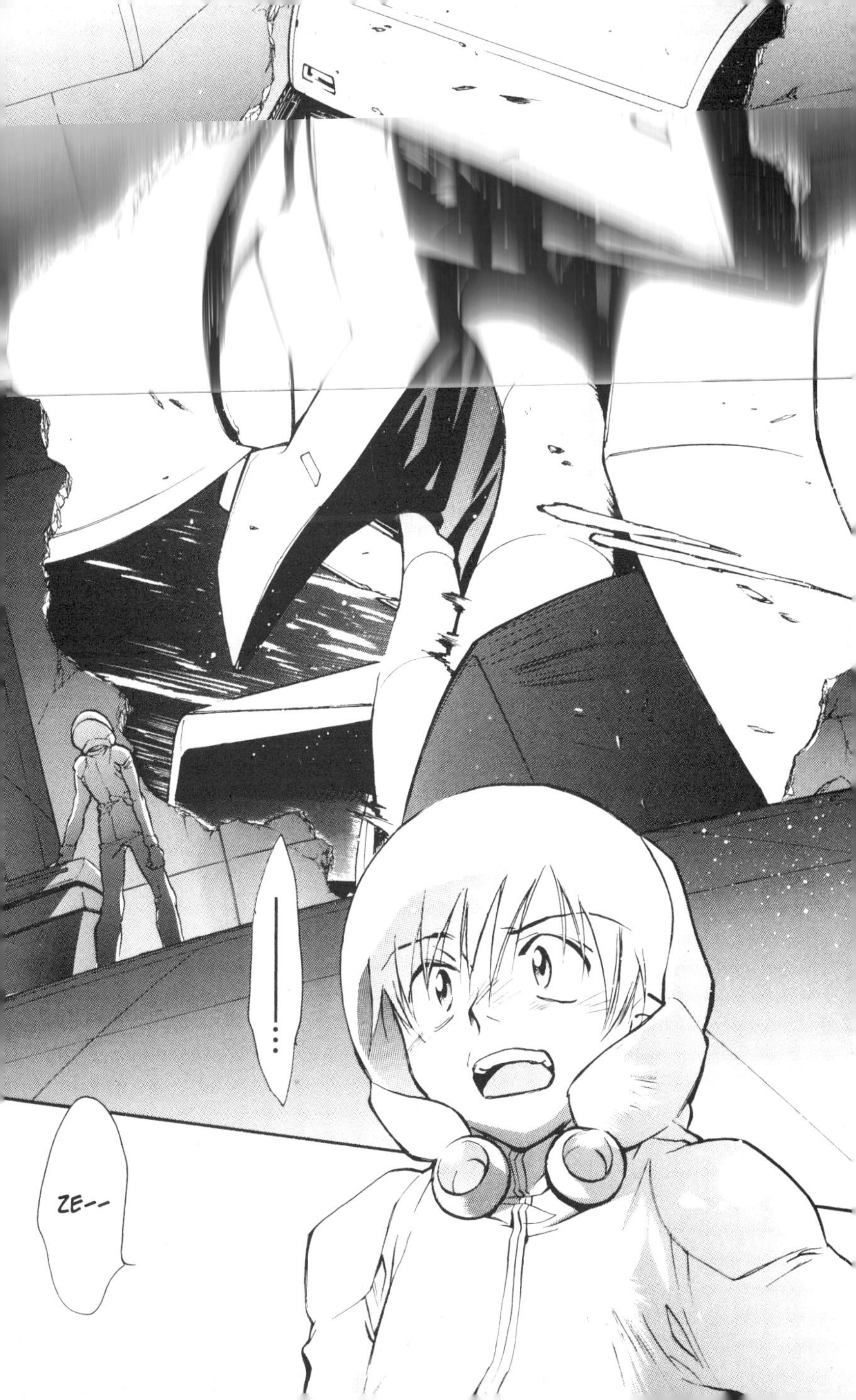
!......
ZE--

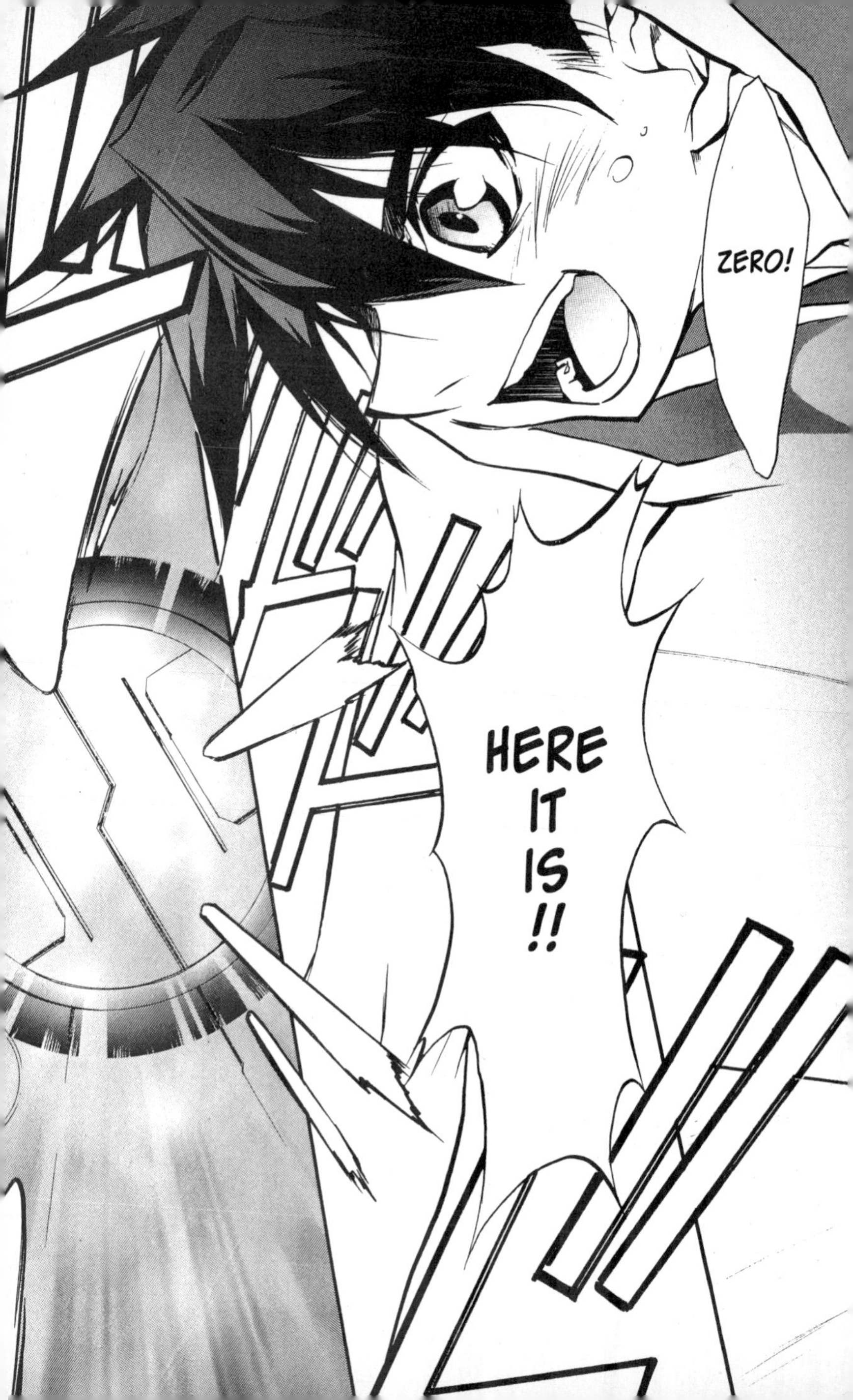
ZERO!
HERE IT IS!!

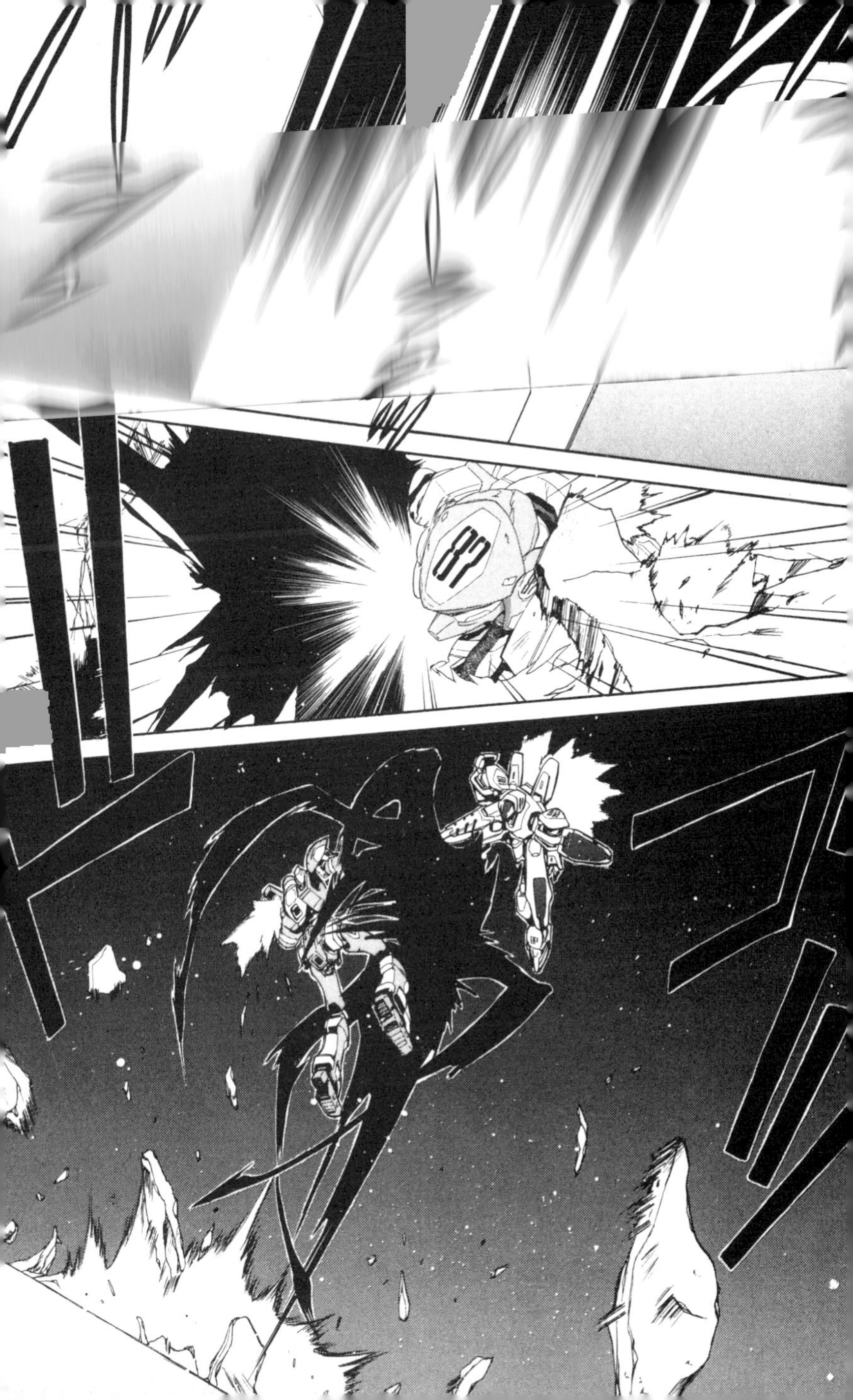

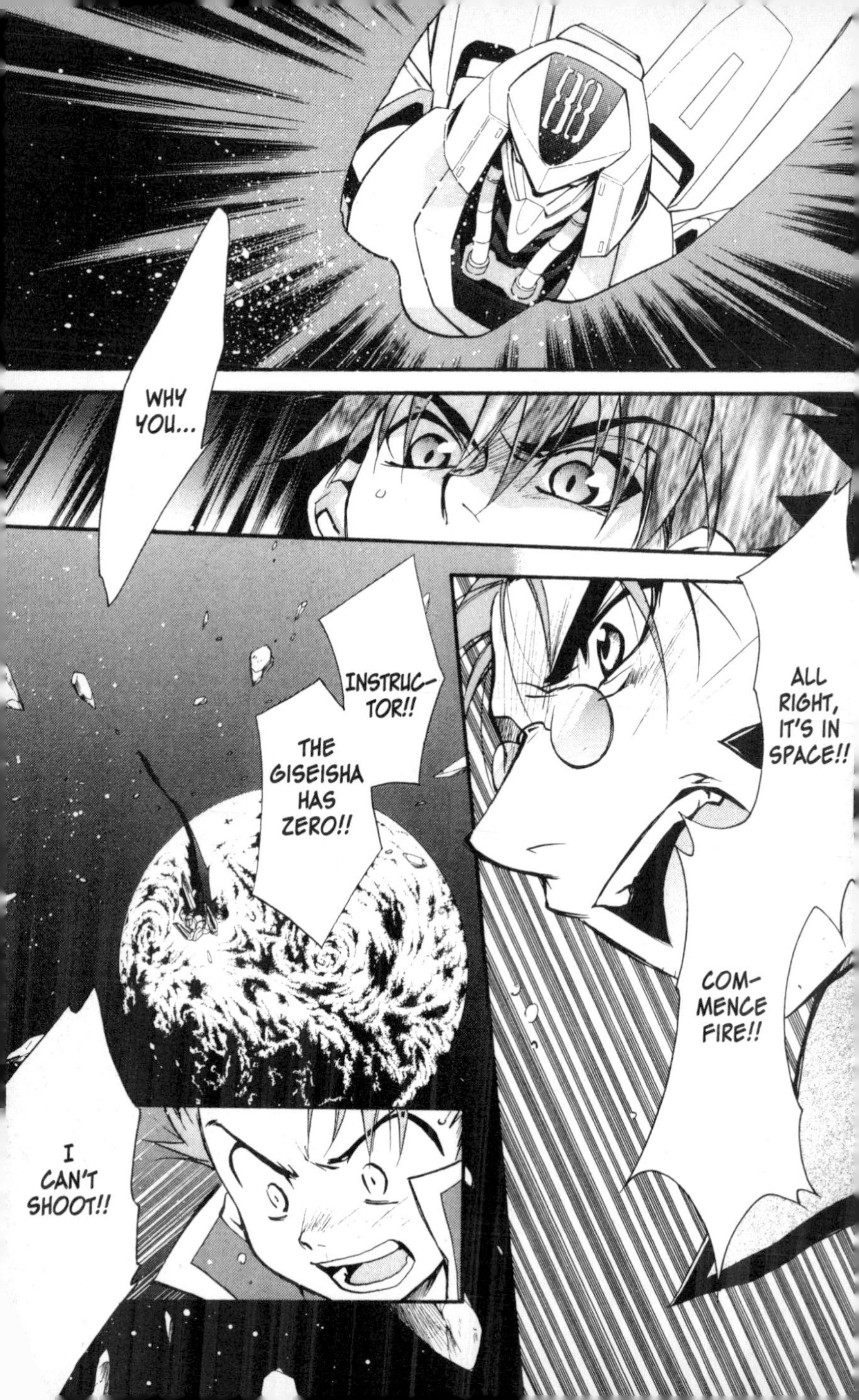
WHY YOU...
ALL RIGHT, IT'S IN SPACE!!
COM-MENCE FIRE!!
INSTRUC-TOR!!
THE GISEISHA HAS ZERO!!
I CAN'T SHOOT!!

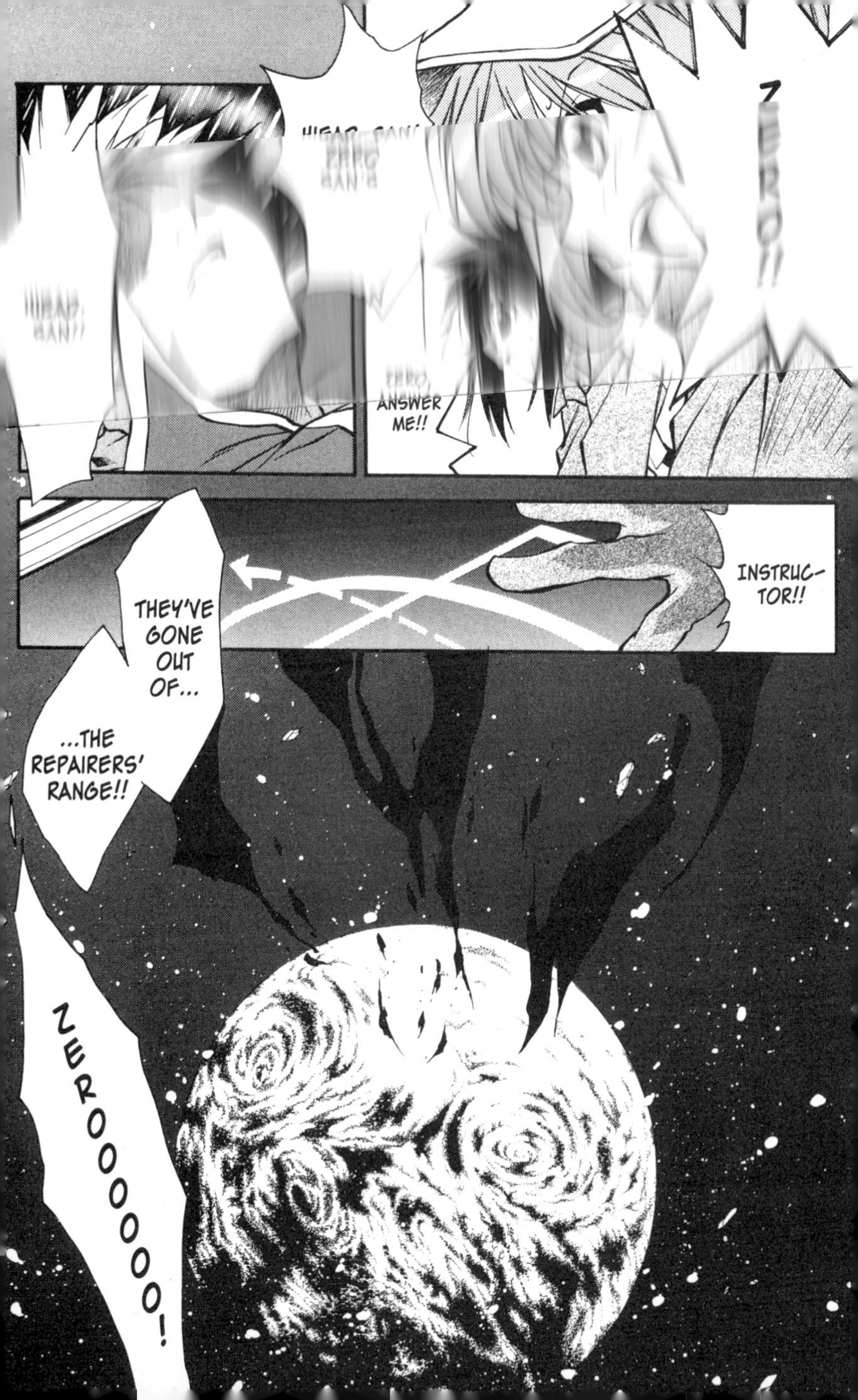
ANSWER ME!!
INSTRUC-TOR!!
THEY'VE GONE OUT OF...
...THE REPAIRERS' RANGE!!
ZEROOOOOOO!

MYTH 25 I'LL REMEMBER FOREVER

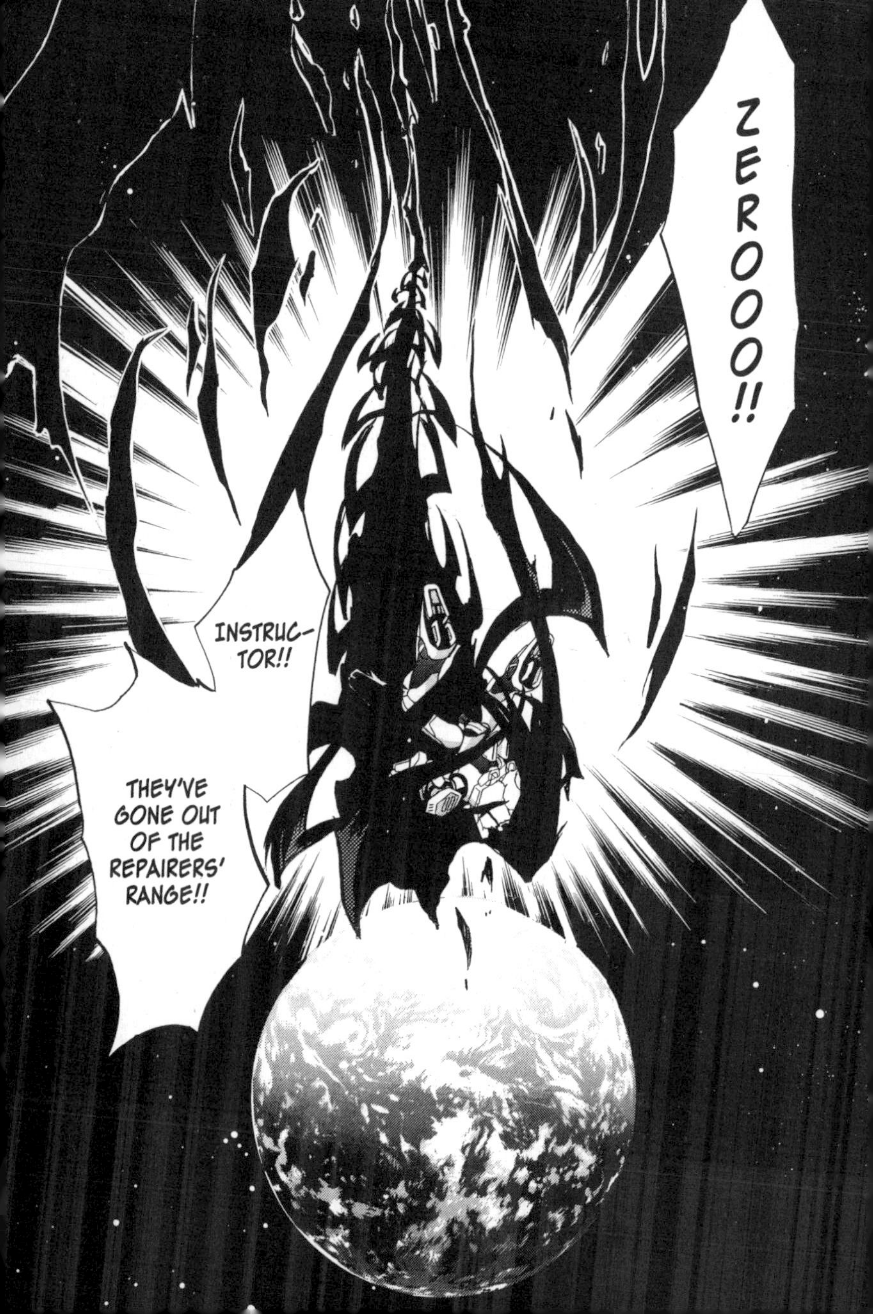
ZEROOOO!!
INSTRUC-TOR!!
THEY'VE GONE OUT OF THE REPAIRERS' RANGE!!

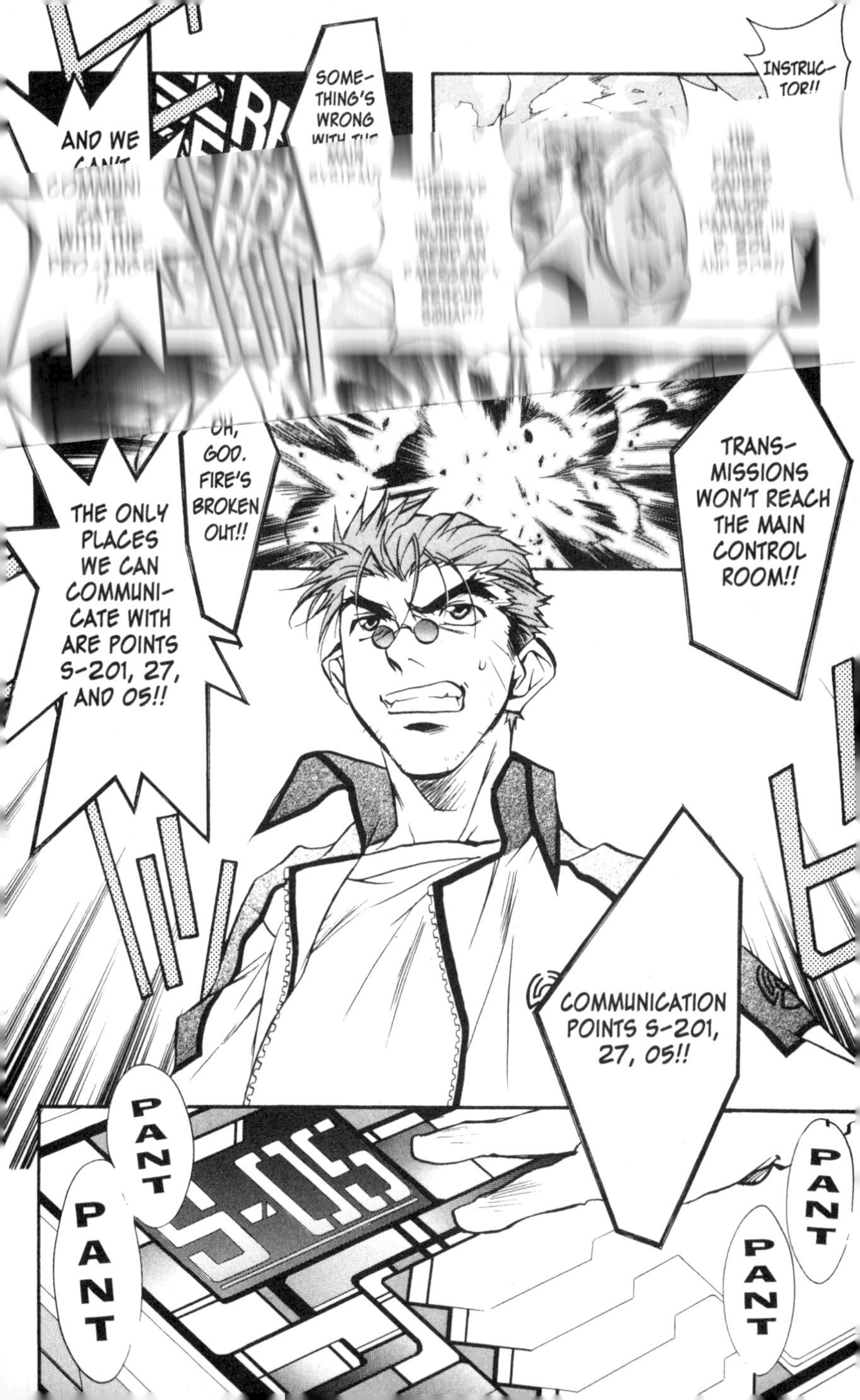
INSTRUCTOR!!
SOMETHING'S WRONG
AND WE
TRANSMISSIONS WON'T REACH THE MAIN CONTROL ROOM!!
OH, GOD. FIRE'S BROKEN OUT!!
THE ONLY PLACES WE CAN COMMUNICATE WITH ARE POINTS S-201, 27, AND 05!!
COMMUNICATION POINTS S-201, 27, 05!!
PANT PANT
PANT PANT

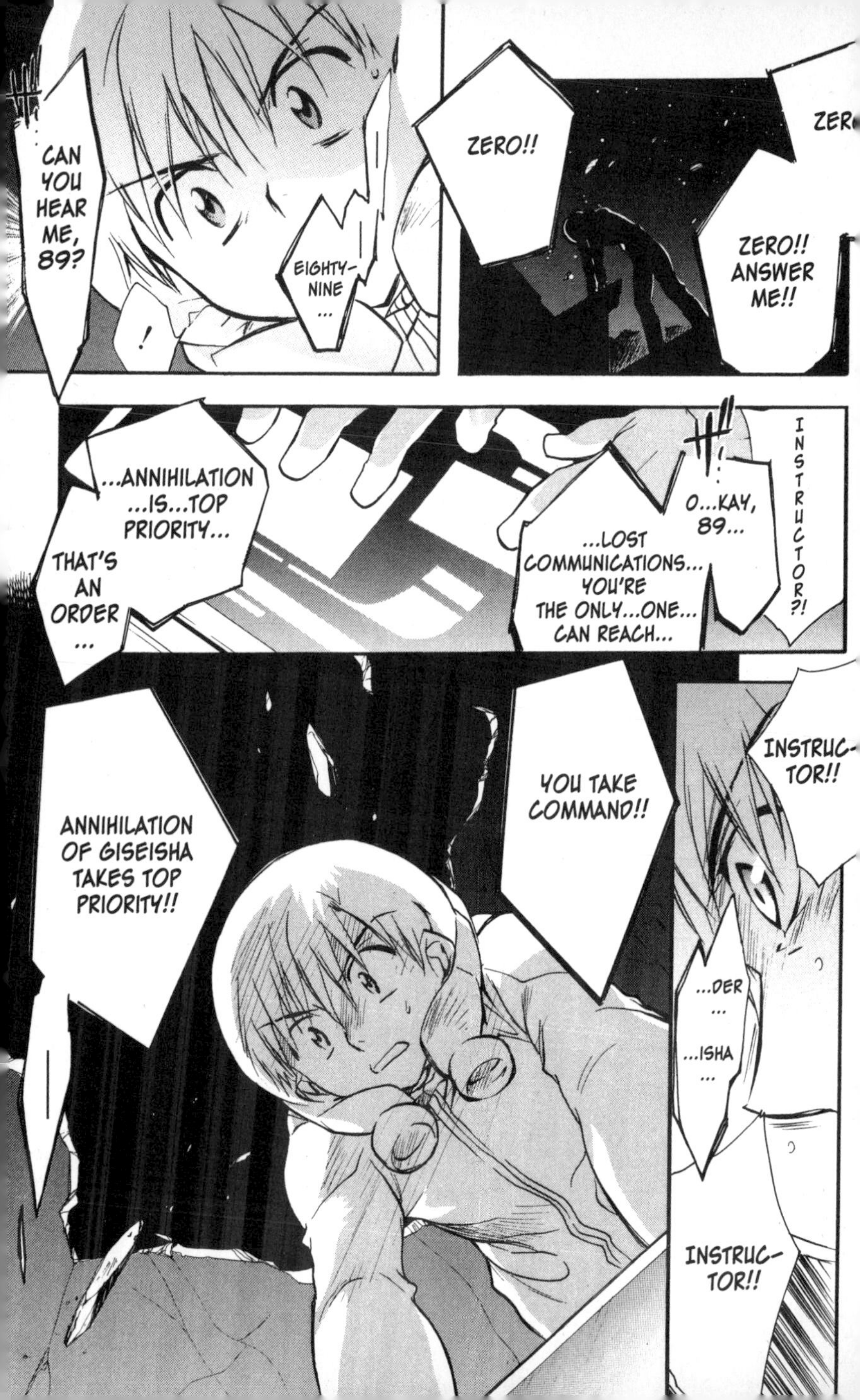
ZER
ZERO!! ANSWER ME!!
ZERO!!
EIGHTY-NINE ...
CAN YOU HEAR ME, 89?
!
INSTRUCTOR?!
!
O...KAY, 89...
...LOST COMMUNICATIONS... YOU'RE THE ONLY...ONE... CAN REACH...
...ANNIHILATION ...IS...TOP PRIORITY...
THAT'S AN ORDER ...
INSTRUCTOR!!
...DER ...
...ISHA ...
INSTRUCTOR!!
YOU TAKE COMMAND!!
ANNIHILATION OF GISEISHA TAKES TOP PRIORITY!!

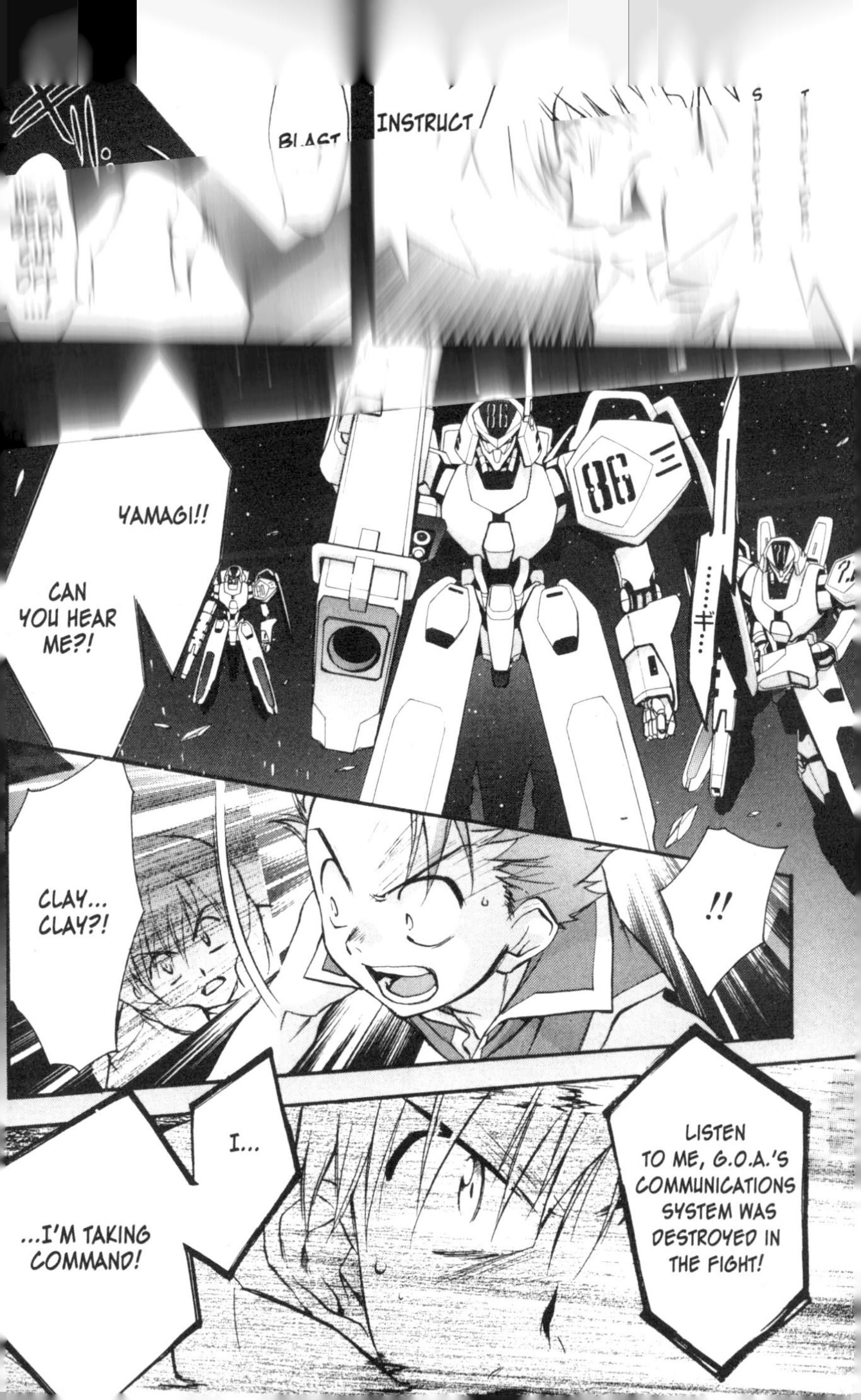
INSTRUCT
BLAST
YAMAGI!!
CAN YOU HEAR ME?!
!!
CLAY... CLAY?!
LISTEN TO ME, G.O.A.'S COMMUNICATIONS SYSTEM WAS DESTROYED IN THE FIGHT!
I...
...I'M TAKING COMMAND!

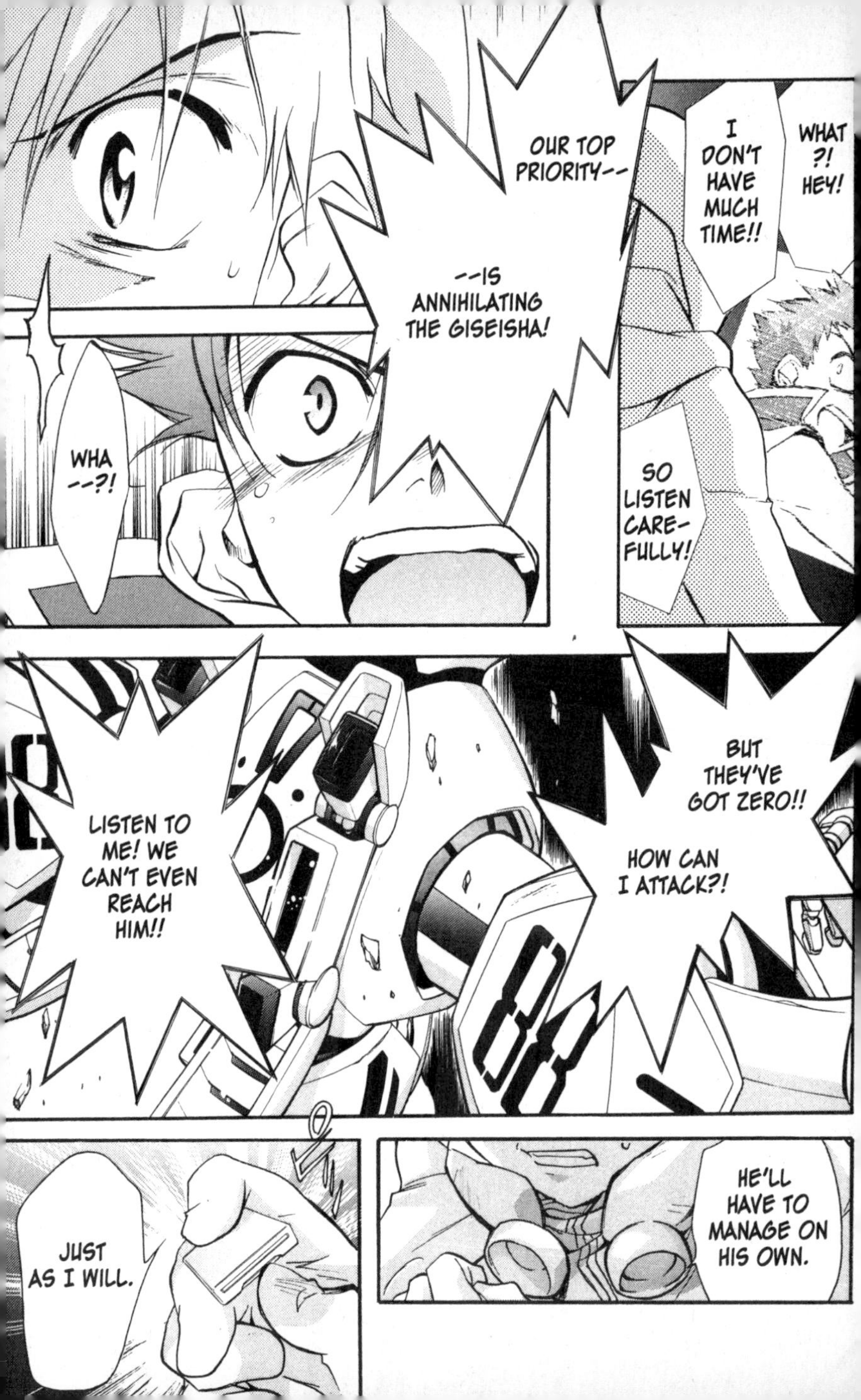
WHAT?! HEY!
I DON'T HAVE MUCH TIME!!
SO LISTEN CARE-FULLY!
OUR TOP PRIORITY--
--IS ANNIHILATING THE GISEISHA!
WHA--?!
BUT THEY'VE GOT ZERO!!
HOW CAN I ATTACK?!
LISTEN TO ME! WE CAN'T EVEN REACH HIM!!
HE'LL HAVE TO MANAGE ON HIS OWN.
JUST AS I WILL.

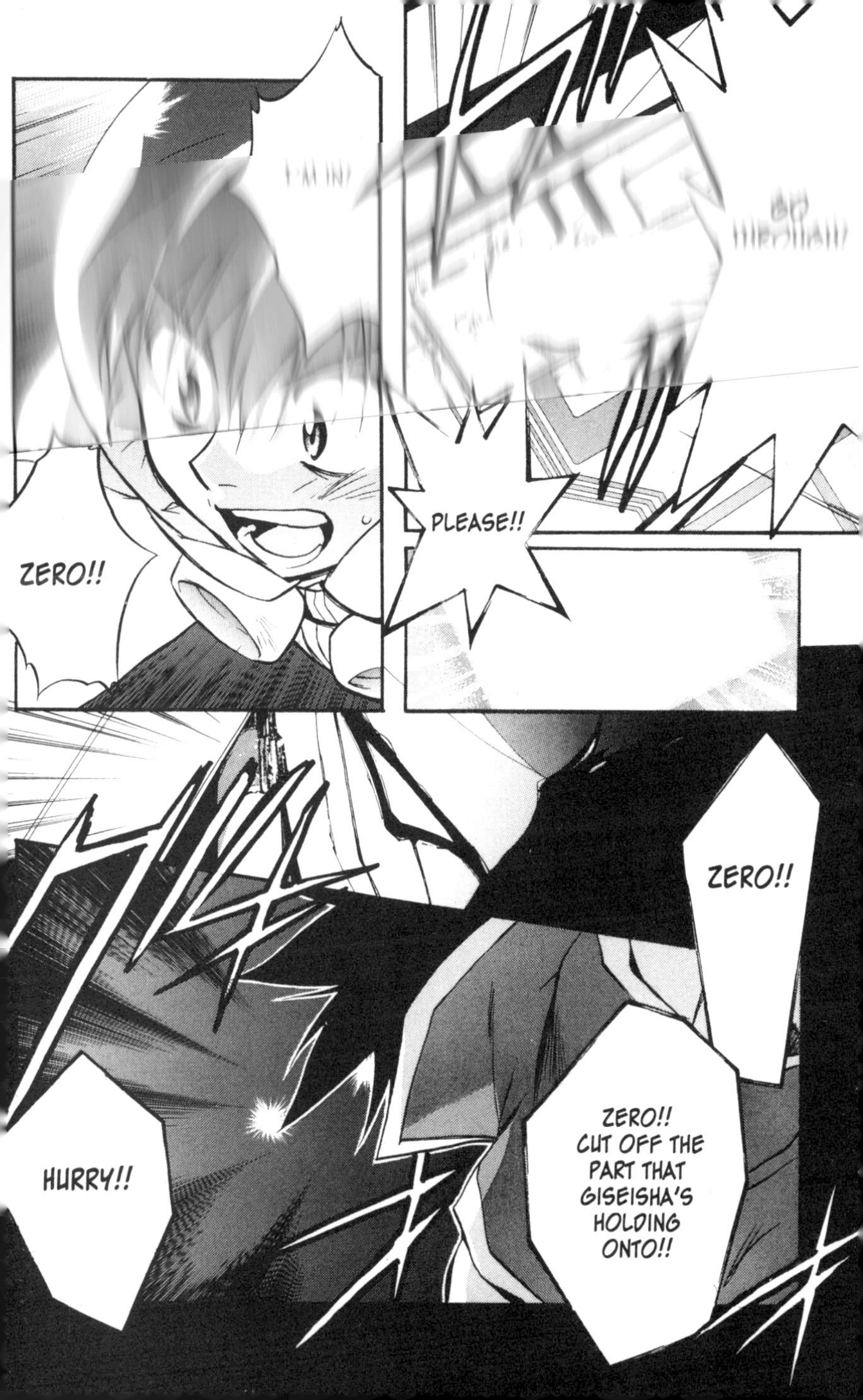
PLEASE!!
ZERO!!
ZERO!!
ZERO!! CUT OFF THE PART THAT GISEISHA'S HOLDING ONTO!!
HURRY!!

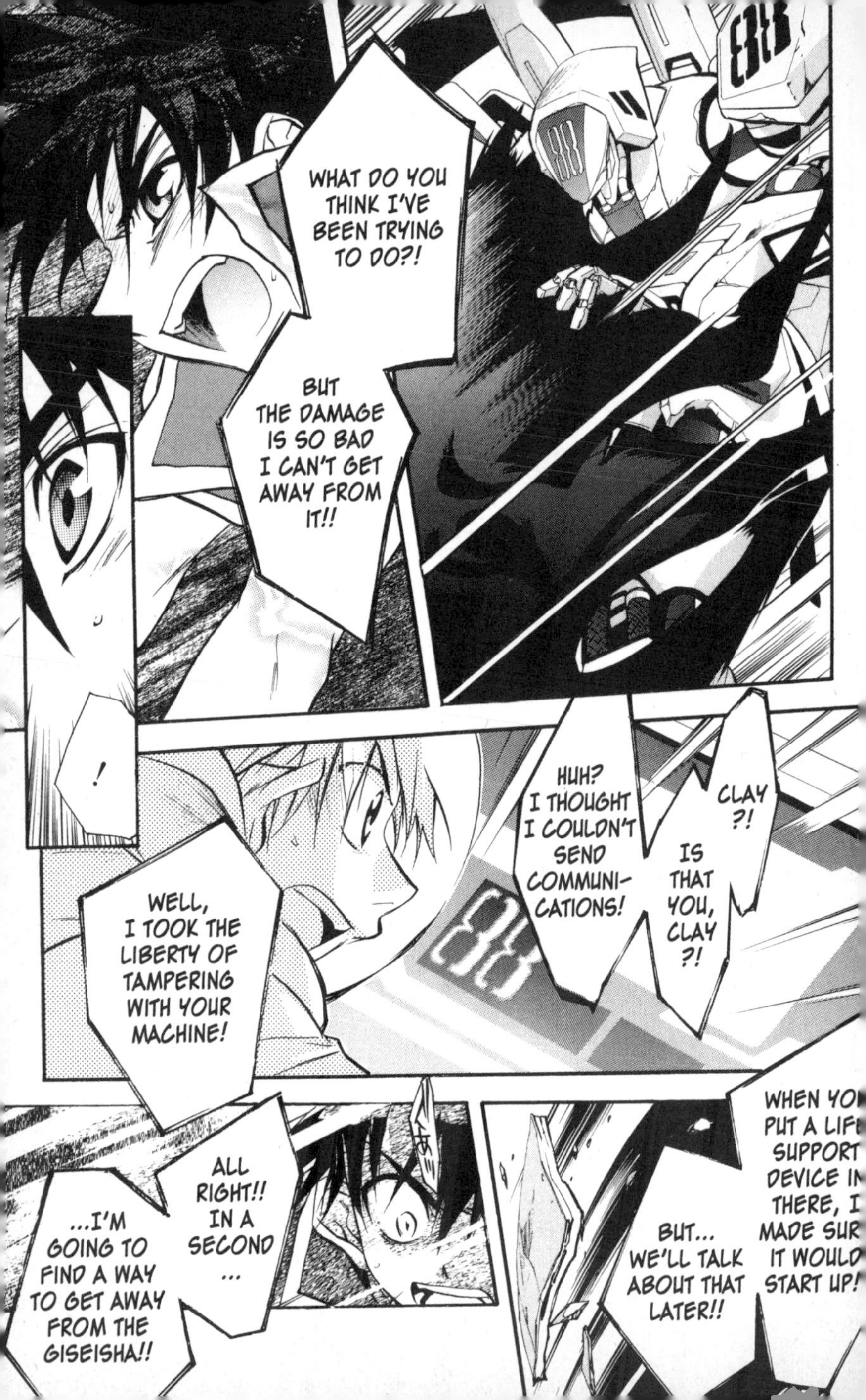
WHAT DO YOU THINK I'VE BEEN TRYING TO DO?!
BUT THE DAMAGE IS SO BAD I CAN'T GET AWAY FROM IT!!
!
CLAY ?!
IS THAT YOU, CLAY ?!
HUH? I THOUGHT I COULDN'T SEND COMMUNI-CATIONS!
WELL, I TOOK THE LIBERTY OF TAMPERING WITH YOUR MACHINE!
WHEN YO PUT A LIF SUPPORT DEVICE IN THERE, I MADE SUR IT WOUL START UP!
BUT... WE'LL TALK ABOUT THAT LATER!!
ALL RIGHT!! IN A SECOND ...
...I'M GOING TO FIND A WAY TO GET AWAY FROM THE GISEISHA!!

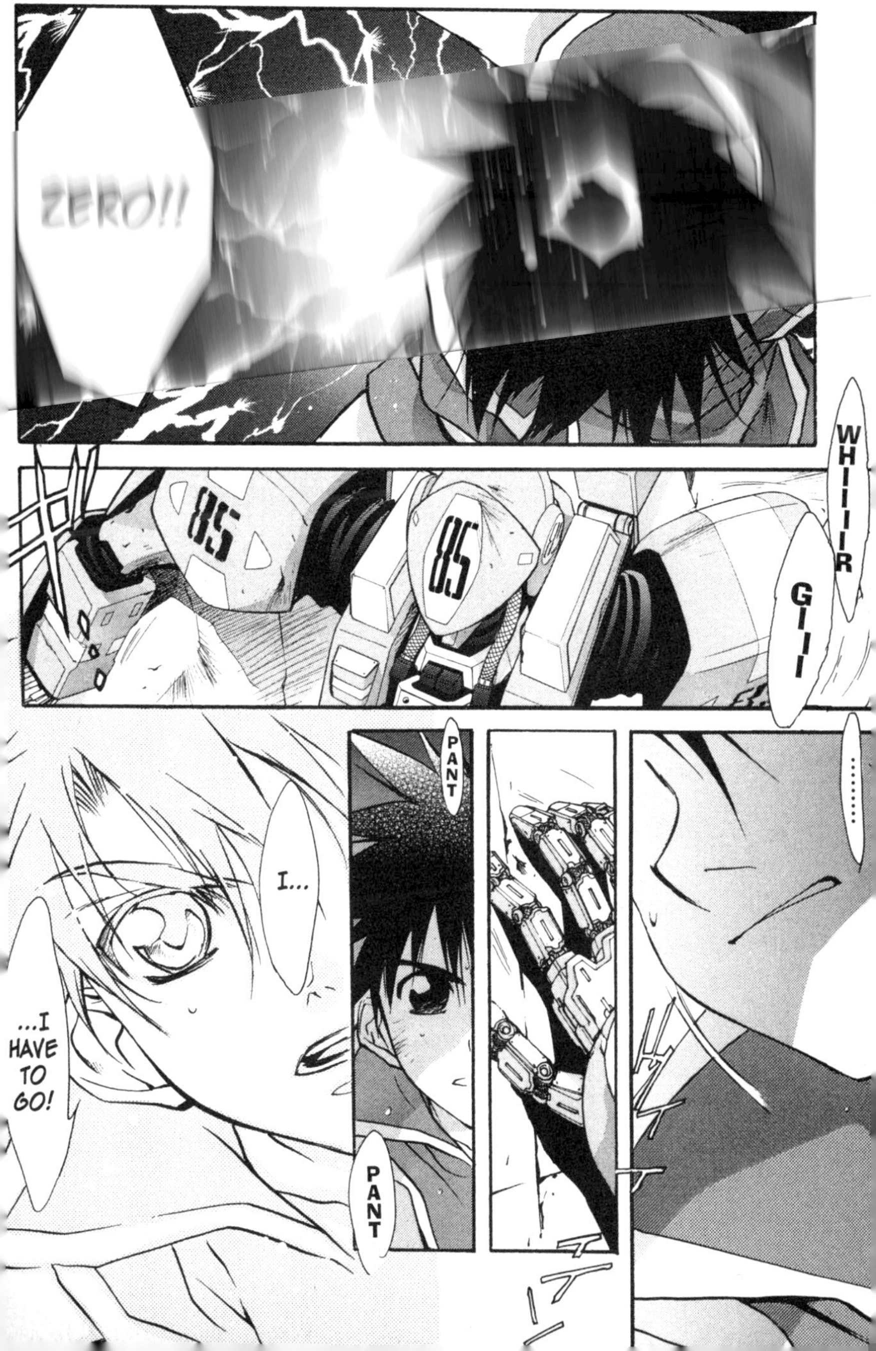
ZERO!!
WHIIIIIR
GIIII
....
PANT
PANT
I...
...I HAVE TO GO!

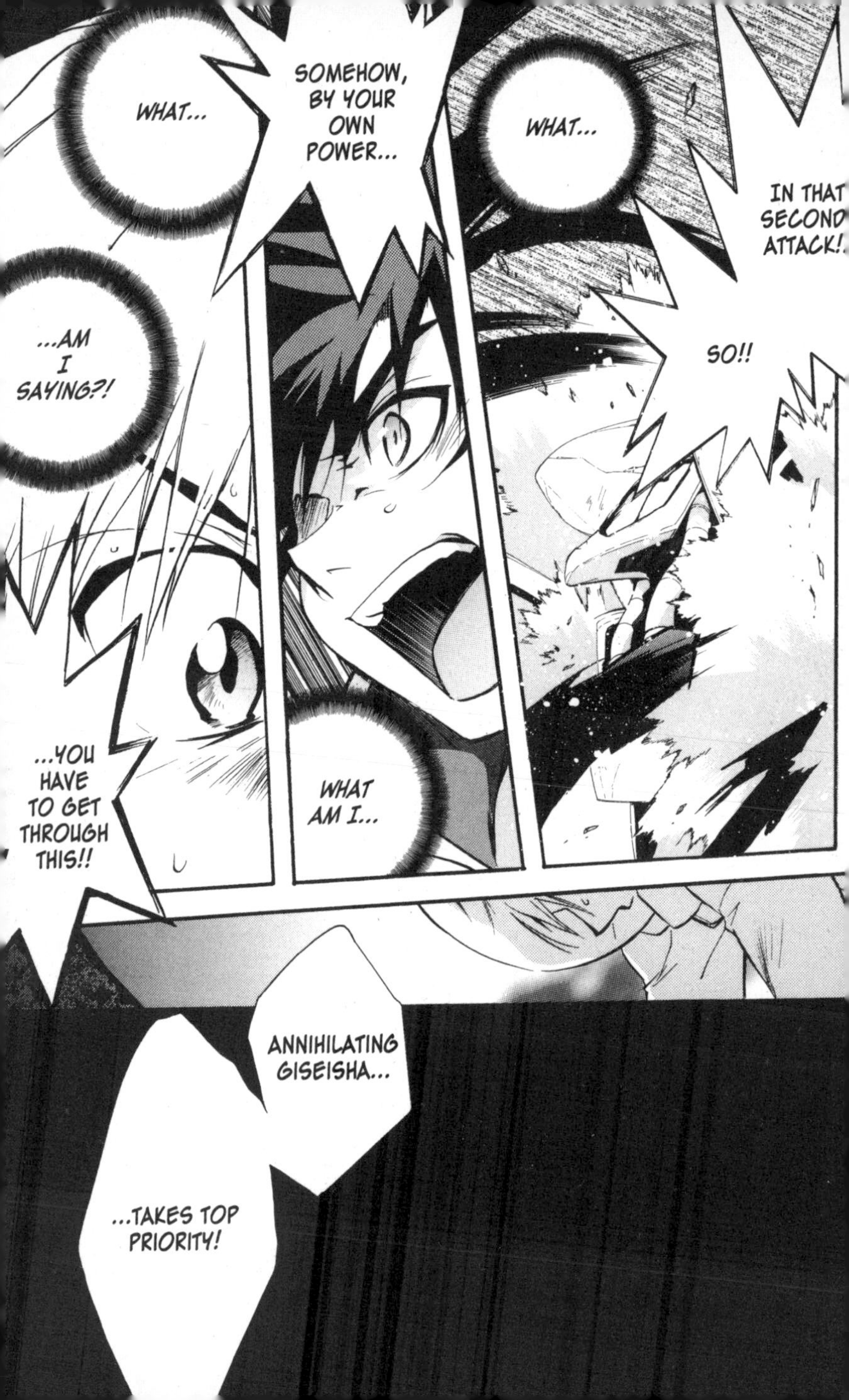
IN THAT SECOND ATTACK!
WHAT...
SO!!
SOMEHOW, BY YOUR OWN POWER...
WHAT...
WHAT AM I...
...AM I SAYING?!
...YOU HAVE TO GET THROUGH THIS!!
ANNIHILATING GISEISHA...
...TAKES TOP PRIORITY!

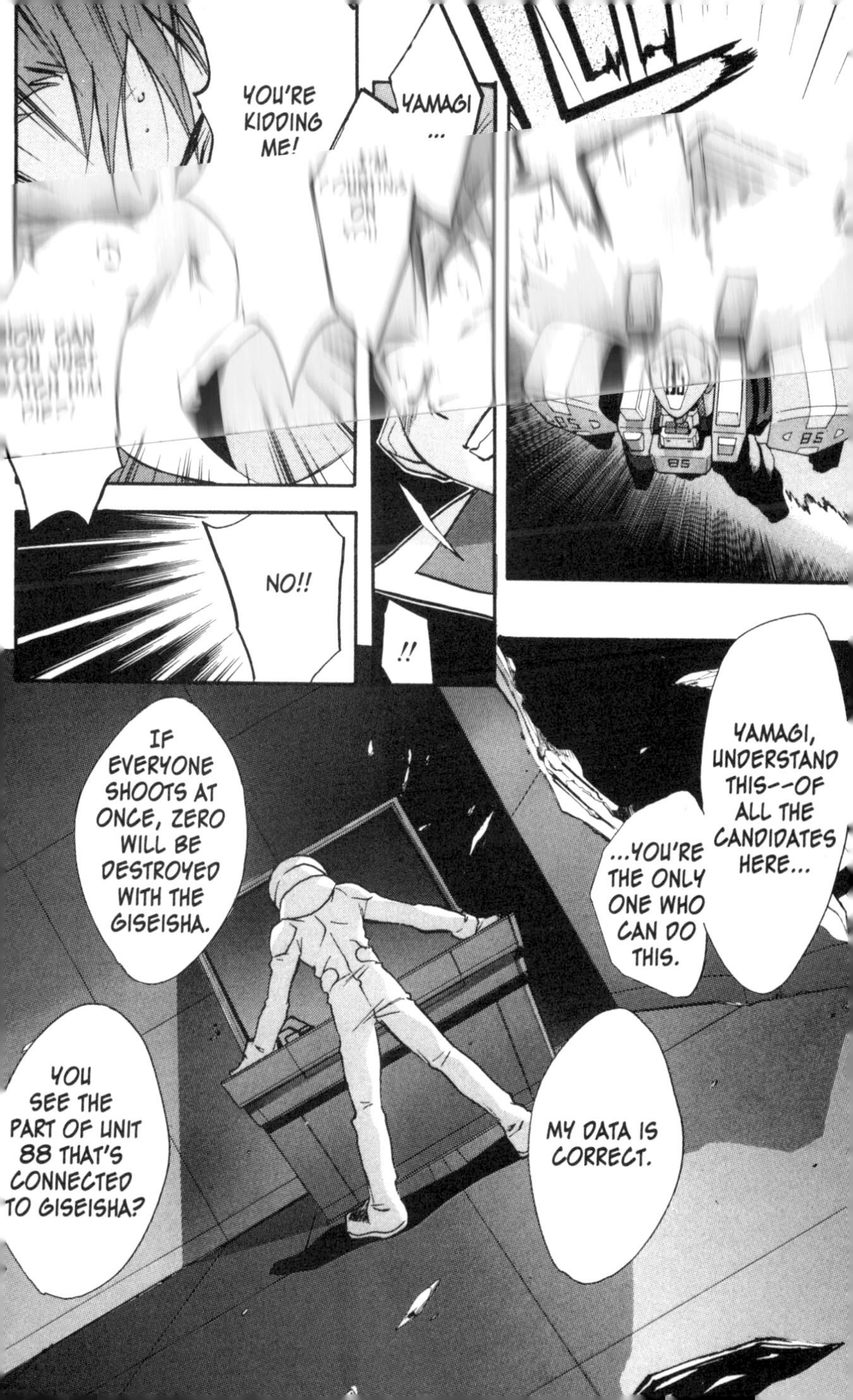
YAMAGI ...
YOU'RE KIDDING ME!
!!
NO!!
YAMAGI, UNDERSTAND THIS--OF ALL THE CANDIDATES HERE...
...YOU'RE THE ONLY ONE WHO CAN DO THIS.
IF EVERYONE SHOOTS AT ONCE, ZERO WILL BE DESTROYED WITH THE GISEISHA.
MY DATA IS CORRECT.
YOU SEE THE PART OF UNIT 88 THAT'S CONNECTED TO GISEISHA?

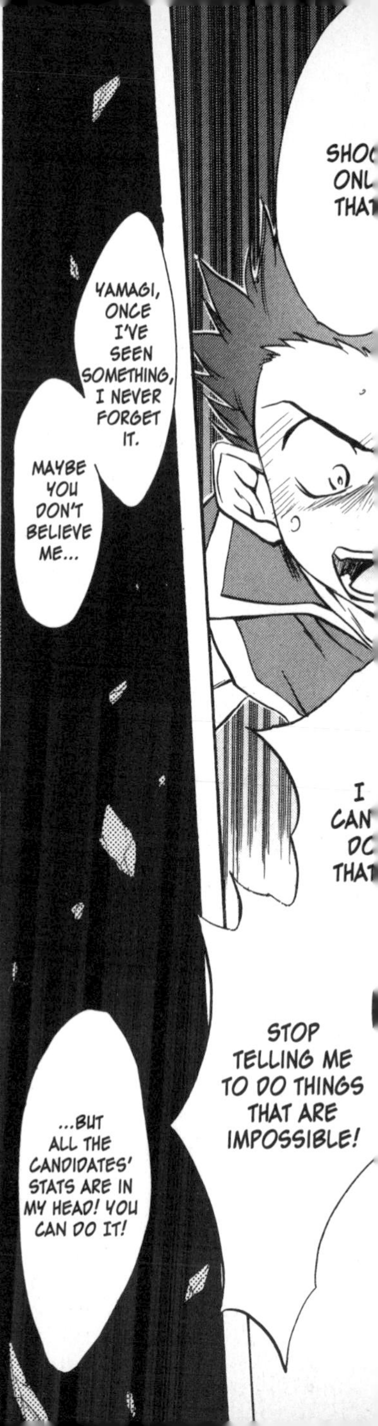
YAMAGI, ONCE I'VE SEEN SOMETHING, I NEVER FORGET IT.
MAYBE YOU DON'T BELIEVE ME...
STOP TELLING ME TO DO THINGS THAT ARE IMPOSSIBLE!
...BUT ALL THE CANDIDATES' STATS ARE IN MY HEAD! YOU CAN DO IT!
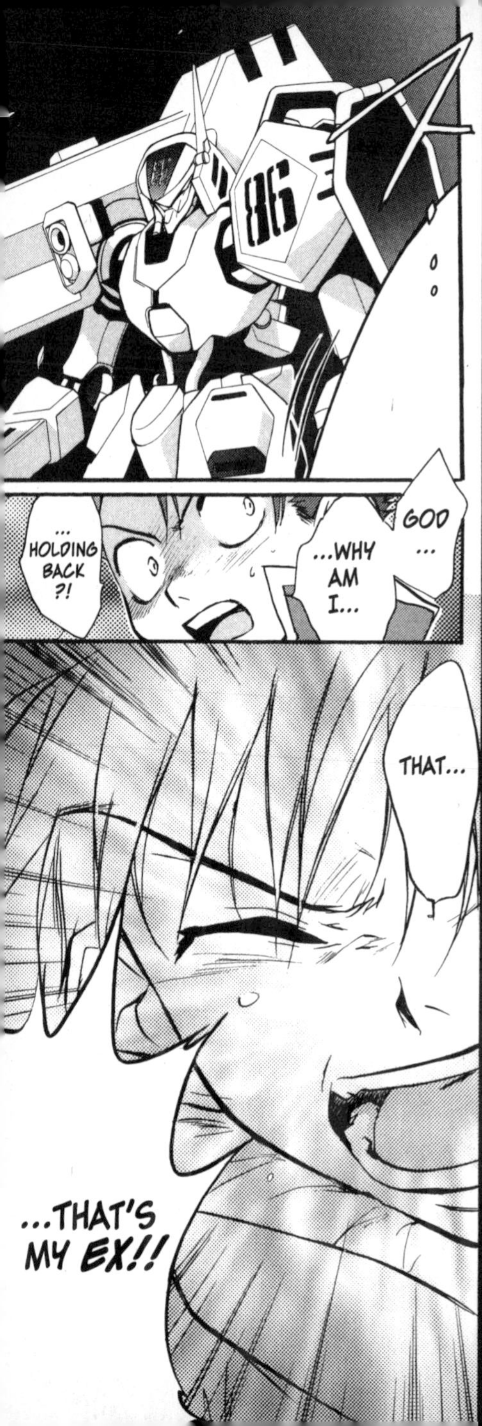
GOD ...
...WHY AM I...
... HOLDING BACK ?!
THAT...
...THAT'S MY *EX*!!

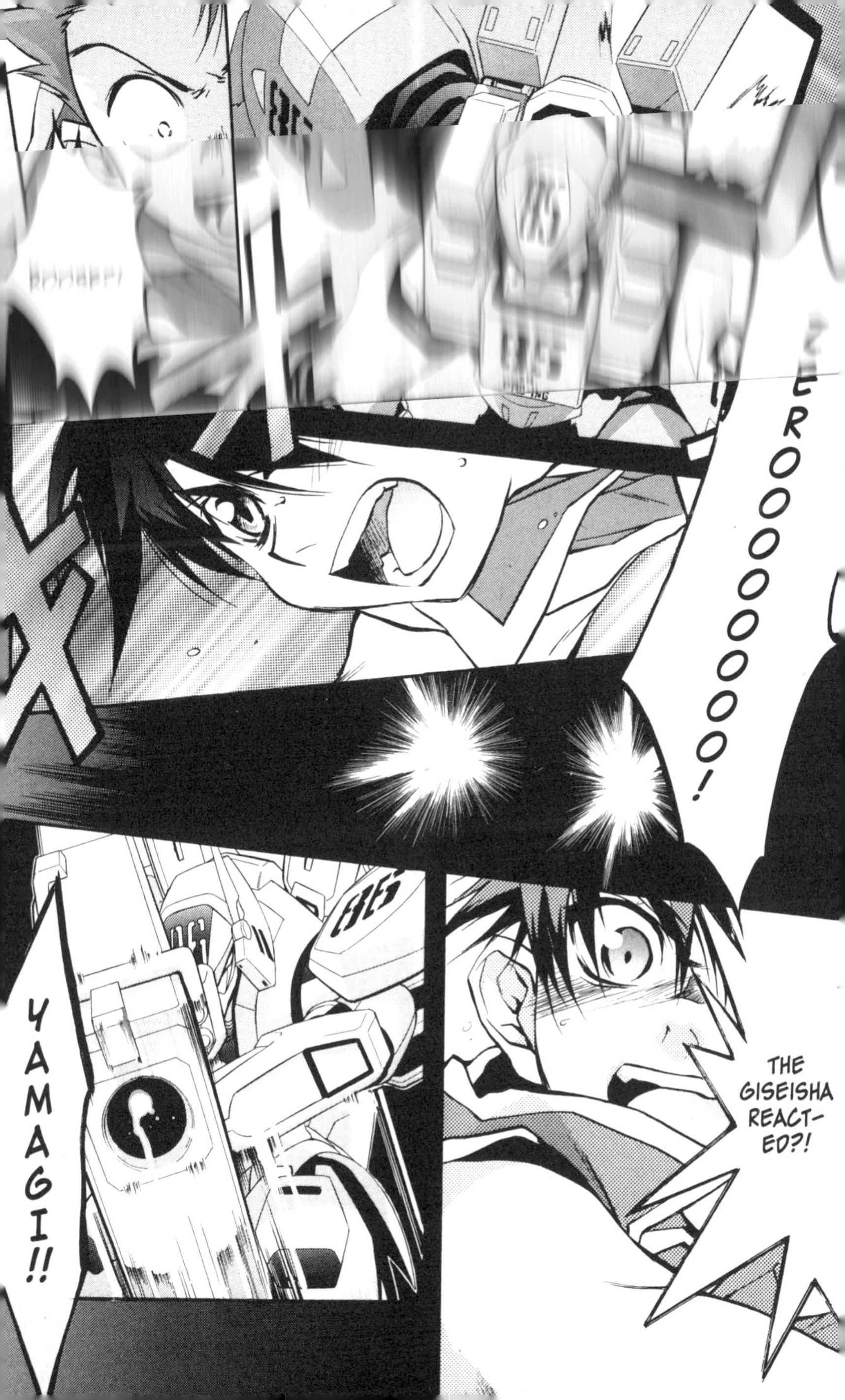

EROOOOOOOOOOO!
THE GISEISHA REACT-ED?!
YAMAGI!!

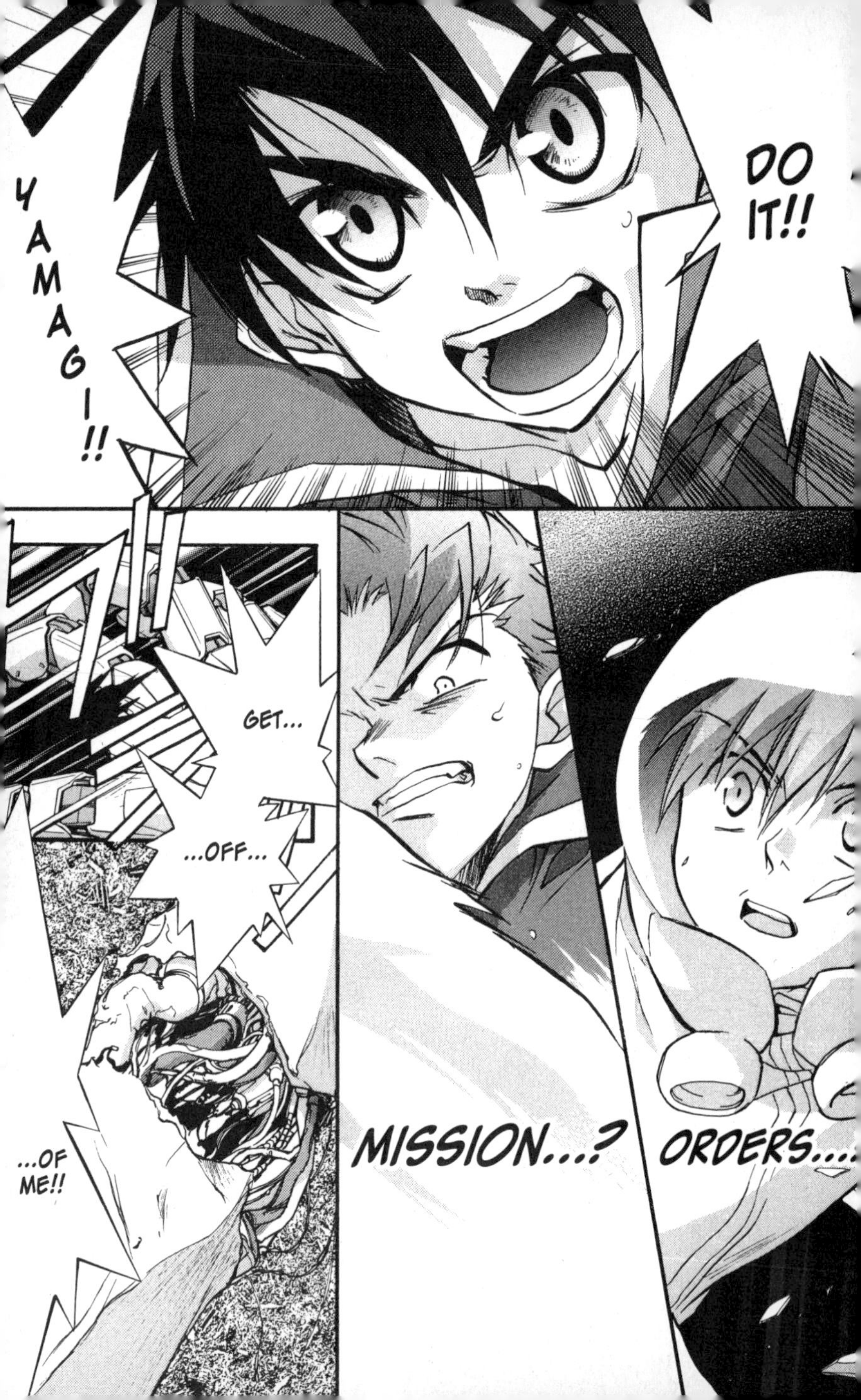
DO IT!!
YAMAGI!!
ORDERS....
MISSION...?
GET...
...OFF...
...OF ME!!

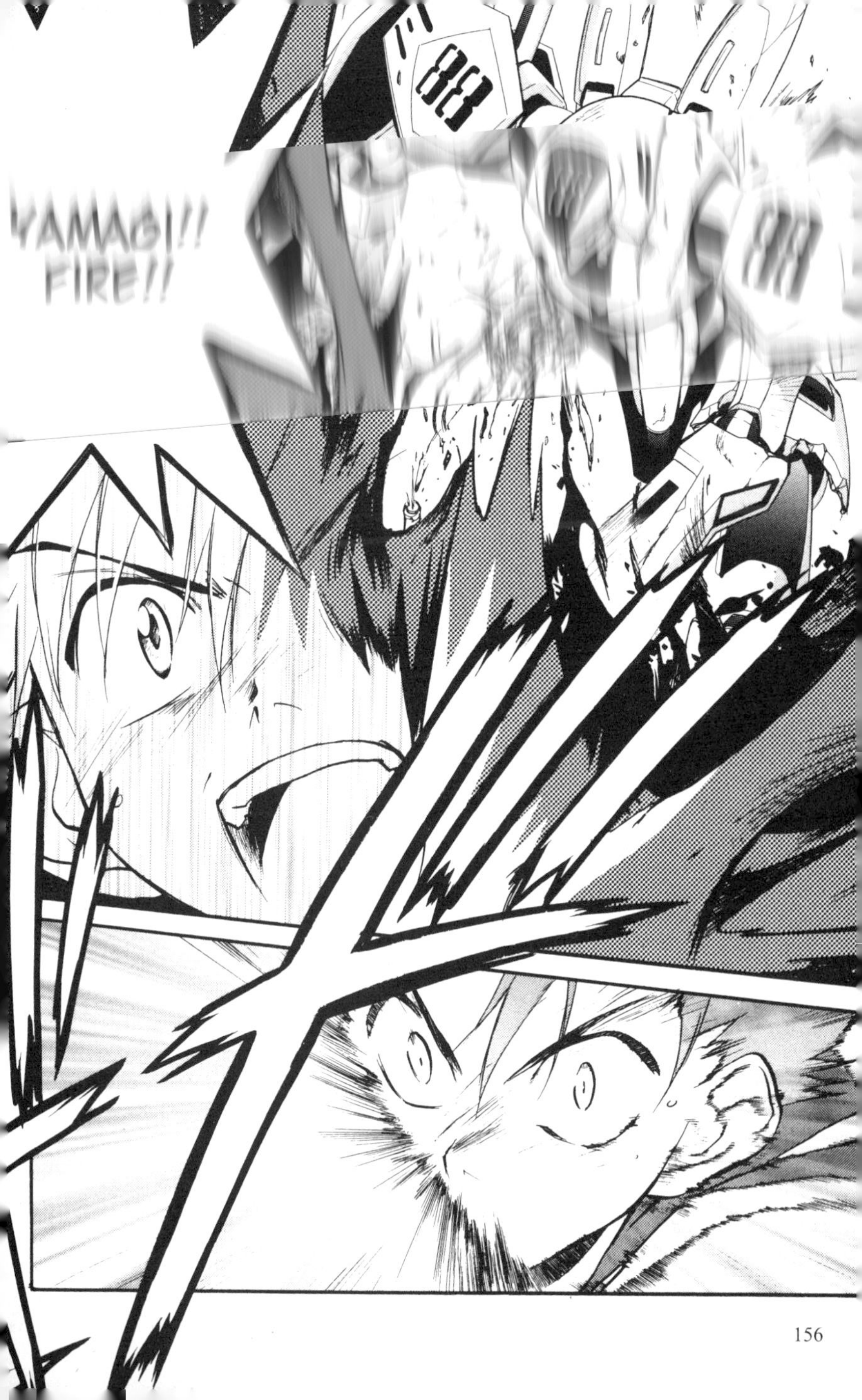
YAMAGI!!
FIRE!!

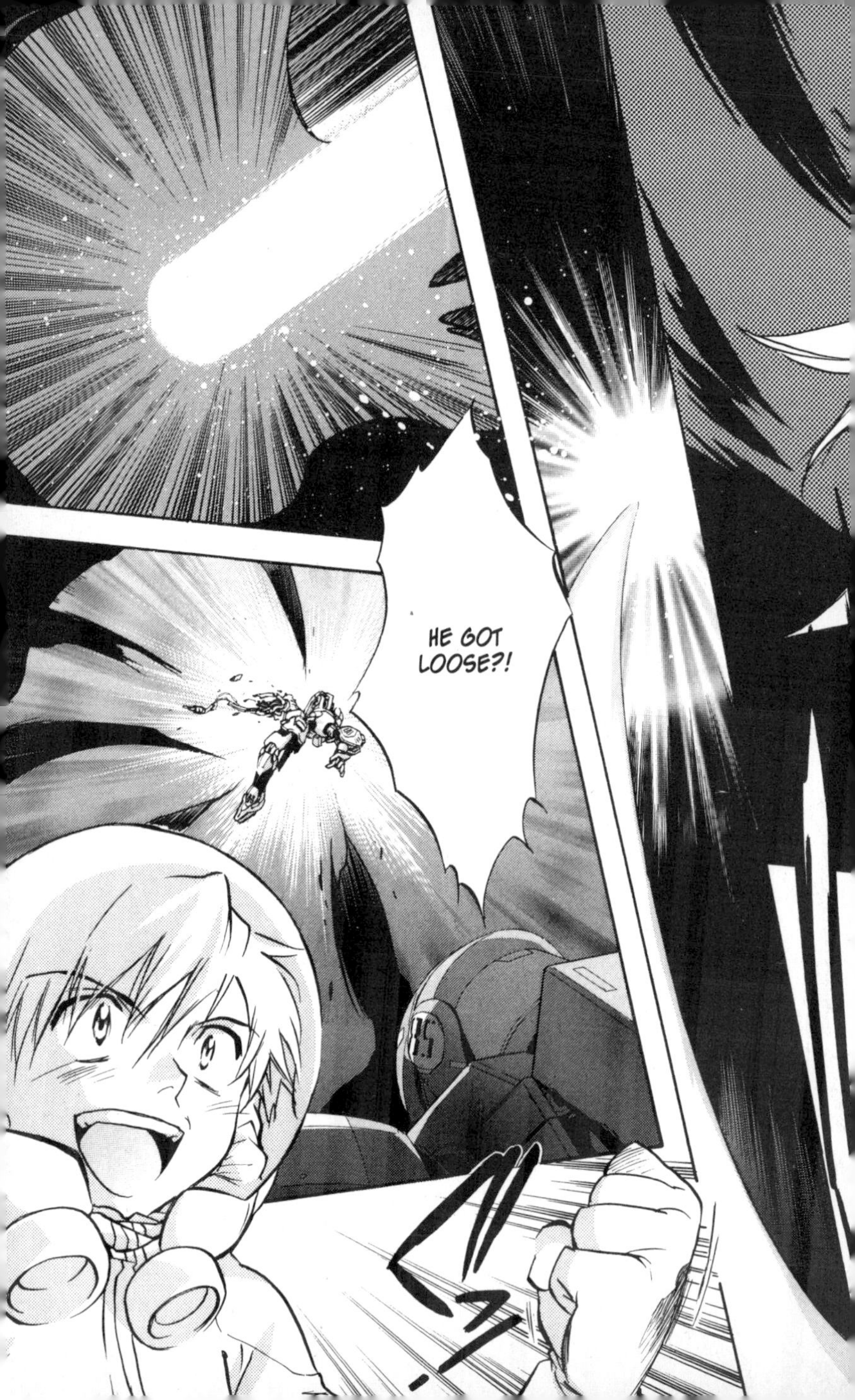
HE GOT LOOSE?!

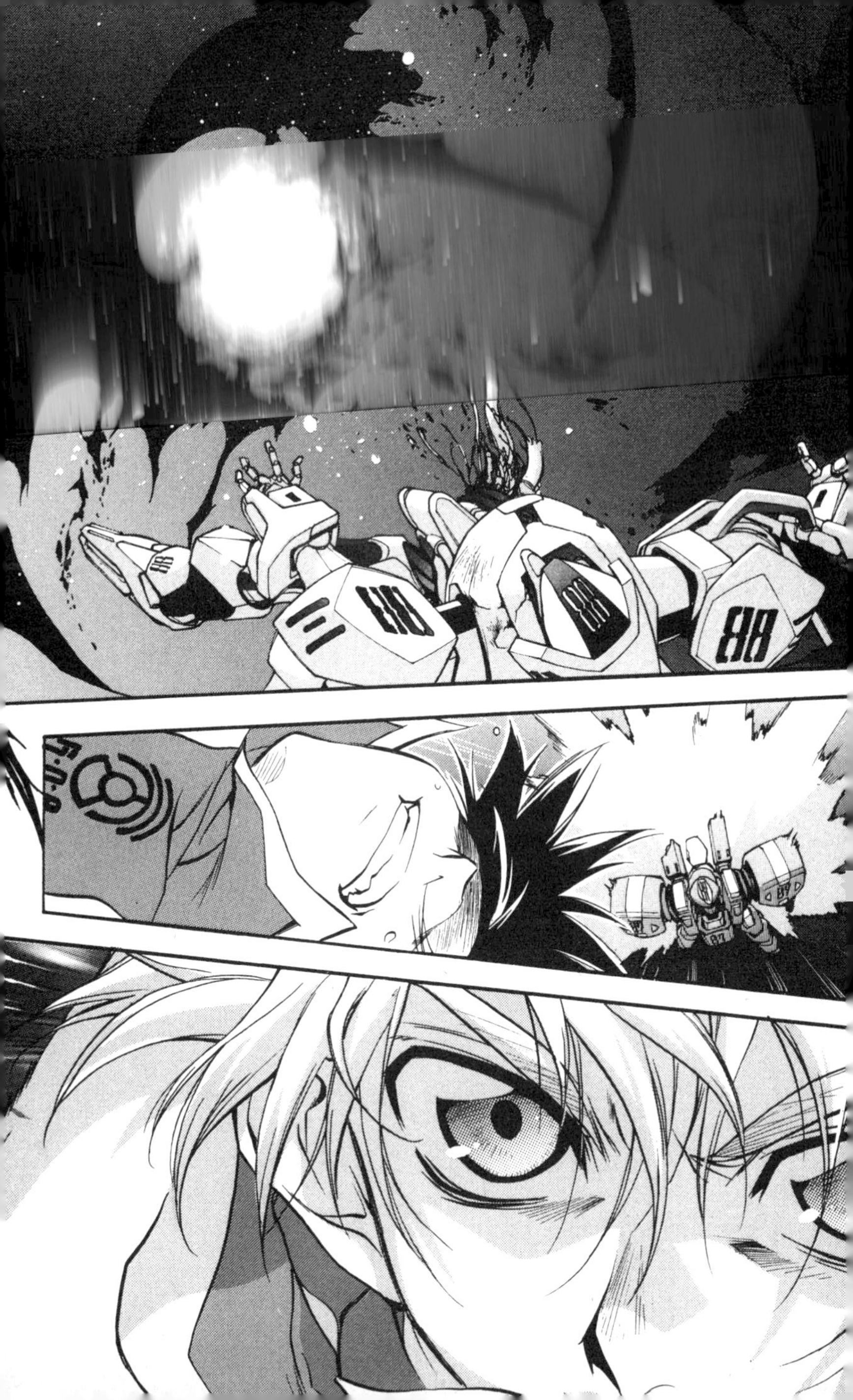

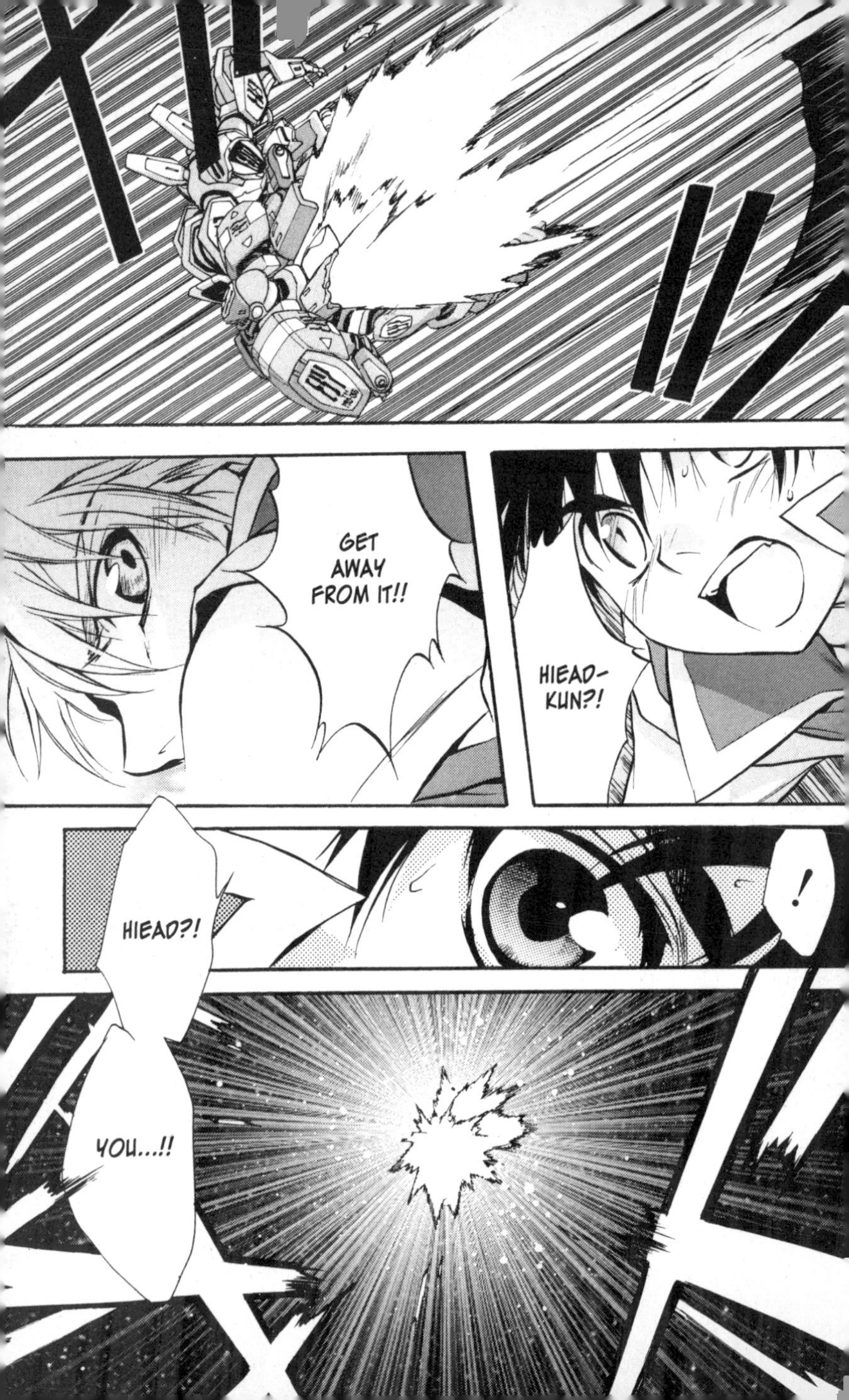
HIEAD-KUN?!
GET AWAY FROM IT!!
!
HIEAD?!
YOU...!!

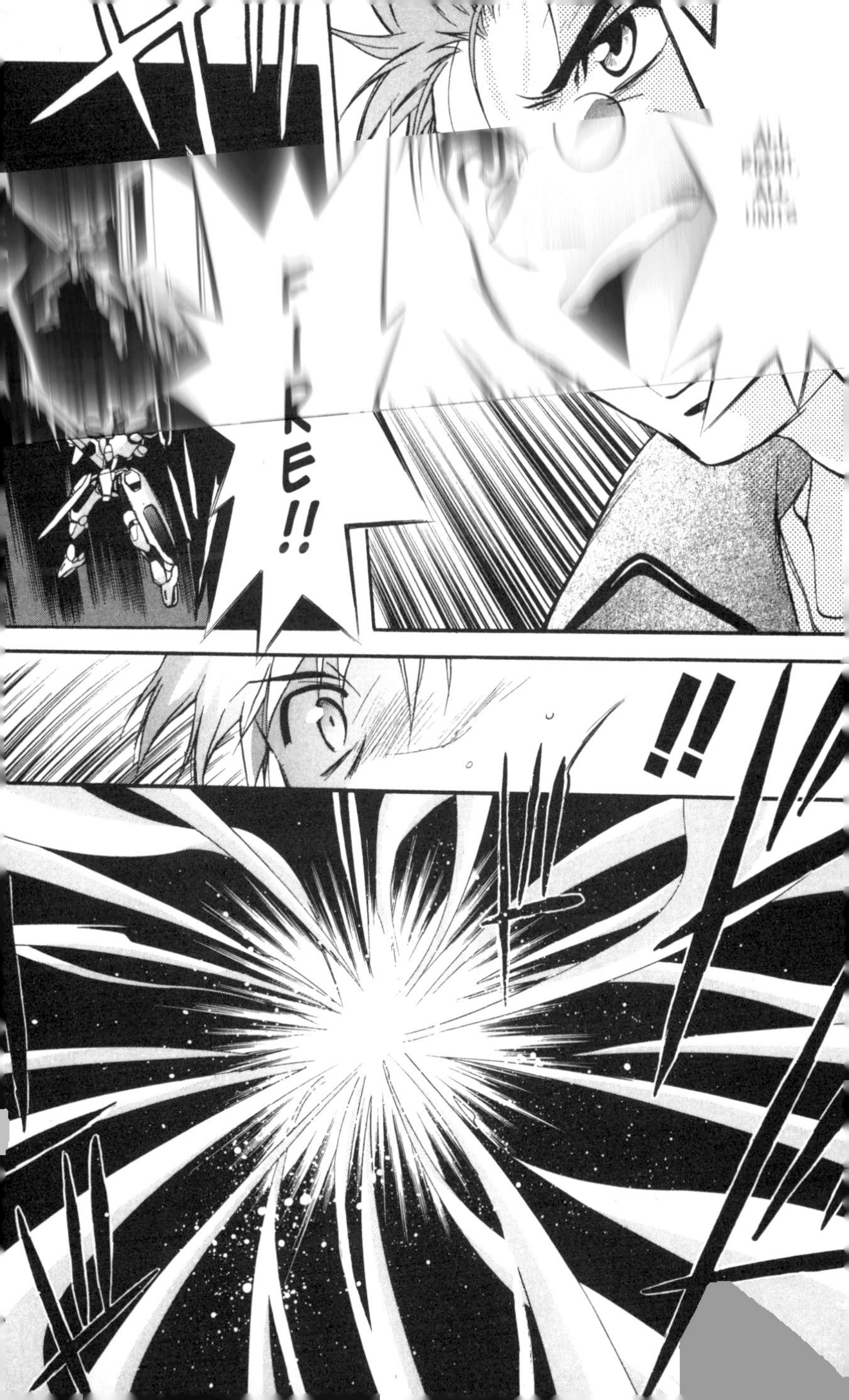
FIRE!!
!!

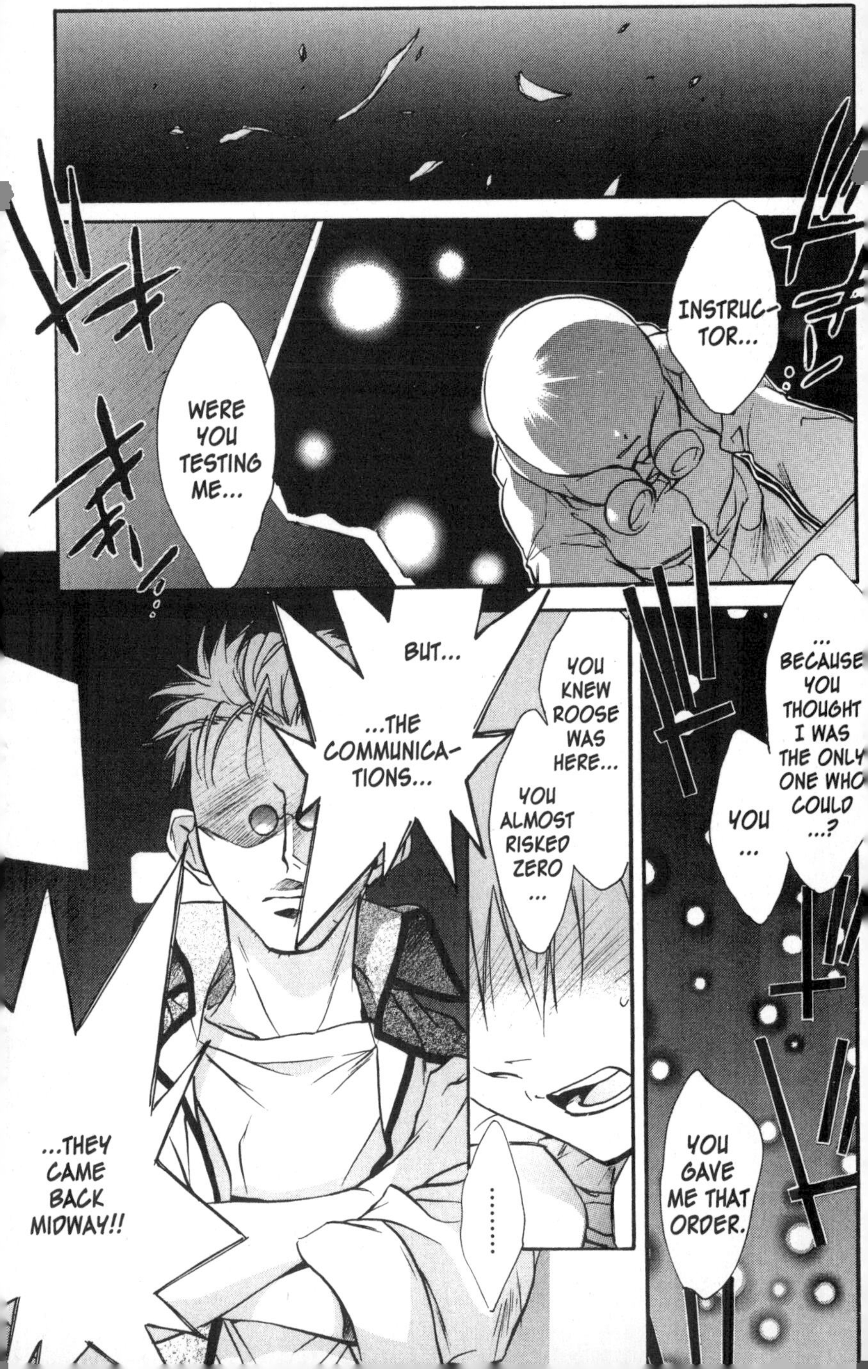
INSTRUC-TOR...
WERE YOU TESTING ME...
... BECAUSE YOU THOUGHT I WAS THE ONLY ONE WHO COULD ...?
YOU ...
YOU GAVE ME THAT ORDER.
YOU KNEW ROOSE WAS HERE...
YOU ALMOST RISKED ZERO ...
....
BUT...
...THE COMMUNICA-TIONS...
...THEY CAME BACK MIDWAY!!

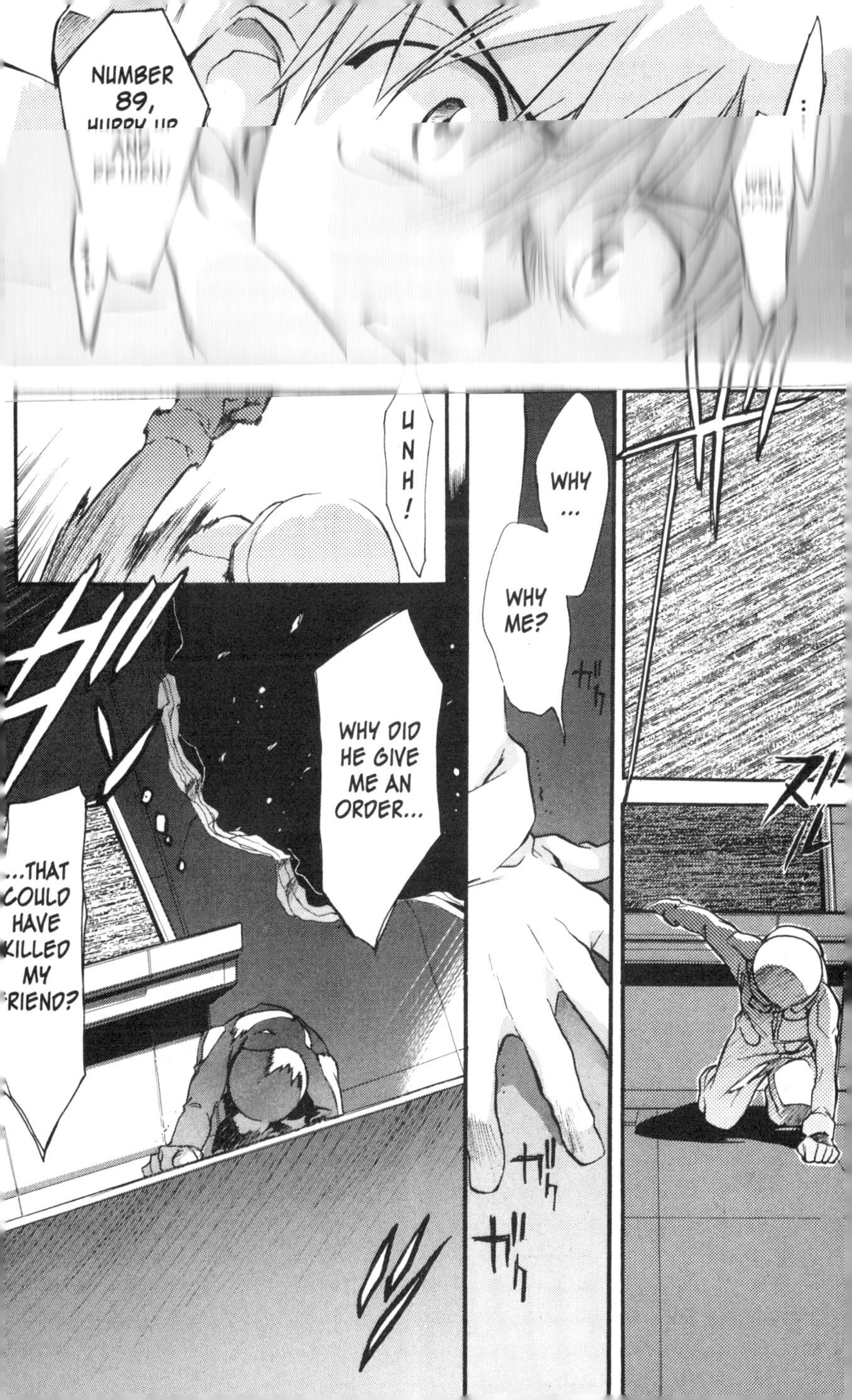
...
NUMBER 89,
UNH!
WHY ...
WHY ME?
WHY DID HE GIVE ME AN ORDER...
...THAT COULD HAVE KILLED MY FRIEND?

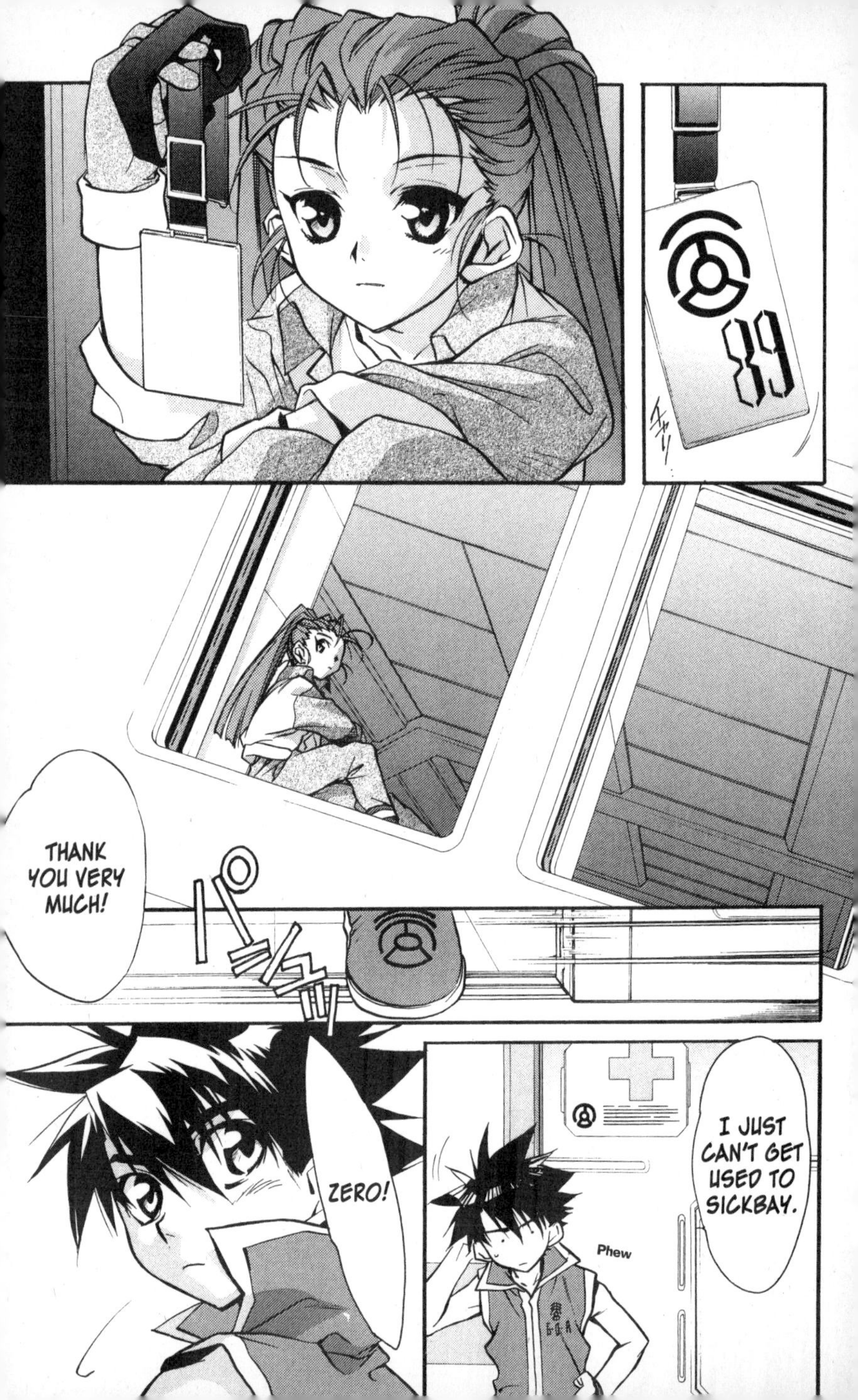
89
THANK YOU VERY MUCH!
I JUST CAN'T GET USED TO SICKBAY.
Phew
ZERO!

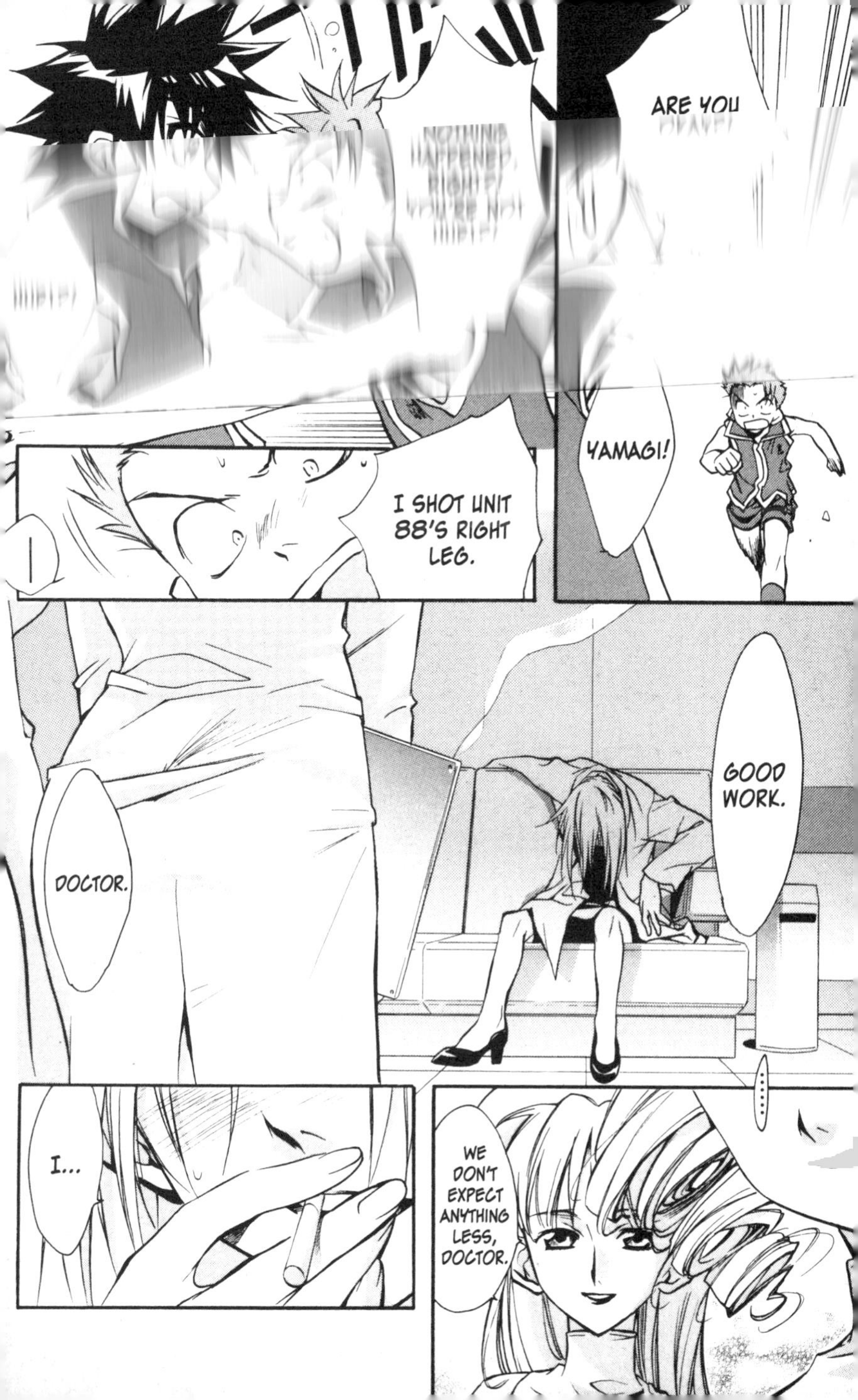
ARE YOU
YAMAGI!
I SHOT UNIT 88'S RIGHT LEG.
GOOD WORK.
DOCTOR.
......
WE DON'T EXPECT ANYTHING LESS, DOCTOR.
I...

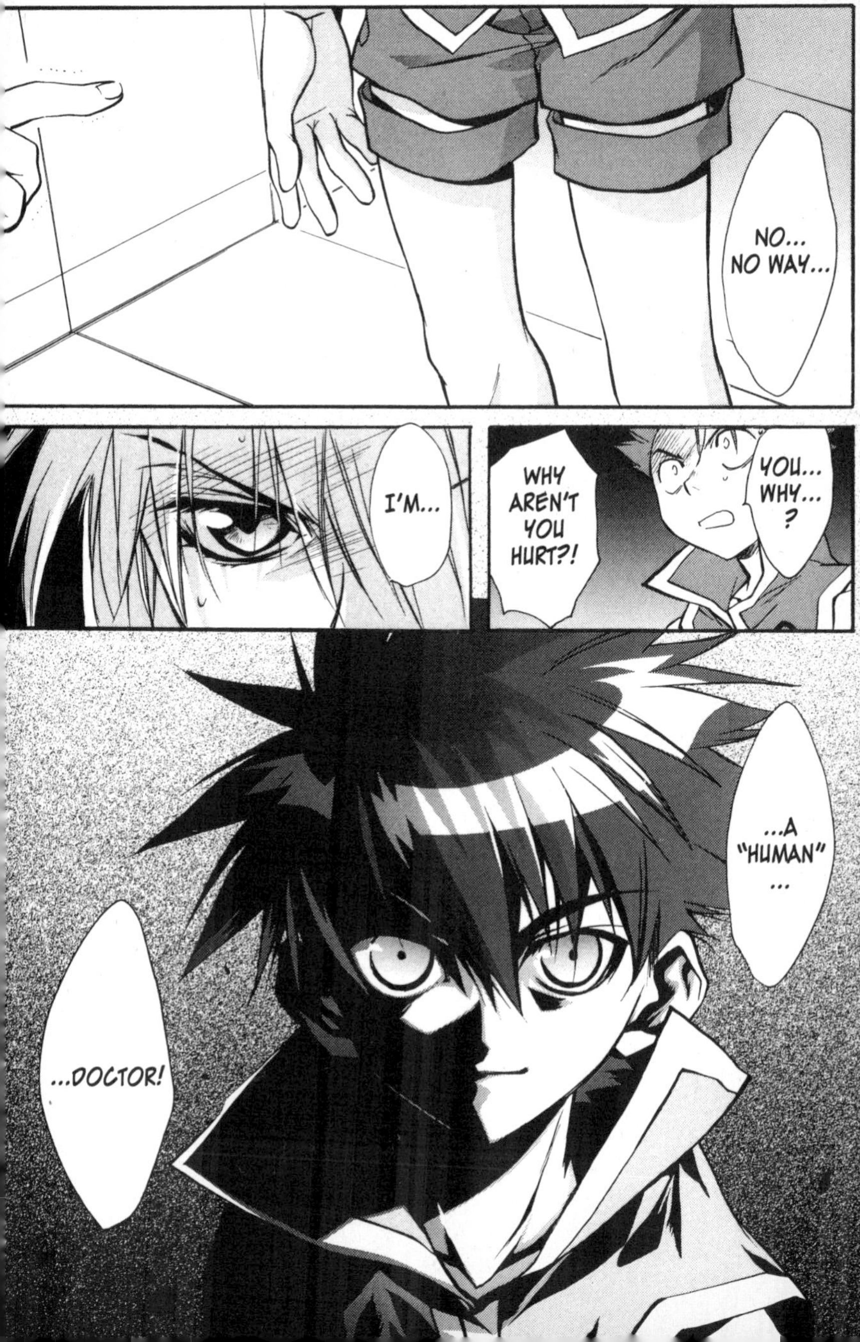
NO... NO WAY...
YOU... WHY... ?
WHY AREN'T YOU HURT?!
I'M...
...A "HUMAN" ...
...DOCTOR!

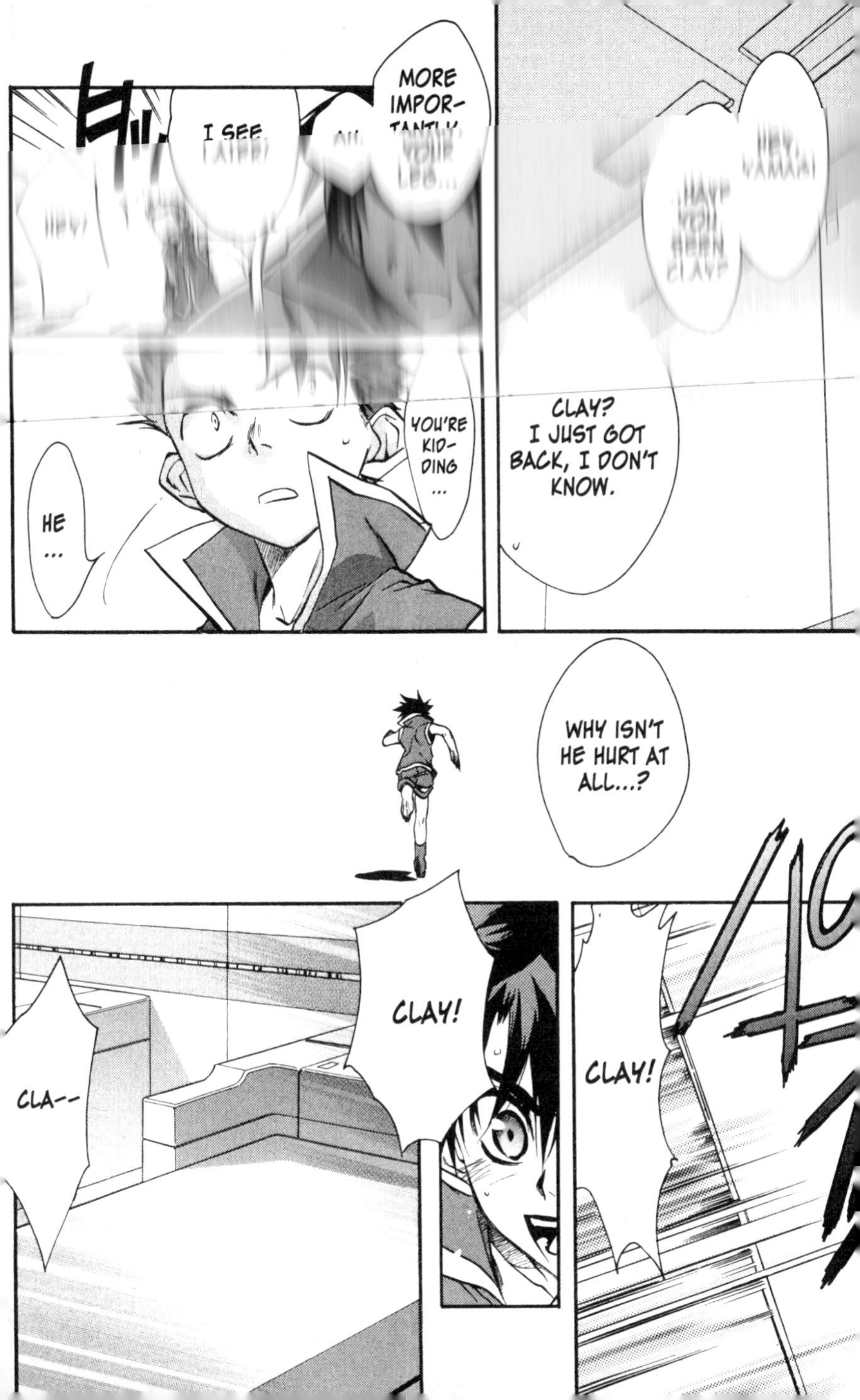
CLAY? I JUST GOT BACK, I DON'T KNOW.
MORE IMPOR-
I SEE.
YOU'RE KID-DING ...
HE ...
WHY ISN'T HE HURT AT ALL...?
CLAY!
CLAY!
CLA--

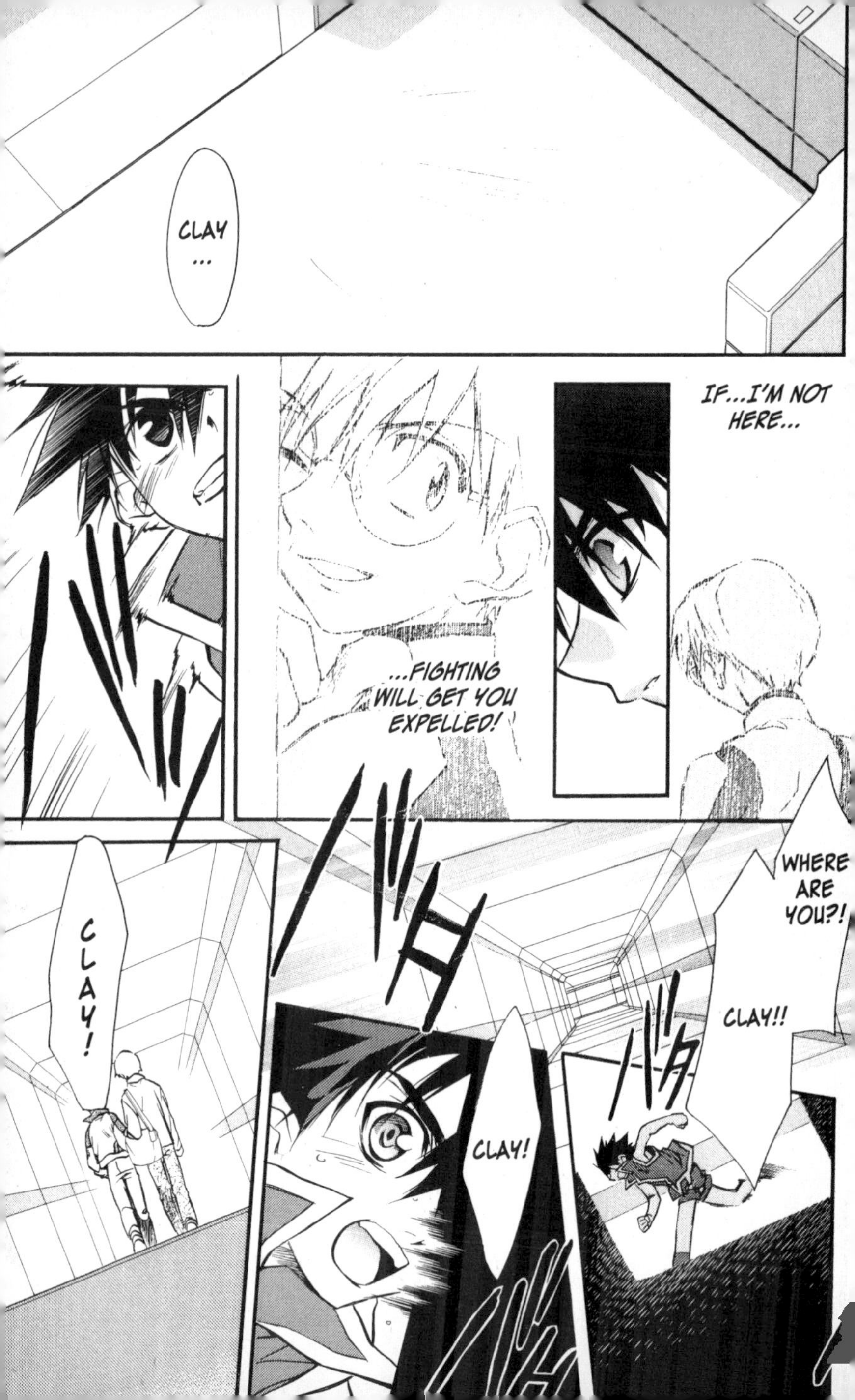
CLAY ...
IF...I'M NOT HERE...
...FIGHTING WILL GET YOU EXPELLED!
WHERE ARE YOU?!
CLAY!!
CLAY!
CLAY!

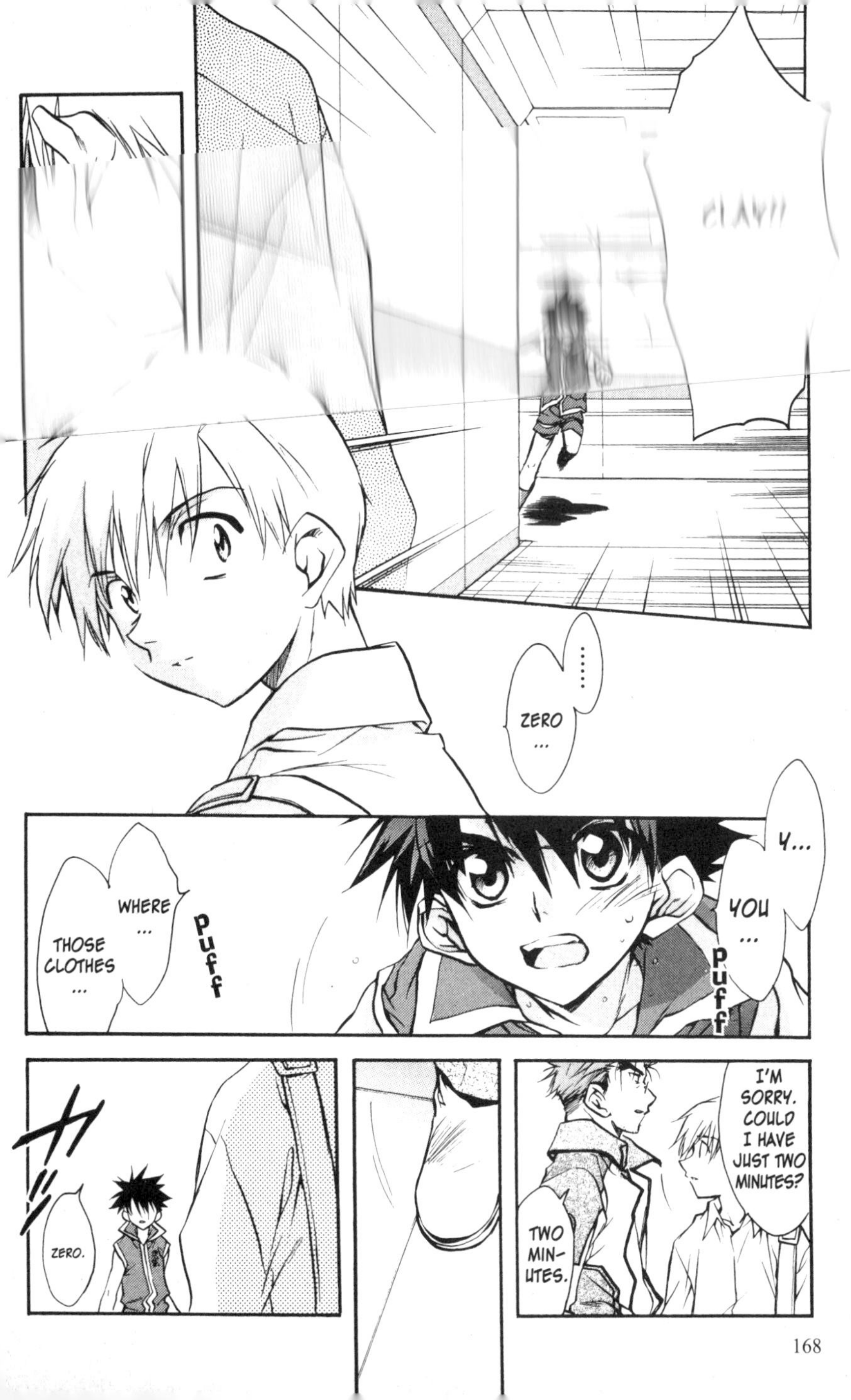

......
ZERO ...
Y... YOU ...
PUFF
WHERE ... THOSE CLOTHES ...
PUFF
I'M SORRY. COULD I HAVE JUST TWO MINUTES?
TWO MIN-UTES.
ZERO.

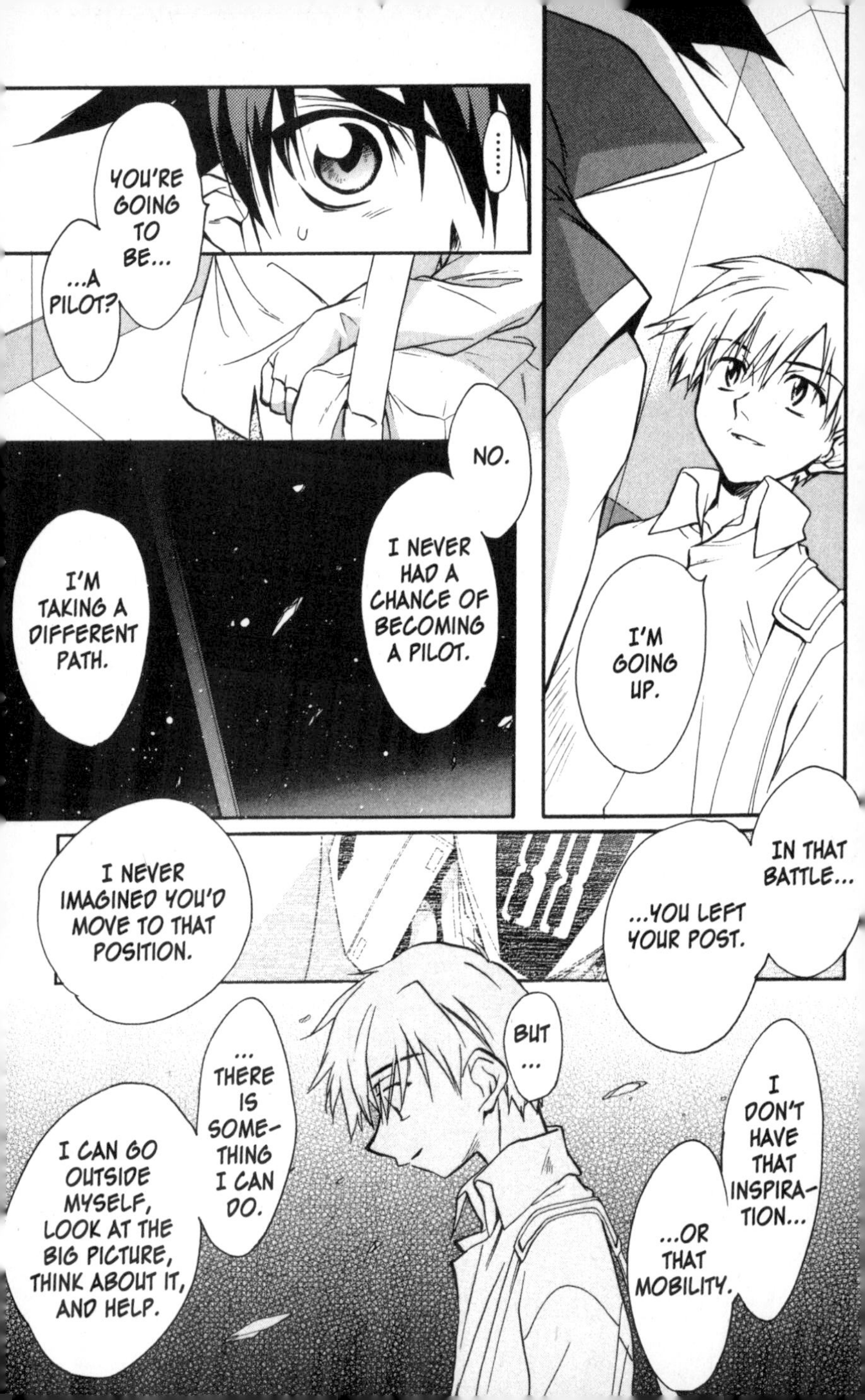
I'M GOING UP.
......
YOU'RE GOING TO BE...
...A PILOT?
NO.
I NEVER HAD A CHANCE OF BECOMING A PILOT.
I'M TAKING A DIFFERENT PATH.
IN THAT BATTLE...
...YOU LEFT YOUR POST.
I NEVER IMAGINED YOU'D MOVE TO THAT POSITION.
I DON'T HAVE THAT INSPIRA-TION...
...OR THAT MOBILITY.
BUT...
...THERE IS SOME-THING I CAN DO.
I CAN GO OUTSIDE MYSELF, LOOK AT THE BIG PICTURE, THINK ABOUT IT, AND HELP.

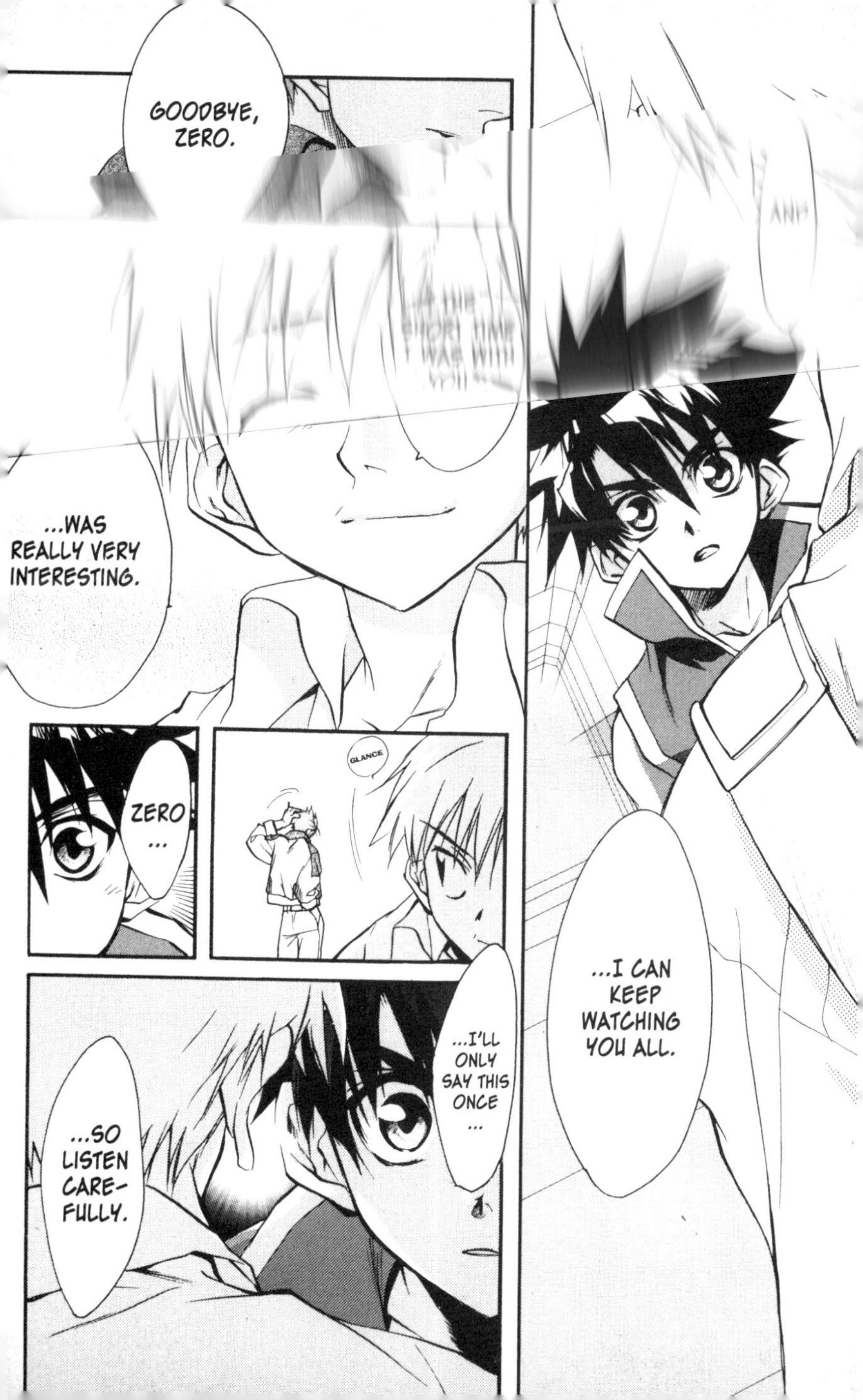
GOODBYE, ZERO.
...WAS REALLY VERY INTERESTING.
...I CAN KEEP WATCHING YOU ALL.
GLANCE
ZERO ...
...I'LL ONLY SAY THIS ONCE ...
...SO LISTEN CARE-FULLY.

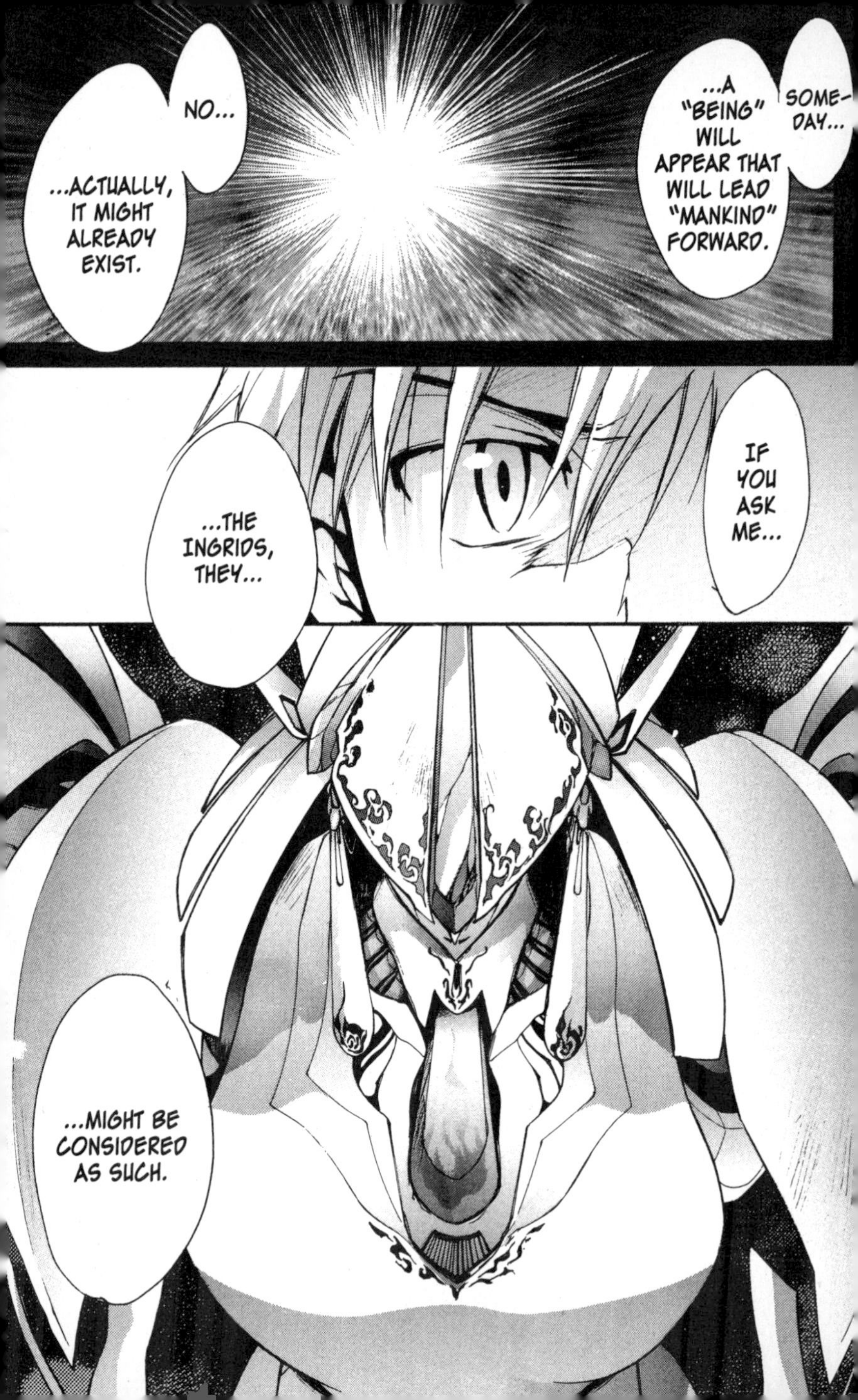
SOME-DAY...
...A "BEING" WILL APPEAR THAT WILL LEAD "MANKIND" FORWARD.
NO...
...ACTUALLY, IT MIGHT ALREADY EXIST.
IF YOU ASK ME...
...THE INGRIDS, THEY...
...MIGHT BE CONSIDERED AS SUCH.

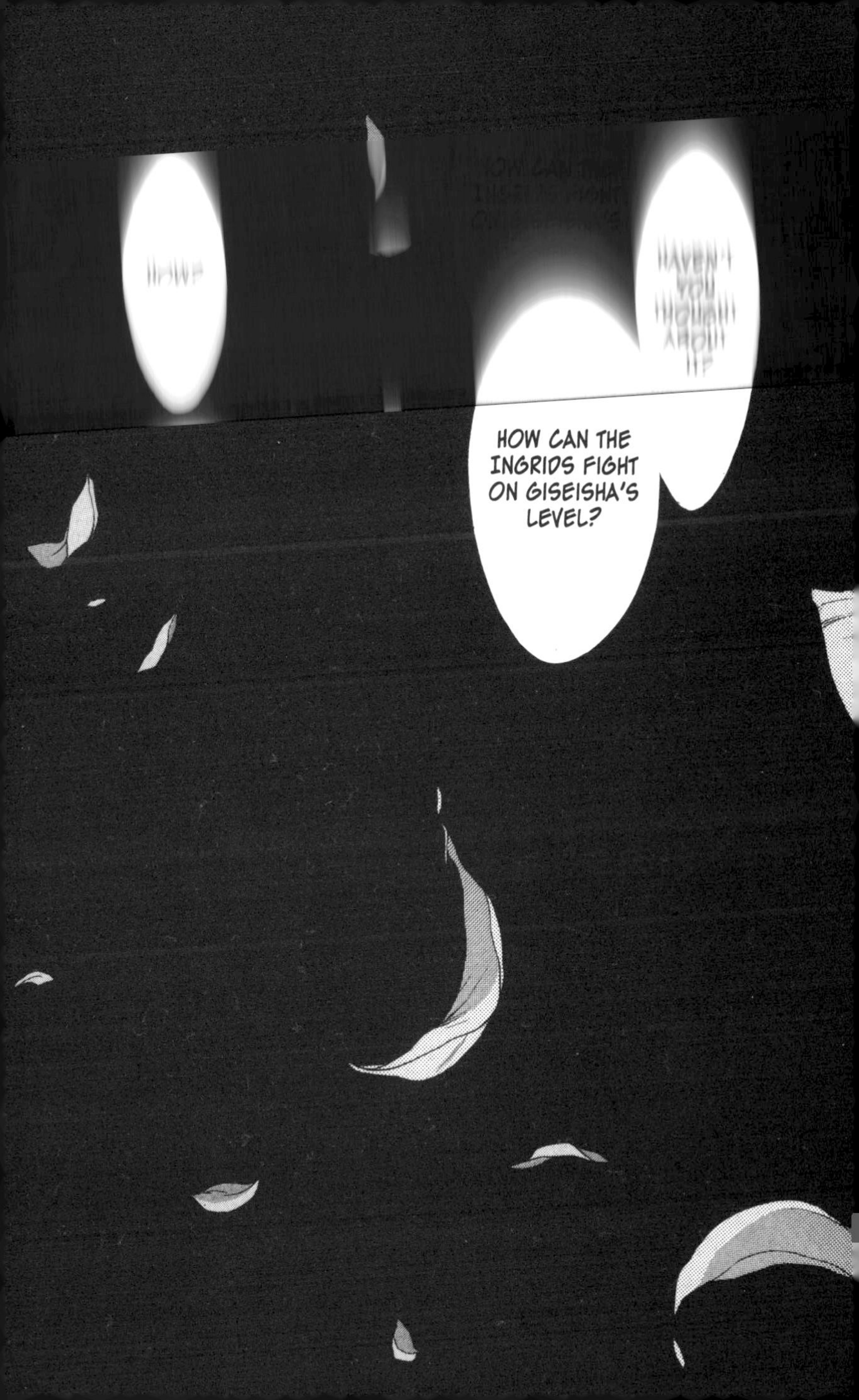
HOW CAN THE INGRIDS FIGHT ON GISEISHA'S LEVEL?

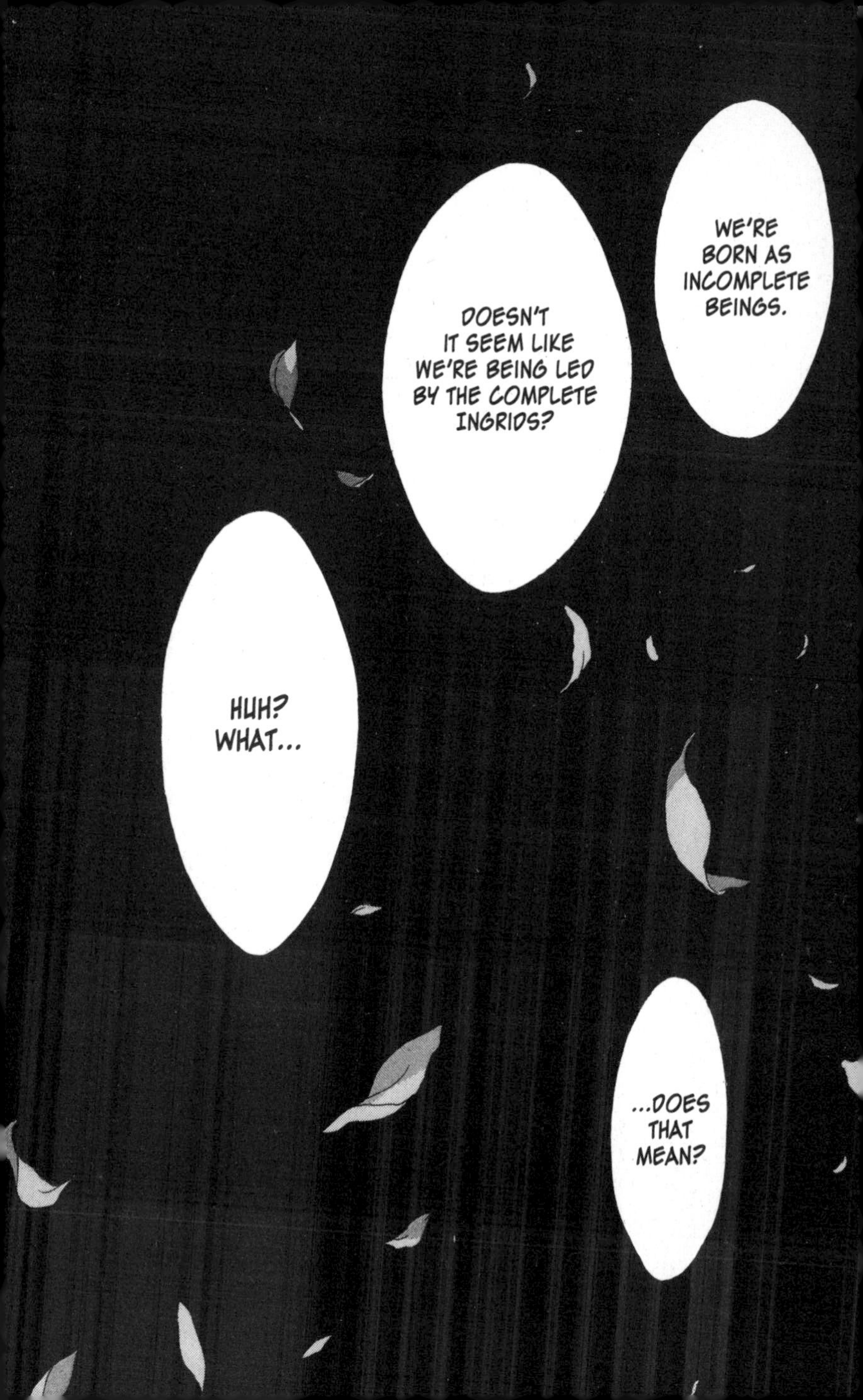
WE'RE BORN AS INCOMPLETE BEINGS.
DOESN'T IT SEEM LIKE WE'RE BEING LED BY THE COMPLETE INGRIDS?
HUH? WHAT...
...DOES THAT MEAN?

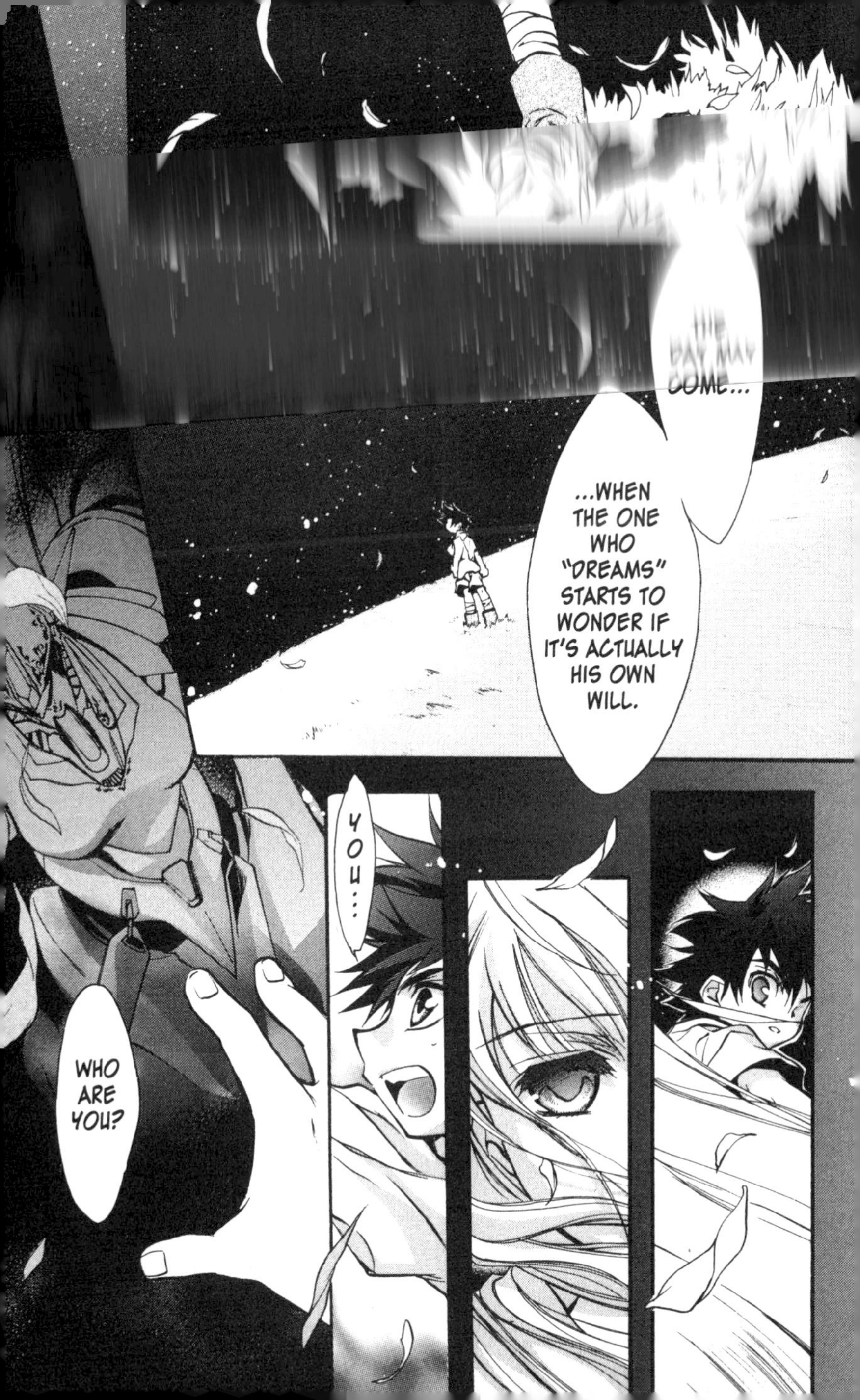
THE DAY MAY COME...
...WHEN THE ONE WHO "DREAMS" STARTS TO WONDER IF IT'S ACTUALLY HIS OWN WILL.
YOU...
WHO ARE YOU?

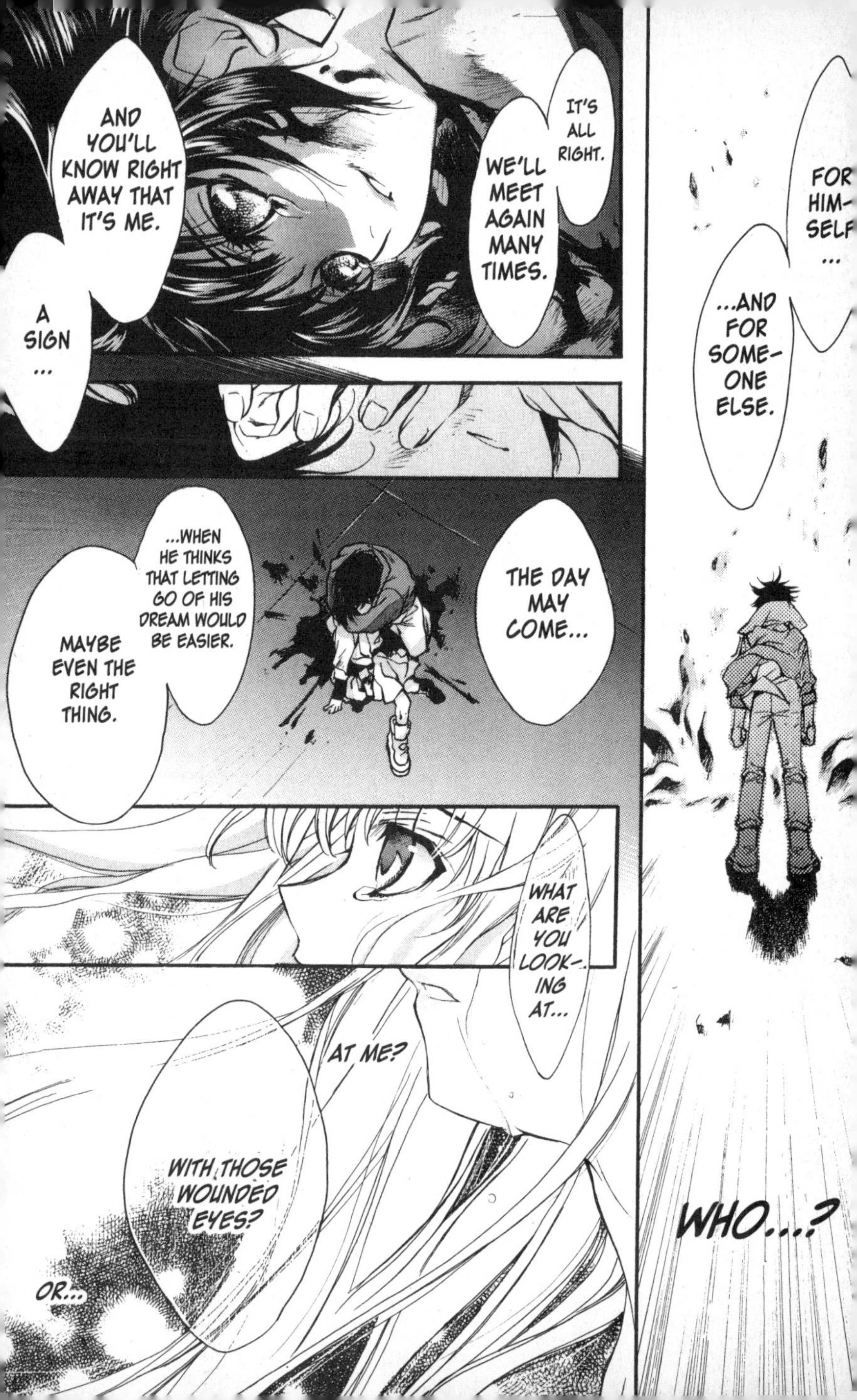

IT'S ALL RIGHT.
WE'LL MEET AGAIN MANY TIMES.
AND YOU'LL KNOW RIGHT AWAY THAT IT'S ME.
A SIGN ...
THE DAY MAY COME...
...WHEN HE THINKS THAT LETTING GO OF HIS DREAM WOULD BE EASIER.
MAYBE EVEN THE RIGHT THING.
FOR HIMSELF ...
...AND FOR SOMEONE ELSE.
WHAT ARE YOU LOOKING AT...
AT ME?
WITH THOSE WOUNDED EYES?
OR...
WHO...?

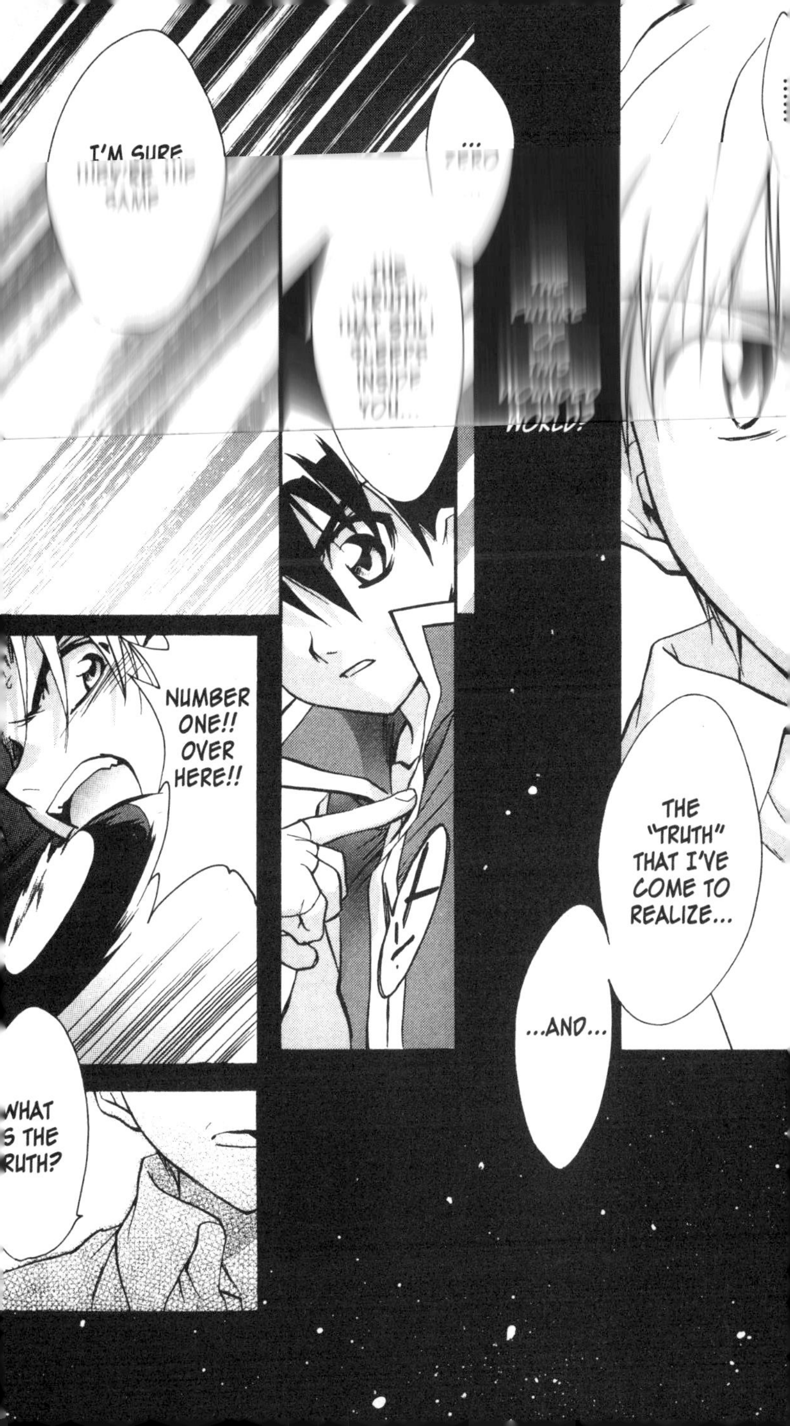
THE "TRUTH" THAT I'VE COME TO REALIZE...
...AND...
...
I'M SURE
NUMBER ONE!! OVER HERE!!
WHAT S THE RUTH?

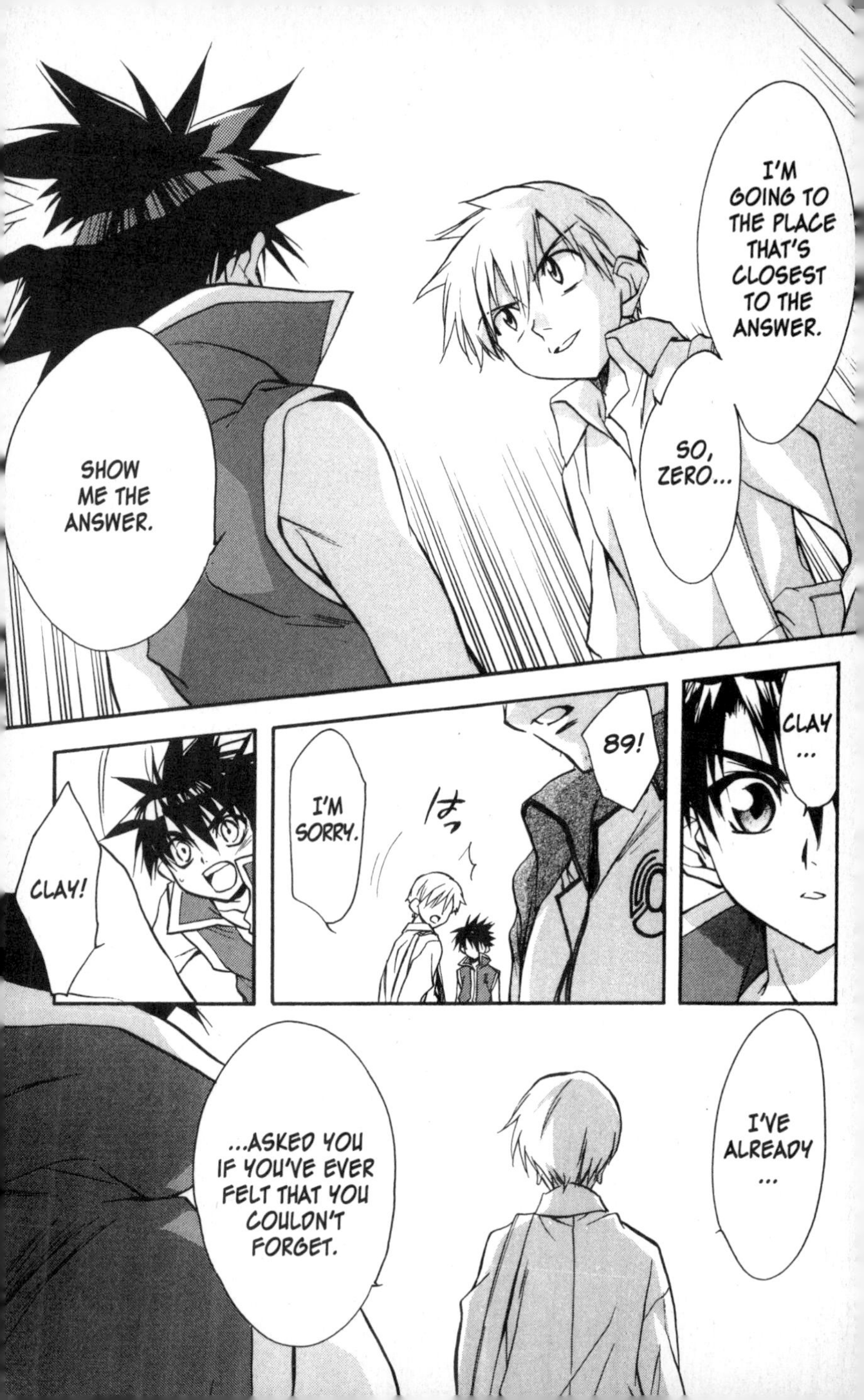
I'M GOING TO THE PLACE THAT'S CLOSEST TO THE ANSWER.
SO, ZERO...
SHOW ME THE ANSWER.
CLAY ...
89!
はっ
I'M SORRY.
CLAY!
I'VE ALREADY ...
...ASKED YOU IF YOU'VE EVER FELT THAT YOU COULDN'T FORGET.

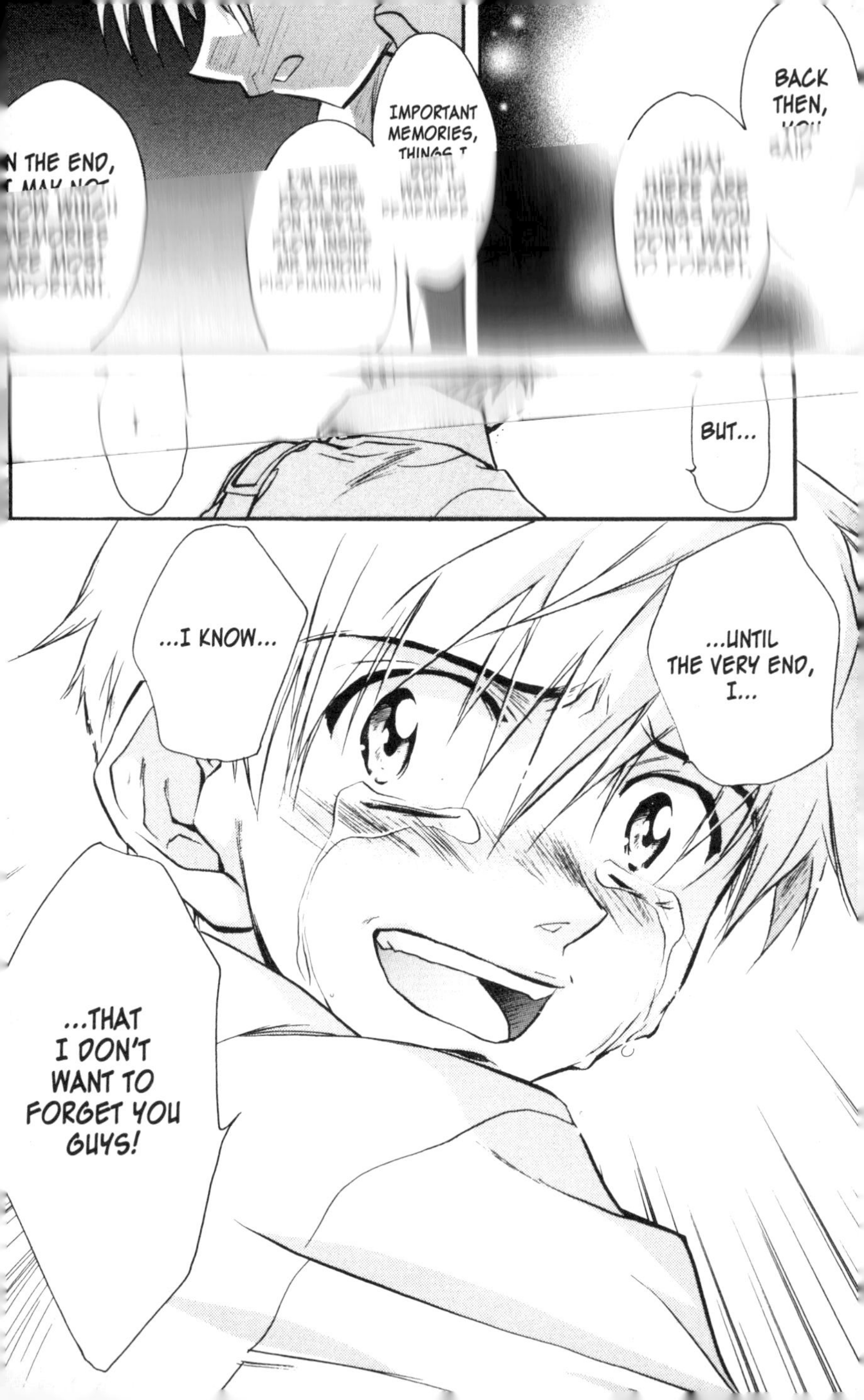
BACK THEN,
IMPORTANT MEMORIES,
N THE END,
BUT...
...UNTIL THE VERY END, I...
...I KNOW...
...THAT I DON'T WANT TO FORGET YOU GUYS!

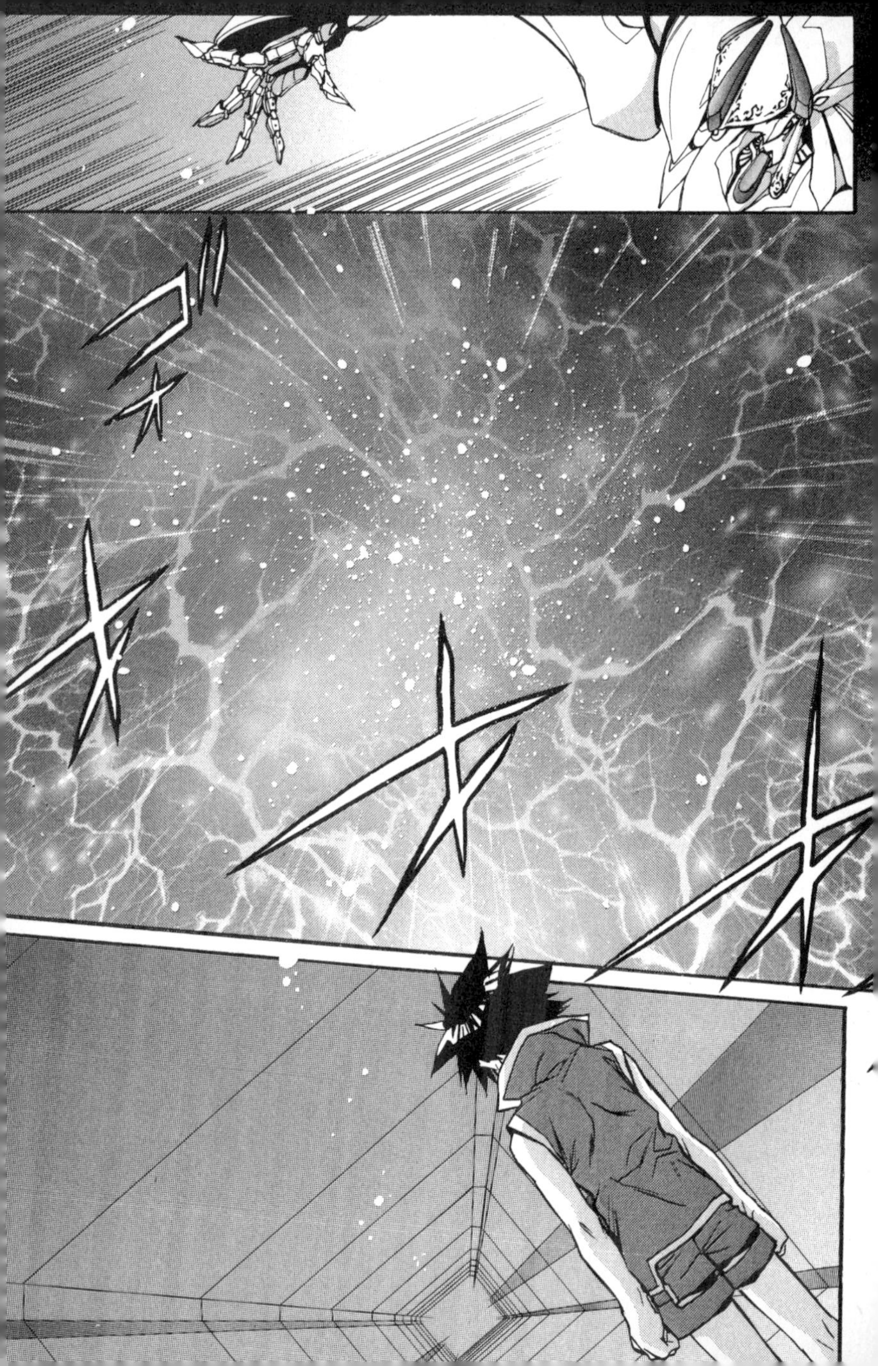
ゴォオオオ

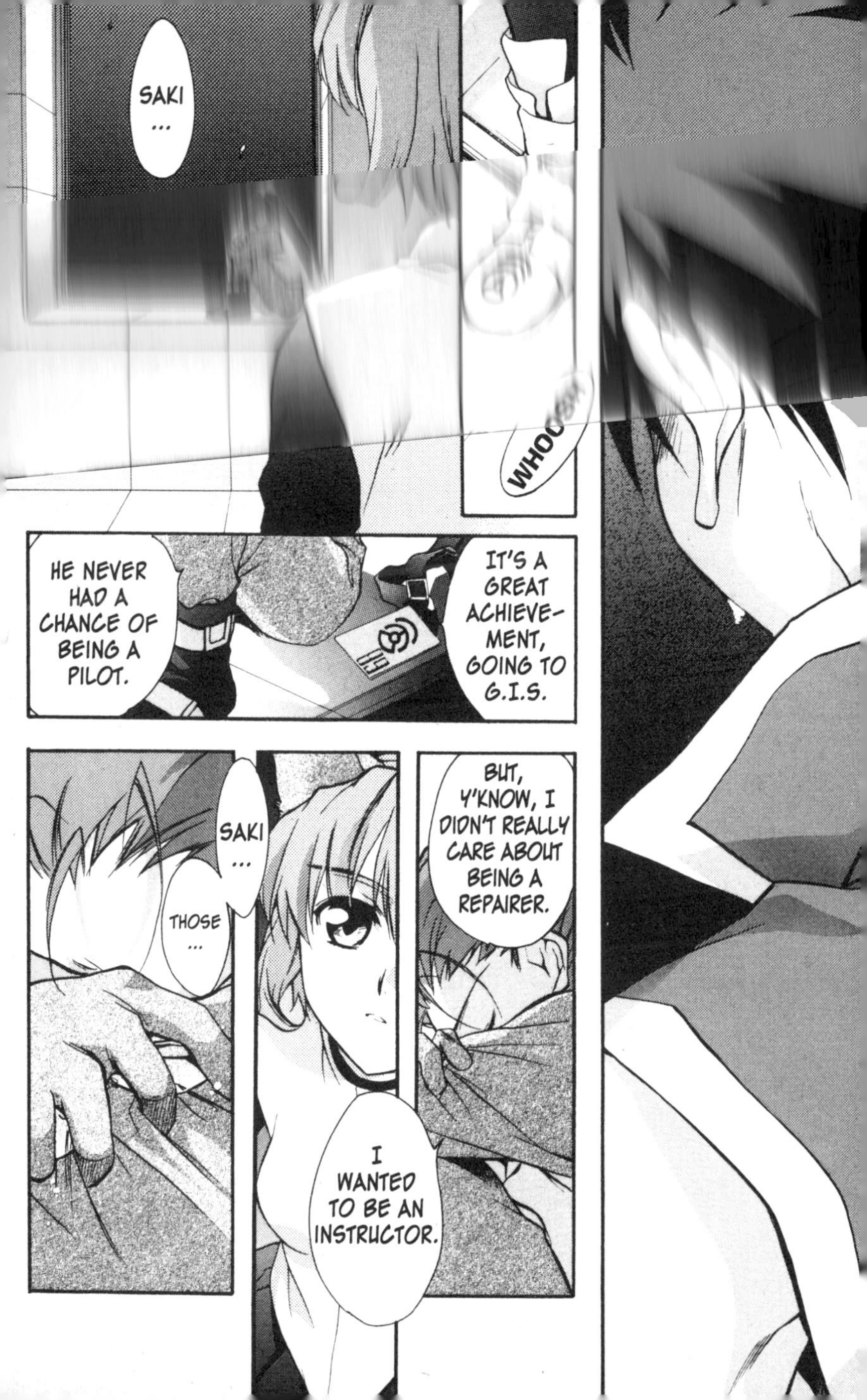
SAKI ...
WHOOSH
IT'S A GREAT ACHIEVEMENT, GOING TO G.I.S.
HE NEVER HAD A CHANCE OF BEING A PILOT.
BUT, Y'KNOW, I DIDN'T REALLY CARE ABOUT BEING A REPAIRER.
I WANTED TO BE AN INSTRUCTOR.
SAKI ...
THOSE ...

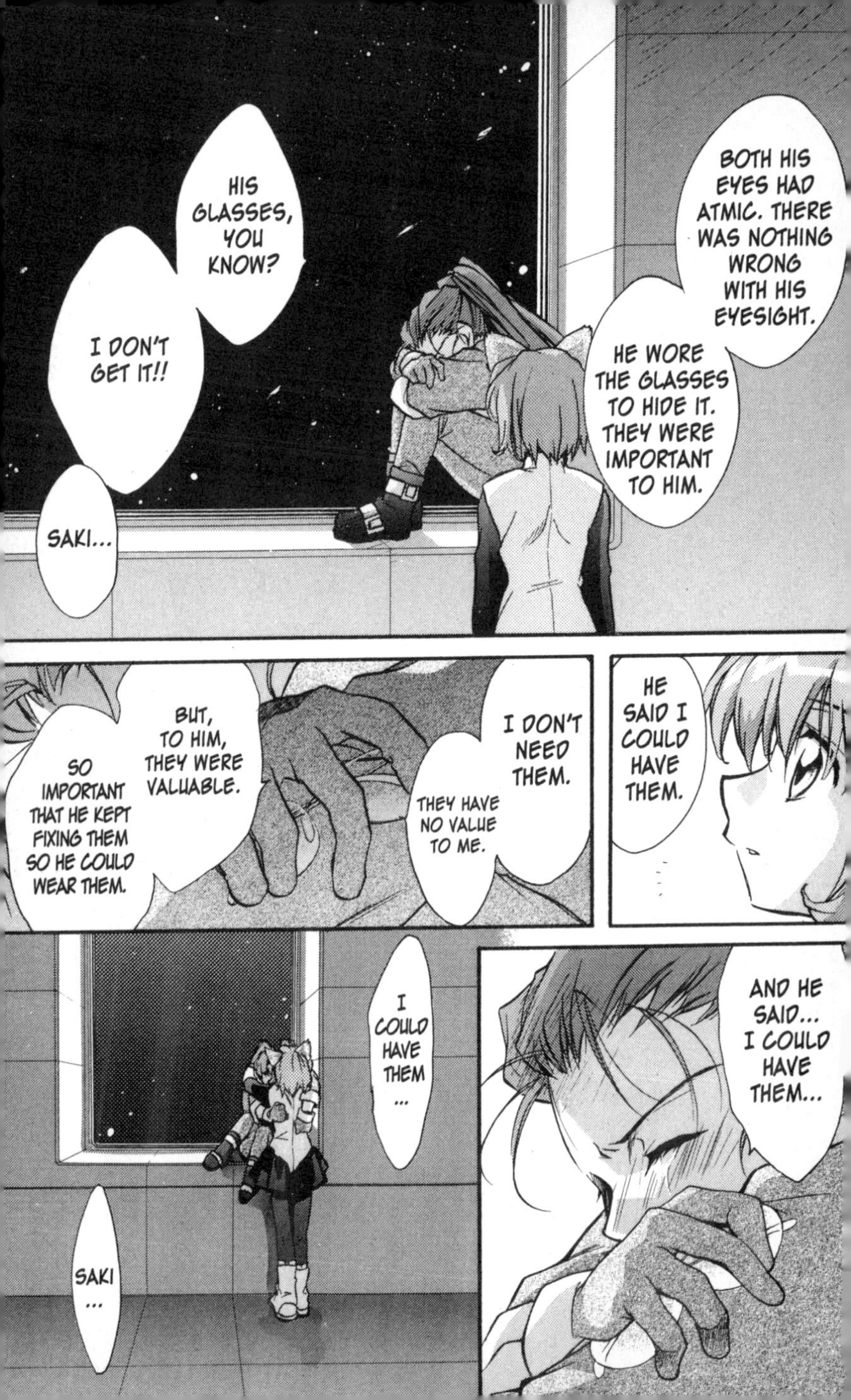
BOTH HIS EYES HAD ATMIC. THERE WAS NOTHING WRONG WITH HIS EYESIGHT.
HE WORE THE GLASSES TO HIDE IT. THEY WERE IMPORTANT TO HIM.
HIS GLASSES, YOU KNOW?
I DON'T GET IT!!
SAKI...
HE SAID I COULD HAVE THEM.
I DON'T NEED THEM.
THEY HAVE NO VALUE TO ME.
BUT, TO HIM, THEY WERE VALUABLE.
SO IMPORTANT THAT HE KEPT FIXING THEM SO HE COULD WEAR THEM.
AND HE SAID... I COULD HAVE THEM...
I COULD HAVE THEM ...
SAKI ...

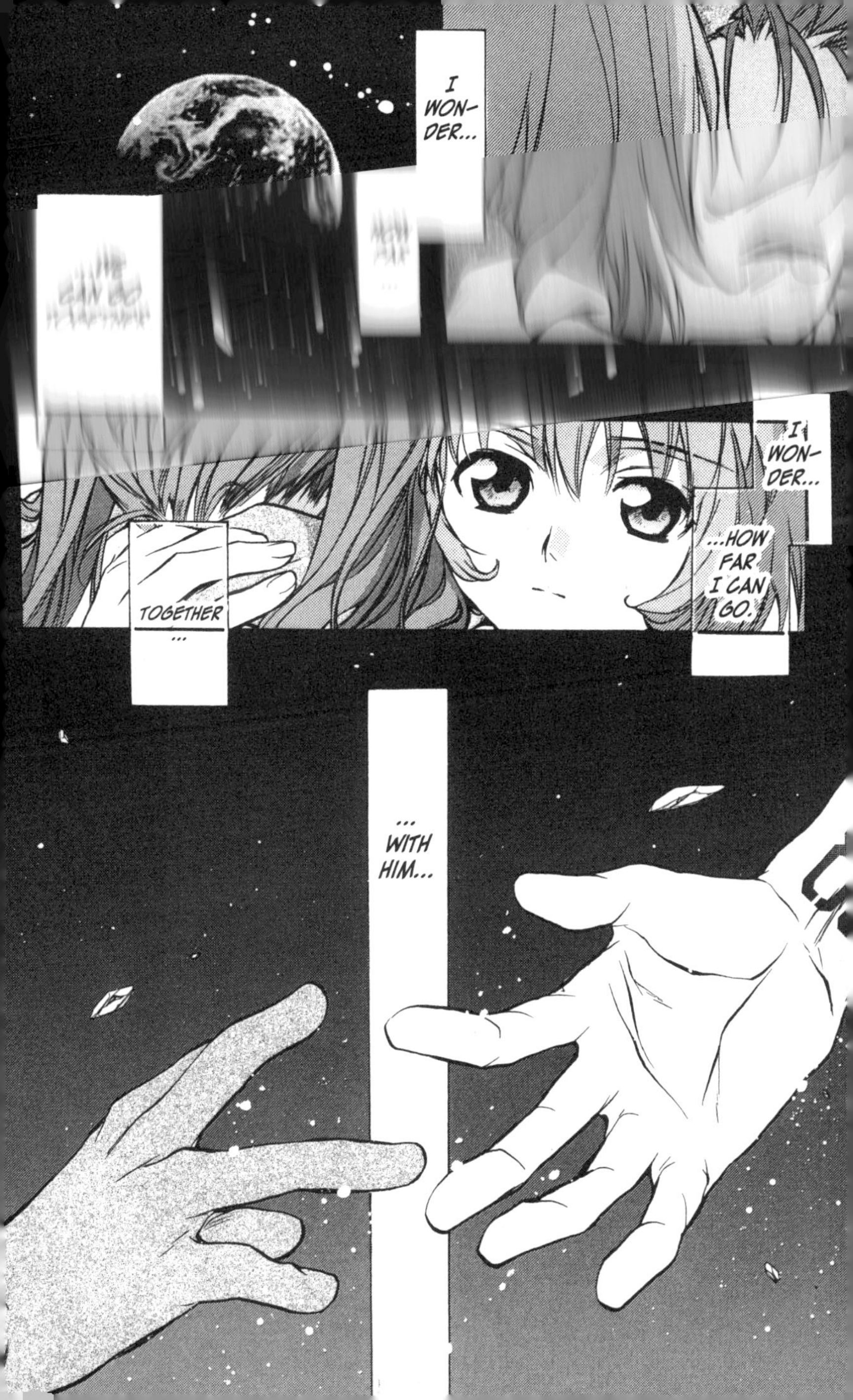
I WONDER...
I WONDER...
...HOW FAR I CAN GO.
TOGETHER ...
... WITH HIM...

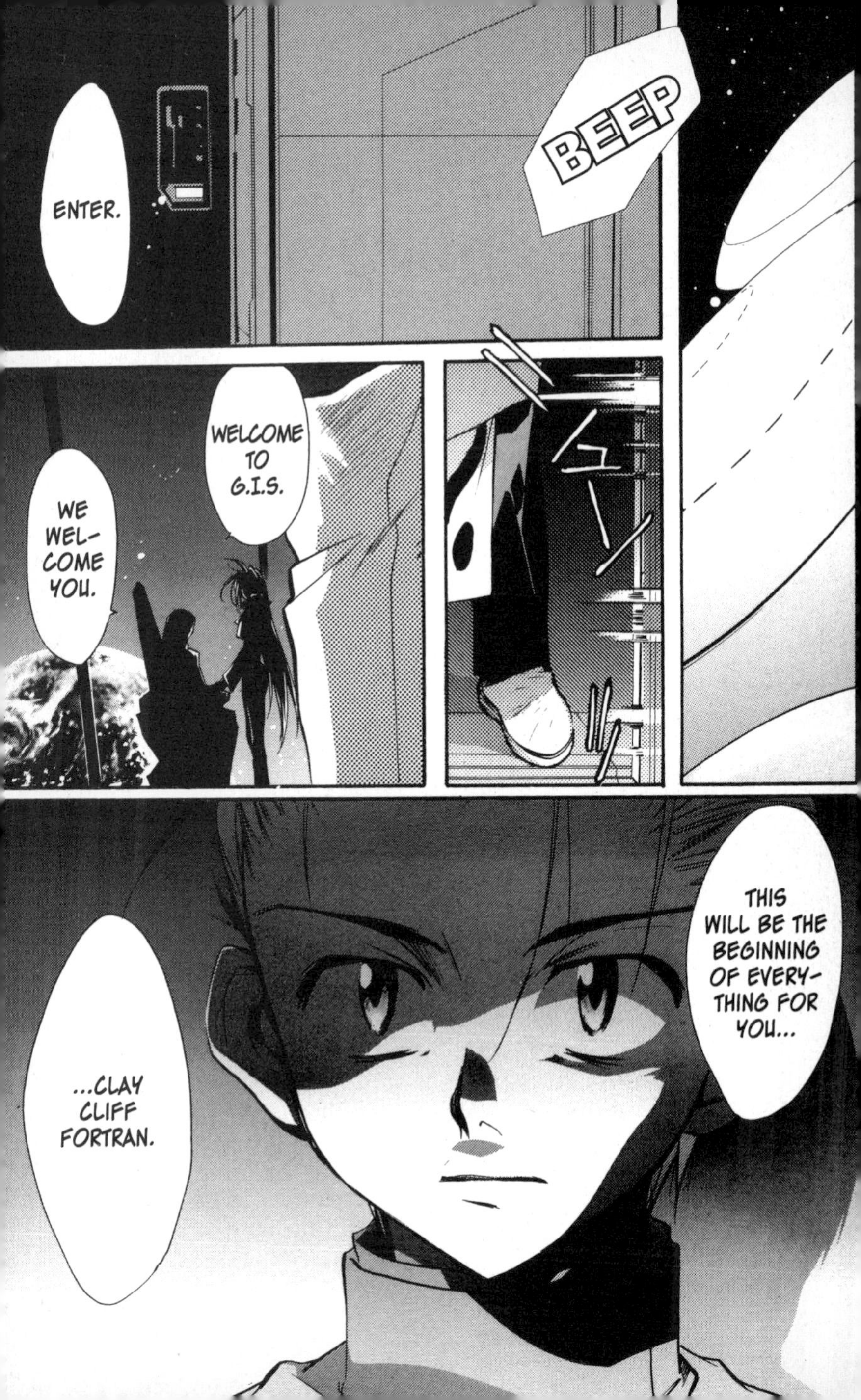
BEEP
ENTER.
WELCOME TO G.I.S.
WE WEL-COME YOU.
THIS WILL BE THE BEGINNING OF EVERY-THING FOR YOU...
...CLAY CLIFF FORTRAN.

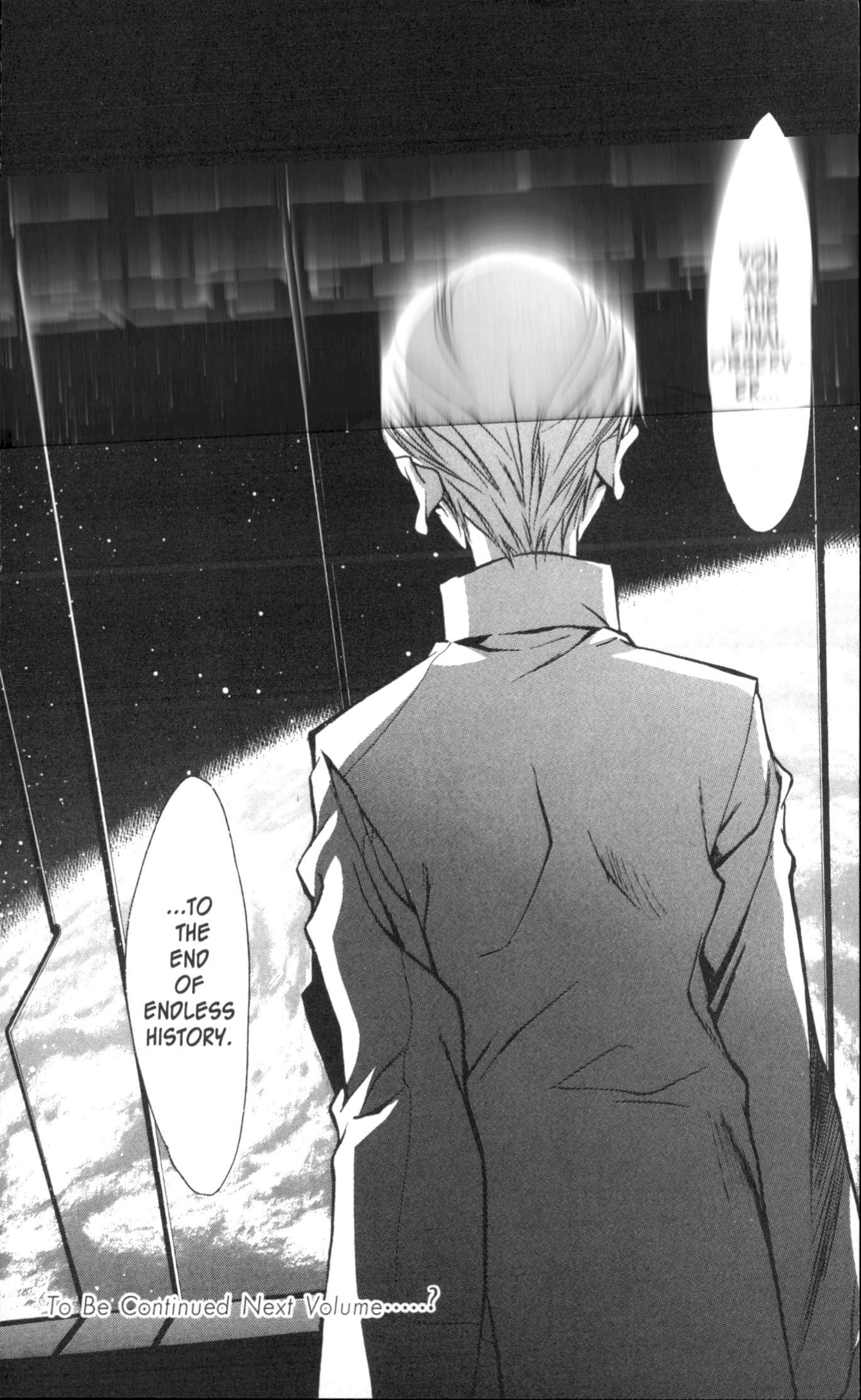
...TO THE END OF ENDLESS HISTORY.
To Be Continued Next Volume......?

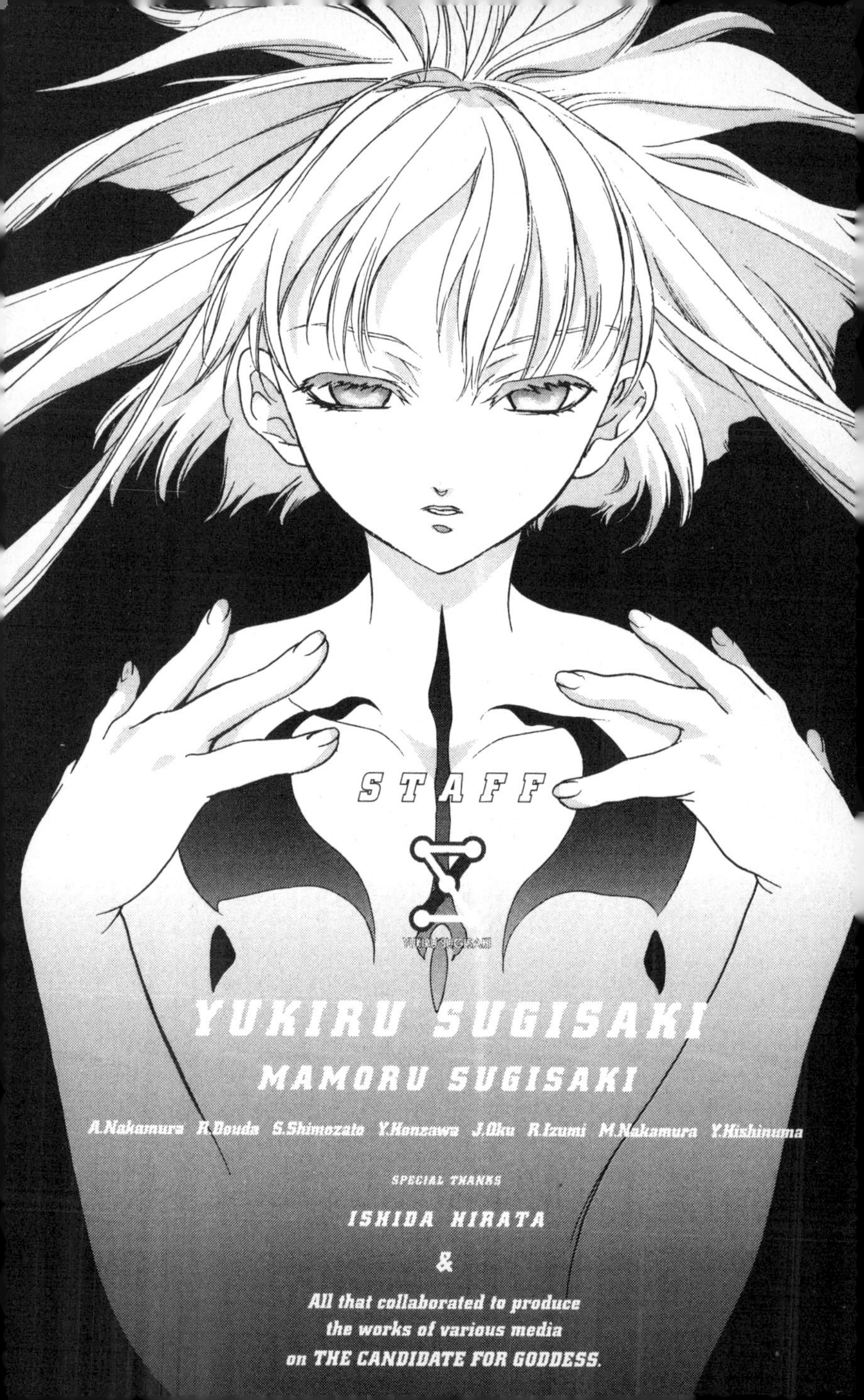
S T A F F
YUKIRU SUGISAKI
MAMORU SUGISAKI
A.Nakamura R.Oouda S.Shimozato Y.Honzawa J.Oku R.Izumi M.Nakamura Y.Hishinuma
SPECIAL THANKS
ISHIDA HIRATA
&
All that collaborated to produce
the works of various media
on THE CANDIDATE FOR GODDESS.

ALSO AVAILABLE FROM TOKYOPOP

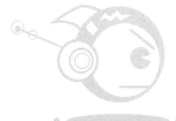

You want it? We got it!
A full range of TOKYOPOP
products are available now at:
www.TOKYOPOP.com/shop

07.15.04T

ALSO AVAILABLE FROM TOKYOPOP®

MANGA

.HACK//LEGEND OF THE TWILIGHT
@LARGE
ABENOBASHI: MAGICAL SHOPPING ARCADE
A.I. LOVE YOU
AI YORI AOSHI
ANGELIC LAYER
ARM OF KANNON
BABY BIRTH
BATTLE ROYALE
BATTLE VIXENS
BOYS BE...
BRAIN POWERED
BRIGADOON
B'TX
CANDIDATE FOR GODDESS, THE
CARDCAPTOR SAKURA
CARDCAPTOR SAKURA - MASTER OF THE CLOW
CHOBITS
CHRONICLES OF THE CURSED SWORD
CLAMP SCHOOL DETECTIVES
CLOVER
COMIC PARTY
CONFIDENTIAL CONFESSIONS
CORRECTOR YUI
COWBOY BEBOP
COWBOY BEBOP: SHOOTING STAR
CRAZY LOVE STORY
CRESCENT MOON
CROSS
CULDCEPT
CYBORG 009
D•N•ANGEL
DEMON DIARY
DEMON ORORON, THE
DEUS VITAE
DIABOLO
DIGIMON
DIGIMON TAMERS
DIGIMON ZERO TWO
DOLL
DRAGON HUNTER
DRAGON KNIGHTS
DRAGON VOICE
DREAM SAGA
DUKLYON: CLAMP SCHOOL DEFENDERS
EERIE QUEERIE!
ERICA SAKURAZAWA: COLLECTED WORKS
ET CETERA
ETERNITY
EVIL'S RETURN
FAERIES' LANDING
FAKE
FLCL
FLOWER OF THE DEEP SLEEP, THE
FORBIDDEN DANCE
FRUITS BASKET

G GUNDAM
GATEKEEPERS
GETBACKERS
GIRL GOT GAME
GRAVITATION
GTO
GUNDAM SEED ASTRAY
GUNDAM WING
GUNDAM WING: BATTLEFIELD OF PACIFISTS
GUNDAM WING: ENDLESS WALTZ
GUNDAM WING: THE LAST OUTPOST (G-UNIT)
HANDS OFF!
HAPPY MANIA
HARLEM BEAT
HYPER RUNE
I.N.V.U.
IMMORTAL RAIN
INITIAL D
INSTANT TEEN: JUST ADD NUTS
ISLAND
JING: KING OF BANDITS
JING: KING OF BANDITS - TWILIGHT TALES
JULINE
KARE KANO
KILL ME, KISS ME
KINDAICHI CASE FILES, THE
KING OF HELL
KODOCHA: SANA'S STAGE
LAMENT OF THE LAMB
LEGAL DRUG
LEGEND OF CHUN HYANG, THE
LES BIJOUX
LOVE HINA
LOVE OR MONEY
LUPIN III
LUPIN III: WORLD'S MOST WANTED
MAGIC KNIGHT RAYEARTH I
MAGIC KNIGHT RAYEARTH II
MAHOROMATIC: AUTOMATIC MAIDEN
MAN OF MANY FACES
MARMALADE BOY
MARS
MARS: HORSE WITH NO NAME
MINK
MIRACLE GIRLS
MIYUKI-CHAN IN WONDERLAND
MODEL
MOURYOU KIDEN: LEGEND OF THE NYMPHS
NECK AND NECK
ONE
ONE I LOVE, THE
PARADISE KISS
PARASYTE
PASSION FRUIT
PEACH GIRL
PEACH GIRL: CHANGE OF HEART
PET SHOP OF HORRORS
PITA-TEN

07.15.04T

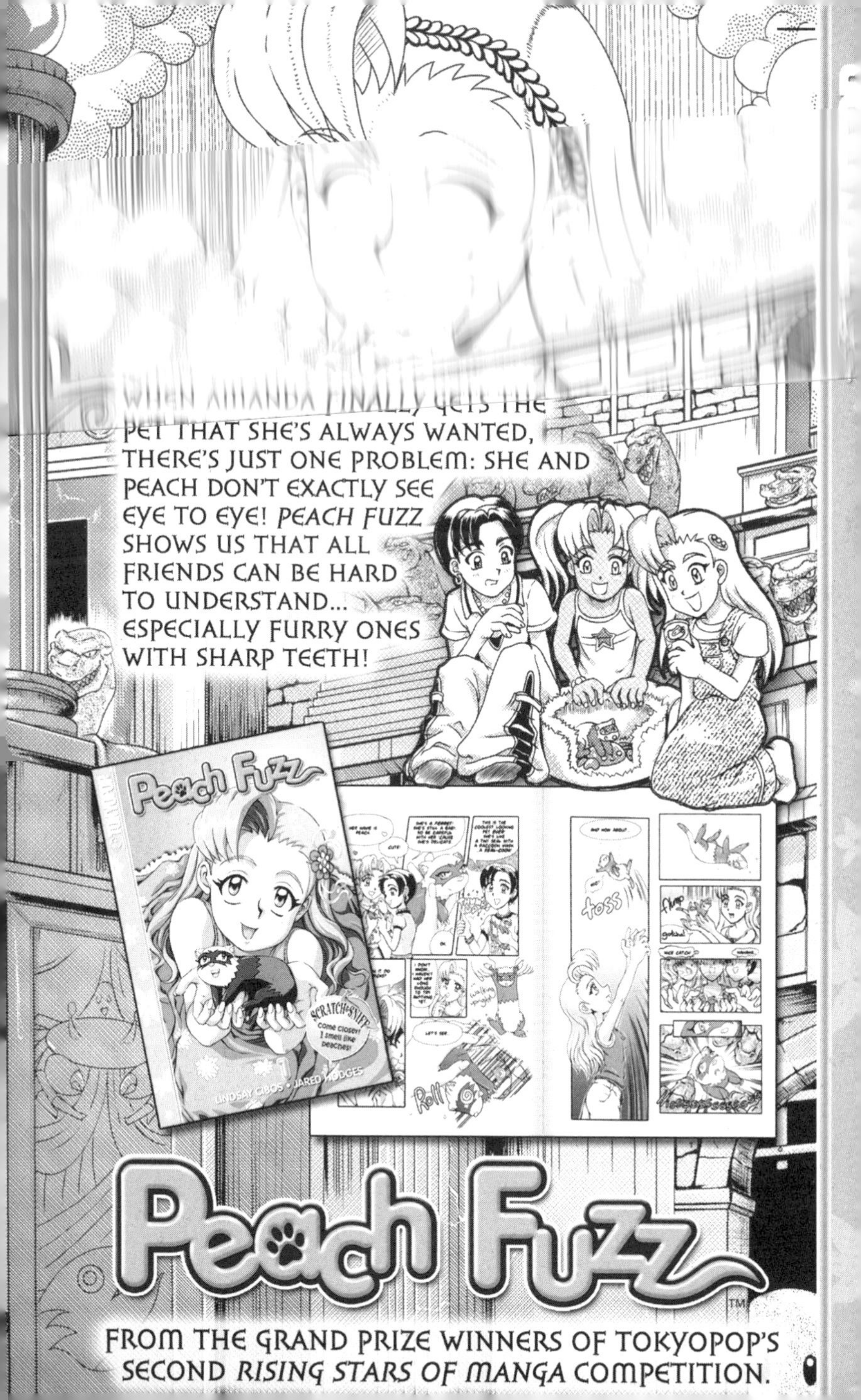

WHEN AMANDA FINALLY GETS THE PET THAT SHE'S ALWAYS WANTED, THERE'S JUST ONE PROBLEM: SHE AND PEACH DON'T EXACTLY SEE EYE TO EYE! *PEACH FUZZ* SHOWS US THAT ALL FRIENDS CAN BE HARD TO UNDERSTAND... ESPECIALLY FURRY ONES WITH SHARP TEETH!
Peach Fuzz
SCRATCH & SNIFF
Come closer! I smell like peaches!
1
LINDSAY CIBOS • JARED HODGES
toss
Roll
Peach Fuzz™
FROM THE GRAND PRIZE WINNERS OF TOKYOPOP'S SECOND *RISING STARS OF MANGA* COMPETITION.

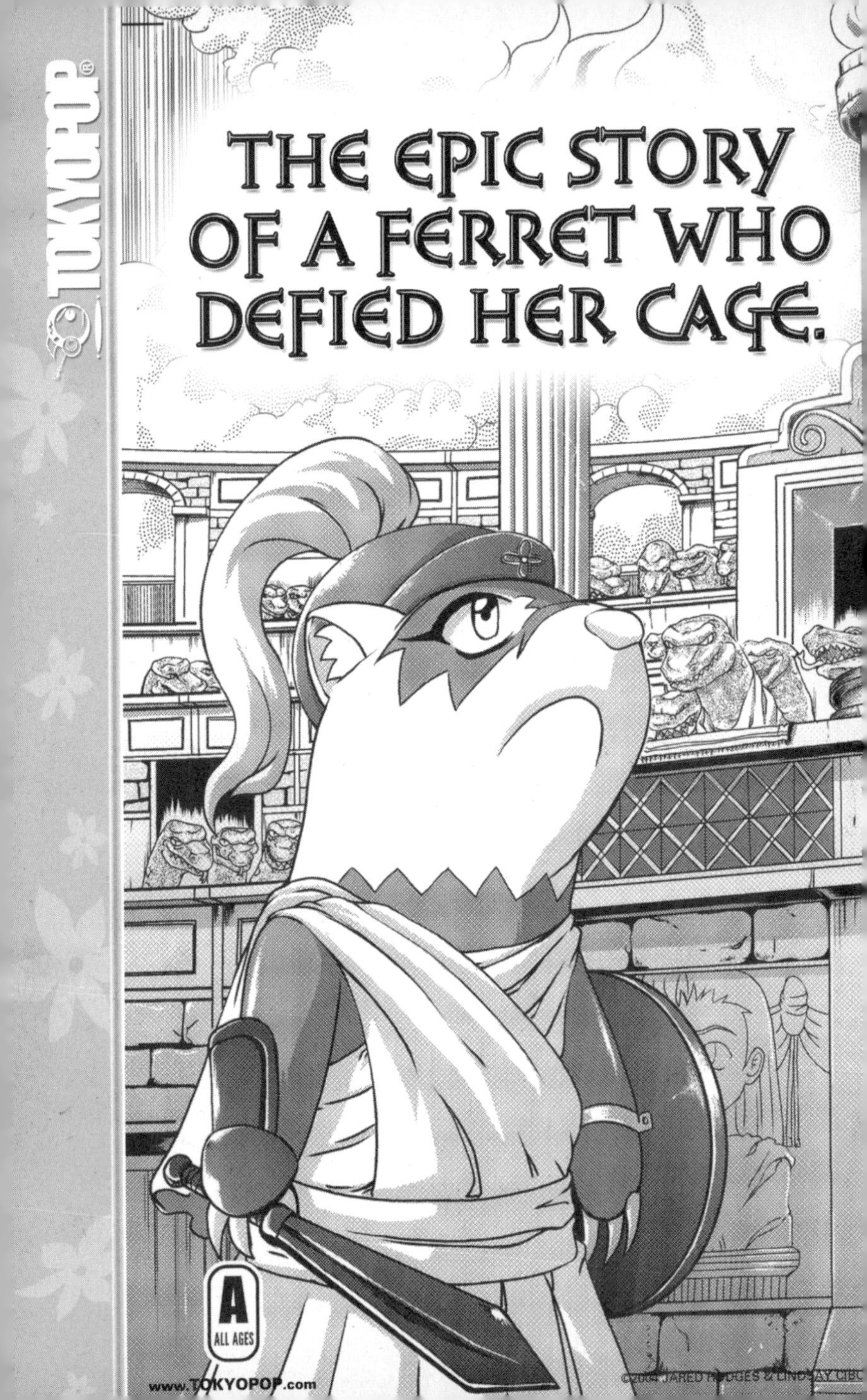
TOKYOPOP
THE EPIC STORY OF A FERRET WHO DEFIED HER CAGE.
A
ALL AGES
www.TOKYOPOP.com
©2004 JARED HODGES & LINDSAY CIB

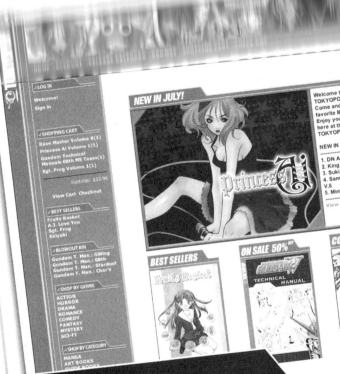

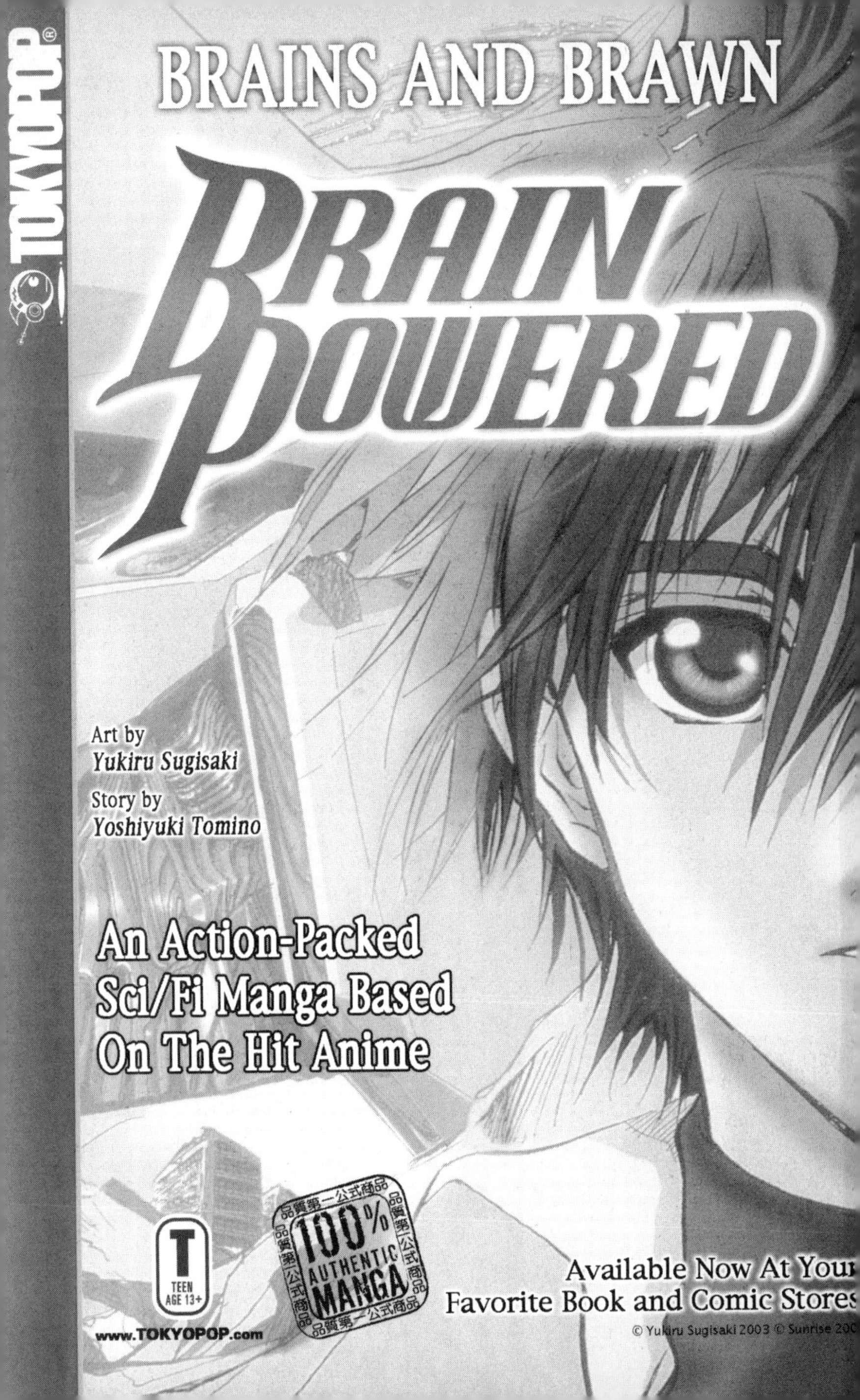
TOKYOPOP®
BRAINS AND BRAWN
BRAIN POWERED
Art by
Yukiru Sugisaki
Story by
Yoshiyuki Tomino
An Action-Packed
Sci/Fi Manga Based
On The Hit Anime
T
TEEN
AGE 13+
100%
AUTHENTIC
MANGA
品質第一公式商品
Available Now At Your
Favorite Book and Comic Stores
www.TOKYOPOP.com
© Yukiru Sugisaki 2003 © Sunrise 200

STOP!

This is the back of the book.
You wouldn't want to spoil a great ending!

This book is printed "manga-style," in the authentic Japanese right-to-left format. Since none of the artwork has been flipped or altered, readers get to experience the story just as the creator intended. You've been asking for it, so TOKYOPOP® delivered: authentic, hot-off-the-press, and far more fun!

DIRECTIONS

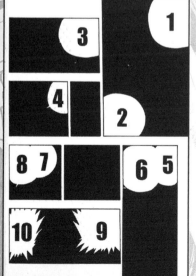

If this is your first time reading manga-style, here's a quick guide to help you understand how it works.

It's easy... just start in the top right panel and follow the numbers. Have fun, and look for more 100% authentic manga from TOKYOPOP®!

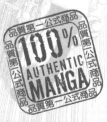